A tzaddik  in our time

SIMCHA RAZ

A tzaddik in our time

the life of Rabbi Aryeh Levin

translated from the Hebrew,
revised and expanded by Charles Wengrov

Foreword by the Chief Rabbi of the United Kingdom

Introduction by Chaim Herzog

FELDHEIM PUBLISHERS
Jerusalem • New York

ISBN 0-87306-986-2
New Edition - 1989

Copyright © 1976 by Rabbi Isaiah Dvorkas
All rights reserved. No part of this publication may be reproduced or transmitted in any form or by any means, electronic or mechanical, including photocopy, recording, or any information storage and retrieval system, without permission in writing from the publisher.

The Hebrew original of this work, Ish tzaddik hayah by Simcha Raz, was first published in September 1972.

**Library of Congress
Cataloging-in-Publication Data**
Raz, Simcha.
   [Ish tsadik hayah. English]
   A tzaddik in our time: the life of Rabbi Aryeh Levin \ translated from the Hebrew, revised and expanded by Charles Wengrov, foreword by the Chief Rabbi of the United Kingdom; introduction by Chaim Herzog. - 4th ed.
     p. cm.
   Translation of: Ish tsadik hayah.
   1. Levin, Aryeh, 1885-1969.   2. Rabbis - Jerusalem - Biography.
3. Chaplains, Prison - Jerusalem - Biography. 4. Jews - Jerusalem-Social life and customs. 5. Jerusalem - Biography. I. Wengrov, Charles. II. Title.
BM755.L446R3813 1989
296' .092-dc20   89-7791
[B]   CIP

Photo credits: City of Jerusalem, Photo Archives | Isaac Freidin, Tel Aviv | Sh'muel Gorr, Jerusalem | Jabotinsky Institute, Tel Aviv | Jewish Agency, Photo Service, Jerusalem | Photo Ross, Jerusalem | Emanuel Prath, Jerusalem | K. Weiss, Jerusalem | Aaron Zuckerman, Jerusalem.

Philipp Feldheim Inc.   Feldheim Publishers Ltd,
200 Airport Executive Park   P.O.B. 6525 \ Jerusalem, Israel
Spring Valley, NY 10977

Printed in Israel

Dedicated to the memory
of the courageous martyrs
who, given strength by Reb Aryeh,
gave up their lives on the gallows
in Israel's battle for freedom and justice
under the British mandate

TRANSLATOR'S NOTE

As I came to Israel in September 1969, months after the death of Reb Aryeh, I had never known the man. I remain eternally grateful for the opportunity to become familiar with his life through the translation of this work. It has been a profoundly moving and ennobling experience. My opportunity to know the man was enlarged when I was granted the privilege of meeting with members of the family, to learn more about this remarkable person, so that the book might present a fuller, more balanced and rounded account of his life. Especially helpful was R. Simḥa Sh'lomo Levin, the source of much of the contents in the Hebrew edition. This fine, unassuming dean of the Yeshiva Ne'ot Aryeh (established in commemoration of his father's life) took precious time from his duties to supply valuable new material.

It is a pleasure, further, to acknowledge my thanks to my good friend Tovia Preschel for his generous help. During Reb Aryeh's lifetime, an organization of his admirers planned to issue a book about him (which alas, never materialized), and Tovia was assigned to meet with him and record his reminiscences. Out of his fund of source material, Tovia Preschel kindly supplied me with an appreciable amount of information, which was incorporated in the work. I was likewise privileged to meet with certain individuals who had known Reb Aryeh, such as Professor and Mrs. S. H. Blondheim and Menaḥem Abramsky, and to record anecdotes out of their experiences. The author, Simḥa Raz, also provided some additional material, of which he learned after the publication of the Hebrew edition.

The entire work (except for last-minute additions) was read in manuscript by Mr George Evnine of London, and it has benefited from his graceful emendations. The shortcomings in style remain my own, of course.

A word of gratitude for the generous provision of photographs is due Yaakov David Perlin, who probably has the largest collection of pictures of Reb Aryeh; and Sh'muel Gorr, whose collection of portraits of rabbinic personages (many historic) is quite certainly unique.

Charles Wengrov

N.B. In keeping with scholarly works, the abbreviation R. is used for Rabbi.

contents

	Foreword *by Dr Immanuel Jakobovits*	9
	Introduction *by Chaim Herzog*	11
1	Prologue	13
2	Some personal history	15
3	Fragments of autobiography	27
4	The woman who shared his life	52
5	A nature of humility	70
6	Making do with little	79
7	Traits of character	85
8	Of kindness and charity	108
9	His ways of hospitality	120
10	Visiting the sick	128
11	Of matchmaking and marriage	142
12	For harmony in the home	149
13	Last respects for the departed	156
14	Comforting the bereaved	172

15	Giving heart and courage	181
16	Within the prison walls	200
17	For the partners in the struggle	260
18	In the sphere of martyrdom	267
19	The gateways of piety and decency	291
20	Of children and grandchildren	312
21	The world of dreams	335
22	Incidents and fragments	350
23	Jerusalem triumphant	364
24	His last years	372
25	In the world of Torah	390
26	His sayings and maxims	408
27	From his letters	417
28	Thoughts on prayer	435
29	Thoughts on the Torah	439
30	From his last will	463

Foreword

The heroes of our time are usually drawn from the bloody field of battle, from the garish world of entertainment, sometimes from the ranks of politicians or journalists, and occasionally from an assortment of scientific pioneers, adventurers, dissidents and other brands of intrepid non-conformists. Only rarely do quiet giants of the spirit and of saintliness achieve lasting fame and popular acclaim.

In the annals of Jewish history, however, such spiritual heroes often took pride of place. Where other peoples erected monuments to their leading warriors or statesmen, we nurtured our children and inspired our national resolve on accounts and supreme acts of faith, selflessness, moral valour and religious fervor, usually sustained by the combination of piety and scholarship.

In our mundane world, preoccupied by the struggles for physical survival and material existence, few men cast in the traditional mould of specifically Jewish virtues have reached popular eminence. Reb Aryeh Levin, however, was such a personality.

Although I was not privileged to know him personally, the extraordinary spell of this Godly man gripped and fascinated me no less than the thousands he uplifted, comforted and inspired by the exceptional qualities of heart and mind which made him a legend in his lifetime and exemplified for a vast many the noblest expression of Judaism.

For him Torah living was virtually meaningless if his boundless dedication to religious learning and practice did not always culminate in his infinite concern for the well-being of his fellow-men. A delightful story related to me in the past indicates his scale of priorities: The editor of a weekly journal once came to interview him, accompanied by a photographer, who, as the interview progressed, tried to snap a picture of the rabbi's saintly visage. Motivated by both his innate modesty and his religious objection to being photographed, Reb Aryeh used his hands to hide his face from the camera, until the photographer grew exasperated. "Rabbi," the editor explained, "by your attitude you are depriving this man of his livelihood."

"Oh," said Reb Aryeh, "you make a living from taking pictures? In that case, take as many shots as you like." And he patiently posed for a number of photographs, suppressing his own religious scruples so as not to cause another Jew even the slightest loss of earnings.

Such stories about Reb Aryeh Levin's greatness are legion. Their spirit breathes through this book. May the immortal message of its pages likewise breathe and flow through our generation, making it worthy of redemption. For, if "Zion will be redeemed through justice, and her inhabitants through righteousness," then the emulation of Reb Aryeh's example can surely be the instrument of our deliverance.

Dr Immanuel Jakobovits
Chief Rabbi, the United Kingdom

Introduction

In the decades which saw the rebirth of the Jewish homeland and the emergence of Israel, the Jewish people were blessed with a host of remarkable individuals, men of stature who led the nation through a most critical period. These were men of dedication and self-sacrifice, whose names will remain indelibly in the annals of Jewish history.

Yet we who lived through the period of valor in our people's odyssey know well that beyond the praise and glory, the honor and acclaim, there stood invariably the anonymous, unknown soldier—the ordinary citizen-soldier who formed the foundation on which the great enterprise of our rebuilt homeland and statehood could arise and endure.

This unknown soldier rarely achieved any reward or recognition. In Israel we knew of such citizens, in every facet of day-to-day life.

Outstanding amongst them was Rabbi Aryeh Levin (of blessed memory).

Whenever I was in his company, I invariably sensed that I was in the presence of a tzaddik, a truly righteous man of piety—not any ordinary righteous man but a tzaddik in every fiber of his being, without a trace of materialistic concern or personal ambition, indeed with no thought but concern for others.

Now the wondrous and luminous canvas of his life has been spread before us by this biography. And inevitably, it has left me with a feeling that despite all the reverence we had in our relations with him, we perhaps never really appreciated this noble, exalted spirit. The author writes that Reb Aryeh was one of the thirty-six concealed tzaddikim whose great merit, according to tradition, sustains the world. When I concluded reading this work on the life of the slight unassuming man who was such a giant in spirit, I too asked myself: could there be another thirty-five like him?

Reading this book recalled many personal memories of Reb Aryeh's strong link with my family, especially with my father (of blessed memory), the first Chief Rabbi of Israel. He was closely bound to my family. When my late father succumbed to his final illness, we instinctively called this tzaddik to pray at his bedside.

Rabbi Aryeh Levin not only left behind him a legend. He is today a legend. This book has succeeded in converting that legend into fact.

Chaim Herzog
Permanent Representative of Israel to the United Nations

A tzaddik  in our time

1
Prologue

It was with both trepidation and happiness that I undertook the task of writing this book, something of the life-story and the activities of a kind and compassionate man, my master and teacher Rabbi Aryeh Levin (may the memory of the righteous bring blessing). I was only one of the many whom he took by the hand (affectionately, as was his way), and he never again let go of me. You see, he did not merely hold fast to you. He upheld you and gave you strength....

He was not tall, but he had immense stature. Short though he was, his heart reached to the very heaven. For his heart came surely from heaven, formed in the divine treasure-house of great spirits. It seems to me I knew him yet before I ever saw him. From his earliest years a person dreams about a wondrous grandfather, a *tzaddik* (a man of great piety), an angel... and suddenly there he was before me....

When he drew me into friendship with him (as he drew everyone) I basked in his light; and I thought: Here is one of the thirty-six hidden, secret, unknown tzaddikim by whose merit the world exists.... Then, as time passed, I thought again: O no, Reb Aryeh cannot be counted among them. How could there be another thirty-five like him in the world?

Our great code of religious law, the *Shulḥan Aruch,* opens with these words: "Let a man gather strength like a lion to rise in the morning for the service of his Maker." Reb Aryeh indeed mustered his strength for the service of his Maker—his life-work. He was not physically strong, yet how much physical force he could store within him. Despite misfortunes and accidents, physical and psychological pain, hunger and illness that he had to bear, he never lost his gentle smile and his words of encouragement for others. With him people found consolation and good cheer, through his ability to comfort so many who suffered and gave way to bitterness.

Our Sages teach that twenty is the age for pursuit and drive in a person's life (*Avoth* v 21). He had truly the strength and drive of a twenty-year-old, to pursue his goals of charity and kindness. He went after the wretched and the miserable, and sought them out—because his heart overflowed with compassion and consolation for people near and distant.

It seemed as though Reb Aryeh had an inner clock, an awareness all his own of the different periods and times in a person's life—and he was always able to respond sensitively to a human being's need.

Of material property and wealth, he had nothing of his own to speak of. Yet he was among the richest of men. He gave more than the greatest philanthropist and donor of charity. He gave of himself. He dispensed love and esteem, generously to all.

The contents of this book come mostly from what I heard from him personally, and in part from what I learned from those who were close to him. It is a book about him and by him, gathering his words and his deeds into one volume, so that those who follow in the chain of the generations may know who this wondrous man was—not just to admire but also to learn, and to follow in his footsteps.

If this book sings his praises and paints a few strokes of his life-portrait, it is my humble hope that it will fulfill in some small measure the wish that this lion of loving-kindness expressed in the last letter he wrote on the bed of his final illness: "... and let it be told unto the last generation that once there was a plain, simple man, without any portfolio or title, who loved your fathers and shared the sorrow and anguish of your families; and the love remained in his heart like a blazing fire..."

2
Some personal history

the nature of a tzaddik

On the ninth of Nissan (March 28) 1969, Rabbi Aryeh Levin (of blessed memory) passed on from this world, in holiness and purity. So ended a life that was extraordinary, a matter of wonder in many ways. The inner focal-point in the activities of this "tzaddik of Jerusalem" was his utter dedication, his readiness to give of himself and sacrifice himself, in his love of Jews and Jewry. This was the great unique, unifying force in him that made him so singular in his generation. It was perhaps for this reason that everyone called him simply *Reb Aryeh*. No descriptive adjectives or titles were added. None were needed to explain just who was meant.

The traits of compassion and love for human beings were implanted in his heart, impelling him to act voluntarily, of his own free choice, as the uncrowned "rabbi of the prisoners" for a quarter of a century. As a general rule, the different branches and communities in Jewry each select their own rabbi. In his case it was he who chose his "congregation": the poor, wretched, abused and persecuted "congregation" of the captured and the imprisoned.

Before the prisoners, there were the lepers he used to visit in the hospital allotted to them in the vicinity of Jerusalem, going to help them in spite of the personal danger of infection. He came to give all he could, and to take nothing. Whatever he did, in his own unassuming way, he did generously, with no intention of getting any reward or recompense.

His energy and his time were simply dedicated to aiding people: to help the needy, uphold the downtrodden in their misery, give courage and strength to failing hands, give ear to every anguished, embittered spirit. He showed that just as there is genius, towering ability, in Talmudic study, so can there be genius in traits of character. Such a genius Reb Aryeh was, wondrously combining and harmonizing within himself a simplicity and whole-heartedness with an uncommon intelligence.

This was a man about whom a mountain of stories and legends had arisen. On Friday the 28th of March 1969, as his body had to be taken to its final resting-place, there came to pay him their last respects and honor the president of the State of Israel, the prime minister and cabinet officers of the land—and noted hassidic rabbis. There came the venerable heads of the great *yeshivoth* in Israel, the renowned Torah academies — and officers of Israel's defense forces and former underground fighters, who acknowledged him as their rabbi. With them, following the coffin slowly on its journey, went Jews in the tens of thousands, of every circle, level and kind—telling of his countless good deeds, which now went ahead of him to the place of judgment in heaven, to speak there gently but eloquently on his behalf.

We ask sometimes, "Who is a tzaddik? What is a tzaddik?" That memorable Friday, Menahem Begin gave an answer: "When a man appears and you watch his ways and his actions carefully—and you are enchanted; you listen to his words, and they touch your heart; you look at his eyes, and they are clear and pure; you touch his hand, and you are drawn to him as though magnetically—then you say in your heart: *This is a tzaddik.*"

Such was Rabbi Aryeh Levin, our spiritual father. His hand touched you, and your heart warmed. A glance from his eyes lifted your spirit.

The man lived in a small dwelling till his last day on earth. Yet his radiance reached far and wide, not only in the land of Israel, but over oceans and seas. How did it happpen? He wrote no essays. He gave no sermons or addresses before an audience of thousands. He never spoke before mass gatherings, or let his voice travel over the airwaves of radio or television. That was not his way.

He lived in his dwelling, and went visiting the victims of misfortune. Only a few knew of it. He went to the sick for whom medicine had no cure. He visited people in prison, sometimes in darkest secret—and not only political prisoners under the British mandate who were living up to an ideal, for which they were ready to give their lives. He went also to convicts who had committed crimes against society. Them too he found it in his heart to comfort and cheer.

His conversation was simple and plain, in the language of ordinary human beings, and was restricted to a very small circle. And yet his influence and reputation spread so very far, to the great mass of his people, reaching past mountains and cities.

The key to the puzzle is simply the love he had for the individual, the Jew, the person, without any conditions or limit. You felt it immediately, once you crossed the threshold of his room. And thus he remained till his last day in his little dwelling, radiating his love and warmth for all...."

So he became a legend in his lifetime.

on the pathway of Torah

Reb Aryeh was born on the sixth of Nissan 1885 in Urla, a village near Bialystok in northeast Poland, the son of the old age of his father Binyomin Beynish, a forester and Talmudic scholar, and his mother Ethel. When his father passed away his employer said of him, "With this man integrity died in the world." The man used to earn twenty rubles a month, and his expense account was less than a fourth of what other foresters claimed. At Reb Aryeh's birth his father was already quite old, and could not work for many more years. After that there was always the distress of want and privation in the home.

One memory particularly remained with Reb Aryeh from the early period of his life, when his father still had regular employment. Away all week in the forest, his father would come home only for the Sabbath. On that holy day of rest, Reb Aryeh remembered his father invariably studying chapters of the Mishnah by heart. This must have left an impression, for through all the decades of his adult life in Israel, as he moved among the imprisoned and the unfortunate on his innumerable rounds of mercy, he too always studied the Mishnah by heart. This remained his own secret, however, and few ever realized how learned a Torah scholar it was who came to bring them solace and cheer in their misery.

Many children all over the world, through the ages, have left home at an early age; and perhaps because of the crushing poverty at home, Reb Aryeh decided to join their ranks, so as not to be a burden to his parents. With him, however, it was no flight into the adventures of the unknown. Imbued with his aging father's reverent love for sacred learning, he went off at a tender age to a place of Torah study. Intrepid far beyond his years, he traveled about, moving on from one yeshiva (Torah school) to another, as he felt the urge to grow and develop in his learning.

(One other wish moved him and spurred him on: the strong desire to know and be close to *g'doley yisrael,* the great Torah scholars of whom everyone spoke with such reverence. It was a wish that would stay with him all his life.)

It was never a problem to find a place to sleep. He learned early to find a comfortable night's rest on a bench in a *beth midrash* (house of study); and if not there, every small town had its *hekdesh,* its public place where travelers and the poor could always sleep over.

One night in a *hekdesh,* as the young boy waited for sleep to come, he heard two beggars talking. Evidently they went on foot from town to town, in search of charity and free meals. Now the young boy heard them discussing householders in the various towns, comparing notes as it were. "Oh, so-and-so in that town is an absolute miser. It is a waste of time to knock at his door. But his neighbor, so-and-so, is a generous gentleman; and he welcomes you with a smile, to boot."

Thus the talk went, until all of a sudden they mentioned Reb Binyomin Beynish of Urla. "That man has a heart of gold," said one beggar. "No one can compare with him in hospitality. He will give a stranger his own bed, and will go spend the night on a bench by the stove."

Gone in a moment was the stoic resolve with which the young lad faced the world. Overcome by nostalgia and longing, he burst into tears.

"What's the matter, boy?" asked one of the beggars. "What happened?"

"The man you were talking about," he answered, his voice choking with his tears, "is my father!"

The next day the news spread among the Jews of the town: The young boy was the son of Binyomin Beynish of Urla. Not only was the man known for his kindness and hospitality (in his dire poverty) but his was a prominent family. As Reb Aryeh was to discover, his father's father had been given to fasting on the days between Rosh haShana and Yom Kippur, and before every new Jewish month. Once the man fasted forty-eight times, and afterward, he said, he felt no more taste in food. Thus he gained a victory over the evil inclination.

Once the townspeople knew who the boy was, young Aryeh was no longer allowed to sleep in the *hekdesh,* with beggars and vagrants, but was allotted a bench in the local *beth midrash.*

Food also was not much of a problem. It was the accepted custom for local families to provide meals for students from out-of-town; and the young boy also learned early to live with hunger. Moreover, in his travels he would seek out and visit relatives, and with them too he was always sure of a meal.

On one visit to a relative he was startled by a piece of information: "Do you know?" said the man. "I believe you are bar-mitzvah. By my reckoning you have passed your thirteenth birthday." Young Aryeh digested the news with equanimity. It simply meant that from then on he was obligated to put on t'fillin (phylacteries) and observe all the mitzvoth of the Torah, like any adult Jew. Without further ado, he borrowed a pair of t'fillin, put them on, and thus said the morning prayers.

Morning after morning he borrowed a pair of t'fillin wherever he was, while he worked assiduously to scrape together enough money, penny by penny, till at last he could buy a pair of his own.

So the one who was to give so much spirit and comfort to others never had a proper bar-mitzvah celebration of his own. Like everything else, he accepted the fact with good cheer.

Such then were the young years of his life, and thus he continued through adolescence. He moved on from one Torah school to another, learning in his teens with great scholars in the noted schools of Slutsk and Slonim. There he became known as an industrious student of prodigious intelligence and learning. And so it was, seeking to progress in his Talmud study, that he traveled on the railroad as a stowaway hidden under a bench, to the town of Volozhin, to seek entry into its renowned Torah academy. On account of his young age, however, he was not admitted.

A TZADDIK IN OUR TIME

Above: Rabbi Goleventzitch, Reb Aryeh's first instructor in Torah, and R. Raphael Shapiro, with whom he studied at the Yeshiva of Volozhin.
Below: the Yeshiva of Volozhin, as it looked when he studied there.

Undaunted by this failure at Volozhin, the young scholar wandered on to other places of Talmud study. As usual at such schools, he was always assigned to various local families, to eat one day a week with each of them. (This was known as *essen teg,* "eating days.") As Reb Aryeh later remembered, he was happier on the days that he ate nothing than when he was fed at the homes among which he made the rounds.

Old enough at last, he returned to Volozhin; and this time he was accepted into the great Torah center.

When he was eighteen something occurred that made it necessary for the young scholar to travel to Brest-Litovsk (Brisk). This is the letter that Rabbi Raphael Shapiro, the sainted head of the Volozhin Yeshiva, sent with Reb Aryeh to his son-in-law Rabbi Ḥayyim Soloveitchik in Brest-Litovsk:

"With the blessed Lord's help / 6 Tammuz 1903 / Volozhin.

... Hoping all is well with you, let me inform you that the student who brings this letter is most estimable and noble in qualities of character, most industrious and diligent in studying in depth, well versed in two of the six orders (sections) of the Talmud. Reb Aryeh is traveling to your vicinity now in regard to a matter of personal importance. I ask of your most esteemed self to give him your friendship in every way possible, and to grant him your good advice in the matter."

It can safely be said that there were not many students in the Yeshiva of Volozhin for whom such a letter would have been written.

In his earlier years, at the Slutsk Yeshiva, he had studied with the noted Talmudic sage R. Isser Zalman Meltzer. The two met again in Jerusalem, when Reb Aryeh had grown to manhood and they became neighbors in the holy city. R. Isser Zalman's memory of him was vague, but seeing what a fine Torah scholar the young man was, he assumed that Reb Aryeh must have been a notable student in Slutsk. While ordinary pupils had been assigned for their meals to families, one per day (for *essen teg*), notable students were given permanent lodgings with the comparatively wealthier families. Hence, as R. Isser Zalman once sat talking with Reb Aryeh about his period of study in Slutsk, he asked innocently, "And where did you have your lodgings?"

Rabbi Isser Zalman Meltzer, Reb Aryeh's instructor at the Yeshiva of Slutsk, who was later his neighbor in Jerusalem.

"Oh," replied the young man, "I was quite comfortably situated. I had a bench in the *shneider shul* (the Tailors' Synagogue) as my regular place to sleep."

"Hmm," grumbled R. Isser Zalman, not altogether pleased at the answer. "And where did you eat?"

"Oh, I had fine accommodations. Let me see.... On Sundays I went to this family; on Tuesdays to that family; and on Thursdays to this other family"; and he named three households in the town.

"But what of the other days?"

"Oh, I managed very well..." said Reb Aryeh; and the Talmudic sage realized that the fine young scholar had simply gone hungry much of the time at his former Torah school. He found the thought distressing. "How can you ever forgive me," he asked, "for having neglected you like that?" Reb Aryeh simply assured him, however, that he had neither suffered nor felt any neglect. He harbored no memories of deprivation.

That night, as the young Reb Aryeh considered going to bed, Mrs Meltzer came knocking at his door. Would he please come at once, she asked. Her husband was unable to go to sleep.... Reb Aryeh found his former teacher sitting up, with tears running down his cheeks. "Whatever will I answer on my day of judgment in heaven," he pleaded, "when they ask me how it is that I never knew that Reb Aryeh slept on a bench, with no proper bed to call his own; that he did not have enough to eat to keep body and soul together, and he studied his Torah in hardship and suffering?" So he continued, without a stop, until at last Reb Aryeh was able to reassure him that he really did not mind what had happened, and bore no grudge whatsoever about it.

Having learned his full measure of Talmud and religious law, the young scholar knew that Europe was no substitute for the land of Israel. War broke out between Russia and Japan, and he decided the time had come for him to set out. (Were he to stay, he was certain to face conscription into the Russian army.) Yet just how was he to go? When he told the head of the great Torah school in Volozhin of his decision, that man of learning asked him what means he had. "I have no means," the young scholar answered. All he requested was a letter of recommendation to the trustees of this yeshiva, who lived in Minsk. Perhaps they would come to his aid.

With this letter in hand the youthful Reb Aryeh set out toward the end of the very same week, asking a wagon-driver to take him to the railroad station in the nearby village of Molodetchna. All went well till they arrived at the station. Then they discovered that the train for Minsk had already come and gone. Reb Aryeh's despair knew no bounds. And the wagon-driver moaned, "Woe is me! Since I first started in this occupation it's the first time my pair of horses was late for the train."

With nothing to ease his despair, Reb Aryeh had to get to Minsk without the vanished train, and as a result he arrived on Friday afternoon, only a short time before the Sabbath candles would be lit. Yet he soon realized that almost as in a fairy tale, the hand of Providence had been at work for him. Had he come as he planned, he would have gone to the community's guest-house for a place to sleep. Under the circumstances he was invited to stay with R. Berl Zeldovitz, a trustee of the Yeshiva of Volozhin who was generous with charity. The letter Reb Aryeh carried was meant mainly for him.

In his home, before the Sabbath, Reb Berl read the letter carefully— and he offered the young scholar three rubles. At so small a sum Reb Aryeh burst into tears. After the Sabbath, therefore, the usually generous Reb Berl went to hold a "family conference." The result was that he raised his donation to some forty rubles—enough to get the young Reb Aryeh to the seaport of Odessa, secure him a passport, and even pay part of his passage to the land of Israel.

In Odessa, the intellectual center of Russian Jewry, the young pioneer came into contact with the Zionist circles that flourished there. A. L. Levinski, a popular writer under the pseudonym of "Reb Karov" (in everyday life he was the agent for Carmel wines from the land of Israel), gave him a letter of recommendation to Zalman David Levontin in Jaffa (there was no Tel Aviv yet) asking him to accept the newcomer—a fine, outstanding Torah scholar, etc.—as an employee in the Anglo-Palestine Company bank.

On the first of Adar (in March) 1905 the Russian ship (on which young Aryeh Levin was almost the only Jewish passenger) arrived at the port of Jaffa. Without a second thought he relinquished his "banking career" immediately, and instead formed a growing friendship with the rabbi of Jaffa, R. Abraham Isaac *ha-kohen* Kook, destined to become the first chief rabbi of the land. They forged a strong bond of affection, that was never severed as long as both were alive.

Soon the young man was settled in Jerusalem, where he continued his Talmudic studies, until he was ordained as a rabbi in 1909 by three outstanding Torah authorities: R. Hayyim Berlin, R. Sh'muel Salant, and R. Kook.

From 1917 till the end of his life he served as "spiritual advisor" and supervisor in the elementary school of Jerusalem's Yeshiva Etz Hayyim. It was a task he dearly loved. More than mere teaching, it meant that he came in living contact with the children every day to appraise not only their intellectual capacity but also their spirit, their character, and their problems. He had a constant chance to become part of their lives and help them.

This is what he wrote in his last will and testament:

> "...I especially recall the school children who were my sacred charge through scores of years, whom I punished beyond the measure of their guilt with harsh words or a rebuke, and I gave them pain without any purpose. For this my heart grieves. Particularly I feel a sharp anguish, to the depths of my being, that I did not fulfill my duties of supervision properly at the beginning of the year 5677 (1917) when I was assigned my position in the elementary school. Yet I embarked on my duties with every fiber of my being, as I found before me a wide fertile field in which to work on the souls of the school children. I was happy indeed. Nothing was too difficult for me..."

This, too, he added in his last will and testament:

> "I relinquish my salary for the last month at the school. But I impose the condition that the money is to be used to install running water for the children to drink and wash their hands—a matter which has caused me great concern..."

Reb Aryeh knew full well the teaching of the Talmudic sages that water is a symbol for Torah: Its study slakes the deeper thirst of the spirit to know the word of the Lord. But he also knew that actual, literal water must be part of the Torah's way of life. It is no less important to relieve the body's thirst than to take care of the spirit's need.

an extraordinary man

This was Reb Aryeh. No other titles were necessary. In Jerusalem when you mentioned "Reb Aryeh" everyone knew you meant the man of kindly piety, Rabbi Aryeh Levin. He seemed to be an essential, inseparable part of the city landscape—the ordinary earthly Jerusalem of daily life, and the heavenly Jerusalem, the holy city that was all spirituality. He was short, with a large head and an oval face adorned with a white beard (it was hard to imagine it as ever anything but white), and handsome. But above all there were his eyes, filled at one and the same time with keen wisdom and tender compassion—a rare combination. In his glance you saw shrewd intelligence and simple sincerity. His eyes radiated light and warmth. They blazed and comforted at the same time. Only a heavenly fatherly love could regard you in that way.

With this love he welcomed everyone he met, particularly a man with a burden of woe, and above all a Jew in whom he sensed dedication, a readiness for self-sacrifice. With a man like that he felt that he himself was as nothing. And so he had an amazing humility. There was a thread of melancholy in him, that he acquired perhaps from the ocean of troubles and anguish of the great many people to whom he went, which he absorbed and bore with them. But he never allowed anyone to talk to him about it. His face always smiled and even beamed, so as to cause no no one any pain.

It once occurred to me that surely this tzaddik must have not only an immense stock of good deeds to his credit, but also a collection of writings, literary works, either published or in manuscript. The truth was that he never wrote any books or created anything in writing. He himself was more wondrous, more extraordinary than any literary creation of morals and ethics. He was an endless wellspring of love for his people.

This was no *rebbe* leading devoted followers in the ways of *ḥassiduth*. He was himself a thorough *mithnagged*, educated and living outside the world of *ḥassiduth*. Nor was he a "miracle man," producing wonders to order (although there were remarkable things in his life). He was something more, something greater.

He was an extraordinary model Jew.

3
Fragments of autobiography
from his own pen

A holy duty lies on every one of us to record for himself the details of all the events, incidents and adventures in his life. In the Torah we read, "from my own flesh I can perceive God" (Job 19:26). With a clear vision you can see His sure hand in the happenings of your own life. Now that most of my years have passed by in the blessed Lord's kindness and abounding compassion, I have decided: Let me relate to my children and grandchildren what happened to me in my days on earth.

childhood and education

According to family tradition, I was born to my dear parents near the town of Urla on Tuesday the sixth of Nissan (in April) 1885; to my father and teacher, Reb Binyomin Beynish the son of R. Yoséf, and my mother, the pious Ethel the daughter of R. Abraham. They were thoroughly poor, but outstanding in the ways of kindness.

Until the age of six I studied with a teacher in my parental home, along with a few other children from surrounding settlements. When I began learning the Hebrew Bible, my father (of blessed memory) sent me to his older brother, my uncle R. Uzziel (of blessed memory) in the nearby town of Narevke, to study our sacred Scripture. There I pursued my learning for almost a whole year, and then returned to my parents, whereupon I continued my education in the nearby town of Urla. There I studied with various teachers, until the age of twelve.

I lost favor in my father's eyes

At that time I developed a yearning to leave my parents' house and go off into "exile," to a place of Torah study far from home, in the city of Brest-Litovsk (Brisk). My sainted father did not like the idea, but the economic situation at home forced me out.

I continued my education at the large elementary school in Brisk. But unfortunately, because of various circumstances I could not remain there more than two months; then back I was in my parents' home. Thanks to this incident, however, I lost all favor and charm in my father's sight, and he had not a good word to say to me.... I did not dare be brazen enough to explain and try to alter his feelings toward me. He must surely have had a good reason for his attitude, and good intentions. After all, in our sacred heritage respect for parents is considered equal in importance to respect for the blessed Lord.

When the festival (*yom tov*) of Shavuoth had passed, I returned to my old place of study, the town of Urla. There I stayed in the *beth midrash* (the public house of learning) pursuing my studies with great diligence and zeal. Whatever was too hard for me to understand, I asked the people in the *beth midrash*. So I became among the first to get there in the morning, and among the last to leave at night. In this way (while continuing to live at home), I studied with great earnestness and zeal for about two years.

"go into exile, to a place of Torah study"

Then I developed again the strong yearning to go off into "exile" to a setting of Torah study. I was sleeping at home during this period, but even in the middle of the long winter nights I would go alone to the *beth midrash* in Urla. No wind or storm, frost or snow could stop me. In this way I managed to draw my sainted father a bit closer to me in friendship. And so I began asking and prevailing on other people to persuade my father, that this time he should agree to the idea of my leaving home.

Just about then a *yeshiva* (Torah school) was established in the town of Fahust near Pinsk. Its distinguished rabbinic emissary came a number of times to our town to speak on behalf of the yeshiva (to raise funds, and so forth) and a desire and longing took hold of me to travel and study there. With the Almighty's help, my attempts were successful. My father consented.

After Passover 1899 I took leave of my parents to make the journey to Fahust; but I did not have the means to get there, lacking expenses for the long trip. I traveled, therefore, instead to the town of Pruzhyna, not far from my home town.

When I arrived in Pruzhyna I was accepted into the elementary school, on the recommendation of the Talmudic scholar R. Eliyahu Feinstein, the sainted head of the *beth din* (rabbinic court), who invited me to eat at his table two days a week. There I studied the Talmud tractate *Gittin* for about half a year, then returned home in time for Rosh haShana (the high holy days, that marked the beginning of the Jewish year).

no place to rest my head

After the festival (*yom tov*) of Sukkoth I made up my mind to travel (with God's help) to the Yeshiva of Slonim together with my friend Alter Heller (who eventually found eternal rest in the holy city of Jerusalem). This time I obtained my father's consent without difficulty.

We traveled by way of Bialystok. But going to the railroad after midnight we were seized by the police. In that time and place travel was severely restricted. You could not go anywhere without a permit, special papers, and so forth. And we had not a single paper of that kind to show. It was only by some sort of miracle that we managed to get free, thanks to a kindly Providence.

Without further trouble we reached Slonim, and praised be God, we were accepted as students of the yeshiva. Then we went making the rounds, knocking on doors, to ask kindhearted home-owners to let us take our meals with them, each for one day a week. This was the time-honored practice of *essen teg* ("eating days") that was followed for generations in the study of Torah. We only had to find seven families (as many as the days of the week) that could and would somehow manage to feed two boys for one day in the seven, and we had the physical means to survive.

Heaven be praised, we were successful, and even found a place to sleep: in the Torah school, near the door, on two benches. We moved the benches together and covered ourselves with one robe—until, thank God, we found our own "permanent sleeping quarters" in the synagogue. For at night every *beth midrash* (study-room) in the yeshiva was packed full with sleeping students, from wall to wall, and in none of those rooms could I find a bench on which to rest my head.

So we spent a whole year in that yeshiva, studying the Talmud tractate *Ḥullin* with the entire commentary of *tosafoth* [by the French-German scholars of the 12th–14th centuries].

One thing remains vivid in my memory from those days. It was the night of Tish'a b'Av (the ninth of Av, the anniversary of the destruction of both the first and second Temples in ancient Jerusalem). Like Jews the world over, we sat on the floor, on low stools, or on overturned benches, chanting the *kinnoth*, the age-old laments and dirges for the *beth ha-mikdash*, the holy Sanctuary that was gone, leaving us bereft in the long, endless exile. Some overly mischievous youngsters entered (probably bored by it all) and began throwing burrs at the lamenting worshippers. At the center, on the floor, sat the great Talmudic sage Rabbi I. Ḥarif, chanting his sorrowful prayers with a keen intensity; and some of the burrs stuck in his beard.

Perhaps a dimly-felt annoyance at the burrs roused him to a greater fervor of lament. Perhaps it was only coincidence. But at that moment, showing no sign that he was aware of the barbed objects in his beard, Rabbi Ḥarif began wailing in a strong voice, "The *beth ha-mikdash* burned down! The *beth ha-mikdash* burned down!"

Only hours later, after midnight, a fire broke out in the neighborhood, and the house where those mischievous youngsters slept was burned to the ground. On the very day of Tish'a b'Av, after the *kinnoth* of the morning were chanted, their charred remains (nothing more was found of them) were brought to burial. And no one thought it was coincidence.

One other event remains in my mind from that period: While there, I spent time studying with a younger pupil, to help him advance in his learning. For this he paid me half a kopek a week. By saving every single coin, I managed to amass about three silver rubles. That was enough to have a tailor sew a new *caftan* (long jacket) for me, for the festivals (*yomim tovim*). When at last I took the finished garment from the tailor, I hung it up in the synagogue where I slept every night. Yet alas, that night, when I went to the synagogue to go to sleep on my regular bench, I could hardly believe my eyes: the *caftan* was gone! I hardly had the satisfaction of gazing my fill at it before it was stolen from me. There are no words to describe the anguish I felt then....

Yet with Heaven's help I managed somehow to get another *caftan*; and as the month of Elul (August-September) ended and Rosh haShana approached, my friend and I rode home together.

my head went round on wheels

Nothing can stand for long in the way of true determination. With the festival of Sukkoth past, I developed a strong wish to transfer to the renowned Yeshiva of Volozhin, which had recently been reopened.

I left home with just about three silver rubles in my pocket, and so (prudently practicing economy) I bought a quarter-ticket for the railroad train (valid for someone considerably younger than myself). To my misfortune, I was caught out immediately, and the quarter-ticket was confiscated. With no choice, I was reduced to using means that were, to say the least, by no means pleasant: to lie still under the long railroad-train seat, behind people's feet, keeping well hidden from the eyes of the railroad inspectors and ticket-collectors. Thus I managed to stay hidden till the train reached Vilna.

It was a distressing experience for me, filled as I was with fear, my head seeming to keep going round, as if on wheels, from the steady churning clamor of the train. When I finally left the train I found a quiet secluded place where I could rest on the ground for a short while from the strain and upset of the journey. From the money I had left I bought a train-ticket to the station of Molodetchna; and there, with my last coins I hired Mr. Peretz, the "coachman" of Volozhin, renowned for the speed of his horses, to take me to Volozhin, where we arrived toward evening.

From afar I could already see the Torah academy, a majestic building on the outskirts of the town, *like a rose among the thorns* (Song of Songs 2:2). I turned my steps toward the yeshiva, and was soon surprised to hear the "tumult" of Torah study, that sweet, strong and mighty sound rising from hundreds of students immersed in their chant of Talmudic study. There is no sweeter sound than the chant of Torah study.

I entered and went to see the head of the academy, that true scholar of the Talmud, R. Raphael Shapiro, and gave him the letter of recommendation that I had brought from the great scholar R. Israel Jonathan, head of the *beth din* (rabbinic court) in my native town. The upshot, however, was that R. Raphael Shapiro rejected me outright; I was simply too young to be accepted; and all my pleading and weeping were to no avail. R. Shapiro and R. Meir Yaslavitz, the distinguished spiritual supervisor of the yeshiva, gave me a letter of recommendation to the learned R. Sh'lomo Golbnitz, head of the Torah school at the noted synagogue *Maskil l'Eythan* in Minsk. In addition they gave me my traveling expenses, and off I rode to Minsk, the tears still streaming down my cheeks as I took leave of them.

"live a life of hardship"

It was shortly before midnight when I reached Minsk, and away I trudged to the Maskil l'Eythan synagogue. A few students who had not yet fallen asleep arose to welcome me as best they could, observing the *mitzvah* (religious good deed) of the Torah, "you shall love the stranger" (Deuteronomy 10:19). They were even able to provide me with a bit of a bench on which to rest my head. Thank Heaven, so tired was I that it was into a most sweet and pleasant sleep that I fell.

The next day the head of the academy accepted me into the school, and my new fellow-students soon made me one of them.

In this locale, where the feet of my fathers and forefathers had never trodden, I was able to arrange a few meals during the week with some families (one day with each, in the time-honored custom of *essen teg*). But in the main I followed the advice of the Sages, "a life of hardship shall you live" (*Avoth* 6, 4), as I suffered quite considerably from hunger-pangs, etc. Yet not once did I think of giving my parents pain by writing them of my situation. On the contrary, I kept writing them encouraging reports, and assured them every time that my situation was in every respect most satisfactory.

Before many days passed, however, I found out that among the young yeshiva students in nearby Kamarauka there was a relative of mine, Joseph Werbin (in later life he became a resident of Be'er Yaakov in the land of Israel). To him I told everything. And he advised me to go to the Yeshiva of Slutzk, where he had studied before coming here.

So when the intermediate days (*hol ha-mo‘éd*) of Passover arrived I set my face toward Slutzk, and took leave from my beloved and revered teacher R. Sh'lomo (of blessed memory).

a new spirit within me

When I came to the Yeshiva of Slutzk it was as though a new spirit possessed me: a mood of happiness. When I entered I found choice, gifted students, true scholars in their own right, studying with a titan of the Talmud, Rabbi A. Z. Cohen. Now the good Lord helped me indeed, and I was accepted into the school.

I took to learning with extraordinary zeal and diligence; and both that prince of Torah known as *Ridbaz* (Raphael Yaakov David ben Z'év) and my unforgettable master and teacher, the great pious scholar R. Isser Zalman Meltzer, head of the academy, befriended me warmly. They wrote quite a few letters about me to my father, in order to strengthen my spirit and resolve. Thank Heaven, in the three years I spent there I acquired a sound knowledge of the Talmud order (section) of *Nashim*, with the commentary of *tosafoth* (except for the tractate *Yevamoth*). The tractates *Gittin, Kiddushin* and *K'thuboth* were known to me by rote, with the *tosafoth*; and I launched into the Talmud order *N'zikin*.

In 1901, when the sainted head of the academy was away, at his home in Slobodka, a movement surged up among various students to introduce *haskalah,* general and Hebraic secular learning—to the bitter dismay of the great Torah scholars who directed the school. Fearing this controversy would interfere with my studies or interrupt them, I decided to travel on to Halusk, there to listen to the teaching of the pious sage R. Baruch Ber (Lebowitz). In the month of Sivan 1901 I arrived.

the inner secrets of my heart

Once I arrived, this fine scholar drew me close to him in friendship, and arranged a set time to give me private lessons in the Talmud tractate *Eruvin* and a bit of the volume of religious law, *Shulḥan Aruch Even ha'Ezer*. My material situation also improved greatly, as the worthy, respected members of the community invited me to have my meals regularly with them. So I studied there an entire year.

Yet I could not comfortably accept this abundance of goodness. I feared it might interfere with my learning (by making me indolent). And back came my earlier desire to go to Volozhin. This wish of mine was not to the liking of my dear revered master and teacher; but he could not gauge the strength of my desire in the inner secrets of my heart.

I took leave of this teacher of mine, the most cherished and beloved of all who educated me, though it was against his wish. For my yearning for the Yeshiva of Volozhin was overpowering.

the mass sound of Torah study

After Passover 1902 I arrived in Volozhin in good order. From quite a distance away that Divine sound could be heard rising and falling—the chant of Torah study by a mass of voices. As soon as I entered the yeshiva I could sense the holiness that imbued and pervaded its every corner, as its dear sons filled every available space.

I made my way once more to the head of the academy, R. Raphael Shapiro. My entire body was shivering in anxiety as I approached this holy man. Would he turn me away again?

To show my degree of knowledge I began discoursing on various topics of Talmud study, particularly from the tractate *Eruvin*, explaining and unfolding the strands of thought. He listened, and Heaven be praised, I found favor in his eyes. He accepted me into the yeshiva, and allotted me the handsome stipend of four silver rubles a month, quite enough for my needs by the normal (minimal) standards of the world of Torah learning.

By good fortune I was assigned to stay in a dormitory with excellent students, outstanding examples of the type; and they befriended me in affection although I reached nowhere near their level of learning. Among them let me mention R. Sh'muel David Levin, a brilliant mind who was fluent in the entire Babylonian Talmud (known afterward by his initials, as Shadal of Minsk); and a marvelously diligent and devout young scholar, R. Mordecai Duker Eidelberg, who in later years wrote *Hazon laMo'éd* and became head of the *beth din* (rabbinic court) in Slutzk.

The greater part of the day I studied with my very dear friend R. Isser Israel, the son of our holy teacher (the head of the academy) R. Raphael Shapiro.

Vivid and alive, as though I still were there, the picture of the Yeshiva of Volozhin rises clear in my mind, with the luster of holiness that graced and filled its every corner, with its precious sons so "learned of the Lord" (Isaiah 54:13). How well I remember the ways of their life in holy times and on weekdays, all their spiritual toil and struggle, and all their spiritual pleasure and delight, which filled my young spirit too, as I shared their emotional experiences. I particularly remember the long winter evenings, when we would study for about five hours at a stretch, the yeshiva filled from wall to wall with the students immersed in their Talmud, serving the Lord with body and spirit, heart and mind.

Had I remained in the Yeshiva of Volozhin for some further time, I would have become the equal of my good friends and fellow-students, all fine notable Talmud scholars; for while among them I was not inferior to them. But "a man's steps are ordered by the Lord" (Proverbs 20:24). I was compelled to leave behind me my parental home and my native land. For in those times war-clouds gathered and darkened the sky, as Russia and Japan met in battle. And in my heart formed and ripened a decision to carry out a hidden dream, a yearning since childhood: to go to the holy land of Israel.

I was about nineteen then, and would soon be of age to be taken by law into the army. I saw no other way but to anticipate the trouble with earnest prayer and form some plan to leave my native land behind me, following the example of my forefather, the patriarch Jacob, who fled from Esau in good time when that brother of his made unbrotherly plans for him.... So I decided that the time had come when, with Heaven's help, I would carry out my long-standing determined wish.

First, I began casting about for some way of getting a vital travel-permit, as I was a young man who had half-disappeared from official notice and records. "But the poor has nothing at all" (2 Samuel 12:3). So I "cast my burden on the blessed Lord." He arranges and regulates all that happens. I simply trusted that He (blessed be His name) would provide me with some plan to make my way overseas, and would form a proper ordered way for me to proceed.

From my parents I could get no help whatever. They simply had no means to aid me at a time of need, and especially not in such a situation of emergency. But in truth the blessed Lord opened a pathway for me, by the clear, open care of His watchful providence, in an obviously supernormal way that bordered on the miraculous.

When I took my leave of the Yeshiva of Volozhin, the matrix of my spiritual life and growth, that true prince of Talmudic erudition R. Raphael Shapiro placed in my hands a letter to two renowned men of wealth in Minsk, the brothers R. Dov Ber and R. Baruch Zeldovitz, asking them to support me in my wish to go to the land of Israel. And the Lord stood by me.

I could not control my tears

On a Thursday morning I left Volozhin, so as to reach Minsk toward evening, the same day. But alas, I reached the railway station only to find that the train had left a few minutes earlier. I had arrived too late. There was no alternative for me but to travel to Minsk early Friday morning, on the day before the holy Sabbath.

It was afternoon when I arrived. The days were short then, in the month of Adar (March), and the Sabbath would soon begin. So I set off at once to find the two men of wealth. I soon succeeded in reaching R. Dov Ber Zeldovitz, a pious, good man of learning, as he sat in his study. He took the letter I brought, read it, and held out three silver rubles. I just remained there standing, dismayed at so small a sum, and tears fell from my eyes. I could not control my weeping, and not a word could I speak; but neither would I take anything from him.

His response was to tell me to go to his brother, R. Baruch Zeldovitz (a wonderful man of piety, who, at the time I write this, lives in Jerusalem). It was Heaven's doing that I did not find him at home; and back I went to the house of R. Dov Ber. He pleaded with me now to stay at his home for the Sabbath, and with all my heart I accepted. I was thus privileged to sit near him at his truly royal table.

Never had I seen Torah learning and grandeur in one place as I saw it harmonized and unified here. There were other guests too, all seated about his table just like the family, in fulfillment of the teaching of the Sages, "let poor people be members of your household" (*Avoth* 1, 5). He treated everyone with charming modesty and good cheer; and the rest of that Friday and throughout Saturday we talked with delight and enthusiasm on topics of Torah. I was then full of all I had learned from that truly pious sage, the head of the Yeshiva of Volozhin—all his original interpretations on the Talmud; and now I was able to expound them in understanding and appreciative company.

When the Sabbath ended (on Saturday night) we discoursed together a while longer on Torah topics; then he called me into a private room, and the two noble brothers gave me enough for my travel expenses. I thanked them gratefully for their goodness and generosity, and took my leave with the fervent hope of seeing them in the holy land of our patriarchs. Blessed be God that I have merited seeing R. Baruch here in the holy city of Jerusalem.

From there I returned to the home of my parents, to make preparations for my journey.

never will I forget

When I returned home my parents almost failed to recognize me. And to my sorrow, I found my dear father seriously ill, and the financial situation wretched indeed. The night before my arrival, the single cow they owned, which helped them stay alive with a bit of milk and butter, took sick and died. I will never forget the great sorrow and anguish that filled my compassionate mother's eyes. It was years since she had last seen me, and to welcome me, she had nothing for the first meal but some dry black bread.

A few days later, my dear father took to his bed in his woeful illness, and on me fell the double burden of attending to him and making the necessary preparations for my long journey to the land of the Patriarchs. For a number of reasons I was compelled to remain with my parents almost that whole year; and I suffered both physically and mentally....

joy and sadness mixed together

After various troubles and vicissitudes I obtained (thank Heaven) what I most needed and desired: a travel-permit (visa) for the land of Israel, all perfectly proper and legal; and I still had barely enough money to cover the travel expenses. I was nineteen then, and it was a time of both joy and sadness for me. On the one hand, as the Psalmist sang, "I was glad when they said to me: Let us go to the house of the Lord" (Psalms 122:1). Yet I grieved at the thought of leaving my dear father with his health declining steadily.

I can see the scene now, as clearly as when it happened. When I came to bid him Goodbye, he put his thin gaunt hands on my head and blessed me, the tears streaming down his face—and I took his hands and kissed them. To this very day, whenever I speak about it, a feeling of immense nostalgia and endless yearning wells up in me. When I finally left he was unable to rise from his bed, and only my dear mother, that most worthy of women, accompanied me to the town of Urla, where I said farewell to her, the mother whom I bore a boundless love, a model of patient suffering and goodness.

I have not the power to describe my feelings for my parents, whom I was hardly privileged to know, appreciate and honor, since throughout my youth I was away, having "exiled" myself to centers of Torah study.

one thing I asked of the Lord

So I took leave of my entire family and traveled down to Odessa. Arriving there on a Friday I made for the house of Rabbi I. Goldschmidt. He welcomed me warmly, and had me stay with him till after the Sabbath. Then I went to a lodging-house, where I stayed the entire week, till I could find a ship bound for Constantinople and Jaffa. During those few days I made the acquaintance of various *maskilim* ("enlightened intellectuals") who still venerated the Yeshiva of Volozhin—principally Mr.

Reb Aryeh's parents

The renowned "Ḥurva Synagogue" and its environs, in the Old City of Jerusalem, where Reb Aryeh came soon after his arrival in the holy land.

L. Levinsky. They begged me to remain in Odessa and obtain a "complete balanced" education (meaning secular, non-holy studies). But as for me, "one thing I asked of the Lord...to see the goodness of the Lord in the land of life" (Psalms 27:4,13)—the holy land. When I refused to yield to their request they gave me letters of recommendation to the most prominent intellectuals in Jerusalem, asking them to befriend me in any way I might wish, and to obtain for me a position in one of the national organizations. All these letters eventually remained with me. I delivered none of them.

in the holy land

On Thursday I found out that a ship heading for Jaffa would sail Saturday on the Black Sea. I hurried off to get my travel-permit validated by the Turkish consul, as required. [The land of Israel, called Palestine, was then ruled by Turkey.] On Friday I bought a ticket for the ship, boarded it, and remained there through the Sabbath. Saturday afternoon the ship embarked peacefully, in good order, from Odessa and sailed for Constantinople.

Aboard the ship I suffered greatly, being the only Jew among hundreds of Russians, devout Christians on a pilgrimage to the "holy sepulchre." Afterward I was joined by another Jew, who was ill. I myself felt sick from the rolling of the ship and the hardships of the journey, until at last we docked at Constantinople on Wednesday, where I left the ship and went to a Jewish lodging-house. There a doctor gave me some medicine, and I immediately felt my health beginning to improve.

On Friday I boarded the ship again, for the second part of the journey, to Jaffa. But once there I immediately turned sick again, and hardly knew myself through the nine remaining days of the trip.

It was early Sunday morning when we reached Jaffa, the port of the holy land, in good order. As soon as I saw from afar this sacred land which the Lord promised our forefathers to give us, I became a completely new person. I was overwhelmed by intense emotion amidst great happiness, as tears fell from my eyes. I felt ready to die (if need be) now that the blessed Lord had granted me the privilege of entering the land of the Patriarchs. Forgotten was all my suffering. I was as if possessed by a new spirit, of boundless ethereal happiness and delight. And at the same time I wept without stopping because by Heaven's mercy I had succeeded in reaching the holy land. I was gazing at the land so many thousands dreamed and yearned to see.

I left the ship and went walking on the holy ground. With every single step I took I sensed that this was sacred land beneath my feet.

Losing no time, I went to find the pious luminary R. Abraham Isaac *ha-kohen* Kook, the learned head of the *beth din* there. He received me with a cheerful, radiant face, as was his blessed way. When I left him to make my way to Jerusalem, he gave me a letter addressed to the learned R. Isaac Winograd, asking him to accept me into his Torah academy.

within Jerusalem's gates

I took the train to Jerusalem, and on the way met R. Isaiah Salomon (of the noted Jerusalem family of that name). I asked him to kindly take care of my bundle of clothing, etc. until I found a place to stay.

Toward evening I succeeded in reaching the city walls of Jerusalem, going from the train to the Jaffa Gate... and there I stood, not knowing to whom to turn. Then I recalled that before I left my home town R. Eliyahu David Lifschitz had given me a letter to bring to his father, R. Yeḥezkel, who dwelt in the Jewish quarter of the holy city. I walked to the section of houses where he lived, arriving in time for *ma'ariv*, the evening prayers; and so I entered a small synagogue to join in the prayer-service. There I found R. Yeḥezkel Lifschitz himself, and gave him the letter, whereupon he invited me to join him for the evening meal.

In the middle of the meal, though, he warned me that I ought to hurry, since I still had to find a place to lodge. Without a word of objection I left his house—to find it quite dark, and myself with no idea where to turn, since my money was all spent and gone. Well, this was not really any new experience for me. Having not a penny to my name, I went looking in the dark of night for a *beth midrash* (a house of study, which also served as a small synagogue), to sleep the night on a bench, as I was accustomed to do since childhood.

Wandering about in the neighborhood, I met an old man, and asked him where a *beth midrash* was to be found. From my question he understood that I had nowhere to sleep; so he replied that if I wanted a lodging for just one night, he could take me into his house. May that worthy, unassuming, Godfearing man, named R. Yaakov, be eternally remembered for his goodness. He put me up in his house until the day I married.

The next day I met a member of my father's family in the synagogue, R. Hayyim Vasser, and he invited me to spend the holy Sabbath with him. That very day my close childhood friend R. Alter Heller, who had moved to the land of Israel a half-year earlier, came to see me; and I felt infinitely better. On the Sabbath we went together to the *kothel ma'aravi* (the Western, or Wailing, Wall), the remnant of our ancient life-giving Sanctuary, from which the *shechinah* (the Divine Presence) has never stirred. Afterward we went to the synagogue called the *hurva* (ruin) of R. Judah the *hassid* (man of kindly piety), where we heard R. Nahum of Warsaw speaking on the biblical Book of Esther.

The next day I made my way to Yeshiva Torath Hayyim, where its principal, the great scholar R. Isaac Winograd, accepted me as a student. If not for his valiant, yeoman work in maintaining this Torah academy, who knows how many fine young scholars, budding great luminaries of Torah who came to the holy land, would have had to make a complete break with their past and forget about further serious Talmudic study, for lack of a proper school. The doors of his Yeshiva Torath Hayyim were ever open to all who came. Let his brother also be remembered for good—R. Yosef Eliyahu Winograd, a righteous, pious learned scholar, of most attractive character, whose ways were always honest and worthy, and whose words were always counted and weighed for their purpose. Together with the distinguished members of his family, he granted me a friendship strong and true beyond measure.

predestined partner for life

About that time I went to visit the noted sage R. Tz'vi Pesah Frank, accompanied by my good friend R. Moshe Ostrovsky. From then on people began raising the subject of marriage with a sister-in-law of his who had recently arrived from Kovno, Lithuania. It soon became clear to me that Heaven intended this modest young woman for my helpmate

Above: R. Abraham Isaac Kook, as he looked in the First World War years; right, R. Tz'vi Pesaḥ Frank, the rabbi of Jerusalem, whose brother-in-law Reb Aryeh became.

R. Sh'muel Salant, head of the Ashkenazic community, and R. Ḥayyim Berlin, who ordained Reb Aryeh as rabbi.

Two early views of Jaffa Gate, leading into the Old City, where Reb Aryeh headed on his arrival in Jerusalem.

in life. Several days later I became engaged to her at a good, propitious moment, in the month of Adar II (March-April) 1905. The formal terms of the engagement (*t'na'im*) were written in the house of the learned R. Tz'vi Pesah Frank himself; and on Friday the eleventh of Tammuz (in July) 1905, in a blissful fortunate moment, we were wed.

Immediately after our marriage we began, with the blessed Lord's help, to be self-supporting. From the yeshiva I received a meager allowance, which was far from enough for our needs. Yet with her generous heart my dear wife sent off 100 rubles to my parents, since they were ordered to pay a fine of 300 rubles on my account, as I had deserted from the army in which I should have served.

Sunday the twenty-seventh of Nissan (in April) 1906 my daughter Rasha was born; Friday the fourteenth of Heshvan (in October) 1907 my daughter Shifra came into the world. And then I began to feel the pinch and pressure of having to support a family.

Going from one subject to another, let me tell a bit about the watchful providential care that the blessed Lord bestowed on me, one person among all His human beings.... I was close to great Torah personages since my early years, in every locality and region.... And truly "the kindnesses of the Lord never cease" (Lamentations 3:22). For a most renowned and beloved Talmudic luminary now appeared on the scene: R. Hayyim Berlin, the son of Jewry's great rabbi, the *N'tziv* (R. Naftali Tz'vi Judah Berlin). Heaven granted that I should find favor in his eyes, and he took me under his care literally as a father befriends a son. It might almost be said that my hand never left his. He linked me closely to him, and in his unassuming modesty he set a fixed time to study with me late in the evening, and sometimes in the morning as well.

He dearly loved my entire family like a good father, and took a great interest in our welfare. On his advice—indeed at his order—I learned the first section of *Shulhan Aruch Yoreh Deyah* (the standard text on the laws of kosher food), and with his great authority he gave me rabbinic ordination.

fourth class, lower deck

After a while, as I found it hard to earn a livelihood, my dear tutor R. Ḥayyim Berlin advised me to leave the country and go abroad, and the good Lord would come to my aid. I approached the various institutions in Jerusalem and asked them to appoint me their rabbinic representative to the Jewish communities abroad (to raise funds in their behalf)—and met with no success. Yet it was all for the best. My dear tutor then advised me to simply change my dwelling-place in the world for a while. Perhaps the blessed Lord would then arrange some new life-program for me, and others would also benefit from my trip.

(In short, I should make a journey abroad, and good Jews would surely help.)

In the month of Kislev (December) 1908 I left my wife and two daughters in Jerusalem and set off to face the vicissitudes of travel abroad.

Arriving in Jaffa, I secured a passage on a ship bound for Marseilles, fourth class (steerage) on the lower deck. On the entire deck I was the only Jew among who knows how many passengers; and uncleanliness ruled everywhere in the vessel. I found a place of my own in the ship's stern, where I suffered greatly, being unused to sea travel. At last, however, we landed safely in Alexandria, Egypt. From this port we embarked again on Friday toward evening.

Just as the ship began moving from the shore, a man was taken aboard: a convicted murderer bound in iron chains. Here his chains were removed, though—and of course, where else should he take his place but next to me, squatting right on my bundle of belongings! I was seized by fear and terror as I heard him engaging me in conversation. Yet somehow I adjusted to the situation, learning to live with my fears for eight days, till we reached Marseilles.

From there I rode on to Paris, where (being without funds) I spent some time in misery and distress, until I obtained (with the blessed Lord's help) the means to get to London. In the few hours from Paris to London I suffered once more from the unsettling effects of sea-sickness. But thank Heaven, I reached London at dawn.

It was Thursday when I arrived at the *Maḥziké haDath* synagogue in

London. The magnificent sight astounded me. With its forecourt it closely resembled a synagogue in Vilna or in the Meya She'arim section of Jerusalem. In that large synagogue one *minyan* (quorum) after another would form for the regular prayer-services, while off to the side, in the *beth midrash* (house of study), many informal classes and study groups were busy learning the Mishnah, Talmud and *Shulḥan Aruch*. In yet another room there were people learning *M'sillath Yesharim,* the classic work on piety and ethics by R. Moshe Ḥayyim Luzatto.

All in all, I found there people outstanding in their pure religiosity and devotion. I saw persons struggling for a livelihood, and yet they devoted their set hours to Torah study, a few hours each night, though it meant toil and exertion. With these people I formed strong bonds of affection and friendship.

It was during those days that I made the acquaintance of a true Talmudic scholar, a man of piety who loved Jewry, R. Abraham Abba Werner, whose fine qualities were endless. He showed me extraordinary friendship (may his great merit protect us all).

At the festive Purim meal that came soon afterward I was seated at his table. A wondrous thing happened there, which I am obliged to tell: It was quite late at night, in the midst of the holiday meal, as I sat with my dear revered host, when all at once two brothers came in, filled with great fear, saying that they must have a word with this worthy rabbi. He told them they could speak freely before me; and they related that about two months earlier their aged father had passed away, leaving the two of them and a married daughter. Two weeks ago, when she was alone in her house, their sister heard a knock on the door. She opened the door, and saw the image of her father, in his exact shape and form. Terrified, she fainted and fell to the floor. Hearing a noise, the neighbors came, and hastened to help revive her; but she would not tell them a word.

On Thursday, which was observed as the Fast-day of Esther, she was alone in her home when the image of her father returned, before her very eyes. Once again she fainted, remaining unconscious until physicians arrived and with great difficulty revived her. And now she was seriously ill.

My host, the worthy rabbi, began by putting them off with all kinds of reasoned explanations, dismissing the whole thing as the result of an overwrought imagination and weak nerves. They stood their ground, however, insisting that it was all true. Bursting into tears, they stated that they knew for certain that their father could find no peace in the Hereafter, since there was no sin or transgression in this world which he had failed to commit, until he died at the ripe age of some eighty-odd years.

Once the good rabbi heard this he changed his tone completely, and told them to give such-and-such a sum to charity for the benefit of their father's spirit; they should solemnly undertake to keep the Sabbath as a holy day of rest from then till the festival of Shavuoth; and they should say *kaddish* (the mourner's prayer) for their father three times a day in the synagogue. In his wisdom the good rabbi understood that if he told them always to keep the Sabbath faithfully, they would not accept at all. But once they became accustomed to it, by the time of the festival of Shavuoth, the Almighty would inspire them with a wish to continue observing the holy day of rest.

They accepted his conditions; and I can bear witness that until the middle of the month of Iyar (May—when I left) I saw them come to the synagogue every Sabbath for the prayers; then, in the afternoon, they would return to attend the classes in sacred study. In addition, they were careful to say the *kaddish* every day. When I asked them how their sister was, they replied that from the time they accepted the rabbi's "terms" she remained in perfectly good health. I wanted to see this woman myself and hear her own account of the matter; but for various reasons I was unable to do so.

the return home

About the middle of the month of Iyar (May) I left London in good order to return to my own home and environment, in the holy city of Jerusalem. On the ship from Marseilles to Jaffa I made the acquaintance of a man of worth and absolute piety: R. Aryeh Leyb, a grandson of the famous R. Israel Salanter. At first, though, he tried to keep his illustrious family a secret, saying not a word about his grandfather.

When we were safely back in the holy land he took to visiting me regularly; and I began speaking to him (since he was unmarried) about my sister Miriam, who was living then in my native town in far-off

Europe. I sent for her, and for my younger sister, Feyge. Eventually Miriam arrived, and the match was arranged most satisfactorily. In the month of Nissan (the following year) they were married.

A while later a man cultivated his acquaintance, presenting himself as a good friend—and he misled my brother-in-law cruelly. He advised my innocent relative to give his money to a certain man of supposed repute... in exchange for shares or certificates in the Yeshiva Torath Ḥayyim and the old-age home (assuring him that it was a most wise and worthwhile investment).

That was the focal point of trouble indeed. Only a little while later the two institutions both went bankrupt under a mountain of debts, having been misled and mismanaged by this same person who made the investment "plan." My brother-in-law was left completely impoverished; and at that very time his dear son Yitzḥak was born to him. It can be imagined how much suffering the man underwent, being entirely unaccustomed to seeking help from others, and suddenly finding himself in need of bread for hungry mouths....

Nevertheless, he accepted it all as Heaven's inscrutable justice, and continued his Talmud studies regularly. It was only at night, when he remained alone in the *beth midrash* in the neighborhood called *Mishk'noth,* that I found him now and then weeping bitterly at his plight.

Yet the merit of his forefathers stood by him. The blessed Lord had compassion on him and sent him some help in his distress, through generous and kindly souls. Especially my dear mentor R. Ḥayyim Berlin deserves to be mentioned. He befriended him as best he could.

Afterward his dear son R. Binyomin Beynish was born, and then the First World War broke out, engulfing the greater part of the globe in blood. Then his situation, too, worsened, and he could no longer bear his troubles. One day he went to the "welfare committee" to see if he could get anything at all in return for the shares or certificates that he had so unwisely bought—anything to keep himself and his family alive. The answer was a flat no: the papers he brought had no value whatsoever.

A few hours later his life-spirit expired, to return in purity to heaven above. An absolute tzaddik disappeared, and no one took it enough to heart to find out why... and this was a man of kindly piety and humility, descended from so great a tzaddik.

myself in a miserable state

The year 1914 saw the clouds of war darkening the skies of the world; and there were many who suffered from the general distress of the times and the shaming plight of hunger.

I too found myself in a miserable state. Yet "not forever shall the needy be forgotten" (Psalms 9:19). In His compassion for us the blessed Lord sent His help from His holiness. With no one's intervention, purely by His watchful providence, I was appointed supervisor and examiner at the Etz Hayyim elementary school, in Jerusalem's Mahaneh Yehuda section. From this time on I would bask in the company of "holy sheep," amid the voices of children innocent of any sin.

Let me record in passing that Saturday the twenty-fifth of Av (in August) 1911 my son Hayyim Yaakov was born, graced by the blessed Lord with great abilities. May the good Lord protect him and guide him ever toward holiness.

But to return to my theme: with Heaven's help I embarked on my work. In 1919 during the ten days of penitence (between Rosh haShana and Yom Kippur) a son was born to me. There is much that could be told about him, from the beginning of his conception... but it would not be worthwhile to reveal it. It could almost be said that from the moment he was born the house filled with light. Yet to my desolation I was not worthy to raise him for more than a month. May we who survive be granted long life.

a Rock of strength, whose work is perfect

In 1920 another son was born to me, consoling me for my previous tragedy, and for earlier misfortunes that befell me (for my many sins) during the years of war, when two dear, precious daughters, Esther-Bluma and Sheyne-Leah, were taken from us. Yet the Torah calls the Almighty "the Rock whose work is perfect" (Deuteronomy 32:4). It is for us to accept His will without question.

This child's birth brought us new joy and consolation. But again a thread of distress wove its way into my happiness. Four days after his birth his dear precious mother contracted a serious illness, and all the physicians despaired of her life. Still, our Torah teaches that Heaven grants the physician permission to heal; and we should never despair. The eighth evening of the child's life, when he had been a week on earth, his mother was taken to the Shaarey Tzedek Hospital, while this tender bundle of life remained at home, awaiting the circumcision on the morrow that would enter him into the covenant of Abraham. With great difficulty and at considerable expense we were able to get a wet-nurse for him [bottle-feeding was unknown there at that time] and thus, by the blessed Lord's mercy, I was able the next day to enter him into the covenant of Abraham. His name in Israel (Jewry) became Abraham Binyomin.

His dear mother's condition, however, was desperate indeed, and she became worse from moment to moment. In all synagogues and elementary schools prayers were said for her recovery to health. At last, by Heaven's abounding compassion for us, her life was redeemed and rescued peacefully. She was given the added name of Tzipporah; and two months later she was well enough to leave the hospital. Nevertheless, that entire winter her health remained weak.

I must mention with a blessing the good woman named Dr. Fabrikant, a devoted physician who showed so much generous compassion, giving no thought to her own body or spirit, either day or night, in order to save my dear wife and ease her illness.

When we were able to greet my dear wife (by Heaven's mercy) at the seder table on Passover, she began feeling somewhat better. A few months later, in the month of Tammuz (July) we decided on the advice of the doctors that she should go to Jaffa for a while, for a change of air. Tuesday the fifth of Av I received a letter from her, from Jaffa, that she was ill with typhus. I traveled immediately to Jaffa, where I left our sweet tender Abraham Binyomin in the house of Nehama Werbin; and I found my wife in the hospital.

Yet alas, that very night my son Abraham Binyomin contracted dysentery. It was with great difficulty that I managed to get him into the hospital. For a variety of reasons though, his condition grew worse from day to day—till I decided to ride back with him to Jerusalem. There was a woman traveling with us, and she advised us (my wife and me) to take him immediately to the Hadassah hospital. That very night I brought the sweet tender child to that hospital, where a woman physician promised to take care of him. It became clear later that she was not giving him any care at all, and we were cruelly compelled to take him back to our home. There that excellent physician Dr. Fabrikant gave him her devoted care without stint.

It was Heaven's decree, however, to take this beloved child from us, and he could not be saved. May those who have remained be granted long and good life.

Yeshiva Torath Ḥayyim, in the Old City, where Reb Aryeh continued studying Torah in his first few years in Jerusalem.

4
The woman who shared his life

the match and the dowry

Reb Aryeh had the fortune to find a wife who shared his blessed ways of behavior. Just as he gave comfort and support to the unfortunate and the orphan, so did she. Just as he sought the company of those who knew misfortune in life, so did she. It was his dear wife Ḥannah (may she rest in peace)—as he loved to tell with a twinkle in his eye—who sewed the many deep pockets into his clothes, into which he stuffed the various notes and messages of the men of the underground fighting movement, to smuggle them either into or out of the prisons where the men were detained. When messages had to be gotten into a prison cell, she would often also fold them up and hide them in the seams of his clothes, so they should not make any rustling sound when he walked and thereby arouse suspicion among the watchful prison guards....

She knew everything, and she never questioned him or had any doubts or misgivings about his activities. On the contrary, in her quiet way she encouraged him. Whenever people would recall good deeds that he had carried out, he would always answer, "But what am I, considering the things *she* did?" And he would add, "She was a great soul, a great *n'shamah.*"

She was intelligent and learned, thoroughly fluent in several languages.

During the First World War, when Turkey and Germany were at war with England, letters from Israel (Palestine, then a Turkish possession) were scrupulously censored. So she amazed everyone by writing letters for everyone in the neighborhood in a clear, fluent German (which the censors could not read).

This too he loved to tell: "Every time I went to visit the women members of the underground movement imprisoned in Bethlehem, my dear wife (of blessed memory) used to accompany me, then turn off at the Tomb of our Mother Rachel [the Matriarch] to pray there for the welfare of those women in prison. When I went back (and she rejoined me) her eyes were always red from tears. You see, she always wept when she prayed for them."

About their courtship and engagement we can gain information from a letter that Reb Aryeh composed when David Tidhar, gathering information for his encyclopedia on the pioneers and builders of the Jewish homeland, asked him to write about his life. I give the letter verbatim, as the style tells much about the man:

> "I have received your proposal to honor me by including me among the pioneers and builders of the *yishuv* (settlement). I do not rank among the communal workers and active leaders, nor am I a research scholar or writer, but since your worthy editorial board has decided to allot me a place among them, I have sought [in my memory] to find some special activity [of mine worthy of mention] which if small quantitatively was not so small in significance.
>
> It will, incidentally, be my pleasure to write for you a memoir of events of over forty-four years ago, when I arrived in the holy land at the port of Jaffa. When I left the ship my first destination was the lodging-house of R. David Schleiffer, to rest there from the fatigue of the sea-voyage. There I went to bed afterward; but I did not sleep the entire night; for in the middle of the night a house collapsed near my lodgings and two persons were killed. The next day their funeral was held; and when I returned from the burial, by good fortune I met a man whose wisdom shone from his face. He greeted me warmly, and as he shook my hand I felt a fatherly affection. He asked me from where I came, whereupon I told him all about myself. Without delay he invited me to come to his house;

but I told him that I had to visit the esteemed R. Abraham Isaac *ha-kohen* Kook (of blessed memory), then the renowned head of the Jaffa *beth din*. We went together to the distinguished rabbi's house, where he received me with every courtesy as a guest and invited me to stay with him (in his usual, blessed way). But the man who came with me insisted that the mitzvah (religious good deed) of hospitality, where I was concerned, was already his.

We then went together to his house; and there I felt just as in my parents' home. He gave me food and drink generously, as the good Lord enabled him—both he and his pious, righteous wife. I found a sweet child there too, with whom I played.

After a few days I took my leave of these wonderful people, to go up to the holy city of Jerusalem; and this marvelous man gave me a letter to give to his good friend in Jerusalem, R. Tz'vi Pesaḥ Frank, who is today the illustrious head of the *beth din* in the holy city. Little did I know the good thought that this man had for me. Afterward, though, I found out his good thought—and praise the Lord, it became a reality. Well, this was it: A sister-in-law of R. Tz'vi Pesaḥ Frank had arrived at his home from Kovno, Lithuania— the daughter of R. David Shapiro and granddaughter of the learned R. Ḥayyim Yaakov Shapiro, who had been head of the *beth din* in Jerusalem. It was my wonderful host's idea that she might make a good match for me.

A month later we were married, forming a lifelong bond. That former host of mine shared in my happiness by attending the wedding and giving us his warm friendship. I received then a dowry of 1,000 rubles. Part of it I sent to my parents, and the rest I entrusted to this man with a *hetter iska,* a legal document that would allow him (under religious law) to use the money in business as he wished, and if there were profits I would receive a share. I took no receipt from him; it was merely noted down in his account-book.

Some time later he contracted an illness, from which he did not recover. It did not enter our minds to think about the money, as our anguish over his illness drove the thought far away, since his condition touched our hearts deeply. When we were informed that the end had come and he was to be brought to his final rest on the Mount of Olives, it was a cold rainy day. Toward evening we joined the funeral procession, with all our heart and mind. It never occurred to us to think about the money. Some time later, however, we received a letter from this poor departed man's partner, Israel Meir Ḥodorovsky, that he had found it noted in the departed man's account-book that such-and-such a sum was due us, plus or minus any profit or loss that it might have brought.

That marvelous man, Mr. Tidhar, was your father—Moshe Betzalel Todrosovitz; and his wife was Esther Rachel, your pious mother—two people whom I will never forget as long as I live. And you (may you be blessed with long life) were the child with whom I played in their home. When your dear mother (God rest her soul in Paradise) was in an old-age home it was a sacred obligation for me to visit her frequently. May her spirit be treasured in the divine matrix of life."

some of her qualities

"What is so unusual," he once asked, "in accepting suffering with love (for the Almighty, in good cheer)? My wife (may she rest in peace) reached such a level of piety that if something was decreed for her in Heaven, she did not even have to accept it in good cheer. She simply did not feel it—any pain, discomfort or anguish. To sense no suffering at all when Heaven decrees it for you—that is a higher level of character than feeling the woe and accepting it."

The devout rabbi was in the habit of saying that all his good qualities came to him from her strength. She never complained; she never worried about tomorrow. Hers was a power of faith that knew no bounds. "If not for her, I could not possibly have withstood the days of hunger during the First World War," Reb Aryeh once said; and he added, "When it came to trusting the Holy One, blessed is He, she was greater than I was; she surpassed me."

In the days of the First World War, the holy city suffered terribly from a shortage of food. Indomitable in her faith, she accepted the trouble without complaint; and her son recalls that one Friday, when there was no

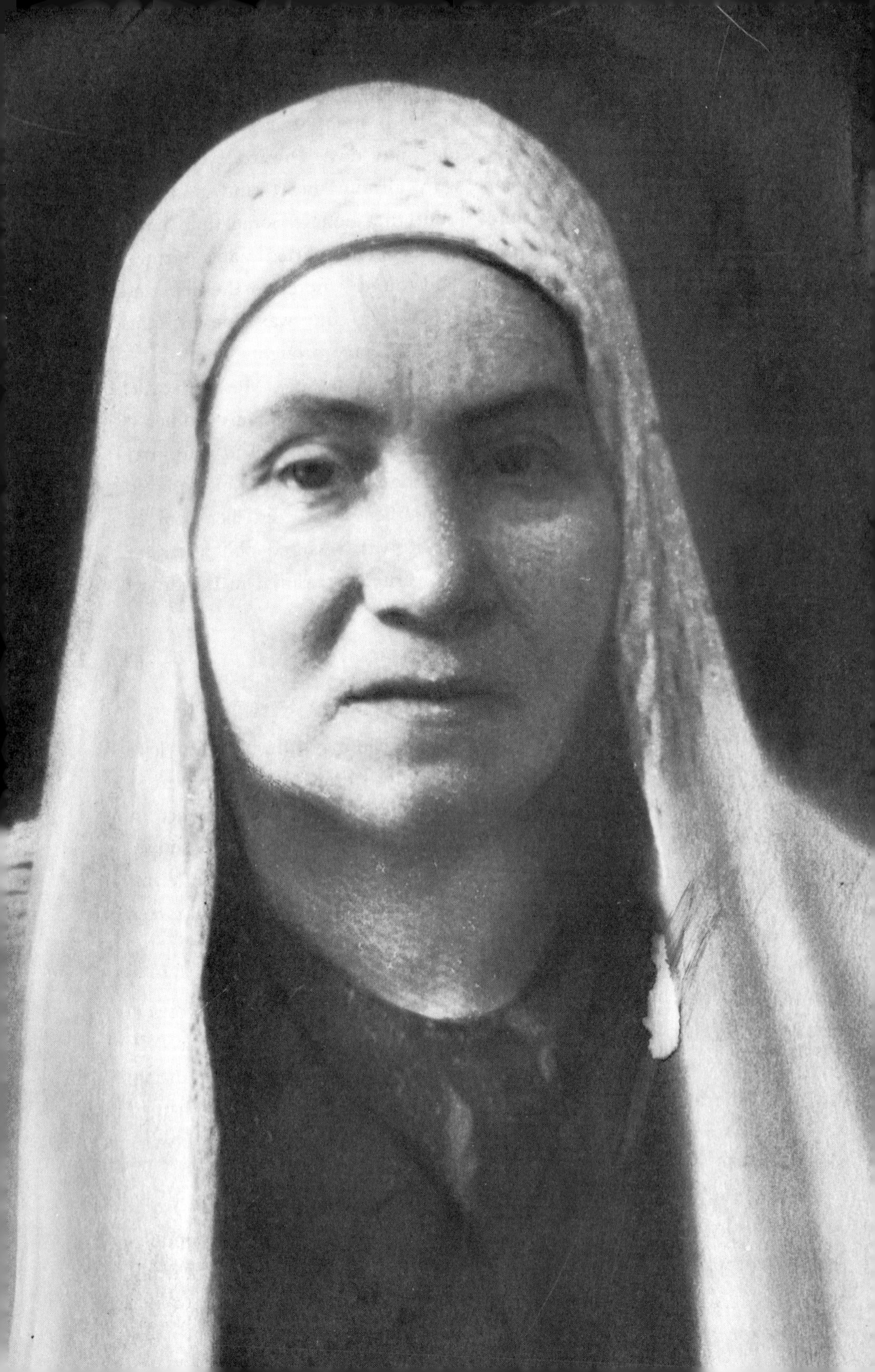

food for the Sabbath in the house, she put up the pots on the stove to give the appearance—should any neighbor happen to drop in—that all was well. However, mealtime came and went on the Sabbath, and the good woman simply forgot to take the empty pots off the stove. A neighbor wandered in, and drew her own conclusions immediately. She knew it would be no use to speak with Reb Aryeh's wife; so she asked the children if they had had anything to eat. They did not know how to lie, and she was soon back with food for the children, and with a good scolding for their mother, for making the children bear her privations.

One woman in Jerusalem had a large supply of rice, and every day she brought some. There was only one trouble: it was thoroughly wormy and had to be thrown out. Every day, though, Reb Aryeh's wife thanked the woman profusely for her generosity, never breathing a word of the truth.

In later years Reb Aryeh often told of the troubles in the First World War. Starving people literally collapsed in the streets of the city. The situation was extremely serious in Jerusalem, simply becoming more than anyone could bear. One day Reb Aryeh went out into the street with no idea of where to find help. At home his children were sobbing piteously: they had eaten nothing for two days.

There was one man in Jerusalem for whom Reb Aryeh had done favors in the past; and now, during the war, it was his practice to lend money to people in need. At his wife's request Reb Aryeh took several valuable holy books that he had and went to this man's house to ask him for a loan against the pledge of the volumes. To Reb Aryeh's surprise and dismay the man simply and utterly refused. "But why do you turn me away," asked Reb Aryeh, "when you lend money to others?" The man replied, "To others I must lend, because they know I am wealthy, and if I refuse they will resent it and bear a grudge against me. But as for you, I know you will hold no hatred in your heart against me if I refuse to give you a loan..."

Filled with utter despair, Reb Aryeh returned home as penniless as before. Seeing no way out, no hope left, he shut himself in his room and gave way to bitter tears. "Because I won't bear a grudge of hate in my heart," he cried, "they refuse to lend me anything, and I must be condemned to starve with my family?"

Gently his wife Ḥannah came over to him with words of comfort and cheer: "Aryeh, Aryeh! Where is your Jewish faith? Where is your trust in the Almighty? Just think a moment why that rich man would not give you any money. Is it because he does not have any?—we know he is wealthy. Is it because he won't give any loans?—we know he lends to all the people in need. Is it then because he will not trust you?—you know that last month you went to knock on his door at midnight, walking barefoot through the streets of Jerusalem because there is not even a pair of shoes in your house—in order to return to him a gold coin that you found in the house after he had changed some money for you here into smaller coins.

"Very well," she continued, "he knows that you are honest. Then why will he lend you nothing? We have to judge a man favorably. So what shall we do when we can find nothing favorable or good at all in what a person has done? We must conclude that something out of the ordinary is going on here. And so it must mean that Heaven prevented that rich man from lending you money—so that your help should come from somewhere else. Aryeh, *cast your burden on the Lord, and He will sustain you*" (Psalms 55:23).

Reb Aryeh grew calm and stopped weeping. He understood that his wife was right. He had to draw strength from his faith....

Incredibly, a short while later the postman came knocking on the door, bringing a letter from America. Reb Aryeh opened the envelope, and found a ten-dollar check inside (worth then many more times its value today)! His amazement grew all the greater when he read the letter that came with it: The writer recalled that several years earlier, when Reb Aryeh happened to be in Petaḥ Tikvah, a man had turned to him and asked, "Aren't you the grandson of so-and-so?" When Reb Aryeh replied that indeed he was, the man continued, "You look like your dear departed grandfather. I knew and admired the man"; and so they parted in friendship. Now it turned out that this American Jew had died; and in his will he had left instructions to send a check for ten dollars to this Jew of Jerusalem, Reb Aryeh, whom he had met years ago. Just now, at this dark hour of his life, the money arrived.

Reb Aryeh realized how right his wife was: It was all Heaven's doing, so that his rescue should come from a different source....

in the face of death

During the fearful, terrible period of hunger Reb Aryeh's young tender child died. It happened on a Sabbath; and his pious wife hid the pathetic news from the neighbors, so that they should not grieve and lament on the sacred day of rest (a time for spiritual joy). Reb Aryeh's own sister came to visit that day and spoke to her, and she had no inkling of the misfortune. Only when the Sabbath ended did she let it become known....

When a second son of his died and the misfortune left him stricken and broken, it was she who comforted him. "I thought," said she, "that I would be worthy enough to see my sons become prodigies in Talmud in the yeshiva here on earth. *Nu*, now we will have two wonderful Talmud students in the yeshiva in heaven, on high..."

During the seven days of mourning, two women came to call and offer solace; and they were quite jarred at her apparent lack of emotion over the loss. As the afternoon wore on, Reb Aryeh's wife excused herself and went to the side to say the afternoon prayers. Her two visitors took the opportunity to hold a conversation in Russian, certain that the pious young mother at the side would not understand a word. In their talk they agreed that she could not be quite right in the head. Otherwise, they concurred primly, how could she take the child's death so calmly?

Her prayer concluded, Reb Aryeh's wife rejoined them, and instead of Yiddish, which she had used till then, she explained in flawless Russian (she was an educated and accomplished linguist) the laws and teachings of the Jewish faith regarding the death of close kin: that the death occurs by Divine will; the spirit of the departed person lives on in another realm of existence; and immoderate grief (giving way to excessive or unwarranted despair or self-pity) is a sinful reproach against the Divine will.

"It would seem," Reb Aryeh used to say, "that she was stronger than I was in submitting to the yoke of God's sovereign rule and accepting suffering."

His son Abraham Binyomin, who died at the age of a year and a half and was buried on the Mount of Olives (in Jerusalem) was indeed a wonder-child. When he died, Reb Aryeh, gripped by emotion, wrote on the back of his picture:

"Who ever saw or heard anything like this? Here was a child of nine months being nursed by his mother—and before beginning to suckle he would say the blessing to thank the Almighty for his food!" (He would cover his mother's breast and say the benediction, "Blessed art Thou," etc.)

What Reb Aryeh wrote when his child died

"From afar you would recognize my voice and call out, *Father, Father!* You would put your hand on my neck to hug me and kiss me, then take me with you to the room where your mother's clothes hung in the closet.

And you kissed the clothing as you wept, crying, *Mother, Mother!*" (This was evidently when his mother was away from home, for some reason, or perhaps in the hospital.)

Whenever Reb Aryeh came to the Mount of Olives the Arab watchman of the cemetery would rush to meet him, saying, "Come: I will show you the grave of the little angel..."

never angry

Perhaps it was because of the loss of these children that she never raised her voice to the young ones who survived and grew up in the home, although at times they drove her to anger, as children will. When they were very difficult, she would mutter between her teeth in Yiddish (the language of the home), "You should only be well!" If some of the children began wrangling and squabbling, she would simply take hold of them and say, "Children, I beg of you: Don't quarrel!"

No improper word ever left her mouth. If a child was late, or something similar happened, she would not give way to worry but remain trustful in Divine providence, that all was for the best. One thing, though, could move her to tears: Sometimes Reb Aryeh came home after listening for a considerable time to people with troubles and miseries, and for a while he would remain unnerved, till he could recover his spirits. At such times she wept silently, in empathy with him.

her prophetic words of comfort

Her grandfather, the noted head of a *beth din* (religious court) in Jerusalem, had a large and very fine library of rabbinic literature. When he felt his end approaching, with Reb Aryeh at his bedside, he turned to him and whispered, "I would like you to have my library when I am gone." He left nothing in writing, however, and as fate would have it, none of the precious volumes ever came into Reb Aryeh's possession.

The good rabbi was greatly saddened to think that from his relationship with his wife's learned grandfather, he had nothing tangible left, not even one holy book from the man's library. Tears fell from his eyes as he spoke of it to his wife.

"Aryeh," she comforted him, "why should you vex yourself? Because you did not get the volumes he promised you? What does it matter? Some day our children will grow up and write their own volumes of Torah learning."

There was prophecy in her words. In his adult life their oldest son, R. Hayyim Yaakov—named after this very grandfather of Reb Aryeh's wife—became the author of two distinguished works on Maimonides' code of law.

when she was jealous

Once his wife said to him, "Aryeh, I must tell you that I am jealous of this-and-this woman, our neighbor." Reb Aryeh was puzzled: His good wife hardly knew what jealousy is. What reason had she to envy her neighbor? And who was this neighbor, anyway?

He soon found out:

There was a rich man in Jerusalem, a person of standing in the community, who lost his wealth in the course of time. Creditors took all he had, until he was forced to move to the Mishk'noth section—the poor, impoverished neighborhood where Reb Aryeh lived, where there were not even bathrooms in the homes but only outhouses in the courtyards. To support his family this formerly rich man now had to go climbing up on a scaffold to work as a repairman on the exteriors of buildings, fixing defects, to earn his small daily wages. Yet every evening the neighbors noticed his wife going out in the street dressed up in pretty clothes and finery.

The neighbors were amazed to see this, and began talking and gossiping about her.... Some time later, though, Reb Aryeh's good wife happened to be talking to the woman, and the reason behind it became clear to her. "You see," said this neighbor, "when my husband returns home from his work his heart is just paralyzed. He is like a dead man. To think of it! He used to be so wealthy, and now he has to work like a common laborer! When I realized how downtrodden his spirit was, I decided that I must make myself attractive and go wait for him out there in Agrippas Street every day, when he comes home from work—so that I can welcome him cheerfully, with a smiling face, just to raise his morale."

"*Nu*," said his good wife Ḥannah to Reb Aryeh, "of that woman I am jealous. I have not reached her level of devotion..."

her ways of charity

She had her own little charity fund (money that she managed to save or collect) from which she gave secretly, anonymously. She never told even him to which needy people she gave. It was "hidden charity," hidden even from him....

Nor was this all. Poverty was never a stranger in Jerusalem, and beggars often made the rounds in search of food. In other homes, if an indigent man was given some cooked dish to eat, it would generally be in a bent or cracked bowl, with a misshapen spoon, and he would be left to eat it outside, at the back door, or off in a corner somewhere. When Reb Aryeh's wife served a poor man food, he sat at the table and was served in the same dishes and utensils as the members of the family. In general, as her children well remember, whoever entered their home for a meal or whatever found himself treated exactly like her own children.

And as a rule, there were other children staying at the home. In one typical case, a man who knew Reb Aryeh arrived in Jerusalem with two small children. Somehow, he had had to leave his wife in Europe. His plan was to find work and a home, and then send for her. For the time being, till he could get his bearings, he would be able to fend for himself; but what to do with the children? Reb Aryeh had an "easy" answer: they would stay at his home (and this in the second or third decade of the century, when food was scarce).

Reb Aryeh's good wife always accepted such children cheerfully. In another typical case, a family in Haifa sent a boy of thirteen to study Torah in Jerusalem. There was no room for him at their home, but Reb Aryeh arranged for the boy to have his meals with various families (one day a week with each, in the time-honored practice of *essen teg*); and for a place to sleep Reb Aryeh found him a bench in a small synagogue (as he himself had slept in his early years). The boy's clothing, however, was washed and dried with the family wash. Under his wife's tutelage, the oldest daughter worked patiently at the scrubbing board—and this boy too had clean clothes—no small thing in those years. And Reb Aryeh's good wife took it all in stride with the grace of an angel.

Moreover, she had a way of turning the home into a wedding hall, if you please. Through the early decades of her married life, there were a

An early picture of Reb Aryeh and his daughter

good many yeshiva students whose time came to be married. Living on next to nothing as they did, they could afford no wedding hall or elaborate celebration of any kind. So the Levin home became the setting for the wedding ceremony, and there the guests were served, by their smiling hostess, Ḥannah.

Yet her biggest charity of all was surely her tolerant and forbearing acceptance of her husband's schedule every single Saturday of the year. Every Sabbath morning, for long decades, the gentle undersized Reb Aryeh trudged off to Jerusalem's central prison, to conduct the morning prayer-service with the inmates; and then he would speak with each and every one, to bring messages from families and loved ones, and to take messages back. Of course, he would not write on the Sabbath (religious law forbids it), but he had no need to. His phenomenal mind recorded everything.

When he left the prison, he headed not for home but for the relatives and close friends of the prisoners (all of whose names and addresses he remembered) to deliver his new, fresh batch of messages. Having trudged through the length and breadth of Jerusalem, he finally came home at an advanced hour, and only then did the family sit down for its Sabbath meal.

People kept dropping in, however, to ask if he had any messages for *them* from imprisoned relatives. This happened every Sabbath of the year, and his dear Ḥannah accepted it with a smile. After all, it was for the sake of a mitzvah.

Slowly but surely her sterling qualities were recognized. One of their neighbors was bitterly antagonistic toward Chief Rabbi Abraham Isaac Kook, to whom Reb Aryeh was always closely attached. Yet when this neighbor died, he left a directive to his daughter in his will, that if ever she needed guidance or instruction, she was to go only to the good wife of Reb Aryeh.

the pearl necklace

In her single years she already had her immense capacity to give with no thought for herself, which made her a perfect mate for him.

Back in Kovno, when her mother died, her sister sailed for the land

The parents of Reb Aryeh's wife

of Israel, while she remained at home to look after her father. In time, however, her father remarried, and she was free to come to the holy land. Before she left, her father gave her a very beautiful and valuable necklace which had belonged to her mother: a double rope of very fine pearls. "Here, Hannah," her father said. "I want you to have this."

Soon after her arrival in Jerusalem, in the course of a conversation, her sister asked her with a touch of eager interest, "Whatever became of Mother's pearl necklace?" Sensing her sister's yearning for it, she replied without hesitation, "Father gave it to me to bring to you."

From her overjoyed sister the necklace passed into that woman's family as an heirloom; and the truth remained known only to Reb Aryeh and his wife, and some of the children when they were grown.

This trait of hers never changed. One of the sons recalls that one day a package of clothing arrived, sent by friends. The young boy rummaged happily through it, found an attractive tie, and grandly put it on. "I think this suits me," he announced. Gently his mother replied, "First you should think of what would suit others in the family."

the happy accident

In the home there was a set of dishes that was an heirloom, fine china inherited from earlier generations. One day they were being washed and dried, when by some dreadful accident the set dropped to the floor and broke—every last dish. His good wife knew that Reb Aryeh would be extremely distressed when he found out, as the set meant very much to him.

When it was time for him to come home from the Etz Ḥayyim school, she waited for him outside. "Aryeh," she greeted him as he arrived, "a wonderful thing has happened—a miracle. Let us thank God together."

"What happened?"

"First let us give thanks." So they recited in unison, *O give thanks to the Lord, for He is good, for His mercy endures forever* (Psalms 107:1).

"Do you know?" she continued. "When a parent gets very angry at a child and feels he must strike him, so to vent his wrath he strikes something else, the child may be frightened and upset at first, but afterward he is thankful that he himself was not beaten. You know the Sages teach that this is why Asaf sang a happy psalm that begins, *O God, the heathen have come into Thy inheritance* (Psalms 79:1). He hymned about the destruction of our holy Temple, yet it was a happy psalm—because the Almighty poured out His wrath on wood and stones, and not on His people. They survived." (Echah Rabbathi 4:14). The good rabbi nodded in agreement. He knew this Midrash.

"Now we know also," his dear wife continued, "that the greater the object destroyed—the more valuable and precious it is—the greater our escape is, because we realize how enormous Heaven's wrath against us was." By now he had an inkling of what she was about to tell him; and when at last she revealed it, he smiled and accepted it with a shrug.

Her whole life was like a praise-song to the Almighty. She relished every moment of her life as His precious gift, even when her last illness brought pain. When she said her daily prayers, she was always in exalted enthusiasm, in a fervor of sublime happiness. Opposite her window there was a small synagogue of Yemenite worshippers. Even in the coldest weather they would open their window in homage to her, so that she could hear their prayer and join in the responses.

Especially toward the end of her life, she achieved an inner peace and utter tranquility, despite all the illness and pain, that left all who knew her, including doctors and nurses, marveling....

When ultimately she passed away, Rabbi Tz'vi Pesaḥ Frank, the rabbi of Jerusalem (and her brother-in-law) wrote of her that in qualities of character he had never seen her equal. Beyond any doubt, he added, she could be compared to our Matriarchs of the Bible (Sarah, Rebekkah, Rachel and Leah).

her departure from the world

Once she told him that she had had a very disturbing dream; and she implored him to take her to the holy mystic R. Sh'lomo Elyashav, to whom they were related by the marriage of their children. She hoped this master of *kabbalah* and Jewish mysticism would convert the dream into a good omen.

What the dream was about, she refused to tell Reb Aryeh, but only begged him to forgive her for keeping it from him. In time, however, it became clear that it had revealed to her the day of her death: it would come in 1952.

What R. Sh'lomo Elyashav told her, no one knows. But when she left him she sent off a letter to her son who was then serving as a rabbi in America, telling him she had dreamt of the day when all the dead are to be brought back to life: It would be in 1952. (This was her way of preparing the family yet sparing them any pain.)

And true enough, in 1952 she passed on to her eternal rest....

In far-off America her daughter-in-law saw her in a dream, dressed in her clean Sabbath clothes, walking in peace and serenity, and entering a beautiful garden, where R. Elijah the famed Gaon of Vilna stood at the entrance to welcome her in.

The woman awoke in agitation and related the dream to her husband, Reb Aryeh's son; and he felt mournful and grieved. When a few hours passed by, a telegram arrived from Jerusalem, informing him that his good, pious mother had passed on.

It happened that S. Z. Shragai (the former mayor of Jerusalem) once accompanied Reb Aryeh on a taxi ride through the holy city, when this pious man of compassion had to return home. "Where is your house?" the driver asked him. "Where do you live?" Reb Aryeh gave no answer.

So the driver then asked, "Where do you want to get off?" He replied, "On this-and-this street."

When they left the taxi, Reb Aryeh told Mr Shragai, "You must have wondered why I gave no reply when the driver asked me where my home is. You see, since my devout and pious wife died, my home just doesn't exist any more. Our Sages spoke truly when they said that a man's home is (in effect) his wife (*Yoma* 2a). So I kept quiet.... When he asked me then where I wanted to get off, that I could answer."

With her departure from life a permanent sorrow seemed to settle over his heart. His longing for her grew stronger and stronger. "Physical details about her," he once told Dr Israel Eldad, "even her physical appearance, become blurred and fade away. But to the same extent, her qualities of character shine ever more brightly in my memory."

Dr Eldad related further that he once happened to meet Reb Aryeh returning from the cemetery. "What were you doing at the cemetery?" he asked him. "A grandson of mine just became engaged to be married," he replied, "and I went to tell Ḥannah the good news."

Another story: One Purim holiday I went to visit him, my good rabbi and teacher; and I noticed the picture of a beautiful young girl standing on his table. I thought it must be a portrait of his granddaughter. "Whose picture is that?" I asked. And he told me it was his dear departed wife. "Well, why is her picture standing on the table today?" I wanted to know. "Today is Purim," the pious rabbi answered. "Everyone is happy and rejoicing. So I too, when I gaze at her portrait I have pleasure and joy."

Finally, here are some paragraphs that Reb Aryeh wrote about her soon after he lost her:

"In the name of the Lord:

My heart is in grief and my spirit mourns. For how shall I find consolation for my great misfortune when my greatest treasure, my crowning glory was taken from me?—*my sister my love, my dove, my perfect one* (Song of Songs 5:2), this utterly devout good woman, Tzipporah Ḥannah the daughter of R. David, may her spirit dwell in the treasury of the highest heavens.

My anguish is great and fearful my woe. Who could ever describe her devotion and goodness? Another like her is hardly to be found—

so pure of spirit, with a heart as wide in generosity as the entrance to a palace, with a sensitivity of kindness and compassion that strove to give and help at every step of the way. She had a cheerful smile for everyone, and spread out her compassion to reach every living being.

She was all kindness and pity, all holiness. Her entire life was an unbroken, uninterrupted song of praise and service to God, the life of the worlds. Every moment of her existence was another stanza, another bar of melody in her song of eternity.

But above all she watched her tongue, to a most extraordinary degree. Her pure precious spirit returned to its place of origin on high, as clean and spotless as on the day it descended into the world [when she was born], but more shining, sparkling and radiant; more grace-filled and pure.

Old age brought her no cause for shame or disgrace. She never saw sin or evil in any man; she never brought pain to any heart. The spirit of God and the spirit of human beings were both pleased with her. Never did she grow haughty or raise her eyes in arrogance—not to the slightest extent. The downtrodden and the wretched were the friends she made. Let them always relate her deeds, chart her ways, and make her qualities their own. She ever turned to those left forsaken in the corner, embittered in spirit, impoverished by need; and the poor and the needy turned to her for comfort—to that spirit as pure and clear as the very essence of heaven. To all those who sought and needed her she did not leave anyone like her in the world."

In his last will and testament this is what Reb Aryeh set down:

"I have prepared my grave near the burial-place of your mother, my wife of blessed memory. The document of right to the plot of ground has been left with the bundle of clothing that I have prepared for my interment at the end of my life. I bought two parcels of clean linen cloth for this clothing. The more choice of the two I allotted for her, since I did not merit to honor her more than myself while she lived, because her spirit abhorred any kind of luxury, anything superfluous. At the time that I paid the burial society everything owing for her, I paid also for myself..."

5
A nature of humility

the root of his character

"I always tried to find the root, the source-point of my father's qualities of character," said his son R. Ḥayyim Yaakov. "I asked myself: What did he do to earn so much respect, such considerable esteem, far more than a vast number of great men ever earn? What was the root and basis of all his activities and of his personality? And at last I plumbed to the heart of the matter: My father (of blessed memory) had one basic quality, which was both the foundation and the crest of all his good deeds and acts. It was simply *humility*. In this he excelled beyond human understanding.

"There is a well-known teaching," continued his son, "in *Pirkey Avoth* (Ethics of the Fathers): Be humble in spirit before every man. We generally explain it to mean even before the smallest, least significant person. But to my poor mind it rather means this: It is very easy for a person to be humble and modest before smaller people, less important and significant than himself. For then his modesty shines through. He shows how big-hearted he is, as he humbles himself in dealing with his inferiors.

"Neither is it so hard for a man to be modest and unassuming toward persons far greater than he is. The real difficulty is to have humility when dealing with people who are similar or equal to you. If a man is to show the quality of humility toward someone like himself, he really has to grow humble so as to make it appear that the other is superior to him. And that is something very difficult.

"So you see, this dictum—Be humble in spirit before every man—does not mean particularly someone more or less important than you, someone inferior or superior, but even someone quite like and equal to yourself.

"Well, I can bear witness," concluded Reb Aryeh's son, "that my father was humble toward everyone. He bowed his head in respect before a person greater than himself; he lowered his head before someone smaller, inferior to himself. But he also behaved humbly with any person who was (or seemed to be) his like or his equal..."

he tore it up

In the Talmud we read: Wherever you find an instance of the Almighty's greatness, there you find His unassuming modesty (*Megillah* 31a). It could be said that in this respect Reb Aryeh was like his Maker. His one touch of pride and joy was that his old upholstered chair in the Torah school where he worked was the very one in which the noted sage Rabbi Joshua Leyb Diskin had sat; and the *tallith* (prayer-cape) in his house was the very one that R. Sh'muel Salant, the acknowledged head of the entire religious community in Jerusalem, had worn. It was R. Sh'muel Salant who had conferred on him rabbinic ordination, signing the official certificate.

Yet in that certificate which gave Reb Aryeh the title of rabbi, R. Salant sang his praises highly. In his great humility and modesty Reb Aryeh was unwilling to accept all those praises that R. Salant heaped on him. He felt them undeserved, and feared they would fill him with pride—so he tore up this precious certificate of ordination!

"and have found nothing of note"

There is a weekly column in easy Hebrew that I prepare, which is printed in several dozen Jewish periodicals all over the world. I devoted one column to this "tzaddik of Jerusalem," and then sent him a printed copy, clipped from one of the periodicals. Hastening to reply, he sent me this note immediately:

> "I have read your letter. Your intention is sound and good: to make noteworthy, outstanding people known through the various publications, so that a great many will read about their activities and follow in their footsteps. In this case, though, to my regret, you did not achieve your purpose—although the fault lies with me and not with you.
>
> I have searched and examined myself thoroughly, and have found nothing of note or value. If perhaps I once did some good, I have already received honor and acclaim a hundred times beyond anything I deserved.
>
> Take then my good advice and choose someone who is really a man of great spirit and achievement, to publicize as a fine model to emulate; someone in whose shining light and sturdy steps it is really worth following. Then I will remain your good friend and admirer, for it will be of value to me too..."

"who am I to bless you?"

The day before Rosh haShana (the beginning of the Jewish year) a man came and asked Reb Aryeh to give him a blessing. "Who am I," said Reb Aryeh, "that I should bless you? But if you are already here to ask a blessing, it would be good for you to get one from my neighbor. You see, I myself go to him and beg him to bless me. For he is R. Hykel Miletzki, a man of great suffering (one of his feet had been amputated) and a great Torah scholar."

who should enter first

One year during Hanukkah a library devoted to the Holocaust and Jewish bravery in Europe under the Nazis was to be dedicated in the Israeli town of Pardes Hanna. At the door Reb Aryeh met the noted scholar R. Reuben Margulies (of blessed memory); and each wanted to give the other the honor of entering first. Finally Reb Aryeh agreed to go first. But, he added, "it is only because I have a holy volume in my pocket. That entitles me..."

the interview

"It is not easy to get Reb Aryeh talking about himself," a journalist once reported. "I was told that he doesn't like to tell about himself. When I try to draw him out, he manages to get *me* talking—about my profession, my job, and so on. I feel he wants me to unburden myself..."

The journalist continued: "Sir," I said when I went once to interview him, "you do not know me; but I have known about you for quite some time. I first heard about you when I still lived abroad."

"Why, where are you from?" he asked; it was as though he were trying to disparage the fact that his reputation had spread beyond the borders of the holy land. "Rabbi," I replied, "I heard of you in China."

He gave me a shrewd appraising glance: "Ah...you are from China." As a rule Jews who came from China joined the militant factions in the homeland under the British mandate, and became members of the underground fighting movements. He guessed that I must have learned about him from friends in the underground movements who were imprisoned by the British and thus came to know him from his helpful, compassionate visits. "Well," he continued, "how do you know that what you were told about me was the truth?"

"You know the people who wrote me, dear rabbi," I replied. "You know they wouldn't lie about you."

He took my hand between the two of his. "Let me tell you a story: A young man once became engaged to a girl. Before the time of the wedding arrived he went to her and said, 'There is something I must tell you.' 'All right,' she replied. 'Listen,' he continued: 'The matchmakers who introduced us and arranged everything for us did not tell you the truth. You cannot blame them; this is their profession, and no one really expects them to be very accurate. Now, however, I must reveal the whole truth to you: I am no genius; I am no saint; and I am not rich—in spite of anything they may have told you.' To this she replied, 'Yet every man must have at least one virtue. Surely you have at least one good quality?' He thought a moment and shook his head. 'I don't know,' he said. 'Perhaps the only virtue I have is the fact that everything I've just told you is the truth!'"

the request for a blessing

Elazar Cohen's task was neither easy nor enviable when Israel was at war. He was in charge of the helicopter squad, and he and his men had to take the helicopters continually into the range of enemy fire in order to rescue wounded soldiers.

Once he went to Reb Aryeh and asked him for a blessing—and the good rabbi refused to give it. "But why?" asked the puzzled army commander.

"Who am I to bless you?" asked Reb Aryeh. "I truly believe your merit before heaven is greater than mine."

a check that was returned

The time came when R. Sh'muel Weingarten, head of Jerusalem's Religious Council, discovered that Reb Aryeh was in financial difficulties. He went to Israel's minister of religion, R. Judah Leyb Maimon, to consider with him what could be done to ease the good rabbi's troublesome situation.

It was decided that R. Maimon should submit a formal request to the Religious Council that a monthly payment be allotted to Reb Aryeh, as it was the practice to maintain the rabbis who headed the various sections and neighborhoods of the holy city. R. Maimon readily submitted the request.

The matter was taken up at the next regular meeting of the Religious Council; and thanks to Moshe deHaan, assistant head of the council, it was voted to grant Reb Aryeh fifty Israeli pounds a month—because he taught a group of advanced students every morning and evening (something he did, of course, with no thought in the world of getting paid for it).

When Reb Aryeh received his first "salary" check, he was taken by surprise; and he wrote the head of the Religious Council:

> "... many thanks to you worthy, noble people for your good thought concerning me, and your good-hearted intention. I have, however, weighed the matter most carefully, and have reached the conclusion that I have no right to accept anything as a rabbi. I will have enough

to answer for in my judgment on high (after my departure from this life) merely for having been ordained a rabbi.

Praise the Lord, my income continues as usual, with no serious lack—for the Almighty will not abandon me.

May the good Lord repay your worthy noble selves for your good thought concerning me; and I herewith return your check..."

"how could I waste his time?"

Dr Feigenbaum was a fine eye specialist at Hadassah hospital, who played the violin in his spare time. One day Mrs Blondheim, whose husband is a professor of nutrition at Hadassah, discovered that Dr Feigenbaum also painted fine portraits as a hobby. Being a good friend of both Dr Feigenbaum and Reb Aryeh, it occurred to her that it might be a good idea to have the amateur painter do a portrait of the good rabbi, and she went and suggested it to Reb Aryeh, half fearing that he would reject the idea out of hand, out of a wish (founded on some religious belief) to avoid having himself ever painted or photographed.

To her surprise, the good rabbi seemed taken with the idea, as he turned it over in his mind. Then he asked in his usual gentle, somewhat shy and diffident way, "How much time would it require?" Mrs Blondheim explained that he would have to sit for several sessions until Dr Feigenbaum had the outline well sketched in.

"Dear me," replied Reb Aryeh after some round reflection, "I do not think I deserve the honor of having so distinguished a professor of medicine come to my humble dwelling and give up precious hours of his valuable time, merely to paint my picture..."

the wistful touch of envy

One day Mrs Blondheim told him of a woman she knew who was devoted to a mitzvah all her own: Every Thursday this woman bought a large quantity of fish in Mahaneh Yehuda, which her own mother, a woman of eighty-five, chopped and made into the famed Jewish delicacy of *gefilte fish*. On Friday the woman took the fish, along with braided loaves of *halla* (soft white bread) and cooked chicken, and she made the rounds of a whole list of deserving individuals and families in the poor sections of Jerusalem, to drop off food for the Sabbath. Where she found bed-ridden people, she would empty bed-pans and do a bit of cleaning, etc.

As Reb Aryeh listened to Mrs Blondheim telling of this woman, there was a wistful touch of envy in his voice. "How I wish," he said in all sincerity, "that I could earn a merit like hers." All the merit he had earned, for his own prodigious list of good deeds, was as nothing in his eyes.

only the truth

After the funeral of Chief Rabbi Isaac Herzog (of blessed memory), as the many who came were leaving the Sanhedria cemetery in Jerusalem, Rabbi S. Z. Landers, one of the founders of the religious community in Ramat Gan, wanted to prove some point, and noticing the good rabbi, he exclaimed (in Yiddish), "Look, Reb Aryeh. You are definitely a tzaddik..." Reb Aryeh was overheard retorting, "Rabbi Landers, here we are standing at the gateway to the world of truth (the Hereafter). Here we have to speak only the truth...."

in flight from honor

For years there were many who wished to have this pious good man awarded the title "honorary citizen" of the city of Jerusalem. Hundreds of people from all walks of life wrote to the city government to ask, "If Reb Aryeh is not granted this mark of high esteem, then who should receive it? Who deserves it more than he?" And in turn many tried to persuade him to accept it should it be offered him; but he refused.

When he reached the age of eighty the mayor at that time, Mordecai Ish-Shalom, went to see him and begged him to accede to the pleas and wishes of so many people—and Reb Aryeh simply stood his ground. He would not agree. Said the mayor, "But look: this is the unanimous request of all the members of the city council. We want to have the honor of honoring you. It will be an honor to us, the people of Jerusalem, if you will agree to join the ranks of our city's honorary citizens."

It was no use, however. Menaḥem Begin was asked to use his influence; perhaps then he would accede. And Reb Aryeh still would not budge.

He explained his refusal: "A man ought not to run after honor. Yet if the honor comes running after him... if people want to pay you tribute without your running after it, perhaps then you have the choice to yield graciously and accept? Still, suppose that I said yes and agreed to accept this fine title. Then after my days on earth, when I stand before the throne of judgment on high, they will ask me: How did you ever agree? Is this something honorable? A man like you ought never to have consented to any awards or tributes.

"And you see (he continued) I will not be able to defend myself and say: I did not know that there was any honor in it. When they heap their tribute on me in other ways, writing whatever they write about me, I could argue perhaps: I did not know... I did not realize that this title bestowed on me contained any particular honor.... But in this case how could I ever say anything like that? The very name of the title tells that you want to pay me tribute: it is called explicitly *citizen of honor*. With the word directly there in the title, whatever will I say on my judgment day in self-defense?

Unable to prevail on Reb Aryeh to become a "citizen of honor" of Jerusalem, former Mayor Mordecai Ish-Shalom honored him with an ethrog at Sukkoth.

"If this title were bestowed on me," he concluded, "it would cause me only unhappiness. All my life I have striven to flee from honor, keeping well in mind the teaching of the Sages: Who is honored?—he who honors human beings (*Avoth* 4, 1). It is quite enough for me that I have been privileged to walk the streets of Jerusalem for more than fifty years."

(When he was no longer among the living, he could not interfere any more with plans to honor him. In his section of Jerusalem [Mishk'noth], the street on which his home stood was permanently renamed R. Aryeh Street.)

the last award

A few days before his life on earth ended, the pious rabbi celebrated his birthday. In honor of the occasion the government of Israel decided to honor this tzaddik with the decoration of *ittur lohamey ha-m'dinah*, "tribute to the fighters for the land," which had been awarded all the fighting men of Israel's underground forces under the British mandate.

In his last days, as he lay ill in the Hadassah hospital, Reb Aryeh learned about the award—and he objected. "What do they want from me?" he asked. "I did not really do anything. If I shared a little of the suffering of persecuted brethren, I have been given more than enough honor for it. When I arrive in the world of utter truth [after this life] they will say: Aryeh wanted honor for nothing in his lifetime..." He found consolation only in the fact that the decision to give him the award was accepted unanimously: "If my small, insignificant self has succeeded in making all the officers of Israel unite their hearts in harmony over one matter of peace and tranquillity; if I have succeeded in bringing about this unity of heart and mind—that is enough for me."

6
Making do with little

why the candle

One winter morning I found him studying a holy volume as a candle burned on the table. "Why the candle?" I asked him. "I am warming myself by its light," he replied.

a dislike of gifts

Menaḥem Begin related this: One day I came to see Reb Aryeh. It was a cold, nasty winter day, that made your bones shiver in the streets. I entered his home, his little dwelling, and I was startled. The tips of his fingers were in the grip of the cold, as Reb Aryeh sat as usual behind his small table, on the chair in which he took pride because it was the oldest piece of furniture there, going back to the days of his marriage (in the early years of the century).

Well, as usual, he ran to greet whoever came in, although we didn't want him to get up from his seat. We shook hands; and he in his usual way took my hand between his two palms and fondled it on both sides—and I felt that warmth in his heart that is so hard to describe. Yet in spite of that warmth I felt the bone-shivering cold that filled the room. He had been in the middle of writing something when I came in. I was

A TZADDIK IN OUR TIME

quite taken by this situation. How could he live in this bitter cold? Yet I did not utter a word, because I knew him well.

My secretary was with me, known then by his nickname in the ranks of the underground movement, "Moshe-le" (he was Dov Alpert, who later lost his life while still a young man). As a child he had been a student of Reb Aryeh, learning Torah from him. Well, I told Moshe-le, "Do me a favor: Go to the Friedman factory and buy a stove, and bring it to Reb Aryeh. Don't say anything and don't ask him." Moshe-le rushed off eagerly to do such a mitzvah—but Reb Aryeh refused to accept the stove. "It would be too much physical comfort," he protested; "too much of a good life here on earth." We begged him, we pleaded with him—to no avail.

Deeply moved by Reb Aryeh's devotion to the imprisoned underground fighters, Menaḥem Begin (who headed one of these resistance movements) remained a grateful admirer throughout Reb Aryeh's life, and continues to revere his memory.

"luxury"

His home was in the Mishk'noth section, a typical neighborhood in Jerusalem that mingled poverty with spiritual purity and loftiness. To reach his home you had to cross little streets and alleys, then one courtyard within another. His "apartment" was simply one long narrow vaulted chamber—only one room, with a partition separating the table and the bed, which was made out of parts of wooden boxes, from the "kitchen," where he had a kerosene stove to boil water for tea, etc. and near it a sink and a shower.

During his wife's lifetime he lived on the floor above. When she was gone he gave that apartment to his daughter, and moved down to the room below. "When my wife was living," he once said, "this was home. Now that she is gone, it is just a lodging-place; and for a lodging-place even one room is enough."

One of his students wanted to attach a soap dish to the wall near the shower, so that he should not have to bend down to the floor every time he needed the soap. But again, Reb Aryeh refused: "What need have I of extra conveniences or comforts?" he asked. "All my life I have shunned luxuries." And he added, "I did not build myself a home or plant myself a vineyard. The radiance and splendor of Jerusalem are really enough for me."

plain modesty

Just as his home was humble so were his quarters at the Etz Ḥayyim elementary Torah school. He made a place for himself under the vaulting staircase and felt quite comfortable there.

When the school expanded its structure, Reb Aryeh refused to have a separate room assigned to him. The officials of the yeshiva finally prevailed on him to occupy the end of the long corridor. There he settled down in a "room" of his own: a part of the corridor separated by a wooden partition.

"I have no need for more"

A time came when the Zionist Revisionist Organization in South Africa resolved to send him every month a certain sum of money for his maintenance (in recognition of his devotion to members of the underground army in Israel under the British mandate, which was linked with the Revisionist movement). The organization even sent the first check. Moved as he was at this mark of their gratitude for his work, Reb Aryeh sent the check back at once, writing, "Inasmuch as I have about 100 Israeli pounds a month for my upkeep and have no need for more, I am returning this money with my feeling of thanks..."

like a real lord

A journalist once came to interview him; and in the course of the talk he asked him, "Reb Aryeh, please tell me: Are you really comfortable and satisfied here? Does the roof perhaps not leak a bit in the winter, when it rains heavily? Do you not find the wooden bed hard? Why, even the doors of the closet here open only with difficulty!"

The good rabbi put his hand on the young man's shoulder. "Listen," he said. "I will tell you. Once I discussed it with my wife (may she rest in peace) and we decided that we would always live and make do with whatever we had. And so it has been. Now, today, the Lord be praised—what do I lack? The room is higher than I am; I do not have to bend down to move about in it. There are luxuries now to be had; but whatever do I need with them? Why run to get something from the third room? Here I have everything at hand in the first room. I have running water and electricity. Indeed I live today—how should we put it?—like a real lord!"

why he asked her name

Once in his life he was the victim of a road accident, when he was struck down by a jeep while trying to cross the street. To recuperate after his brief hospital stay, he went off for a while to a convalescent (rest) home, with a few of the children to keep him company and attend to his needs.

One day a woman in some distress came to see him there, seeking advice. Her son, a pilot in the Israel Air Force, had been reported missing in action quite some time before. The months went by, and there was no word at all about him. The poor woman was racked by doubt: Should she go on praying and hoping against hope? Or should she accept the doleful fact that in all probability her son was no longer alive? Should she dispose of his clothes and belongings and try to put him out of her mind, as we do with any close kin who has passed on?

In his usual way, Reb Aryeh spoke long but gently, till some of his own dauntless hope and faith permeated her being, and she knew she would keep her son's belongings intact, praying and waiting for his return. Then she admitted: she had been first to see the *Hazon Ish* (Rabbi Abraham Isaiah Karelitz of blessed memory, an outstanding Torah scholar in B'ney B'rak), and he had given her the same advice. Yet somehow, she added, his words had failed to calm her fears and persuade her. Now she felt clear and at peace....

At home it was always Reb Aryeh's custom to get up and accompany visitors for a bit down the road when they left. It was a mark of his unfailing respect for human beings. Now, however, he was still unable to walk properly, and so he asked his daughter to accompany the woman to the bus stop. Before the woman turned to go, moved by some impulse, he asked her for her name and address; and when she told him, he jotted it down carefully.

His son Simha Sh'lomo looked up in surprise. What was this? His father had an ironclad rule never to ask for the name and address of anyone who came for advice. He felt people would be less embarrassed and more at ease if they were left in their anonymity. Why did Reb Aryeh break the rule now?...

In a few moments the good rabbi's little daughter was back, with happy news: The woman had given her an envelope with a tidy sum of money, to give to her father.... Reb Aryeh, however, was not happy but aggrieved. Under no circumstances would he ever take money from those he helped in any way whatever. This was an absolute law. And now the well-meaning woman had taken advantage of his little daughter to foist money on him. What to do?

Suddenly Reb Aryeh's face brightened, as he remembered: He had her name and address. It was the work of a moment to address the envelope and send his son to the post-office with it, to return the money by registered mail.

Now both Reb Aryeh and his son understood why he had broken his rule to let people remain anonymous when they came to him for help. His impulse to take her name and address had been a directive from heaven, to enable him to keep his rule about payment for help.

from here to there

Abraham Axelrod, the late deputy-mayor of Jerusalem, related: I chanced to be standing once near Reb Aryeh during a funeral at the Sanhedria cemetery. After the grave was filled he said to me with a smile "Many times people have tried to persuade me to move to larger, more comfortable living quarters; and I have refused.

"Come and see (he continued). After his long life on earth is over, a man is brought from his home—here. For me the move, the transition will not be hard; because between my room and here the contrast is not so very sharp. But when a man has grown accustomed to living comfortably in a splendid home, how hard it will be for him at the end of his days to move his 'residence' to this small bit of space..."

7
Traits of character

a noble quality

R. Abraham Isaac *ha-kohen* Kook, the first chief rabbi of Israel (then called Palestine) was once asked what reason he had to recommend Reb Aryeh to the British officials in charge of the prisons (under the mandate), for the position of rabbi (chaplain) of the prisoners—to deal with criminals and law-breakers. He replied, "In Reb Aryeh there is the quality of kindness, the disposition to do favors personally, by his own physical activity. This is the inner essence of his spirit, and in this way he will achieve his spiritual perfection in this world."

one spirit bound to another

In turn Reb Aryeh held R. Kook in deep affection, admiring and revering him greatly; and he was a faithful member of the chief rabbi's household. R. Kook returned the affection, until one spirit was veritably bound to the other.

Once one of the great Torah scholars in another land asked Rabbi Kook, "What is the reason that you are so fond of Reb Aryeh Levin?" The chief rabbi answered, "I have not one reason but three. For twenty years he has been frequenting my home, and in all that time (1) he has never flattered me; I have yet to hear him utter a single word in my praise; and if ever he saw me do anything which he did not understand, he questioned it or commented on it; (2) he never once told me of anything said by my fierce opponents, who were continually denigrating and defaming me; (3) and whatever he asked of me, it was never a favor for himself but only for others."

R. Kook would sometimes say, "If there were three Jews in our generation like Reb Aryeh, the Messiah would come..."

seeing only the good

Just as he never spoke in praise of anyone who respected and admired him, so that his words should not sound like flattery, so never in his life would Reb Aryeh speak in disparagement of any member of the Jewish people.

Once he was told of R. Joel Teitelbaum, known as the *rebbe* of Satmar (who holds the same extreme views as the members of the *n'turey karta* group in Jerusalem), that this religious leader, while living in the United States (in Williamsburg, Brooklyn, to be exact) was defaming and denouncing the state of Israel and its leaders.

Gently Reb Aryeh replied, "I do not know him personally. But I have heard that he possesses three good qualities: he loves Jews, is very learned in the Torah, and he promotes charity and acts of kindness."

judging every man favorably

He always strove to judge every single member of Jewry favorably, and would never see any evil or wrongdoing in anyone. In extreme cases, where he seemed to have no choice, he would retort, "But do we know everything about that man?" Or he would prefer to keep silent and turn the conversation to something else.

Once he told me how he reached this level of behavior: "One day I attended the funeral of R. Eliezer Rivlin, one of Jerusalem's fine, pure-minded Jews, who served as the secretary of the old-age home and was responsible for the collection and distribution of its charity funds. That esteemed and worthy man had a dear friend for many years: none other than R. Sh'muel Kook (a brother of the first chief rabbi). The two had been very close, sharing a splendid harmonious friendship while both lived; and they worked in one and the same field thirty years.

"All at once I saw this true friend of his leave the funeral procession, that was just beginning on its way to the cemetery. He was not accompanying his dear friend on this last journey, to his final resting-place, as he certainly should have done. Instead, he entered a flower-shop nearby to buy a pot for planting!

"*Nu*, I thought to myself: Is this how a man should act toward a true friend who has passed away—a friend who treated him so well while he was alive? Could he not give him this last kindness and pay him this last honor? Could he not find some other time to buy the flower-pot? Did he have to buy it right now, during the funeral?

"Well, you know, the Torah commands us: You shall not hate your brother in your heart; you shall surely rebuke your neighbor (Leviticus 19:17). So I went over to him and scolded him to his face: *Teach me, so that I also will know. Were you not more like a brother than a friend for so many years to this man who has departed this life? Then why did you leave the funeral procession to go buy a flower-pot?*

"That man explained: For years (he said) I have been visiting and attending a Jew stricken with leprosy. Yesterday he died, and for obvious reasons the doctors—who are gentile—ordered that all his clothes and possessions must be burned. Among his possessions there is a pair of *t'fillin* (phylacteries); and I rebelled with all my heart at the thought of the holy *t'fillin* being burned. Well, I spoke earnestly to one doctor, and it was agreed that I should bring a flower-pot today before noon, and then the *t'fillin* would be placed in this earthenware container and buried thus in the ground—in accordance with our religious law. So you see, I was compelled to hurry off now and buy the flower-pot, in order to bury the *t'fillin*.

"Since then," said Reb Aryeh, "I firmly resolved to judge every person favorably."

he had a trained ear

He saw only the good in human beings, even those for whom others rarely had a kind word. "That man," he would say, "is really wonderful. You simply do not know him well enough. I know him very well"; and he would go off on a list of praises.

"But rabbi," a listener would object, "people say about him that..."

"O, people say about me also things that are not true. The ear has to get accustomed to hear only what we are allowed to hear. Otherwise it will become stuffed up with evil reports and no room will be left for the truth!"

"the same outside as inside"

The truth is that from the time he made the resolution, he kept it. His son R. Simḥa Sh'lomo related: One of the heads of the anti-Zionist zealots in Jerusalem (*n'turey karta*), named R. Amram, was once arrested after a (rather violent) demonstration against the Israeli authorities, and he was imprisoned along with other members of his group. As soon as my father learned of his arrest he hurried over to the place of detention, in the "Russian compound" section of Jerusalem, taking with him a Torah scroll, so that those imprisoned souls could have the *sidrah* (the weekly portion) chanted from it on the Sabbath.

When he arrived there my father pleaded with the police officer in charge to bear in mind that these prisoners were pious Jews, and he should try to treat them with consideration. When he saw that the room of imprisonment was dark, my father spoke to the officer with gentle persuasion, asking him to move R. Amram and the others to another, lighter cell.

When he had done speaking with the officer in charge, my father turned back to see the arrested men once more before leaving. Well, noticing my father, that irascible R. Amram covered his eyes with his hands and exclaimed, "It is forbidden to look at that face!" (Since my father was closely linked in friendship with Chief Rabbi Kook, R. Amram thought him too wicked, under religious law, to look at.) The officer in charge was dumbfounded. "Is this the gratitude you get," he asked my father, "for all the trouble you have taken?"

With a shrug and a smile my father replied, "He is a just and straightforward man. His mouth and his heart are in exact accord. What he feels in his spirit he puts into words. Here you can see it is so: he is not ready to be bribed by the kindness I have done him, into changing his views about me. He is the same outside as inside—true to his beliefs."

the deserter from Brisk

Given as he was to acts of compassion and kindness, few suspected that Reb Aryeh also had an element of iron in his character, and when necessary he could break the resolution of the strongest man, merely by talking to him.

In his early years as self-appointed "rabbi" to the inmates of the central prison in Jerusalem, he was shown an interesting letter by his former instructor in Torah who was now his neighbor, the famed Talmud scholar R. Isser Zalman Meltzer. It was a letter that Rabbi Meltzer had received from R. Velvel of Brisk (Brest-Litovsk), a member of the noted Soloveitchik dynasty of great Talmudic scholars.

R. Velvel wrote of a certain Jew of Brisk who had simply picked himself up one day and disappeared, abandoning his wife to the misery of a life as a grass widow. There was reason to believe, R. Velvel added, that the man had headed for the land of Israel. So R. Velvel gave whatever details he could of the man's appearance, and he sent the man's family name and his Hebrew given name plus his father's given name.

R. Velvel ended his letter to R. Isser Zalman with a plea to keep a sharp lookout for the man; and should he find him, he should move heaven and earth to make the man send his wife a divorce, so that at least she would be free to remarry.

Reb Aryeh read the letter through carefully. "You know," said R. Isser Zalman, "I do not mingle much among people, whereas you do. Perhaps you will run across him."

Saturday mornings at the prison, it was Reb Aryeh's practice to speak briefly with every inmate before beginning the prayer-service; and he took a special interest in newcomers. One Sabbath morning he found one new inmate there, imprisoned for illegal entry into the land. Reb Aryeh began talking with him, and asked his name and his country of origin. The man hemmed and hawed and muttered something. In short, he left Reb Aryeh to conclude, he was just a Jew from somewhere. In the good rabbi's mind an idea glimmered: Could this be the deserter from Brisk?

All his conversations finished, Reb Aryeh began the prayer-service; and eventually the time came for him to chant the weekly portion of the Torah scroll. As usual, he would call up seven people to the Torah, and one for *maftir* at the end, and for each he would read a part of the weekly portion. When the time came to call up the fifth person, he sang out, "*ya'amod* (Arise) So-and-so the son of So-and-so"—using the Hebrew given names that he remembered perfectly from the letter of R. Velvel of Brisk. (In other words, he called for the man who had fled Brisk to come up to the Torah.) And out of the corner of his eye he watched the illegal immigrant with whom he had spoken.

Sure enough, the rabbi saw the man start from his seat. But then the man caught himself and sat back with studied indifference, ready to show whomever it might concern that the name meant nothing to him. Reb Aryeh waited a moment, and seeing no one come forward, he called up a different man. After the prayer-service, though, he headed straight for the new prisoner, took him to a private room, and began talking to him like a Dutch uncle.

No one knows what words passed between them; but a short while afterward, the man sent his wife a divorce through the proper channels of the religious courts.

the check that was never cashed

The time came when Reb Aryeh married off the daughter born to him in his middle age. The occasion made the political prisoners in Israel decide to present their rabbi and chaplain with a gift, as a token of their esteem and appreciation. Very slowly, bit by bit, they collected their coins (through their own channels of the prison grapevine) till they had a total of twenty-five Israeli pounds (an appreciable amount in those days); and then they turned to their *muchtar,* the uncrowned "king" of the prisoners, Moshe Segal, with the request that he should find some way to smuggle the money out through the prison walls and get it into the hands of their good rabbi. Segal obtained a check for this amount and transmitted it to Reb Aryeh, accompanied by the *mazal tov,* the very good wishes of the prisoners on the occasion of his daughter's marriage, as well as words of deep appreciation and gratitude for all that the good rabbi had done for them, striving always to help them with no thought of any personal gain.

Reb Aryeh never cashed the check. In his letter of thanks, written with a quill in his gem-like handwriting, he explained to the prisoners that he wanted this mitzvah of his, this religious good deed of visiting the imprisoned and giving heart to their families, to remain whole and perfect for him in his heavenly account. Never would he agree to exchange it for money—not for all the wealth in the world.

Nevertheless, Reb Aryeh asked to be allowed to keep the check as a remembrance: for he treasured and cherishd it, since it would let him feel anew every day how much "his" prisoners appreciated him (which in turn encouraged him to continue).

"men of qualities"

Another story: The staff of Israel's radio network once came to interview him, in preparation for a program in the series called *anshey middoth* ("men of noble quality"). A while afterward they sent him a check for twenty-five Israeli pounds, as they generally did after interviewing someone.

Without hesitation Reb Aryeh sent it back. "You must surely have made some mistake in sending me the check," he wrote. "For clearly you had expenses in connection with this broadcast; and I rather thought that it was for me to pay you for the honor that was given me to appear on the radio—and certainly not for you to pay me."

a sign from heaven

When he first came to Jerusalem, as a young man, Reb Aryeh rented a room in one of the houses of the old *yishuv* (religious settlement) that belonged to one of the organizations which ran the community. In the lease it was stated that he had to leave the room at the end of a year, or else he would be excommunicated—as the custom was in those times.

Well, this was in 1914; during the year that he lived there the First World War broke out. When his year ended Reb Aryeh wanted to leave his rented room, as agreed. But the directors of the organization that owned it assured him, "Look: there is no need for you to move out now.

We planned to place new immigrants in it—people coming from abroad who are connected with our organization. But since it is wartime, no one is coming to the holy land at a time like this." Reb Aryeh accepted the explanation, and he stayed.

The next year he again wanted to move out of the room. This time, however, it was a season of epidemics; and again no outsiders wanted to set foot in Jerusalem. Once more they begged him to remain—and he did.

During the festival of Sukkoth, like very pious Jews the world over, he slept in his *sukkah* (his booth roofed with greenery) every night during the week of the festival. Friday night during Sukkoth, as he lay there sleeping, he suddenly awoke in confusion and fright. A fire had broken out, and his *sukkah* was in flames. With great difficulty he fled to safety.

Without delay Reb Aryeh hastened to the head of the organization. "It is a punishment from heaven," he insisted, "because I did not honor the terms of the lease to which I put my signature; I did not move out of the room at the end of the year, as I promised."

He went then to live in the poor neighborhood of Mishk'noth.

the letter of thanks

In 1948, as the War of Independence raged in full force, Jerusalem lay under siege, and food and other necessities became extremely scarce. Thoughtfully, some good friends of Reb Aryeh sent the family packages from time to time. Once, though, by mistake the post office delivered one parcel to someone with a similar name; and he simply kept it. In a while, having received no word from the good rabbi about it, the sender made an enquiry, to try to trace it. Once Reb Aryeh realized what had happened, seeking to spare the man who had received it any embarrassment, he sent off immediately a warm letter of thanks for the package, as though he had received it.

he insisted on the price

This is an anecdote told by Yaakov Gellis of the education department in Jerusalem's city government: One day he visited the office of Yeshiva Etz Ḥayyim (where Reb Aryeh worked) and he had with him a copy of his book, *Seventy Years in Jerusalem* (just published). Reb Aryeh came into the room, saw the book lying on the table, and began leafing through it. He found that one chapter was devoted to the sainted rabbi of the religious settlement, R. Sh'muel Salant, whom Reb Aryeh had revered in his lifetime.

"Who wrote this book?" Reb Aryeh asked. "I did," Yaakov Gellis answered. Wanting to buy it, Reb Aryeh then asked for the price. "Three pounds," said Mr. Gellis. Reb Aryeh took the amount from his pocket and paid the author.

Some time later Reb Aryeh set out walking to find where Mr. Gellis lived. He climbed up the four flights to the man's apartment, and came in with a complaint: "Why did you ask me for three pounds for your book? I came across a copy of it in a bookstore, and it had a printed notice that its set price is five pounds."

This was right enough, the author replied: The fixed price of the book was indeed five pounds. But, he said, to yeshiva students he gave a discount, and the price for them was only three pounds.

"But I am not a yeshiva student," Reb Aryeh retorted. "I only work as a sort of teacher at the Etz Hayyim school." And he insisted on handing over the difference in the price.

that others should also benefit

Driving his car out toward the Hadassah hospital, which is quite far from the city proper, a man noticed Reb Aryeh walking, leaving the Ir Gannim neighborhood and setting out on foot up the long road leading to the Hadassah hospital. Knowing Reb Aryeh quite well, the man stopped his car and asked the good pious rabbi to get in. Reb Aryeh refused at first, insisting that he preferred to go on foot. Finally he yielded, however—but on one condition: "that we should take with us the people waiting at the next bus stop."

concern over a bridegroom's worry

One of the fine young Talmud students at the Yeshiva of Hebron (relocated in Jerusalem since the 1929 riots in Hebron) was about to be married, and he invited Reb Aryeh to the wedding. The bridegroom made arrangements with a good friend of his to bring the rabbi by car from his home to the ceremony, which was scheduled to take place at five in the afternoon.

The bridegroom's friend knew, however, that the ceremony would not begin until several of the *roshey yeshiva* arrived—the distinguished Talmudic scholars who taught at the Yeshiva of Hebron; and hence the act of marriage under the wedding canopy was bound to be delayed. The young man therefore decided that it was better to bring Reb Aryeh a bit later, so that he would not have to fritter away his precious time waiting.

The young man arrived at Reb Aryeh's home and brought him to the place of the wedding twenty minutes late. Then he explained his reason for arranging the delay. Reb Aryeh, however, was displeased: "Today, when that yeshiva student is getting married, his head is full of worries and concerns. Is it right for me to add another worry to his burdens, to make him wonder for twenty minutes why I have not appeared? It were better for me to waste an hour in the wedding hall rather than cause the bridegroom needless concern over my lateness."

the apology

When he was well past eighty, he found himself once seated in a crowded bus, with a woman standing in the aisle, right next to him. Apologetically, he explained that he suffered from water on the knee, and asked her to excuse him for not giving her his seat.

the willing witness

At a wedding that Reb Aryeh attended, he noticed the wedding party asking a plain Jew, a worthy man who earned his living by honest work, to serve as one of the two formal witnesses to the marriage, which the Jewish law requires; and the man happily agreed. Then the wedding party asked a very dignified Talmudic scholar if he would serve as the second witness. He felt his dignity so strongly, however, that having seen the choice for the first witness, he felt it would be beneath him (as a Talmud scholar) to be coupled with a plain Jew. So he declined the honor, on the grounds that under the Jewish law he was disqualified as a witness by a technicality.

This scholar may have thought he had been clever, but his real reason was only too obvious; and Reb Aryeh saw the other Jew (the first witness) blanch and turn pale, fairly stunned by the insult. In a moment Reb Aryeh was beside him and speaking to the wedding party. "Here," he said with his infectious smile, "I am perfectly qualified and ready. Let *me* be the second witness." His offer was gratefully accepted, and then the first witness's face was also wreathed with a smile.

in honor of the mother

When a certain orphan boy became bar-mitzvah (on his twelfth birthday rather than his thirteenth, because he was an orphan), Reb Aryeh went to the family's celebration of the happy event. He had known the boy's late father and grandfather, both very learned and pious Jews. So there he sat amidst the family, radiating and sharing the joy he felt, as he reminisced genially about the boy's father and grandfather. The members of the family were honored and warmed by his amiable and distinguished presence.

Having finished his talk and paid his respects, the good rabbi gave the boy his blessing and left. Some fifteen minutes later, however, he was back. "Reb Aryeh," came the question, "why have you returned?"

"Oh," he replied, "on my way from here I learned that this boy's mother was the daughter of a fine scholar who wrote a noteworthy volume of Torah learning. The boy deserves to be honored anew for the sake of his mother's father. So I have come back." And his beaming face brought fresh joy to the family group.

"please forgive me"

On a winter day filled with rain he was walking through the little alleys of Jerusalem paved with smooth stones, when he slipped and fell in the mud. Someone happened to be passing by, who was evidently a member of a rather extreme group that denounced R. Abraham Isaac Kook (a dear and close friend of Reb Aryeh) ever since he became the first chief rabbi of Israel (then called Palestine). Recognizing Reb Aryeh lying in the mud, the man exclaimed, "It serves you right! That is just what you deserve! Such is the fate of everyone who follows Rav Kook!"

Reb Aryeh picked himself up, wiped the mud from himself, and went over to this man. "*Reb Yid* (dear fellow-Jew)," he said, "I see that you are vexed and angry. Perhaps you have some complaint against me. Maybe you were once hurt or injured through me? If so, please forgive me..."

Taken aback, the man continued on his way without another word, ashamed at his outburst.

the good trait

In the synagogue where he prayed every morning at sunrise, one man fell into disfavor with the people with extreme views, because of a very remote link with the "heretical Zionists," and they left an order in the synagogue forbidding him to be called to the Torah. On a certain weekday morning when the Torah was read, Reb Aryeh gently insisted that the man be called up. This aroused one person's wrath, and he came over and almost tore the t'fillin from the good rabbi's head, insulting him roundly to boot, within everyone's hearing.

Without a word, he accepted the disgrace and went home, pained and hurt. Many came afterward to cheer him and ask him back, but he came to that synagogue no more. One man, though, asked him, "Do you know perhaps *why* you were punished by that man's act and words of deep insult? Do you know the underlying reason?"

"It may be that I sinned toward God."

"O no," said the other man, himself one of the extremists. "It is because you are so close and friendly with that rabbi." He meant R. Abraham Isaac Kook, then the chief rabbi of the holy land, whom he would not deign to mention by name.

"Tell me," said Reb Aryeh: "Was I right to keep silent and say nothing?"

"Certainly," the other answered. "That is a very fine quality you have. You know that our Sages said: Those who accept insult and do not mete it out, listen to their disgrace and make no reply—about them Scripture says, *those who love Him* (God) *are as the sun rising in its might*" (Judges 5:31; Talmud, *Shabbath* 88b).

"Well, you should know," said Reb Aryeh, "that I learned this trait from *that* rabbi."

the meaningful silences

Always, when he was asked for an opinion or a comment on something or someone controversial, where the topic involved friction or rancor, his answer was silence. Not a word would he utter. If he was pressed—"*Nu, Reb Aryeh, what do you say?*"—he would shrug his shoulders: "I have nothing to say."

Once a son of his asked him, "Father, what do you mean by these silences, when you refuse to speak?"

"I will tell you," the good rabbi replied. "You have studied the great compendium of religious practice by R. Isaac Alfasi (the *Rif*—printed at the back of each volume of the Talmud). What did that great scholar do? He merely copied out whole passages from the Talmud; but he omitted the parts that are not to be followed in actual religious practice. That is the meaning of his silences...."

the holy wares

Walking through the city one day, Reb Aryeh saw a peddler standing in the street, offering his assorted merchandise for sale. Among the wares, the good rabbi noticed a few old holy volumes, some of them torn. He felt pity for the holy books exposed like that on a peddler's stand, and with his last few coins he bought them. At home he examined them, only to find a small old prayer-book among them, with the signature of the famous 18th-century scholar and bibliophile R. Joseph Hayyim David Azulai—a valuable autograph!

faced by the camera

The editor of an Israeli magazine once came to interview him, accompanied by a photographer. As they talked, the photographer tried to get some good candid shots, but Reb Aryeh managed to avoid the camera and foil his efforts, having no wish to let his face appear in print. When it became clear that the photographer was not going to succeed, the magazine editor turned to him and said, "Rabbi, this photographer is a new immigrant from Vilna, and you are preventing him from earning a living—because he earns money for those pictures of his that I publish in the magazine."

Reb Aryeh was taken aback, and now he posed calmly for the photographer. "My dear man," he said, "if it is to earn your living that you are pursuing me with that camera, I am completely at your service. Take all the pictures you want."

Similarly, during his frequent visits to the Western Wall after it was back in Israel's possession, people veritably pulled at him from all sides with their requests to let them take his picture. With his little smile turned to an infectious grin, he would generally comply. "Why not?" he said. "It is a great thing for a Jew to do kindness *b'gufo*, personally—with his physical self."

another's honor

In his last years, when Reb Aryeh was in his eighties, it was hard for him to stand on his feet. On his doctor's orders one of his students, Yaakov David Perlin, would come every day to massage his feet. Yet under no circumstances would Reb Aryeh ever let him untie his laces and take off his shoes: for that might perhaps be a slight to the honor of this student. It cost him an effort to bend down, yet he always took off his own shoes, allowing his student to do no more than massage his feet.

A few days before his end came he told me, "In the world of truth also [in the Hereafter] I won't forget his kindness toward me."

his thoughts for others

Through all his married years it was his custom (he thought it his privilege) to serve every Yom Kippur as the *ḥazzan* (reader of the congregation) for the senior students and faculty of Yeshiva Merkaz haRav, the fine Torah academy founded and headed by Chief Rabbi Kook of blessed memory. The select congregation (which also included relations and friends of the chief rabbi) valued him not for his fine voice and cantorial technique, which he had not at all, but because he prayed with a moving simplicity and honesty before his Father in heaven.

On the last Yom Kippur of his life, almost six months to the day before his end came, when major illness was an inseparable part of his life, he refused to give up his custom. Mustering his strength, he served as *ḥazzan* for *Kol Nidrey* and the evening service that followed; and late the next afternoon he led the *neʿilah* service, that ended the Yom Kippur worship. After *maʿariv* (the regular evening service) it was Reb Aryeh's custom to recite the benediction of *havdala*, marking the separation between the concluded holy Day of Atonement and the ensuing non-holy time.

Reb Aryeh refused to begin, however, till he found and set out the pieces of cake that he had prepared the day before—so that all could break their fast of some twenty-six hours immediately after *havdala*. He had hidden the cake in several places about the room, and as neither his memory nor his agility was what it had been (he was eighty-three) it was a short while before the task was done. The worshippers kept urging him to recite *havdala*, have the wine, and then look for the cake. He would not hear of it. He would not break his own fast before he had provided for all.

his own life insurance

So great was his wish to trust only in the Almighty and not in human beings (in accordance with Jeremiah 17:5, *Cursed is the man that trusts in man*) that he would not buy any life insurance.

One day an insurance agent who knew him well came and did his best to convince the good rabbi of the need and value of life insurance. Knowing that the man needed to sell policies to earn his livelihood, Reb Aryeh gave the matter some thought. Then he gave the agent his answer — something like this:

In the Torah we read, *The Rock, His work is perfect; for all His ways are justice. A God of faithfullness and without iniquity, just and right is He* (Deuteronomy 32:5). At first sight this seems puzzling. Suppose you saw a judge, and within his hearing you told a friend, "That man is a fair judge, really honest. He will never give any crooked decisions." That man would be highly insulted: What need is there to say such a thing? With his record and reputation, how could anyone even suspect him of anything less than perfect integrity?

An important point lies hidden, however (said Reb Aryeh), in these words of the Torah.

Assume that the police catch a man in a shop late at night, stealing money and merchandise. He is arrested and brought to trial. The judge will take his circumstances into account: Was he poor? Was he driven to steal by the need to keep body and soul together, or to feed his family? Witnesses who know him will testify about his character. The judge will ascertain if this is his first arrest, or if he was convicted of crimes before, etc.

Quite possibly, the judge may sentence the man to two years in prison. Everyone will agree that the verdict is just; the judge has done his duty well. Alas, though, the sentence has consequences: Now his wife will probably have to leave the shelter of her home and go looking for a job. She will have to work eight hours a day. Then what will become of the children? Left without a father or mother to supervise them, they may turn delinquent and live blighted lives.

Do the wife and children deserve their fate? Certainly not: they committed no crime. Yet no one would dream of accusing the judge of having passed an unjust sentence. He has no duty to consider the impact of his sentence on innocent people.

The Almighty, however, acts differently—"for *all* His ways are justice." When Heaven metes out punishment, every last effect of the sentence on any given individual has been taken into account; and the Almighty's decision is that this individual deserves the bad consequences.

Assume now (said the good rabbi) that, Heaven forbid, I committed some terrible sins for which I deserved death. There would be a trial before the Almighty, and He would prepare to give the fatal verdict—when suddenly an angel would rise up and say, "Wait a moment. The man has a wife and children. What of the great hardship they will suffer if his life is ended? Do they deserve that?" So to speak, the Almighty will shake His head and will prepare to cancel the verdict, to let me live so that I can support my family—when suddenly another angel will arise and say, "Yes—but the man has life insurance!" (So he bought no policy.)

to rest on the Sabbath

Whatever letters arrived on Friday after the middle of the day, it was Reb Aryeh's custom not to open them—so that bothersome thoughts and worries should not trouble him during the Sabbath, the holy day of rest.

and not to disturb its peace

He was very devoted to his nephew (his sister's son) R. Binyomin Lipkin (of blessed memory), a brilliant Talmud student, of fine character, and a direct descendant of R. Elijah the Gaon of Vilna. Unfortunately this nephew died in his young adult years, stricken by a malignant illness.

The death occurred on a Friday. On Saturday Reb Aryeh met a friend who had not heard the sad news. "How is Reb Binyomin?" the friend asked. "*Nu*," Reb Aryeh replied, "it is the holy Sabbath today..." And he said not another word.

with a cheerful greeting

For over sixty years, without missing a day, he rose before daylight every morning to join a group (*minyan*) in prayer at the rising of the sun, following the practice of R. Elijah the Gaon of Vilna. Even when his health began to suffer he kept this practice faithfully, with devotion—and so even when a curfew was in force.

On his way to the synagogue he made it a point to greet everyone he met on the street; and he was especially careful to wish a good morning to the street-cleaners, who also rose early to work.

Once he told me why he did this: "I have an affection for the street-cleaners. Just look: When everyone is still asleep they take the trouble to come and clean the streets of Jerusalem, so as to support themselves by their own honest labor. Their work is not respected; they are not esteemed for it; their salary is niggardly. And still they take pains to do their task faithfully."

his quality of devotion

Where did Reb Aryeh learn his quality of devotion, his readiness to give of himself utterly?—from something that happened.

In 1929 the *rebbe* of Lubavitch, R. Yosef Yitzhak Shneersohn (head of the *habad* sect of *hassidim*, the father-in-law of the present rebbe of Lubavitch) came on a visit to the holy land, and he was put up in quarters in the Old City of Jerusalem.

R. Abraham Isaac Kook, the chief rabbi of the land of Israel, wished to visit this renowned hassidic figure, and he asked Reb Aryeh to accompany him. In turn Reb Aryeh asked his son-in-law R. Sh'muel Aaron Yudelevitz, who was with him, to come along with them. When they reached the room of the rebbe, R. Kook entered alone, while Reb Aryeh was compelled to remain outside. When R. Kook realized this he turned around to the hassidim, the devoted followers of the rebbe who filled the room: "Is this how you treat someone who accompanies me?" The hassidim made way, and Reb Aryeh entered also, with his son-in-law. All three were present as R. Kook engaged the rebbe of Lubavitch in a conversation that concerned the most important and burning issues in the world of Jewry and Judaism. R. Kook and the rebbe spoke long and earnestly, and Reb Aryeh listened attentively to every detail.

Reb Aryeh later related how R. Kook explained to the rebbe his approach, his idea of *k'lal yisra'el* (the Community of Israel) and the reconstruction of this people and its homeland. The chief rabbi's words were as radiant and illuminating as the Torah given at Sinai.

"At that meeting," said Reb Aryeh, "I learned a fundamental law that prevailed in the thought of this master teacher (R. Kook): When it comes to rescuing our brethren, members of Jewry, the concept of *m'siruth nefesh*—dedication, readiness for self-sacrifice—cannot be limited to giving of your physical self (work, energy, effort) or your money or property for the sake of others. It has to be enlarged, expanded to include even the readiness to sacrifice your spirit, your soul. Even if you think that the matter will cost you your life in the Hereafter, your eternal reward in the Afterlife, you must go ahead and work to rescue your brethren.

"Now, this," Reb Aryeh continued, "I learned also from something that actually happened with two pious, devout brothers, disciples of R. Elijah the Gaon of Vilna, named R. Moshe and R. Yitzhak. Living entirely within the laws of the Torah, R. Moshe spent the whole year traveling and wandering among the villages, teaching Torah to the children of the country people, the rural folk. Thus he barely eked out a meager livelihood with difficulty, while remaining devoted to Torah and prayer in his discreet, unnoticed way; and he would return home only for the main *yomim tovim* (festivals), with the bit of money he managed to gather for his family's sustenance.

"In that earlier generation it was also the practice of the people of

TRAITS OF CHARACTER

piety that everyone would devote himself particularly to one *mitzvah* (religious obligation) being ready to go to any length to observe it fully, far beyond the pure call of duty. For his 'special' mitzvah R. Moshe had chosen *tzitzith* (the ritual tassels or fringes that have to be worn at the corners of a four-cornered garment, as a reminder of all the mitzvoth). This pious man would refuse to move four cubits (about six feet) without fit and proper *tzitzith* about his body.

"Once, early in Nissan, as the festival of Passover approached, the pious man was returning home after an absence of a good many months, bringing with him a little hoard of money so that the family could have what it needed for Passover. He rode along with a plain Jew who drove his horse-and-wagon, until, during the journey, he got down from the wagon and went over to a boulder a good distance away from the road (probably to say his prayers).

"Somehow, while R. Moshe was at the large rock, one of the tassels on his four-cornered garment caught on a notch of the boulder, and it tore off.

"Needless to say, R. Moshe remained true to his way of observance. He would absolutely not move four cubits without wearing proper *tzitzith*. So now he remained at the rock as though stuck fast, and would not budge. At the top of his voice he called to the wagon-driver, sitting in his wagon a good long distance away. This plain, simple Jew knew of R. Moshe's utter dedication to the mitzvah of *tzitzith,* and he understood the situation well enough. But he thought that at the present such strict behavior by R. Moshe was unwarranted. After all, it was an emergency.

"He went over to the boulder and argued with R. Moshe—to no avail. The pious man would not budge. Finally the wagon-driver agreed to ride to the nearby village and bring him a new *arba-kanfoth* (four-cornered garment). But in his annoyance at this extra trouble, the driver demanded a stiff price: the entire purse of money that R. Moshe held—the small amount he had gathered to support his family through Passover and perhaps some months afterward.

"R. Moshe did not hesitate or think. Immediately he put his bit of collected money into the wagon-driver's hand, knowing full well what he was doing. He readily exposed his family and himself to suffering and want for the next weeks and months, sooner than violate the way that he had undertaken to keep the mitzvah of *tzitzith*. This was his Divine way.

"Well, the story is told that the wagon-driver just took off with the money and never came back. And this pious man stayed in his place for a whole twenty-four hours, until someone passing by took pity on him and lent him a good *arba kanfoth* (four-cornered garment), so that he could return home. You cannot imagine the anguish and suffering of the man's family that Passover (trying to make do on nothing or a bit of borrowed money, or credit)....

"Some time afterward his equally devout brother, R. Yitzhak, known and esteemed through all Lithuania, fell so seriously ill that the physicians gave up hope for his life. So people sent for R. Moshe to come from the villages where he was wandering about. Perhaps he could entreat Heaven's mercy for his brother and so save his life; the gates of tearful prayer are never shut there, you know.

"R. Moshe came without delay, entered the room where his brother lay ill, and asked everyone there to kindly leave. When the two brothers were alone in the room, R. Moshe stood up, took off the *arba kanfoth* that he wore, and put it on his brother's bed. *Sovereign Ruler of the world,* he said to God, *there is one mitzvah that I have kept with all my strength: the mitzvah of tzitzith. I hereby give up all the reward for it that I am to get in the Afterlife. I yield my reward—to my brother. Just let him be credited with whatever merit I have earned, and let him recover from his illness.*

"A few neighbors were peering through the cracks in the old wooden house of R. Yitzhak, and they saw it all. They told about it afterward, describing the poignant emotion and heart-rending tears of R. Moshe as he gave up the most precious thing he had, the Divine merit he had earned for keeping the mitzvah of *tzitzith* with so much utter self-sacrifice—to have his brother cured.

"By the merit of his prayer, the pious R. Yitzhak did recover, and he lived another fifteen years."

Reb Aryeh added: "From this I learned how much *m'siruth nefesh*, how much readiness for devotion and self-sacrifice we need to rescue members of our people. A Jew has to be ready to give up everything he has and is—not just physical well-being, life and wealth, but even his life in the Hereafter that he has earned. For that is *true* self-sacrifice."

"this was my father"

Talking once with his son R. Ḥayyim Yaakov (the rabbi of Pardes Hanna in Israel), the journalist Geula Cohen mused, "I can see before me the living image of your dear departed father (of blessed memory). While he was giving his help to the underground fighter, the Israeli soldier in the days before the Jewish state was established, at the very same time he found the means and the spirit to extend his hand in encouragement and comfort to a thief who had befouled his life. In the morning he would give heart to a condemned prisoner going to the gallows, and in the evening he gave solace and comfort to the woman who had thus become a widow. With him, it seemed, there was no before and after, no sense of what must come first and what could be put aside for later. Somehow the big, important things never blocked the little things from his view. Did he rate such things at all, in terms of what should come first?"

This was the reply of Reb Aryeh's son:

If he made no such rating or distinction in his humane activities, it is because there could be no order of preference or importance in love and affection for fellow-Jews. The pain of an individual is everyone's pain. For my father (of blessed memory) it was never a matter of big things and little things to do. For him every human being was a whole world, and the whole world in turn was one unity.

As a rule people see only the things called great, important, and not what we call insignificant or minor. But here we can really see the difference between physical, material force and spiritual force. Physical strength and prowess is generally described or indicated in terms of external size or quantity. On the other hand, spiritual strength is measured precisely by the power to see the small, unnoticed things that are hidden from the eye. Loud, stormy voices any ordinary person can hear. But a stilled moan, a sob within the heart, only a man of spiritual powers, such as my father, could hear. Great people also see small things. Great things are also seen by small people.

It truly needs this kind of ability to hear and see human pain. You cannot hear a melody from musical notes. You must have violins, with the strings vibrating to produce the notes. So here too it requires human beings who are akin to violins, able to vibrate to signals of pain and suffering and be shaken by them. But in addition, it is also a matter of training: You can train yourself to hear things; you can work to develop your sensitivity. Some are privileged to be born with the nature and spirit of a tzaddik. But we believe that in every human being there is the capacity to become good.

My father trained himself to do acts of goodness. He knew how to learn the Torah, and indeed he studied a great deal. Yet to do and to act you cannot learn from volumes or from scholars, but only from the actions of tzaddikim, devout good people. I remember my father telling me how he had a great yearning and longing, from his childhood years, to bask in the presence of tzaddikim; and he would go traveling great distances when still a child, just to see the face of a tzaddik and learn to follow his ways faithfully.

This was the answer of Reb Aryeh's son. Geula Cohen then asked him, "When you said just now, 'to cling to his ways,' you reminded me that whoever came into your father's proximity, into his world, was simply drawn to him and affected by him. I remember how in your father's presence, without his saying a single word to preach or rebuke, we not only wanted to improve but we actually felt that right there we were becoming better human beings. Is it indeed so that when a human spirit is itself drawn to goodness, it automatically draws and raises others also to the good?"

To this R. Hayyim Yaakov Levin, Reb Aryeh's son, replied:

There are certain human spirits so pure that they can be affected by no stain of impurity. Filth will simply not cling to them; on the contrary, they attract and draw to themselves only the clean and the good. Every material element has the capacity to draw certain things to it, while other things it repels. Thus for example it is not possible to write with ink on every kind of paper. Some papers absorb and retain ink, and some reject it. You can have a coat that absorbs the rain and becomes wet, while another coat lets the raindrops pass across its surface without penetrating it. Some materials absorb dust and dirt, and some do not.

Well, if something absorbs dust and dirt, that is an indication that there is some connection between it and the dust and dirt. And so there are some human spirits which even if they fell down a chimney would not be blackened. There are certain spirits—and I personally am convinced that my father was one of them—that draw, like a magnet, only good things; spirits that arouse in another human spirit the good, pure inclination, thrusting away the dark and evil elements. And goodness and purity exist in every human being.

There are some spirits which, once you come across them, do not let you remain indifferent. At times an encounter with a tzaddik opens your heart. Or it can happen that a person's heart is opened by some specific singular event that happens to him. Then as it were a passageway is opened either in his mind or in his heart, and through it he can perceive things that he never saw before. Great troubles and tribulations are a kind of key to open such a passageway; but it is necessary to know how to use this key for troubles to open the passageway. For just as dire and serious troubles can be a key that opens the heart, so they can lock the heart and harden it.

In my father's hand (Reb Aryeh's son concluded) there was always the key that fit.

8
Of kindness and charity

who taught him compassion

In his memoirs Reb Aryeh wrote:
> I recall the early days, from 1905 onward, when it was granted me by the grace of the blessed Lord to go up to the holy land, and I came to Jaffa. There I first went to visit our great master R. Abraham Isaac Kook (of blessed memory), who received me with good cheer, as it was his hallowed custom to receive everyone. We chatted together on themes of Torah study. After an early *minḥah* (afternoon prayer-service) he went out, as his hallowed custom was, to stroll a bit in the fields and gather his thoughts; and I went along. On the way I plucked some branch or flower. Our great master was taken aback; and then he told me gently, "Believe me: In all my days I have taken care never to pluck a blade of grass or flower needlessly, when it had the ability to grow or blossom. You know the teaching of the Sages that there is not a single blade of grass below, here on earth, which does not have a heavenly force (or angel) above telling it, *Grow!* Every sprout and leaf of grass says something, conveys some meaning. Every stone whispers some inner, hidden message in the silence. Every creation utters its song (in praise of the Creator)."

OF KINDNESS AND CHARITY

Those words, spoken from a pure and holy heart, engraved themselves deeply on my heart. From that time on I began to feel a strong sense of compassion for everything.

in response to emergency

It did not take him long to become involved with deeds of charity and help for the poor. During the First World War, when regular funds from abroad for the religious community often failed to arrive, Jerusalem suffered cruelly from hunger and want. A man named Sh'muel Lerner was in America at the time, while his wife and children were in the holy city. Concerned for their welfare, he sent money for their support to a supposedly worthy gentleman, whom he believed to be above reproach. Human nature has always been far too fallible, however; and in dire difficulties himself, that "worthy gentleman" simply pocketed the money.

On a day before Yom Kippur, Reb Aryeh happened to look in on Sh'muel Lerner's family, and he saw that there was not even a tablecloth spread on the table. He did not need any fine Talmudic reasoning to conclude that there was probably not a bite of food in the house to eat, in preparation for the solemn day of fasting that would soon begin.

At that time Reb Aryeh owned some valuable old volumes of Torah learning—rare editions, and so forth. Without hesitation he went home, took one of these precious volumes, and set off to see Mendel Rand. Mendel Rand was a rarity in his own right: a wealthy member of the religious community who loved rare old volumes and was always ready to purchase them for his fine collection. Happy at Reb Aryeh's offer, he paid a good price for the work; and so the good rabbi gave Sh'muel Lerner's wife and children the means (a "loan" payable at any time whatever) for a good festive meal before Yom Kippur.

"why should the poor suffer"

In time Reb Aryeh's reputation spread as a man of integrity and devotion to the poor, who could be trusted with money for charity; and in consequence he became a mainstay of support for a number of worthy but indigent families in Jerusalem. Yet he himself never suspected how far his reputation traveled.

Once Rabbi Judah Leyb Maimon (of blessed memory), Israel's Minister of Religion, had to make a trip to America, accompanied by his secretary, Israel Friedman. At a meeting with observant Jews in Chicago, one man approached Israel Friedman. "Do you know Reb Aryeh Levin in Jerusalem?" he asked.

"Certainly."

"Then please give him this"—and he handed Friedman a check for a thousand dollars (worth far more then than today).

"But from whom is it?" asked Friedman. "Reb Aryeh will want to know."

"What difference does it make?" asked the man; and he moved off into the crowd. At that Israel Friedman went over to Rabbi Maimon and told him about the check. "I believe the man is standing over there," he added. "Can you recognize him, perhaps?" Rabbi Maimon was rather near-sighted, however, and he likewise answered, "What difference does it make?"

In Jerusalem, though, Reb Aryeh refused to accept it. "For myself," said he, "I never take gifts. Thank Heaven, I earn enough at my employment. And if it is for charity, I do not know for whom or what it was intended, nor do I know the source of the money. For all I know, it may have been acquired dishonorably...."

In frustration, Israel Friedman consulted friends; and they went to see R. Tz'vi Pesaḥ Frank, the rabbi of Jerusalem and Reb Aryeh's brother-in-law. He took the check and sent for Reb Aryeh at once. "Look here," he said. "I know how many families depend on you for their subsistence. Why should they suffer because you do not know who gave this money? For yourself you can have all the qualms you want—but not at their expense."

Reb Aryeh took the check and cashed it.

"this mitzvah is mine"

As he was walking once along one of Jerusalem's alleys or side-streets an impoverished Jew reduced to begging suddenly turned to him and asked for a bit of charity. Reb Aryeh searched his pockets and found not a single coin. As he was walking with R. Abraham Gneḥovsky, Reb Aryeh asked his companion to lend him ten Israeli pounds. "Why lend it?" asked R. Gneḥovsky. "Here is the money, and do as you like with it." But this Reb Aryeh refused: "The mitzvah that I have now been given the chance to do is mine, and I am not ready to miss the opportunity in any way (by giving him your money instead of mine)."

your own poor come first

It is told that a certain man once came to Reb Aryeh's house and wished to give him a handsome donation for the yeshiva that now bears his (Reb Aryeh's) name. Reb Aryeh would not take it, however. "For you," he said, "it is forbidden to give any contribution."

The man was amazed to hear this. "Why?" he demanded. "I am a man of means, you know." Reb Aryeh's answer was simple: "You have relatives and family members whose situation is quite distressing. As long as you do not help them I may not take your donation. The Torah says plainly: do not hide yourself from your own flesh (and blood; Isaiah 58:7). And the Sages teach that the poor in your own city must come first, before other needy people, when you give charity" (Talmud, *Bava M'tzi'a* 71a). Under no circumstances would he take the man's money.

Reb Aryeh's words made a deep impression on him, and from then on he began supporting the members of his family who were in difficult circumstances.

"I came to ask permission"

It was the custom of the Gneḥovsky family twice a year to send Reb Aryeh a substantial check, accompanied by a note that read, "to use for any purpose you wish." This they did deliberately, because they knew how strictly Reb Aryeh obeyed the religious law that money intended for one charitable purpose is not to be used for any other charity. Hence they left their gift open to his discretion.

Once, on the day before Yom Kippur (the Day of Atonement) Reb Aryeh suddenly appeared at the home of Dov Gneḥovsky (a senior economist of the Bank of Israel). Astonished, the man asked, "Whatever are you doing here just a few hours before our most solemn holy day begins?"

The pious rabbi answered, "You know, just as always I received the check from your family this year too. But since they did not include a note about a purpose for the money, I think they must have meant to donate it to the yeshiva. Well, that is the problem. I want to use the check for charity in situations that are really urgent. And so I came to ask permission, to find out if I have the right to do so."

"Certainly you have the right," said Dov Gnehovsky. "It was only by an oversight that the usual note, 'to use for any purpose you wish,' was not added. Was it for this that you had to trouble yourself now, before our holy Day of Atonement?"

Reb Aryeh was not finished, however. Then and there Dov had to telephone his uncle Nahum Gnehovsky in Tel Aviv, whose signature was on the check, that he too should give his consent to use the money for the pressing cases of which Reb Aryeh knew.

"take and act"

This pious rabbi once related: Whenever the festival of Passover approached, it was my custom to distribute money among the needy. One year, however, the times were very hard and I simply had no money for this charity. Passover was drawing near, and I was in confusion and despair. How could I face these people who looked to me to help them in their utter poverty?

When it was at last the very day before Passover, I set out for the *kothel ma'aravi* (the Western Wall). I took my son and went to take the bus to the Old City. A long line of people was waiting for the bus, the heat was intense, and there I stood in my misery. Suddenly a bare-headed Jew in shirtsleeves came over to me, thrust some money into my hand, and asked me to distribute it among the poor.

I seized him by the hand. "Who are you?" I demanded. "Why are you doing this? And what reason did you see to choose me particularly to be the emissary for this mitzvah?" The man grew a bit angry with me: "If you are given money, just take it and act!"

I hurried off to my widows and orphans and gave them all that they were waiting for, and more. But who that man was or where he came from, to this day I do not know.

they are also in God's image

When the news reached us in Israel of the massacre in the African country of Biafra, a campaign for rescue funds was started. As soon as Reb Aryeh heard of it he asked the campaign manager to be kind enough to take his contribution too, even if it could only be a modest, token amount—for "they too were created in the Divine image."

The time came for the representative of Magen David Adom (Israel's equivalent of the Red Cross) to fly out to Biafra, to rush Israel's help for the suffering and needy there. The head of the rescue-fund campaign came over to him and said, "Here is Reb Aryeh's contribution. Keep it with you. You know what the Sages teach—that emissaries on their way to do a mitzvah will never come to harm" (Talmud, *P'saḥim* 8b).

When the representative of Magen David Adom returned from his trip, he went to Reb Aryeh and told him all that his eyes had seen—all the terrible suffering, and the help that Israel had given. "You have sanctified God's name in the world," said Reb Aryeh; and he doubled his contribution to the fund.

the charity became anonymous

It was Reb Aryeh's practice to support (out of his charity funds) a fine young Torah scholar who was both learned and devout, but lived in great privation. In time, however, the young man adopted the extreme views of others; and when he learned that Reb Aryeh was among the close friends of the chief rabbi, R. Abraham Isaac Kook, he refused to take any more charity from him.

Reb Aryeh knew, however, the difficult and distressing circumstances in which the young Torah scholar lived, and he was determined to continue to support him. So it became his practice to get the money to the man through an acceptable intermediary (R. Shalom Eisen), and the young scholar never knew from whom the money really came.

"share your bread with the hungry"

It was not only money that Reb Aryeh gave in charity. He gave as well of his own self, his energy and strength. In 1948 the State of Israel was born into a desperate battle for survival in the War of Independence, and Jerusalem found itself under siege. The city suffered a severe shortage of food. The members of the underground fighting movements, however (Irgun Tz'va'i Leumi and Lohamey Ḥéruth Yisra'él), stationed at their army posts, were well stocked with supplies. Remembering their rabbi (chaplain) who had done kindnesses for them in the days when they were imprisoned (under the British mandate), these soldiers would bring Reb Aryeh parcels of food for his family. Losing no time, Reb Aryeh would take the parcels and hurry out of his house, to distribute the food among all his neighbors....

not to cause shame

The noted Talmudic scholar R. Tz'vi Pesaḥ Frank, the rabbi of the Jerusalem community, knew Reb Aryeh quite well, as they were related by marriage (a sister-in-law of his was Reb Aryeh's wife). Knowing how good-hearted and sympathetic his relative was, R. Frank forbade him to co-sign as a guarantor on any IOU's or similar documents of financial obligation. For more than once Reb Aryeh was thus exploited by borrowers who did not meet their obligations, and so left him in a quandary, facing bitter troubles.

Once Reb Aryeh was summoned to appear in court, to face a demand to pay a debt for which he had co-signed as a guarantor. The good rabbi was amazed. He did not remember at all having signed on any IOU like that. Still, he went to court as required. There he had a look at his signature on the document, and saw at once that it had been forged—while right before him stood the poor debtor with his eyes lowered, unable to look Reb Aryeh in the face, since it was he who had forged the signature.

Well, the judge wanted to know, was it his signature? So as not to shame the guilt-laden debtor, Reb Aryeh acknowledged it as his, but asked the judge as a kindness to let him pay off the debt in monthly installments (as he could not clear it off all at once). For several years Reb Aryeh paid out twenty-eight Israeli pounds a month for an IOU that he had never signed, just to avoid subjecting a man to mortifying shame in public.

in the role of "go-between"

Under the British mandate there was no more unity among the Jews of Israel (then called Palestine) than there is today. During his entire career, Rabbi Abraham Isaac Kook (eventually the first chief rabbi of the land) and his followers maintained close friendly relations with the Zionists. On the other hand the group of very pious Jews in Jerusalem called *neturey karta* ("guardians of the city") bitterly opposed and denounced the Zionists, and hence were always hostile toward Rabbi Kook.

Once the daughter of one of the heads of *neturey karta* was stricken with a difficult and dangerous illness. The doctors who examined her had but one conclusion: She must be sent abroad, to Professor So-and-so in this-and-this country; he was the world's greatest specialist in his field.

This leader of *neturey karta* made inquiries, and he learned that the professor in question was a very busy man; a great number of patients made demands on his time. If his daughter came to this renowned physician as just another patient, it was not likely that he would give her case much attention. Moreover, the fee required was far beyond the man's means.... But then the sick girl's father learned something more: The professor was a very great admirer of Rabbi Abraham Isaac Kook. Should the man receive a personal request from Rabbi Kook to treat the sick girl, he would put all else aside and devote himself to curing her.

The girl's father was now definitely in a quandary. If he approached Rabbi Kook directly with a plea for a letter to the professor, he would die of embarrassment and shame. As a leader of *neturey karta* he had subjected Rabbi Kook to contumely and disgrace in public more than once.

Then the man had an idea: He knew that Rabbi Kook bore Reb Aryeh a profound affection and there was a strong bond of friendship between the two. He went to Reb Aryeh and asked him to kindly serve as a "go-between" and speak to Rabbi Kook for him. Needless to say, Reb Aryeh readily agreed and went off post-haste to the renowned rabbi's house.

Once Rabbi Kook understood the problem, he too readily agreed: "Of course I am prepared to give the man a letter to the professor. What does this have to do with the difference of opinion between us?" He took paper and pen and wrote the letter carefully, taking pains to depict the sick girl's father in very favorable terms—because he had reason to resent the man, so that (as he explained to Reb Aryeh) "I will let no personal bias influence me as I write this."

The precious letter in hand, Reb Aryeh left the room in great happiness at being the successful go-between for such a great mitzvah. Leaving the house, he met two distinguished rabbis who, he knew, could never forgive the extremist pious Jews of Jerusalem for their hostility to Rabbi Kook. He greeted them pleasantly and went his way.

As he walked along, Reb Aryeh suddenly heard his name being called from Rabbi Kook's house. He was being summoned to return. In momentary confusion he thought that those two rabbis whom he had met at the entrance might have persuaded Rabbi Kook to change his mind, and he now wished to take the precious letter back. For a moment Reb Aryeh stood there hesitating, irresolute. Then he decided, "I cannot demur. If the rabbi calls me I must go"; and with trembling heart he returned.

"I had another thought," said Rabbi Kook to him. "The trip abroad is very expensive. I remembered that there is a shipping line which respects my requests and recommendations, and gives a considerable discount in the fare to those in need. Let me give you a letter to that company as well."

the short-term loan

This is an incident told by his grandson, R. David Levin:

Once my grandfather needed a loan urgently. Although all his life he avoided borrowing, this time he felt bold enough to ask a shopkeeper in the Maḥaneh Yehuda market to let him have what he needed, knowing that in the evening he would receive his monthly salary. So he went to the shopkeeper and asked him for a loan of fifty Israeli pounds till the evening. The man readily agreed.

In the evening he wanted to repay the loan, but a heavy snow had begun falling during the day. He told his wife about it, then asked her, "How can I walk such a long distance to his house in this weather?" (He quite certainly did not have the clothing, especially the shoes, for it.) "Maybe I will wait and give him back his money tomorrow?"

"O no," his good wife replied. "A man must stand by his word. If you promised to return him his money this evening, you have to make an effort and pay your debt as you promised."

On his two feet he tramped to the far-off neighborhood where the shopkeeper lived. As he came close to the door he heard the man's wife raise her voice: "Whatever made you lend that man money? Who gave you a guarantee that he will pay it back?" Then Reb Aryeh heard the answer: "You can trust Reb Aryeh that he will keep his word. There is no reason for worry." While their words were still coming thick and fast and loud, he knocked on the door—and the woman came to open it. "Really, Reb Aryeh," she exclaimed when she saw who it was. "For this loan you had to walk your feet off in this nasty, miserable weather? Could we not have waited till tomorrow?"

the séfer torah that returned

Early one fine morning Reb Aryeh knocked on the door of Sarah Herzog, the widow of the land of Israel's second chief rabbi. Mrs. Herzog opened the door, and saw Reb Aryeh standing there pale with intense emotion. Alarmed, she asked him, "What is the matter? What happened?"

This was his answer, once he entered her apartment and sat down:

Twenty-five years ago I rode with your dear late husband, the chief rabbi, to the prison in Latrun where the British kept the captured fighters of the underground. The prisoners told us they needed a Torah scroll (to read aloud from it at the Sabbath morning prayer-service, and so forth). But since they were moved about from one prison-camp to another, it would be best to bring them a small *séfer torah,* that was easy to carry.

I told the chief rabbi that I had a miniature Torah scroll with me, which was rare and precious. I was gladly willing to let the prisoners have it and use it. But I was afraid that with the passage of time it would be forgotten to whom exactly the scroll belonged, and I was uncertain if it would be returned to me. The chief rabbi's answer was: "I will give you an acknowledgment in writing that this *séfer torah* is your private property. I will even write you a guarantee in the same document that you will get it back."

Once I heard that I went ahead without hesitation and gave the Torah scroll to the prisoners, who kept it with them for a few years.

Chief Rabbi Isaac Herzog

Since the early years of his adult life, Reb Aryeh always kept a careful record, in his crystal-clear hand, of all money he received and gave for charity.

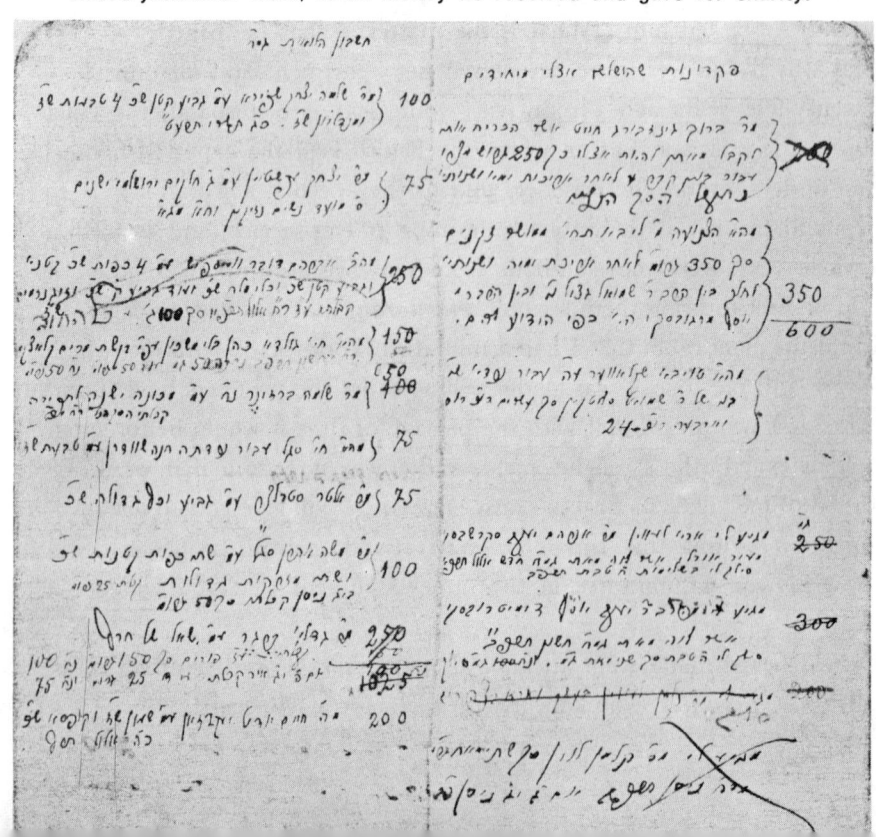

Time went by, the State of Israel was proclaimed, the prisoners were freed from their places of internment—and the small Torah scroll disappeared. It was nowhere to be found; no one knew where it was. And so I suffered great anguish about it—especially as the written acknowledgment and guarantee by the chief rabbi had also disappeared and was lost and gone. Then the day came when the chief rabbi himself passed on from this world to his eternal reward.

In my heart I mused: The *séfer torah* is gone, the rabbi is gone, the written acknowledgment is gone. Now whatever am I to do? *Nu,* with the passing of the days and the months I gave up all hope of ever getting that miniature Torah scroll back, and the matter vanished from my mind.

Well, today I rose before dawn as usual, to be able to say my morning prayers with the group in the synagogue at about the time of sunrise. But before setting off for the synagogue I looked in my bookcase for a particular volume that I needed. As I was searching, a sheet of paper came loose and fell on the floor. I bent down and picked it up—and what else was it but the acknowledgment of the chief rabbi about that Torah scroll which I had lent years ago to the interned soldiers! I was shaken to the core; and suddenly I felt again the old anguish at my loss of this miniature Torah scroll which had been so precious to me. And I felt too a twinge of resentment at the dear departed chief rabbi, since it was at his persuasion that I had taken the *séfer torah* from my home and given it to others.

Hardly had a few hours gone by when I returned from my morning prayer, to find a man waiting for me at my home, with a bundle in his hand. "Are you Reb Aryeh?" he asked, and I nodded. "I have a package for you." And what else did he bring me but that lost little *séfer torah*!

"And so I came to tell you," said Reb Aryeh to Sarah Herzog, the widow of the holy land's second chief rabbi, "that the rabbi kept his promise. The lost object was returned to its owner!"

9
His ways of hospitality

the thief

One of the thieves imprisoned among the criminals in their prison ward in Jerusalem served out his sentence and was set free toward evening. Since he lived far from Jerusalem and had no money whatever in his pocket, he went off to find Reb Aryeh, whom he knew from the pious rabbi's visits to the prison, to try to get some pocket-money from him.

Reb Aryeh and his good wife welcomed the man like a distinguished guest. They gave him some money, and then added that they would not let him ride home before he sat down to a good meal. The "guest" accepted, and soon felt relaxed and happy. The meal over, Reb Aryeh remarked, "I am grateful to you for visiting us. Thanks to you I had the unexpected opportunity to fulfill two mitzvoth (religious good deeds): offering hospitality and helping someone in need. But do me one more favor. It is late. Why trouble yourself to go traveling in the dark? Be our guest a bit longer and stay the night with us." They prepared a bed for him, and eventually bid him good night.

Before dawn Reb Aryeh rose as usual, to prepare to go to the synagogue for morning prayers at sunrise. As he moved about, it soon became painfully clear to him that his "dear guest" had stolen his wine cup (that he used for *kiddush* on the Sabbath) and the silver Sabbath candlesticks, and vanished into the night....

Reb Aryeh woke his good wife and told her what had happened. "Well," he added, "I forgive that poor thief completely. Let Heaven not punish him on my account." Then he said as an afterthought, "But let us promise each other and really resolve in our heart that this little incident will not mean anything for us in the future, and it will not prevent us from inviting other thieves into our home!"

the safe-cracker

One of the people kept in the central prison of Jerusalem was a criminal who had been sentenced to a long period of detention for "breaking and entering" (to commit theft). He was an expert at cracking open iron safes; but he was just as much an "artist" at talking and telling stories. With his skill at breaking through iron doors that hid valuables, he had a good warm heart, and he was privileged to form a close friendship with Reb Aryeh (who used to refer to him as "a man with a great soul").

One day a man named Ḥayyim Dviri was arrested by the British (who then ruled Israel) for his activity in the underground movement, and he was put into the same cell as the safe-breaking "artist." It did not take long for the two to become firm friends.

The time came when the safe-breaker confided to his cell-mate that he was simply "fed up" with sitting in prison. He could tolerate it no longer, and he was absolutely determined to get free, either by escaping or in some other way. So Ḥayyim Dviri was not surprised when soon afterward half of his cell-mate's body seemed to have become paralyzed and could not move....

The physicians rushed the man to the hospital, where he lay for several months, officially "unable" to get off his bed. The prison warden, an officer named Steele, soon lost his patience. "With me," he shouted at the man, "you're not going to be an 'artist.' This whole performance of yours won't help you one bit!" But the evidently sick safe-breaker remained unchanged, holding fast to his illness, unable to move half his body—and the doctors confirmed it.

It was decided to transfer him to the government hospital for a thorough examination. There the doctors held a consultation, and their unanimous decision was that the man was indeed paralyzed. The officer named Steele held fast to his own "diagnosis": "Believe me," he expostulated, "that man never began to be sick. He just has an iron will, and he can convince not only others but even himself that there is something seriously wrong with him." Yet what could he do? The physicians stuck pins into the hand and foot of the "paralyzed man" and he never budged or twitched a muscle. Whatever Officer Steele's private thoughts, the official verdict was paralysis; the man had to be sent home.

The prison authorities contacted his family in Petaḥ Tikvah and informed them that they were ready to discharge the man. But his wife was dismayed: "What will I do with an invalid like that? How can I take care of him?" And she refused to take him home.

The safe-breaker was non-plussed. "Take me to Reb Aryeh," he told the prison officers. "I hope and trust that he won't turn me away." The prison authorities complied with his request, and brought him to Reb Aryeh's humble little home in the Mishk'noth section of Jerusalem. As of then the innocent pious rabbi knew nothing whatever of the whole incident, not even that the man had been taken "ill." When he saw the ambulance arrive and the man carried in on a stretcher, he was simply stricken with alarm and confusion. The prison guards who brought him told the good rabbi the whole story then, including the fact that the man's family refused to have him home, since this "invalid" would be an unbearable burden to them.

To the amazement of the guards, Reb Aryeh and his wife were immediately agreeable. Without hesitation they gave their consent: Yes, they would take the man in and care for him to the best of their ability. And all that time the man lay there "paralyzed."

As soon as the guards were well away with the ambulance, the man whispered to Reb Aryeh, "Now don't you worry, Rabbi. I won't be a burden to you for long. I am not sick at all. I only pretended to be paralyzed. Let me stay in your house a few days, till I learn to walk properly and regain the full use of my muscles. Then I will be as normal as any man." And that is exactly what happened.

One fine day, years later, Ḥayyim Dviri (himself freed when the British rule of Israel ended) met the man strolling jauntily on the streets of Tel Aviv. In the meanwhile one of the man's sons became a chief army officer in Israel's Defense Forces. (Such are the ways of Providence.)

HIS WAYS OF HOSPITALITY

not through any agent

Once a man visited Reb Aryeh at home, and the good rabbi asked if he would have a cup of tea. When the visitor consented, he went to his bit of a "kitchen" to prepare it, and returned carrying the cup of tea in one hand and a plate of cookies in the other. The visitor wanted to help him, but Reb Aryeh would not allow it.

After it was all set down properly on the table, the pious rabbi said, "There was a teaching of the Sages in my mind: When our father Abraham (the Patriarch) wanted to attend to his guests, what did he say? *and I will fetch a morsel of bread* (Genesis 18:5). In other words, the master of the house himself served his guests. So the descendants of Abraham, the Israelites, were privileged to have the Almighty Himself give them their 'bread from heaven,' the manna: *Behold, I will rain down bread from heaven for you* (Exodus 16:4). But now, what did Abraham tell his guests about water? *Let a little water be brought* (Genesis 18:4), which means by some servant or agent of his. What was the result for his descendants, the Israelites? There was quarrel and bitter argument with Moses over water: *These were the waters of contention, where the people of Israel contended with the Lord*" (Numbers 20:13).

no ashtray

The mayor of Rishon l'Tziyon once visited Reb Aryeh at his home, and began smoking a cigarette. He asked for an ashtray, but in the rabbi's house there was none to be found. Realizing that this was not a house of smokers, the visitor asked, "Perhaps the cigarette smoke bothers you, and it would be better if I stopped smoking."

"O no," said the rabbi. "On the contrary, please continue. I enjoy seeing a person enjoying something."

repaying a call

An acquaintance of his once met Reb Aryeh walking, looking for the Kings Hotel (*m'lon ha-m'lachim*) in Jerusalem, "Why do you need to find the Kings Hotel?" asked the curious acquaintance.

"I came home," said the good rabbi, "and I found a note in my door from someone who has come from abroad on a visit. He wrote that he wanted to see me, but did not find me at home, and he is staying at the Kings Hotel. *Nu*, if he took the trouble to come to visit me, perhaps he needs me for something. So I am looking for him to ask him how I can be of help to him."

he asked to be forgiven

It was his practice to escort everyone who came to see him at home, for a short distance down the street when the visitor left. Once he was confined to bed with an illness, and during the time a man came seeking his advice. When the visit was over, the good rabbi asked the man to kindly forgive him for being unable to get up from bed and accompany him a bit on his way. He would not let the visitor go till he told him explicitly that he pardoned him for it.

place for a new arrival

One day a young man arrived in the holy land who was a member of the family of the noted Talmudic scholar R. Raphael Shapiro, the head of the Yeshiva of Volozhin, where Reb Aryeh had spent happy and gainful years of study. Unfortunately, this new arrival suffered from tuberculosis, and there was no one who would agree to give him a place to live.

When Reb Aryeh learned of this, he sent word at once to the young man that he was ready to put him up in his own house—this despite the fact that Reb Aryeh was then burdened with several small children in the house.

Since he lived then in an apartment of one room with a kitchen, Reb Aryeh's good wife took to sleeping in the kitchen, and the sick young man took up his quarters near Reb Aryeh's bed.

"we can talk outside"

One evening I went to see Reb Aryeh, to talk something over with him. I found the door locked, and people told me that he had gone to teach the neighborhood class of the *daf yomi,* the study-group that learned a double page of the Talmud every day. I returned after an hour, only to be told that he had gone to the celebration of some religious family event. Two hours later I came back, and was told that he had gone to comfort mourners for a departed parent.

When I came a fourth time I found two others waiting for him at the door. I asked them that when the good rabbi came they should be kind enough to let me speak a few words with him alone. Late at night he finally arrived, walking at his usual slow pace, and he began greeting the people who waited for him. I asked him to please come inside into the room with me, since there was something I wished to tell him in private, and the two other visitors were willing to wait outside for a bit. Nevertheless the pious rabbi asked them to come inside, which left me wondering. Once we were all within he asked them to sit on his bed, then asked them to excuse him, and he went out with me into the street. "We two," he said, "can talk outside just as well. Why should we make the visitors wait in the street?"

no room at home

His son R. Simḥa Sh'lomo related: My father would often say: When a man lived in a single room, he had space enough to let a guest stay with him in his "apartment." When he enlarged his living quarters to two rooms, he was no longer able to accommodate a guest. When he prospered and attained an apartment of three rooms, the space became too small even for him: He and his wife would eat in the kitchen. And once he had four rooms, they would take to eating in the restaurant.

Evidently in keeping with his own maxim, the good rabbi would invariably invite guests for the Sabbath to his one-room dwelling. His son attests that there was hardly a Sabbath without a few outsiders at their table. At the synagogue on Jaffa Street that Reb Aryeh attended there was a *hachnasath orḥim,* a room where travelers, newcomers and homeless persons could stay; and from there the good rabbi always brought a few home with him on Friday evening. If no one was to be found there, he was ready to go scouring the streets in search (emulating the conduct of Abraham the Patriarch, as the Sages describe it).

In this way he sought to educate his children in the practice of hospitality.

"see what I lost"

When he reached the eightieth year of his life, a celebration was arranged in his honor in the courtyard of the "Russian compound" in Jerusalem, where the prison used to be located in the time of the British. Thousands came from all parts of Israel to take part in the happy event.

As it was his birthday, though, from the morning hours people started streaming to his home to wish him many more years of life. Needless to say, Reb Aryeh was deeply moved, as these visitors were all "clients" of his from the past, members of the underground fighting forces detained, interned and imprisoned by the British in the years before 1948. During the afternoon I went with the former mayor of Rishon l'Tziyon to see him; and we pleaded with him to take a little rest and gather some strength. As we might have expected, he refused. We even offered to hang a sign on the door asking visitors to wait till three o'clock, when he would get up from his rest. This too he would not allow, saying that he had never yet put a sign on the door giving hours when he was "open to the public."

Shulamith Katznelson, the director of Ulpan Akiva in Netanya (where newcomers to the land learn Hebrew) was there with us; and she offered to go stand outside the door herself, to tell all visitors to kindly come back later, after three o'clock.

With a smile Reb Aryeh answered, "Let me tell you a little story: Once on a Purim day I felt very miserable and downhearted; and I thought: Here people will be coming to visit me, and they will even be bringing *shalaḥ manoth*, Purim presents of food; and I do not have anything at all to give them in return. *Nu,* I decided, let me go and lock the door. In that way I will avoid insulting my visitors by giving them nothing in return.

"Well, I locked the door. And a few minutes later someone came knocking. It was my firm resolve to pay no attention, since I had decided not to open the door to anyone. So I made no reply whatever. Yet in my heart I felt I was not acting properly.... Just then there was the sound of knocking again on the door. And as I was hesitating whether perhaps to open it after all, I heard the footsteps of this visitor fading off down the street. With my conscience now troubling me, I went to the door and opened it wide immediately. But the figure of my visitor was already far off and fast disappearing.

"How bad I felt when I was able to recognize the figure from the back, and I realized that I had forfeited a visit from a most worthy guest. You see, that visitor was you, Shulamith.

"*Nu,* there you are," Reb Aryeh concluded. "Once when I locked the door I missed the visit of a good guest; and now you suggest that I should lock it again?"

With his son R. Raphael Binyomin listening, Reb Aryeh is shown giving advice to two of the countless hundreds who brought their problems to him.

10
Visiting the sick

the lonely and the forgotten

It was Reb Aryeh's custom to go to the hospitals of Jerusalem every Friday, to visit the sick who were confined there. First he would always go and speak with the nurses, to find out from them who the patients were that received no visitors as a rule. At the beds of these forgotten souls whom no relatives came to see, he would linger, caressing each one's hand and giving him words of encouragement and cheer.

Once, having finished his rounds at the Sha'arey Tzedek hospital, he left and started to cross the street, only to be struck down by a swiftly careening jeep. Miraculously, however, he escaped with relatively minor injuries, to the amazement of the doctors who treated him. He needed to be hospitalized, of course, and then there was a period of convalescence; but under the circumstances he "got off very lightly".

To Reb Aryeh, though (at least, so he said), there was no miracle about it. "It is a clear rule in the Talmud: Emissaries for a mitzvah, a religious good deed, are not harmed, neither going nor returning. If Heaven decreed this accident, for my sins, the mitzvah of visiting the sick protected me."

the wretched and lowly in spirit

There are some downtrodden, downhearted people whose spirits can be cheered, to bring them out of despair; and there are others with whom it cannot be done. With them there is a need to descend, to come down to their level, and sit with them. This is what Reb Aryeh's son R. Hayyim Yaakov Levin related:

My father (of blessed memory) worked on both fronts. Those whose spirits could be raised he strove and put in effort to restore to good cheer. With those for whom it could not be done he descended to their level, went and sat with them, whether it was in a leper-hospital or in a hospital for the mentally ill.

It was my father's practice that every *rosh hodesh* (first day of a Jewish month) in the afternoon he would take a small parcel from the house under his arm, and go. On *rosh hodesh* the classes at the elementary school of Yeshiva Etz Hayyim (where he was employed) ended at noon, and he had free time. At home we knew already that we were not to ask where he was going and why. It was a practice that he kept up for a good many years.

Once I went with him, though; and as we were walking, a man came over to my father and asked, "How is your relative getting along in the mental hospital?" My father answered, "The Lord be praised," and we continued on our way. "Father," I asked, "what relative do we have that is in the mental hospital?" Then he told me that once he visited the hospital to ask or recommend that someone be taken in for treatment; and since he was already there he went visiting through the wards. One man there caught his attention: the poor soul was full of welts and wounds, and needless to say, my father became interested in him at once. (He always heard the still voice of another's pain.)

Well, the other patients explained: "After all, we are ill, you know; and there are moments when we get wild and out of control. Then the orderlies restrain us by force, and at times they even hit us. Now, we all have relatives and families. So the orderlies are always a bit afraid that a visitor will come and find that they have injured his relative, and of course he will complain and raise a hue-and-cry. That poor invalid over there is the only one here with no family, no relatives at all. So the orderlies really treat him roughly. Whenever they lose their temper he bears the brunt of it..."

Without a word my father went over to the orderlies and told them that this patient was his relative. From that time on he remained my father's "relative"; and so he went to visit him every *rosh ḥodesh,* and brought him little presents.

So it remained commonly accepted knowledge at the hospital, and eventually outside it, that this was a relative of Reb Aryeh.

among the lepers

It was his practice, furthermore, to risk his own health and pay regular visits to the lepers' hospital in Jerusalem. How did he get into that habit? This was his answer:

One Friday, before the Sabbath, I went to the *kothel ma'aravi* (the Western Wall), and there I found a woman weeping bitterly. I tried to calm her, and asked her whatever was making her cry so intensely. She told me that for her child there was no cure: The poor boy was locked up in the lepers' hospital, in the Talbieh section of Jerusalem.

There and then I made up my mind to visit the boy. When I arrived at the hospital I found twelve Jewish patients surrounded by 300 Arab lepers, with Christian nurses to take care of them all. When they saw me they burst into tears. It was years, they said, since they had the privilege to see any visitor from the outside world.

I could not shake hands with them; but I took to speaking with them, just chatting about this and that, and heartening them a little with my words. Then I read to them from the Hebrew Bible (the Five Books of Moses) with the commentary of Rashi. This I made into a regular habit: to go to them every Friday.

[It should be added that when he came, Reb Aryeh found them living in filth and squalor. The living conditions were subhuman, a morass of neglect and despair. From the start he approached the authorities and sought to have the Jewish inmates housed separately. It took effort and perservance, but he succeeded. Through the years he made it his business to learn of new medical advances in the treatment of leprosy, and he kept after the medical authorities at the hospital to apply them.]

Once they told me, "You know? every time you come to see us, it is as if for the last time. We just wait here for the angel of death. This place has a firm reputation that whoever comes in through its gates never goes out alive."

On one visit of mine they asked me to try to arrange kosher food for them. I went directly to David Berman, in his shop of housewares in the Mahaneh Yehuda section, and told him the whole story. Then I asked him to kindly take a share in this mitzvah (this religious good deed). To my amazement he insisted on giving me all the dishes and utensils I would need.

My wife Hannah took to cooking regularly for them, and I would take the prepared food to the hospital.... When Rosh haShana came (the solemn festival that begins the Jewish year) my sons went along with me, and gave the patients the great privilege and satisfaction of hearing the sound of the shofar (the ram's horn—one of the most important mitzvoth on Rosh haShana). My sons had no fear of the hazard to their health that this involved. You know the teaching of the Talmud: "Those on their way to do a mitzvah are never harmed" (*P'sahim* 8b).

the early-morning visits

An acquaintance of his once came to Reb Aryeh in great distress: His son was seriously ill with pneumonia. The lungs were abcessed, and the boy's life was in danger. Would Reb Aryeh please pray for the boy, asked the distraught father. The pious rabbi told him not to despair: "There is a great master Physician in heaven."

Some time afterward, when the father visited his son in the hospital, the woman doctor on duty came over to him and asked, "Who is that old, man who comes to see your son here every morning at five o'clock?" The man was amazed, and did not know what to say. He discovered later that it was Reb Aryeh who thus came faithfully every morning to see how the boy was getting along—without letting him (the father) know anything about it.

the baby-sitters

It was nothing new for Reb Aryeh to be with a sick child in hours when people normally sleep. There is an instructor at the Etz Ḥayyim school whose memory goes back many years to a time when a child of his was seriously ill, and his wife and he had to stay by his bedside at night—until the effects began telling on his nerves and health.

One night Reb Aryeh and his wife turned up at their home. "Go to sleep now, both of you," said the good rabbi. "The two of us will stay with your child. You see," he explained with his own brand of genial, charming apology, "we have to talk something over, very important, and we cannot do so at home, where the children may eavesdrop...."

the vigil that cured

In another case, when the good rabbi sat by a sick child's bedside, the effect was far greater. A child of a man named Abraham Axelrod became deathly ill. The poor father sat by the little one's bedside night after night, without a bit of sleep, and saw no improvement. And at last the doctors on the case despaired of the child's life. They saw no hope.

One night Reb Aryeh came and told the distraught man to go to sleep, and he would watch the child. The grateful father accepted the offer... and in the morning the child was on his way to recovery, to the frank amazement of the doctors.

Had anyone suggested that Reb Aryeh and his prayers had anything to do with the boy's return to health, the good rabbi would have been incredulous. But the happy father, who served for many years as deputy mayor of Jerusalem, became so attached to the good rabbi that under his influence the man returned from irreligiosity to a full observance of the Torah.

care for a Torah luminary

All his life he yearned to be close to great Torah scholars, and he formed strong bonds of friendship with them. Thus he became attached to the noted Rabbi Yeḥezkel Abramsky when that brilliant Talmudist moved from London to Israel.

VISITING THE SICK

In the course of time, it did not escape Reb Aryeh's attention that the learned scholar had taken to walking too fast, and it might be injurious to his health. One day he met him in the street, and he said in his own genial way, "Rabbi Yeḥezkel, people are talking about you in Jerusalem."

"Why, what do you mean?"

"They are saying that you walk too fast."

Had he told him in any other way, Rabbi Abramsky would probably have brushed the matter aside. In this way, the point struck home.

At another time, this noted scholar became ill. The sickness began on a Sunday and continued through the week. Thursday night he felt extremely sick; and as he slept he dreamt that his father-in-law (a noted rabbi in Eastern Europe) appeared, whereupon he told this visitor his mother's Hebrew name, so that his father-in-law could pray for him (since prayers for a sick person always mention him by his and his mother's Hebrew names: So-and-so the son of So-and-so).

It needed no skilled or recondite dream interpretation to tell Rabbi Abramsky that his dream boded him no good. If his father-in-law had to pray for him, it meant that things were black indeed for him.

Reb Aryeh in animated conversation with R. Yeḥezkel Abramsky

In the morning, though, who should knock on the door and come in but Reb Aryeh. The good rabbi had never come to the house before. What brought him now? "I have come," he said, "to ward off, undo the effects of a dream. I have a tradition handed down from R. Ḥayyim of Volozhin that it helps." He said certain prayers, etc. and left.

Told afterward by Rabbi Abramsky himself, this story is not open to doubt. That very Friday he felt himself recovering. The next day he gave his regular Sabbath lecture in Talmudic learning!

"I came to keep a mitzvah"

When he was in his last years, a third son was born to his former student Yaakov David Perlin, who remained devoted to him till the end. The happy father invited Reb Aryeh to be the *sandek*, to have the honor of holding the infant on his lap during the circumcision. The good rabbi refused, however. Knowing that the child's grandfather (Perlin's father-in-law) was alive and well, he insisted that the honor belonged to that man. Only after Yaakov David Perlin assured him that his father-in-law had been the *sandek* for his oldest son would Reb Aryeh relent and accept the honor.

(To this firm policy of his, never to serve as *sandek* at a circumcision where a grandfather of the baby was available, the Blondheim family can bear witness. He already accepted the honor for the forthcoming *b'rith* of a newborn son of theirs, only to learn a day or two afterward that meanwhile Mrs Blondheim's father had arrived from America. Nothing on earth could move him then to be the *sandek*.)

Reb Aryeh serving as **sandek** at the **b'rith** of Yaakov David Perlin's infant son.

Three days after the Perlin child's *b'rith,* as the city sweltered in heat, Reb Aryeh came trudging up at his usual gait to see the baby—old and feeble as he was. Amazed, the parents expressed their surprise that in his condition he had taken the trouble to walk such a long distance in the heat. The good rabbi smiled.

"I came to keep the mitzvah of visiting the sick," he replied. "This is the third day since the child's circumcision. And the Torah tells us that the Almighty Himself came to visit Abraham our father on the third day after his circumcision (since he was sick then as a result). We have to follow in His ways..."

he did not want to be deprived

R. Isaiah Aryeh Dvorkas recalled: In 1949 I was serving as a chaplain in the Schneller Military Camp in Jerusalem. It was agreed between Reb Aryeh and myself that once a week I would come to his house and take him to visit the soldiers lying in the military hospital. Reb Aryeh was always careful to be waiting for me punctually, at the appointed time, to go with me.

Once it happened, though, that for a reason beyond my control I did not come to take him for our weekly visit to the hospital. The next day I received a postcard from him, complaining that I had deprived him of his rightful due. Then he added his earnest plea, beseeching me that in the future I should make every effort to come promptly and punctually and take him to see the wounded soldiers, since he was not prepared to give up this great mitzvah.

"we were all there together"

After the Six-Day War (June 1967) he went visiting the wounded soldiers who were receiving care in the hospitals of Jerusalem. Surprised at his friendly approach, one soldier asked him, "Where do you know me from, dear rabbi?" With a twinkle he answered, "The feet of all of us stood together at the foot of Mount Sinai when the Torah was given." (He had in mind the teaching of the Sages that then not only the Israelites who left Egypt were there, but the spirit of every Israelite and Jew who was to be born in every generation.)

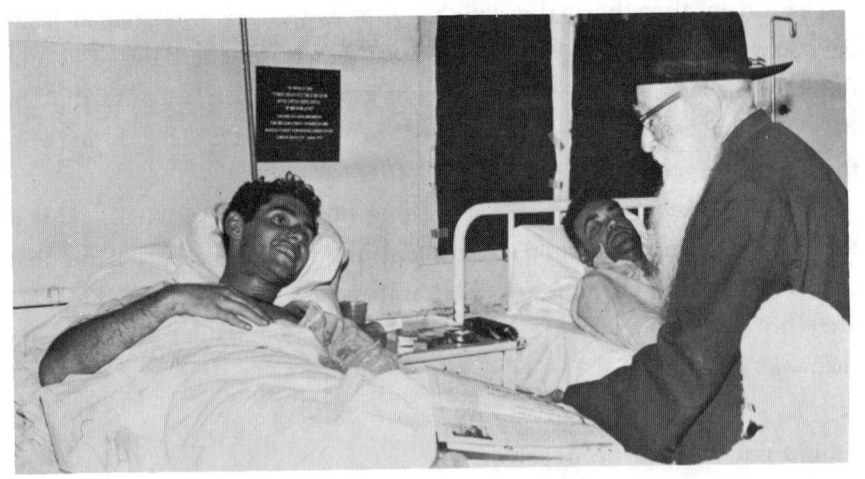

Reb Aryeh's usual friendly self at the bedside of a wounded soldier.

a kiss of blessing

Simḥa Holzberg adopted the compassionate way of his rabbi and teacher Reb Aryeh, and he made it a point to visit the wounded Israeli soldiers and bring some happiness into their hearts (and thus he became known as the "father of the wounded"). Once, when he was on his way to bring some of them a gift, he went first to see Reb Aryeh briefly. Reb Aryeh embraced him, took from his hand the package that he was taking to the soldiers—and the pious rabbi kissed it.

in the middle of Yom Kippur

In the very neighborhood where he lived, there was a woman bedridden by a long, severe illness. This was Rivka Weiss, an active worker in religious Jewry in her time, who was known for her charitable work and her Jewish learning. Now, during her difficult illness, it was Reb Aryeh's custom to visit her at least once a week.

Reb Aryeh knew how devout the woman was. On Yom Kippur (the Day of Atonement), the most solemn day of the year, she would certainly want to fast (as the Torah commands all healthy people, whose life is not endangered by fasting). So right in the middle of this solemn holy day, wrapped in his *kittel* (white robe) and *tallith* (prayer-cape), Reb

Aryeh left his place in the Etz Ḥayyim synagogue and set out for the home of Rivka Weiss, the sick lonely widow who had to remain alone. When he entered he made straight for the kitchen and prepared a cup of tea. Then he searched and found some biscuits in the pantry, put them on a plate, and entered the woman's room. He ordered her to take the tea and biscuits and start eating at once. And under his compelling gaze she could not refuse.

After she had obeyed and eaten and drunk, her eyes lit up. And at his command she promised that she would eat more on this most holy day, just as on any other day.

the prayer and the recovery

One Friday afternoon he was making his rounds as usual among the patients in the Sha'arey Tzedek hospital when he was stopped by a woman he knew. "Rivka Weiss is seriously ill," she told him. "Please make sure to look in on her."

It was the widow whom he had visited in the very middle of Yom Kippur, to serve her tea and biscuits and to make sure she would not fast, since she had been so ill.... Now he found her hospital bed completely enclosed by curtains on movable frames, and for a moment his heart sank. This was the sign that the doctors had given up hope for her, and she was not expected to last much longer. He thought of all the good that the dear soul had done when she had had her health; he thought of the young children she was struggling to raise, without the help of a husband; and tears came to his eyes.

He went to the door of the hospital ward and put his hand on the *m'zuza*. And then the sobs and the words of prayer came pouring out together: "In the Torah You are called the Father of orphans and the Judge of widows," he wailed like a child in distress. "This woman is a poor *widow,* trying to raise her children—*orphans* with no one else to look after them. How can You sentence her to lose her life? Be merciful and compassionate..." And so he continued for perhaps half an hour, oblivious of anyone who might have stared at his behavior. Unable to stay longer, he gave a last pitying look at the unconscious woman and sadly took his leave.

About another half hour went by, and the woman stirred and opened her eyes. After lying still a while, she asked a nurse for some water, and then for food. She had been unconscious for some time, and now was hungry. The next few days saw her slow but steady recovery to complete health, to the amazement of the physicians who attended her. To this day, it is said, there is no medical explanation for her return to health.

his gift of healing

More than once he was able to cure people with mental illness, where the best of doctors failed. Quite often his good friend Professor Halperin, head of the neurology department at the Hadassah hospital, would send mentally ill people to him with the request that he should please help them. And time after time Reb Aryeh succeeded.

On one occasion Professor Halperin asked him: "Tell me, what is your secret? What do you say to these people with sick minds and emotions whom I send to you?"

"I just listen to them patiently."

"O yes," Prof. Halperin rejoined. "Listening is a wonderful method of healing. This is an important rule in psychiatry."

"But I do not stop at listening alone. I also reveal a touch of empathy, of sharing in their troubles, and these sick people sense it and respond."

The Jews of Jerusalem indeed tell of a young woman of a fine family who suffered for years from a severe emotional ailment. Her parents took her to the best medical doctors, to no avail. They sent her abroad, and she returned unchanged. When the good rabbi was seventy-six, she met him, and the two had long conversations several times, both alone and with her father present. Today she is quite normal, married and the mother of children.

When Reb Aryeh himself fell sick and had to be taken to the Hadassah hospital suffering his own full share of pain—even then, once he was permitted to leave his bed he would go across to nearby rooms to cheer and hearten lonely people with severe illnesses.

One day Prof. Halperin came to the hospital to visit a patient of his stricken with painful sickness, and he found him in high spirits. "Aha," said the doctor, "Reb Aryeh must certainly have paid you a visit today."

the added years of life

Not long after the great Talmud scholar R. Isser Zalman Meltzer passed away, a son of his, a rabbi in Reḥovoth, suffered a serious heart attack, and was taken to the Bikur Ḥolim hospital in Jerusalem, where he was to spend the next three months. While in the hospital he suffered another one or two attacks; and his future became for him a dark uncertainty.

As luck would have it, Dr Tycho, Israel's leading eye specialist, was placed in the bed next to his at about that time. Dr Tycho too was suffering from a heart ailment; and a few days later he expired. In the bed after his lay a *shoḥet* (a ritual slaughterer of kosher fowl and animals) from Beth Shemesh, a learned man who hailed from Rumania; and in a day or two *he* passed away from a heart ailment. Then (truth being stranger than fiction) a new patient was placed in the bed next to R. Isser Zalman Meltzer's son; and all too soon he also was gone—from a heart ailment.

R. Isser Zalman's son grew haggard and broken in spirit. Utterly dejected, he lay haunted by worry over what fate held in store for him. And needless to say, the tormenting worry did his health no good whatever.

Having been his father's pupil and close companion for many years, Reb Aryeh visited the rabbi from Reḥovoth regularly. His discerning eye detected the situation soon enough, and he knew drastic measures were needed. The man could simply worry himself to death. So Reb Aryeh suggested "casting the Scriptures" for him—using the method described below (page 165) which pious Jews in Jerusalem call *goral ha-g'ra*, "the lot-casting of the Gaon R. Elijah" (of Vilna), since it is said that he first used the method to identify unrecognizable victims of massacres and pogroms.

With his usual poise and calm Reb Aryeh turned the pages of the small Hebrew Bible this way and that, counted leaves and pages, columns and verses, words and letters; then he searched patiently for the deciding sentence. It was Isaiah 38:5, *behold, I will add to your days fifteen years*—which the Almighty told Ḥezekiah when he prayed for mercy after the prophet had told him that he was going to die.

"You can stop fretting and worrying," said Reb Aryeh with complete certainty. "You shall live another fifteen years.". . . And so the man did.

reward for footsteps

Once the assistant minister of health arranged that a car from his ministry should pick up Reb Aryeh every day at his home and take him to the hospitals, so that the aged pious rabbi would not have to wear out his feet walking across Jerusalem to visit those confined to the hospital beds.

But Reb Aryeh declined the service: "Look," he said, "I am old. The Torah I do not study properly. The little that is left for me is the mitzvah of visiting the sick. I would rather go on foot, so that at least the heavenly reward for walking will remain mine..."

"about this my heart hurts"

R. Yaakov Rakovsky, the rabbi at the Hadassah medical center, recalled this:

When Reb Aryeh fell victim to his last, difficult illness and was confined to his bed at the hospital, how much anguish and tears I saw on his face. Then he told me what his anguish was: "Reb Yaakov, can I not go around visiting the sick? How can that be?"

"But," I answered him, "you yourself are ill." Immediately he retorted, "Is a sick person free of the obligation, the mitzvah to visit the sick? Is a poor man who lives from charity free then of the mitzvah to give charity?"

And he was not to be stopped. As soon as his condition eased, he put on a hospital robe and went to see how the patients in the nearby rooms were doing. And when the news spread to the patients in the hospital generally that Reb Aryeh was there, day after day they came streaming to him by the dozens, so that he should bestow his blessing on them. His room became a corner of prayer and supplication to the merciful God.

Once he told me (R. Yaakov Rakovsky continued), "O, Reb Yaakov, who knows if I fulfill my obligation in the Almighty's eyes, truly and wholeheartedly? There ailing people come to me that I should pray for them, and they look forward in hope and yearning for the Lord's rescue. Yet at times there sneaks into my heart what the Sages taught in the Talmud: Whoever pleads for Heaven's compassion for someone else (to be granted what he needs) and he needs the same thing himself, he is answered first—he gets Heaven's help first (*Bava Kamma* 92a). The result is that I do not do my task honestly, faithfully—because probably in my unconscious mind, when I pray for them to get well, my intention is that *I* should be cured first. My heart is sorely troubled by this. So I implore the Holy, Blessed One that first He should really answer the prayers of all the sick people who come to me."

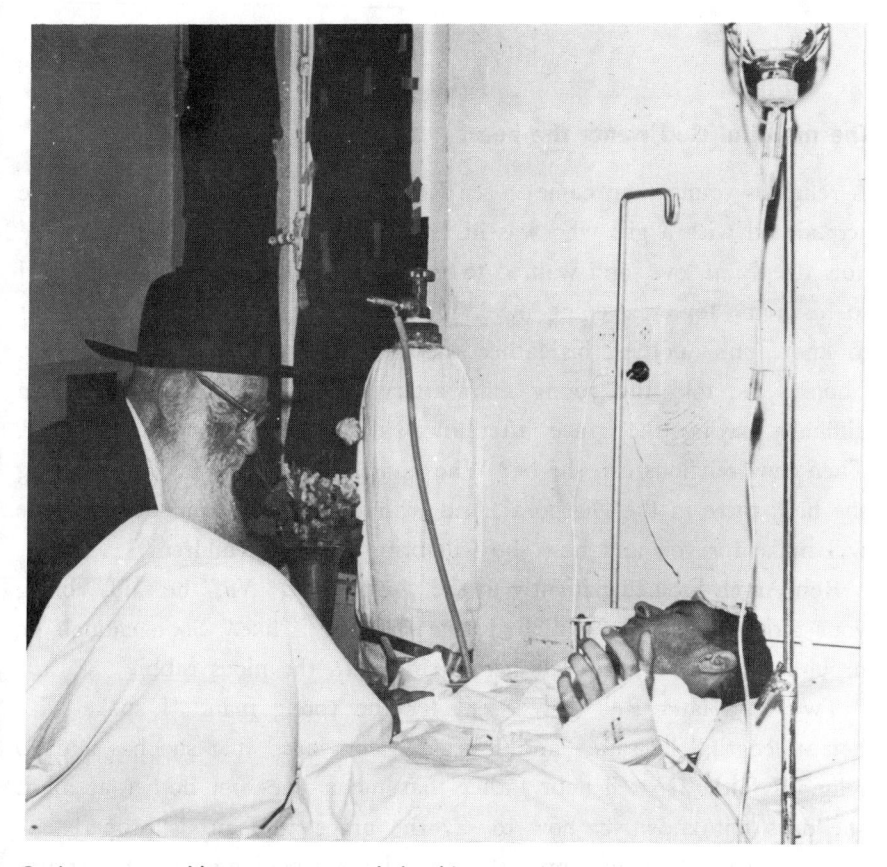

On his innumerable visits to wounded soldiers in the hospital, he always found the means to cheer them up.

11
Of matchmaking and marriage

The merciful God wants the heart

A religious young man came to see Reb Aryeh one day. He had become acquainted with a girl who was in Israel as a tourist, and the two were now deeply in love, and wanted to marry. But when he brought the girl to his home for an evening meal, so that she and his parents could get to know one another, his father was not altogether pleased with her. "Look," he told the young man afterward, "you saw how she had difficulty saying the grace after meals (*birkath ha-mazon*) properly. Then how religious can she be? Who knows what kind of an upbringing she had, there in the Diaspora? And who knows what kind of home she will make for you and how she will bring up your children?"

Reb Aryeh listened patiently to the young man. "*Nu*," he said, "bring your girl to me, and I will find out what she is like." Soon enough he brought his fiancée, and left her talking with the pious rabbi.

Two days later Reb Aryeh sent for the young man. "I spoke with her at length," he said, "and I became convinced that she has a deep religious faith. Go tell your father that me it does not bother at all if she does not know yet how to say the grace after meals properly.... Not only that. You tell your father that I am myself prepared to arrange and perform the wedding ceremony."... And this is just what happened.

in that case there is nothing more to be said

A good friend of Reb Aryeh, who was divorced, wanted to marry again. The pious rabbi went to see him and tried to persuade him that he should agree to remarry his first wife, and thus patch up their quarrels and heal the rift. "But I cannot do that," said his friend. "I have already given my word to another young lady that I will marry her."

"*Nu*," said Reb Aryeh, "I am ready to go to this young lady's parents and explain to them why the courtship has to be dissolved."

"That," the young man replied, "you cannot do. The girl that I am about to marry is an orphan. She has no father."

Once he heard this Reb Aryeh rejoined, "In that case there is nothing more to be said. An orphan girl is poor and helpless. She has no father to pour out her pain and suffering to him. She will be hurt if you break off your wedding plans with her, and will never forgive you. You go ahead and marry her."

another virtue

A young man dropped into Reb Aryeh's house one day to ask his advice about a match (marriage with a certain girl) that was suggested to him. The young man began listing all the fine qualities and virtues of the girl. "But," he added, "she comes from poor parents."

Reb Aryeh interrupted him: "You have listed just now another virtue with which the girl is blessed."

to make him happy

Late in his life Reb Aryeh went to a great deal of trouble to arrange a marriage for a certain woman who was related to him. When the woman saw the efforts that the good rabbi—already bedridden by illness—was making for her sake, she realized how much it pained him that she was without a husband. She thereupon agreed to be married, knowing it would bring him considerable satisfaction....

the decreed wedding

He was ready to go to any lengths to arrange matches and help people marry. Once, at the close of Yom Kippur, a friend remarked, "Reb Aryeh, why don't you do something to help this young man? It is high time he became engaged and married." (As noted earlier, Reb Aryeh spent every Yom Kippur with a "select congregation" of the senior students and faculty of Chief Rabbi Kook's Yeshiva Merkaz haRav, and the chief rabbi's friends and relatives. The young man under discussion was one of Rabbi Kook's grandsons.)

Reb Aryeh looked at the man thoughtfully. Intent (like his grandfather) on the inner, spiritual aspects of life, the young man tended to neglect his personal appearance, and he looked quite unprepossessing. Thus, sad to say, he had begun getting on in years without succeeding in finding a girl to marry.

"You are perfectly right," Reb Aryeh told his friend; and he called two distinguished men of learning and piety, members of this Yom Kippur congregation, to sit down with him. "Come," he told them. "Three Jews can constitute a *beth din* (a religious court). We have just spent the day in fasting and prayer, in a state of holiness like the angels above. Surely we have some spiritual power now. Let us decree that this very year he shall become engaged and will be married. And as we decree it here on earth, below, so may it be ordered in heaven above."

The three pronounced the edict together, in formal terms. And strange as it may seem, that very year the young man became engaged, and later married, to a very fine young lady of a distinguished family who left people wondering: How did he ever get a wife like that?

"like a daughter"

When the time came for Alizah Shwartz, one of those who used to frequent his house, to go and get married, she begged him to honor her wedding with his presence. But Reb Aryeh apologized and pleaded with her to excuse him. He simply did not have the strength. Then he added, "Look: even to my grandchild's wedding, only last week, I did not go."

"What does that prove?" she asked in response. "I am like a daughter to you. Didn't you go to the weddings of your children?"

"You have answered well, my child," said Reb Aryeh. And he gathered his strength and came to her wedding.

the secret wedding

In the days of the British mandate, Yitzḥak Shamir, one of the leaders of the *le-ḥee* underground movement (the initials of *loḥamey ḥéruth yisra'el*, "Fighters for the Freedom of Israel") was in the habit of meeting his fellow-underground-fighter Moshe Segal (a fine religious bearded Jew) in Jerusalem's Reḥavya synagogue. There both would sit together over volumes of the Talmud, bending down, swaying back and forth as they chanted and discussed the ancient words of Jewish learning, for all the world deeply immersed in their study. But interspersed in the apparent (or intermittent) study they transmitted to one another secrets and messages of the underground activities.

At that time Shamir had a young girl from Bulgaria serving as his "liaison officer" or "go-between," maintaining contact between him and other *le-ḥee* members—a sweet, simple girl who fulfilled her duties with loyalty and devotion.

One day, as the two sat swaying over their volumes of Talmud in the Reḥavya synagogue, Moshe Segal suddenly asked his friend, "Look here: I know how busy and burdened you are now, since we are living in this time of tension and emergency. But why don't you pay some attention to your liaison officer—this girl who is so devoted to you? Why don't the two of you get married?"

Shamir gave his friend a strange, puzzled look. What business did his friend have getting involved in the relationship between him and the girl? How did his friend suddenly turn into a matchmaker?

Moshe Segal was persistent, however. He went on talking to his friend, to persuade and convince him. "Look," Shamir finally answered, "even if I already wanted to marry her, I cannot. How can I go and get myself officially registered in the marriage bureau of the community council? Officially I do not exist. The British must never know about me. I have to live and stay 'underground,' alone and unseen."

"Very well," said Segal. "Tomorrow I will ask our rabbi, Reb Aryeh, for his advice." (Reb Aryeh had a high regard for Moshe Segal, as he had been the first to sound the shofar at the *kothel ma'aravi*, the Western Wall, at the end of Yom Kippur in 1930, after the official commission on the Western Wall forbade ever sounding the shofar at the *kothel*.)

The next day Segal went to Reb Aryeh's house and explained the situation. Reb Aryeh embraced him. "Blessings on your head," he exclaimed. "As our Torah teaches, we were not put on this earth to live separately. It is not good for a man to live in isolation. Shamir will do well to get married."

Then the pious rabbi got up and went to see R. Tz'vi Pesah Frank, the rabbi of the Jerusalem community (to whom he was related). Privately, in complete confidence, he explained the problem to him, and asked R. Frank what to do.

R. Tz'vi Pesah Frank gave him a note to R. Abraham Adler, head of the office for rabbinic affairs in Jerusalem, ordering that a wedding should be arranged for a young couple without any record of it being made in the official files, and no unnecessary questions asked.

A date for the wedding was set; Reb Aryeh's good wife prepared the food and refreshments; and R. Abraham Adler, casting a sharp, puzzled look at the man who was marrying his wife in secret, performed the wedding. The two witnesses (required by religious law) were Moshe Segal and Reb Aryeh Levin.

Except for these people, not another soul attended this secret, unrecorded ceremony.

the letter

This is a story told by one of the leaders in the underground fighting movement:

When I was interned by the British in the prison in Jerusalem, Reb Aryeh used to come to visit me every Saturday; and more than once he happened to see there a fine girl from a good religious family in the old *yishuv*, the old religious settlement in Jerusalem—who came to visit me, always bringing with her a parcel of food for me.

The day before my release, the good rabbi asked me, "This girl who comes always to see you—she is your *ḥaveyra* (girl-friend)?" When I told him yes, his face darkened with a touch of dismay or displeasure. I realized at once that he had not really understood me. He was not accustomed to our "street language" of those times, and he imagined that if she was my *ḥaveyra*, "my girl-friend," it must mean we were physically intimate, etc. So I made the situation clear: "Look, dear rabbi: This girl, who lives in the Meya She'arim section, is my 'go-between' in the underground movement. In the food parcels that she brings me she smuggles in messages. Like myself, she is a member of *le-ḥee* (the Fighters for Israel's Freedom). But she is not my personal girl-friend."

I could see that Reb Aryeh felt a sense of relief.

Well, when I left the prison behind me, the good rabbi tried to persuade me that it was time to get married and have a home and a family. Then he asked me, "What do you think of that girl who always came to visit you in the prison?" When I said that she was not my heart's true choice, he smiled.... But that did not close the discussion. He then asked me what I thought of a certain other girl—and he took me by surprise. That young lady was also a member of our underground movement, but she was Viennese, used make-up, smoked, and was not particularly religious.

Anyone would have expected the good rabbi to be more in favor of the fine religious girl. Yet there he was, urging me to take as my partner in life the other young lady, whom he knew through his contacts with people in the underground movement. (It was only much later that I realized that with his intuitive discernment the good rabbi sensed that the religious girl from the old yishuv would not really suit me.)

Now I became busy protesting: "But how do I know that the girl will want me?"

"I will talk with her," said Reb Aryeh simply. And true to his word, he went and spoke with her in his gentle persuasive way that she should agree to marry me. And there I was, still hesitating and unsure.

One day the spirit moved me (as one might say) and I wrote a long letter to the young lady, explaining why I could not marry her. Yet for some reason I did not send it off right away.

A day or two later the good rabbi asked me, "*Nu?*" I took the letter out of my pocket. "Here," said I. "Read what I have written to her,

147

and you will understand for yourself." And he took the letter home with him, to read.

Two days later I went to see him, with my knees shaking. "Did you read it?" I asked him.

"You will not get angry at me?" he asked in reply. "I found your words so charming that I felt a need to make a copy of the letter. Then do me a favor: give the copy I made to the young lady, yourself, with your own hands, and let me keep the original as a memento." Then he added, "But if the young lady will be convinced by your letter—that I do not know." And he smiled... leaving me surprised and puzzled again.

Well, I followed his advice and took the letter to the young lady— the copy written in Reb Aryeh's hand.... She was so impressed by the fine reasons I gave, written in flowery, poetic language and imagery, to explain to her why we could not marry — that we became man and wife. And the man who performed the ceremony was our good matchmaker, Reb Aryeh himself.

Ever since then (the leader in the underground movement concluded) it became a custom for my wife to go up to Jerusalem every month to visit him. If, however, she happened to come to Jerusalem in any case, for some other reason, then she would not go to see him. Once I asked her what her reason was. "To Reb Aryeh," she said, "it is hard to drop in just like that, by chance. To him you have to go specially" (as on a pilgrimage).

12
For harmony in the home

words from the heart

Once he discovered that a few members of a different Jewish community (originating from a different part of the world) who lived quite near him, did not treat their wives with respect. The next Sabbath he went to their synagogue and asked to be allowed to preach in the late afternoon, between *minḥa* (the afternoon prayer-service) and *ma'ariv* (the evening service). His subject would be a man's duty to respect the woman who shared his life.

His former teacher in Lithuania, the renowned scholar R. Isser Zalman Meltzer (of blessed memory) was living then in the neighborhood, and he came to this synagogue to join in the prayers and listen to the sermon. When it was over he approached Reb Aryeh and said, "Your words touched my heart deeply. I have taken a good account of my conduct, and you have made me aware how I fall short of my obligation toward my dear wife. From now on, however, I will know how to improve my attitude toward her."

"Imagine that," Reb Aryeh replied. "I was directing my words mainly at one of the regular worshippers there. (I hear that he treats his wife miserably.) And he did not realize it at all; my words hardly affected him. But my dear master teacher, you certainly give your wife respect.

On the contrary, I am certain that there is much to learn from you on how to treat a wife with esteem."

"Well," said R. Isser Zalman, "my Beyleh-Hindeh copies out my *ḥiddushim*, my novel thoughts in the Talmud, in her clear fair handwriting, so that I can give them to the printers. Sometimes she makes an error in the copying, and I lose my temper. But from now on..."

to swear an oath

A sharp quarrel once broke out between a certain married couple, and the two came to Reb Aryeh to have him settle the matter. The woman argued that her husband was unfaithful to her, and she was ready to live amicably with him again only if he would consent to swear to her a solemn vow of faithfulness. The husband felt hurt and insulted by such a demand, and he refused.

To bring harmony back into their home-life, Reb Aryeh announced quite simply that he was ready to take the oath for the husband, that the man was indeed true to her....

how to treat a wife

One of his students, of marriageable age, was about to embark on the seas of matrimony. So he came to Reb Aryeh and asked, "How should I behave toward my wife? How should I treat her?"

Reb Aryeh looked at him in wonder. "How can you ask a question like that? A wife is like your own self. You treat her as you treat yourself."

And indeed, when his own good wife Hannah felt pains, he went with her to Dr Naḥum Kook and told him, "My wife's foot is hurting us..."

To a young Talmud scholar who was recently wed, the good rabbi gave this prescription: It is a mitzvah, a precept of the Torah that a man *shall make his wife happy* (Deuteronomy 24:5). How should he make her happy? It is a woman's nature to find pleasure in finding favor in her husband's eyes. She looks to him, yearning to have him find her pleasing and charming. It is therefore up to the husband to try to show his wife love and endearment by open affection, and by encouraging and pleasing conversation. This is the intent of the Divine wish upon the creation of the human being, that *they shall be one flesh* (Genesis 2:24). And our Sages teach that when there is peace and harmony between a man and his wife, the *shechina* (the Divine Presence) dwells with them.

A man (he continued) has a duty to treat his wife with respect and courtesy. Still, he should take care that the attitude of respect should not lessen the relationship of intimate affection between them. So it is necessary to behave in a way that will blend respect with love and intimacy—so that nothing will interfere between them, just as nothing interferes between one's right and left hands, since they are both part of him.

Should any misunderstanding occur between them, he should never talk to her "impersonally," saying for example, "See what she is doing. Just look at her conduct." Instead, he should face her and speak directly: "See how you are behaving. Think of what you have done to me."

When he leaves the house, he should tell his wife where he is going. When he comes back, he should tell her where he was and what he did—and so with all little matters like that. For the purpose of all this is to strengthen the bond between them, to reinforce their love and cheer the heart....

When his oldest grandson was about to marry, he gave him this advice: When you come home, do not go and leave things strewn on the bed, for your wife (and children) to clear away. Do not impose on her, that she should serve you needlessly.

so that they should not be seen

Reb Aryeh would generally not go to bed till two o'clock in the morning. Almost every night he would sit up at home and busy himself with restoring peace and harmony between married couples—listening to their quarrels and arguments, and responding with his sage advice and solutions.

Once I asked him, "Why do you arrange for a couple to come to your home so late at night when they need your help?" His answer was: "There are families whose home life has become broken by discord, and they are among the prominent and distinguished families in the city, or even beyond our city limits. They come here to have their conflicts smoothed out, but they want no one to see them coming here, so that people should not gossip and start tongues wagging. So they come, together or separately, late at night—at times even at midnight—when the neighborhood is asleep.

"*Nu*," he concluded "there are many couples that follow such a procedure, and the result is that they all manage to come here in the late hours of the night."

"she remains faithful to you"

Among the political prisoners interned by the British under the mandate, there were those who suffered greatly from the long enforced separation from wife and children. It had a bad, injurious effect on their emotional well-being. Especially vulnerable were those who left behind a fiancée wearing a new engagement-ring, or a young newly-married wife. They were tormented by doubts and uncertainties that perhaps... who knew? ... what if...; and so to their physical suffering, psychological pain was added. Unable to withstand the severity of isolation and loneliness in the long prison sentence, they were stricken by gloom and melancholy; and they took to pacing back and forth in their cells like a caged lion. More than once, many of them would toss and turn on their prison beds at night, unable to sleep, adding mental torture to physical suffering.

It sometimes happened, too, that the long, endless imprisonments led to family tragedies and serious discord between married couples, especially if they were only recently wed. Then a young wife, finding her husband in prison, could see a dark picture ahead. In her mind's eye she could see herself already a grass widow, alone and abandoned for life, should her husband be deported to a far-off land.

Reb Aryeh had a special gift or faculty to sense what was going on in such people's hearts. As though an angel gave him secret information, he knew just who among the prisoners were suffering from depression. With them he would spend a great deal of time talking, getting at the psychological sores that festered inside them. For them he did not consider it enough just to pass written messages and bring greetings from family members on the outside (and it should be mentioned that the pious rabbi had an extraordinary memory, like a cemented cistern that never loses a drop of water; he always remembered a person's relatives and family members). To them he would add a remark: "You know, I am full of admiration for your fiancée. How much that girl loves you!" Or: "By the way: I met your aunt the other day, and she was just full of praise for your wife, that she just remains so faithful to you." Or again, "Your neighbors are telling wonderful things about your wife..." And so forth.

Simple words that warmed a person's heart, they were like oil to lubricate the very bones and nerves of those worried, melancholy prisoners.

no way but forgiveness

A woman once lashed out at her husband with some vicious stinging curses. Troubled by her conscience afterward, she sent Reb Aryeh a letter begging him to make sure that her curses would not strike home to her husband. And in the letter she included some money for charity.

In his reply the good rabbi returned the money to her, explaining patiently that even if she gave ten times as much to charity, she could not be forgiven till she made peace with her husband and received his forgiveness. And he added: "Since you have quarreled with your husband I would assume that he does not know of the donation to charity that you wish to make. Then in this there is also a suspicion of theft" (since she was giving the money without his knowledge and consent).

A few days later the good rabbi received a second letter from her, telling him that she followed his advice and asked her husband to forgive her—and now they were reconciled. In the letter she again enclosed an amount for charity—twice as much as in the first letter. And at the end of her message there was a note by her husband that the donation was by his knowledge and with his good wishes.

a gift for her would be better

A couple that took to quarrelling with each other came to Reb Aryeh to ask his help. When he succeeded in restoring peace and harmony to their life together, the man sent him a donation for his Torah school. The pious rabbi promptly sent it back, and wrote, "Rather than give money for the yeshiva, it would be better for you to spend the money for clothing and jewelry for your wife, and thus cheer her up."

on the husband's behalf

In one case Reb Aryeh had to put in months of energetic labor and effort to restore peace and affection between an estranged couple. When he succeeded at last, the delighted husband forced him to accept a personal gift of fifty Israeli pounds.

The good rabbi went and bought a fine present with the money, for the woman in the case (the man's wife), and then he gave it to her in her husband's name—"to strengthen the harmony in their home," he explained when he told about it.

the surprise package

On a Friday in 1956 he was returning home to prepare for the Sabbath when, passing by a window in Mishk'noth, the section of Jerusalem where he lived, he overheard a woman berating her husband in anger. He stopped a moment to listen, and realized at once that the quarrel was over the lack of money. The husband simply did not have enough to provide adequately for the Sabbath. The good rabbi went on his way, and in perhaps a quarter of an hour a youngster arrived at the home of the couple, with a large package of groceries. "What is this?" asked the woman of the house. "Who sent it? Who paid for it?" The boy had no answer to give. He worked at the grocery a few blocks away, and had been told to deliver it. It was paid for.

After the Friday evening prayers, Reb Aryeh passed by on his way home, and he stopped to wish the couple a good Sabbath. The husband told him of the mysterious package, and he received the news with an air of surprise and wonder. So happy was the woman of the house that she invited the good rabbi to their Sabbath meal (he was then a widower, living alone); and he accepted.

Some eleven years later two couples met: this one, and the man and wife who ran the grocery that had supplied the package. As they talked together at length, the first couple discovered the truth about the package at last.

the ideal time

There was one time in the year that he found ideal for making peace between estranged couples: the day before Yom Kippur. Then people's thoughts turn to seeking forgiveness for misdeeds and sins; the heart grows softer at the approach of the most solemn day of the year, when all pray in the synagogue for the Almighty's pardon; and then people are more likely to forgive one another for words and acts of cruelty, and to become reconciled. So if Reb Aryeh knew of a couple living in mutual hatred and hostility, thinking of divorce, in many cases he dropped in the day before Yom Kippur.

Rabbi Nissan Zaks, a fine Talmudic research scholar in the holy city, recalls how the good rabbi turned up at his home on one such day, at about ten in the morning, insisting that both must go at once to see an estranged couple and make peace between the two. Rabbi Zaks knew the husband, and Reb Aryeh believed the Talmudic scholar could influence him. It did Rabbi Zaks no good to protest that he had to attend a funeral just then. Reb Aryeh simply insisted that the needs of the living should take priority over the consideration of the dead. So off went the two, to use their powers of persuasion to the utmost.

Not always was the good rabbi successful; but he would never leave a conflict-laden home before he felt that he done everything possible to bring harmony. And always he would plead, "Do me a favor—for my sake — make peace between yourselves!"

13
Last respects for the departed

elevated by suffering

He gave his kindness not only to the living but also to those who departed this life. Once his friends met him on the street, on his way to a funeral. "Who passed away?" they asked him. "I do not know," he replied. They looked at him in astonishment: He was going to someone's funeral and did not know who the departed man was?

Reb Aryeh explained: "I saw in the obituary notices posted on the walls that the man died after severe pain and suffering. Then obviously he was a man of stature in the eyes of the Almighty. So I am going to give him the last kindness, pay my last respects, and accompany him to his final resting-place."

just for the mitzvah

One year, the entire winter in Jerusalem was cold and difficult, with frequent rain and snowfalls that blanketed the city. On a miserable Saturday night in December a cantor named Weinberger met the good rabbi in the cemetery of *har ha-m'nuḥoth* (the Mount of Repose) walking in a funeral procession to bring some deceased person to his eternal rest. (In Jerusalem no dead body may be left overnight as a rule, and funerals on a Saturday night are a common occurrence.)

"Reb Aryeh," asked the cantor, "what are you doing here on such a miserable winter night? Is this some close relative of yours, to whom you have to pay your last respects?"

"O no," said the good rabbi, "no relation whatever, In fact, I do not even know for sure whom we are bringing to his last resting-place. But I will tell you: In the Ba-tey Broido section of the city, quite close to my home, I heard someone walking about and proclaiming, *Good Jews, come to a funeral! Come to escort the dead!* I knew then that a departed person needed to be given proper burial, with a *minyan,* at least ten Jews, attending. Well, I thought to myself: Who will come out on a chilly wet night like this for the funeral of some unknown man? I was afraid there would not even be a minyan. So I came."

he knew the family

This is an incident that Reb Aryeh himself once related:

One evening I was walking from Meya She'arim to my home in the Mishk'noth section of Jerusalem. Leaving Ethiopia Street to turn into Reḥov haN'vi'im (the Street of the Prophets), I was undecided whether to go down to Jaffa Street by way of Reḥov Rav Kook, or to continue on Reḥov haN'vi'im, which would take me past the old (former) Hadassah hospital (now called Ziv, attached to the Bikkur Ḥolim hospital). For some reason unknown to me, I continued walking straight on Reḥov haN'vi'im.

I was soon passing the gates of the hospital, inside which there was the mortuary room, for patients who expired. But I heard the sound of weeping coming from the room, and I went in to investigate. I saw a woman of middle age with three young girls, evidently her daughters, standing and wailing over a dead person.

I turned to a poor Jew (a beggar) who was there. "Who is the dead man?" I asked him. "Someone from Ḥadera," he answered. Well, Ḥadera is quite a distance from Jerusalem; and I realized that this family was here all alone in the world, with no one to share their anguish. So I could not leave.

As I stood there I heard the woman say to the dead man in her lament, "May your holy forefathers go out (in heaven) to welcome you!" Unable to control my curiosity I went over to her and asked, "Perhaps you could tell me who his forefathers were?"

With some annoyance she replied in her despair, "And if I tell you, you will know?" Stubbornly I persisted, "Still, who knows?..." So the woman yielded "Reb Elyenke [a diminutive of Eliyahu] of Lida was his grandfather."

The name rang a bell. "What?" I asked in surprise. "R. Eliyahu Schick of Lida was his grandfather? Who was his father? R. Pinyele perhaps?"

The woman was amazed. "Father in heaven," she cried, "how in the world did you know? That is right: Reb Elyenke's son Reb Pinyele [a diminutive of Pinḥas] was my husband's father. And my husband himself, R. Moshe Aaron, was a rabbinic authority in Odessa. But here no one knows us, no one has heard of us..."

Needless to say, I did not stay idle but went to work, doing all I could to arrange a fitting funeral for this worthy man, to pay him the last respects properly. I went into the street and stopped every friend and acquaintance who happened by; and in that way a bit of a gathering assembled. I made an effort, and a burial garment of good quality was provided. Words of eulogy were said (a *hesped*), to praise the departed soul properly and give him due honor. Then we escorted him to his final resting-place. Afterward I even paid a visit to the woman and her daughters where they were "sitting *shivʿah*," spending the seven days of mourning, to comfort them in their sorrow.

Several months later I received mail from the family in Ḥadera: an invitation to a wedding. One of the three daughters was to be married. I very much wanted to attend, but alas, I was unable to make the trip.

A few months passed by, and a young man arrived, telling me that he was the new bridegroom in the family that I knew in Ḥadera. He was in Jerusalem now, he said, to try to find employment. I received him cheerfully, and asked him to come and see me again if he would remain in Jerusalem. He promised to do so.

A week later, however, I received a notice from the Hadassah hospital to come there. I went, and found that the young man recently married into that family in Ḥadera, who had been to see me only a week before, was lying there in a hospital bed after a serious operation. His condition was critical, and there was little hope of his recovery.

As I found out, he had come to Jerusalem originally on account of the surgery he needed. He had told me that he came for work only because he did not wish to cause me sorrow. And in the hospital he had given my name as the nearest of kin, whom to notify of anything that happened.

The unfortunate young man lived on only a few more days, in great pain and suffering, and then succumbed. But in those few days that I saw him I was able to see that he was of fine character and truly religious. The hospital nurses too, and everyone who came in contact with him, spoke strongly in praise of him.

This new tragedy for the family in Hadera, so hard on the heels of the earlier one, touched my heart deeply; I felt broken by grief and sorrow. This funeral too I attended. Like the other one, it took place late in the evening (in Jerusalem, as a rule a departed person is not to be left overnight without burial). It was a troubled time then, though, of riots and unrest, and the funeral procession to the Mount of Olives was not without danger. For this reason two armed policemen accompanied the procession.

Before the funeral began its way to the cemetery, I approached the manager (*gabbai*) of the burial society to have a word with him. "Look," I said, "I knew this departed young man. He was truly devout. And I also know who his father-in-law was: a fine rabbi from a very distinguished family. The father-in-law is buried on the Mount of Olives, in the new cemetery. There must surely be a vacant plot of ground right near his grave. It would be only fitting to bury the son-in-law near the father-in-law. For him it would be like being laid to rest in his fathers' graveyard."

The *gabbai* looked at me with some asperity: "I am truly very surprised at you, that you can talk like that. You know this is a time of danger; armed policemen are coming along with us. We are taking our lives in our hands, marching to the Mount of Olives at a time like this. So we are going to do our task there just as fast as possible. We will go to the first grave that we find open, bury the dead person in it, and run back at once to the city. Are we to go looking for special graves and plots there at a time like this, and put Jews in added danger?"

At these words of stern reproof I lowered my head in shame, because I knew he was right. So I answered him quickly, "Reb Yaakov, it is indeed as you say. I did not consider what the present situation is. Now I understand, and I will not ask this any more."

The funeral procession moved swiftly on its journey of last respect. And true enough, it all happened as the *gabbai* had predicted. Everything was done rapidly, in great haste. Fearing for their lives, the people who came to the new cemetery brought the body to its final resting place in the very first open grave they found.

Now, in order to mark the place of this new grave in his record-book, the *gabbai* lifted the stone lying on the grave next to it. That was as yet without a tombstone, and the flat stone which he now raised had on its lower side—as a temporary record—the name of that dead person. So the *gabbai* looked at this stone and read out, "R. Moshe Aaron the son of Pinḥas Schick."

When I heard that a shiver went through my whole body. I turned to the *gabbai* and told him in a shaking voice, "Do you know who lies buried here, right near the new grave? It is that young man's father-in-law! It was precisely next to this grave that I asked you to place his body."

The *gabbai* could hardly contain himself: "Whatever are you saying? Nothing as extraordinary as this has ever happened to me before!"

for the honor of the dead

Midway in the month of Iyar (May) 1948, when heat waves came frequently, the waves of bombs and explosives fired at Jerusalem also grew more intense. After all, we were in the midst of our War of Independence, when the State of Israel, newly born, had to fight not to be stillborn. The guns of the Arab Legion were mounted at Shuafat and Nebi Samuel (just outside the holy city) and trained on the heart of Jerusalem.

Samuel Weingarten worked then as a cashier in a bank, and also served in civil defense for an hour or two a day. This is what he remembered:

As I was walking along King George Street, a shell landed and exploded with a mighty boom in the hollow where the great *menorah* stood (outside the old Knesset building). The people walking in the street hurried to take shelter. But along came a second shell, and it landed in the entrance of one of the nearby buildings, wounding a woman who was standing rather close to it. The ground quaked and heaved; and with every added shell

A Jerusalem street hit by shells during the 1948 War of Independence.

that detonated, it crumbled into dust, and beams of the building collapsed.

In this tumult and confusion of the dance of cannon-fire, I saw the figure of Reb Aryeh Levin approaching. I was astounded: What business did Reb Aryeh have strolling on the street on a day of wrath like this, with bombs exploding to our right and left, fore and aft? Yet there he was, walking at his usual slow measured pace, as though all this was no concern of his. When I asked him this, his answer was, "Every shell has its own address, its own marked destination. If one is meant for me it will get to me even if I stay at home, and even in the bomb-shelter. Look: a shell landed in my apartment and wounded a grandchild of mine. If it is meant for someone he cannot escape it."

"But dear rabbi," I protested, "it is written in the Torah, *be very careful for your lives* (Deuteronomy 4:15). We are ordered by the Almighty to take great care of ourselves!"

"*Nu*," said Reb Aryeh, "people out to do a mitzvah do not come to harm. And now I am occupied with a great mitzvah. Forty deceased persons are lying in the mortuary room of the Bikkur Ḥolim hospital, with no one to guard the bodies. The widow-panes are smashed from the bombing, and hungry cats have come licking the fresh blood from the wounds. We have even discovered human jackals disguised as watchmen, who came to examine the fingers of the dead and see what rings they could remove. Then they took to searching in the pockets.... So I am on my way to find volunteers who will really guard and watch."

I went along to help him, and we soon rounded up a few older friends of ours from the Haganah, and members of the civilian guard. Afterward, yeshiva students came regularly to watch the bodies of victims of the Arab bombardment, until they could be given proper burial.

"casting lots" for the fallen

It was a long time after Gush Etzyon fell in Israel's War of Independence (1948) till the bodies of its defenders could be gathered—the brave fighters who had given their lives trying to hold it against overpowering odds. The bodies were found in trenches and ditches. Some were discovered around the settlements of the Gush, while thirty-five heroic fighters, who met their death on the way there, when they were rushing to come to its rescue, were found buried in a temporary grave, with only a thin layer of earth covering their bodies. But that bit of earth protected them from both human and animal scavengers of the desert.

When the bodies were all gathered, under the initiative and leadership of the chief army chaplain R. Sh'lomo Goren, attempts had to be made to establish their identities. The thirty-five met their death while the Gush (the group of settlements) was still fighting for its existence. Under the enemy fire they had been hastily buried by their brethren from the Gush, with a superhuman effort to observe the laws of Jewish burial and to keep the order of their identity. But the frightful battle conditions did not allow the brave men who buried them to be entirely careful and prepare an exact, precise system of identification, with a chart or diagram, to identify later every temporary grave.

The thirty-five sealed coffins were brought to Jerusalem, and every effort was made to establish the identifications. They made use of whatever sketches or charts *had* been made by those who had given them the temporary burial, the memory of those who might recognize objects or characteristics, and various photographs, especially of teeth (to be checked against dental records).

Twenty-three could be identified absolutely, without any shadow of a doubt. As for the rest, they only knew that these were the twelve remaining martyrs who had given their lives for their land; and they had a list of the names. But there was no way to link a particular body with any one of the names.

It would be hard to imagine or describe the pain and anguish of their parents. When a mother stood bowed down over the grave of her son, cut down in his youth, the channels of prayer and weeping opened for her. She could pour out her tears and her woe, and Heaven listened. How intensely sharper was the grief and agony when the parents did not know to which grave to go, to seek words for their heart's unhealable wound.

All those who devoted themselves to bringing in fallen soldiers from behind the enemy lines, to give them Jewish burial, made every possible effort to identify these twelve. They used every conceivable means and technique. And to no avail.

Solemnly the thirty-five young martyrs were reburied in Jerusalem's military cemetery, on Mount Herzl. On twenty-three, markers were placed (and later, tombstones). Each grave had its name. Yet twelve remained unmarked. The twelve names for them were known. But no one could say which name belonged to which grave.

Whatever was to be done? There were perhaps some slight clues for identification in certain cases, but no clear proofs by any means. So a few of the bereaved parents made their way to R. Tz'vi Pesaḥ Frank, the chief rabbi of Jerusalem, recognized as a foremost authority on religious law. It was only natural that they should turn to him.

Rabbi Frank considered the matter carefully from every aspect; and he decided that lots would have to be drawn to provide an answer. It would be by a certain special, unique way of drawing lots, known only to the wise elders of Jerusalem, which was said to have originated with R. Elijah the Gaon of Vilna. Among the pious elders of the holy city (although they never spoke of it) the tradition was that this way of

A TZADDIK IN OUR TIME

The reburial, in the Mt Herzl military cemetery, of the 35 who fell in defense of Gush Etzyon.

drawing lots traced its origins back to a most holy ancient practice, stemming from the ancient rule to go to the *kohen gadol* (the high priest) in the Sanctuary, and ask of the Urim and Thummim—consult the precious stones on the breastplate that he wore.

This was not a system of divination or wizardry. They would not claim black-and-white certainty for it. It was simply appropriate to use it in certain situations, and how well it worked depended on the spiritual purity and sanctification of those who made use of it.

Who should actually draw the lots (work the method to find the answers)? The people involved had but one choice: Reb Aryeh. It seemed natural, self-evident to them that this pious Jew should undertake the solemn task. When they came to ask him, however, he wanted to decline, and asked them to choose someone else (as might be expected, he was sure that he was unworthy and unequal to the task).

The grieving parents went back to Rabbi Frank: What to do? Well, he despatched a messenger to implore Reb Aryeh again, and to persist until the pious man agreed. In short, the plea of the people grew so strong that Reb Aryeh could not continue to decline. Shaking with trepidation, he went to begin the holy task.

This is how one journalist described the event:

It was Thursday at night. The people went up to the yeshiva (Torah school) that Reb Aryeh maintained on the upper floor of his small humble home in the neighborhood of Mishk'noth. In the room filled with darkness they lit twelve candles (one for each of the fallen) which lit up the eastern wall, where the *aron kodesh* (the holy ark with the Torah scrolls) stood. The people there were Reb Aryeh, his son-in-law R. Aaron Jacobovitz and his son R. Raphael Binyomin, and two of the stricken parents (one of them the Israeli publisher Reuben Mass).

They began by saying *t'hillim*, paragraphs from the Book of Psalms. This room knew many difficult and bitter hours in the past when *t'hillim* was said with fervor. Now the ancient words of prayer resounded naturally, raising the people to an exalted level of devotion. They had never before experienced something like this: a holy, quivering hope and prayer that the Almighty would grant them to find the truth. The sounds of prayer rose from them in an intensity that surprised themselves as well as those who heard it from afar. Rarely had such prayer been heard even in this neighborhood, steeped though it was in Torah study and supplication.

By the tradition, for drawing the lots a certain Hebrew Bible was to be used, with two columns on the page, that was printed in Amsterdam in 1701—and which Reb Aryeh had in his care. Its pages were yellowed with age, but still whole. Where a page was slightly torn it was pasted with scotch tape, to keep it whole. There were a few notes written occasionally in the margins in a clear, pearl-like hand. The title-page had an engraving of an *aron kodesh,* adorned with a sentence from the Bible: "With this shall Aaron come into the holiness" (Leviticus 16:3). Now, with this Bible, the people entered a realm of holiness to draw a most unusual kind of lots.

A hallowed silence reigned over the room, as the flickering candles added to the solemnity and awe. Reb Aryeh opened the Bible entirely at random, to whatever page chance would bring him. Then he continued turning batches of pages this way and that, haphazardly, seven times. Now he turned over exactly seven single leaves, going forward. Next, he

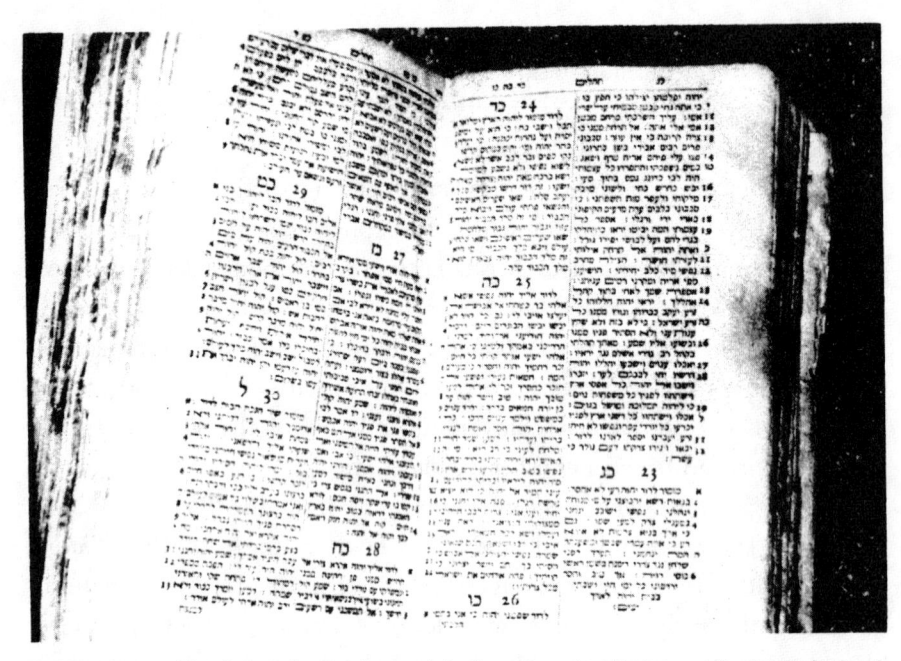

The Hebrew Bible that Reb Aryeh used in "casting the Scriptures"; the holy book is quite small, measuring only about 3½ by 6 inches (9 by 15 centimeters).

went forward seven single pages; after that, seven columns; then seven verses; then seven words; and finally seven single letters. Thus it was "seven times seven": seven batches, leaves, pages, columns, verses, words, letters. Whatever the seventh letter was, Reb Aryeh now looked for the very next verse which began with that letter. By the verses of Scripture found in this way, he would assign a name to each of the twelve unidentified soldiers who now lay reburied in the military cemetery on Mount Herzl.

There was one basic rule: For each "casting of lots" (turning of pages) they chose one of the twelve graves, to find a name for it. The deciding sentence in the Bible, to which they came at last, had to contain or refer to one of the twelve names. And that would be the name for the grave.

There was excitement and astonishment when the first sentence that came up was: "The earth is the Lord's, and all that fills it, the world and those who dwell therein" (Psalms 24:1). The first Hebrew word in it is usually pronounced *la-shem* and is written with the letters *la-med hey*. But those two letters stand for the number 35—and it was a total of

LAST RESPECTS FOR THE DEPARTED

thirty-five courageous soldiers who died on their way to defend Gush Etzyon!

Likewise, every page to which they came dealt with battles of courage and mitzvoth (religious obligations) in the land of Israel which were linked and connected with this very situation.

There was one further rule yet to remember: If the sentence at which they arrived did not relate in any way to what they needed to know, they would take the last letter in it and look for a sentence on the page that began with that letter, and try to find, directly or by inference, the answer from that.

This was the procedure they followed eleven times. There was no need for a twelfth time, because once eleven names were assigned to eleven of the unmarked graves on Mount Herzl, the last name would automatically be given to the remaining one.

To everyone's amazement, each sentence at which they arrived gave a clear and definite message. One after another, the sentences produced the answers they sought.

(Joshua 21:4, "and from the tribe of Benjamin by lot," identified the body in the first grave under consideration as Benjamin Boguslavsky. I Samuel 9:21, "Am I not *ben yemini*, a Benjaminite"—Odéd ben-Yemini. Genesis 46:26, "All the persons belonging to Yaakov"—this identified the body in the grave under consideration as Yaakov ben-Attar. Genesis 47:16, "And Joseph said: Bring your cattle"—Joseph Baruch. Hosea 7:10, "the pride, *gaon*, of Israel answers"—Eytan Gaon. I Kings 17:23, "And Eliyahu took the child"—Eliyahu Hershkovitz. Deuteronomy 33:18, "And of Zevulun he said"—Yitzhak Zevuloni. Psalms 132:9, "Let your *kohanim* be clothed with righteousness"—Alexander Cohen. Psalms 110:4, "The Lord has sworn and will not change His mind: you are a *kohen*"—Yaakov Cohen. Jeremiah 51:49, "Babylon must fall for the slain of Israel"—Israel Merzel. Psalms 27:4, "One thing *sha'alti*, have I asked"—Sha'ul Panueli.)

The people there finished this process of identification in the early hours of the morning, but sleep came to none of them that night. They felt too strongly the strangeness and wonder of the experience. And no one had the slightest doubt that the determination was accurate—that every one of the twelve out of the thirty-five had been rightly identified.

in defense of Gush Etzyon

(Those marked with an asterisk were identified by Reb Aryeh by "casting lots" with the Scriptures.):

Oded ben-Yemini *

Yaakov (Jordan) Cohen *

Eliyahu Hershkovitz *

Benzion ben-Meir

Alexander Cohen *

Yitzhak Halévy

Yaakov ben-Attar *

Yaakov Caspi

Sabo Goland

Yosef Baruch *

Yehiel Calev

Yitzhak Ginzberg

Israel Aloni (Merzel) *

Benny Boguslavsky *

Eytan Gaon *

Judah Bitansky

Hayyim Engel

- Yaakov Kotik
- Amnon (Michel) Michaeli
- Daniel Reich
- Yosef Kufler
- Eliyahu Mizraḥi
- Daniel Şabari
- Tovya Kushner
- Shaul Panueli *
- Yaakov Shmueli
- Yona Levin
- Baruch Pat
- Daniel Tur-Shalom
- Alexander Lustig
- Moshe Avigdor Perlstein
- Yitzḥak Zevuloni *
- Daniel Mass
- Benjamin Persitz
- David Zwebner

The very next day they went and told R. Tz'vi Pesaḥ Frank all that had happened. He was deeply moved, and ruled that the identifications were to be regarded as definite.

The bereaved parents accepted the results as final; and according to these results the names of the twelve were inscribed on the tombstones of their places of burial on Mount Herzl.

a final kindness

One of the stalwart pioneering doctors of Hadassah, who used to travel about on horseback to help the early settlers battle malaria, was Benjamin Bakman. For a long time he provided the only medical service in the Negev. In the years of the underground resistance against the British, it is said, he kept a medical bag packed and ready, and upon any signal or message from the underground fighters, he was off to attend to their wounded friends. As a result, though advanced in years, he spent periods of time in various prisons and detention camps; and thus he became firmly linked in friendship with Reb Aryeh.

Fate was not kind to him, though, and he lost his only son in the War of Independence.

As time brought him close to the end of his life, on his hospital bed he made out a check to Reb Aryeh for his private yeshiva, in fulfillment of a solemn promise he had made, fearing that if he waited much longer, it would be too late for him.

The following day, his end came. As his widow left the hospital, there was Reb Aryeh coming to meet her. "Do not worry," he told her. "I know he did not leave a son. I will say *kaddish* (the mourner's prayer) for him..."

with determination

While Reb Aryeh lay old and ailing in the Hadassah hospital, the late prime minister of Israel, Levi Eshkol, passed away. In response to the news, the medical staff of the hospital gathered for a memorial meeting to pay tribute to this devoted public servant who was now gone.

When Reb Aryeh heard of this gathering he begged the nurses to take him to the hospital courtyard, so that he could take part in the memorial

LAST RESPECTS FOR THE DEPARTED

assembly. But he was quite weak, the state of his health was quite precarious and wavering, and indeed all his body was ailing and stricken with pain. So the doctors did their best to dissuade him and get him to change his mind. But he would not yield. "If my illness prevents me from attending the funeral to pay him my last respects, let me at least take part in this memorial assembly."

So it was that supporting himself with crutches, Reb Aryeh was led to the courtyard of the Hadassah hospital, to fulfill his wish.

When a séfer torah was accidentally burnt in a fire and had to be buried, a saddened Reb Aryeh came to that "funeral" too.

14
Comforting the bereaved

to strengthen faith

Reb Aryeh was especially scrupulous and careful to go to homes where people sat in mourning for a departed member of the family, to comfort them and give them new heart. Once he explained to me why this was so important to him: "When a misfortune or tragic event befalls a man, apart from his anguish and suffering his faith also becomes injured to some extent. When a person goes to comfort someone in mourning, not only does he give him new spirit and courage, sharing in the mourner's sorrow; he also returns the other's faith to its original strength."

everyone mourns and he exults

A former mayor of Rishon l'Tziyon who knew Reb Aryeh well had lost his family in the Nazi holocaust. Once, while in Reb Aryeh's house, he revealed the burden that weighed down his heart: "The truth is that my faith in the Almighty was shaken by that tragedy. What sin did my little child ever commit, that this should happen to him?"

Reb Aryeh rose from his seat at once, took the man's hand in both of his, and began caressing it. "There is a tzaddik," he said, "a righteous, devout person; and there is a ḥassid, a man of kindly piety. But a *kadosh,* a hallowed person, is only one who was put to death for his religion and his faith. Then I have to stand in your presence, because you offered up not one sacrifice to sanctify God's name, not one *kadosh*—but two."

"You know," he added: "when a child is born and comes into the world, all are rapturous with joy—and the child itself cries and wails. When someone dies and his life-spirit leaves the world, all mourn and grieve— but that living spirit itself exults and rejoices. It has gone from a world of darkness to a world of light..." In this vein Reb Aryeh continued talking and explaining, till he sensed that his words were reaching and calming the bereaved father, to bring him some inner tranquility.

From that time on there was a strong bond of friendship between the two.

when no one else came

A learned religious Jew known as Reb Yeraḥmiel the Maggid (preacher) passed away the very night before Passover, while a steady rain fell on the holy city. As the rule is not to let a deceased person remain overnight in Jerusalem, the funeral was arranged in great haste and he was brought immediately to his final resting-place.

The next day his son, R. Ben-tziyon, "sat *shivʿah*" (observed the law of the seven days of mourning) only till noon, as the religious law requires on a day before a *yom tov* (festival). But that entire morning no one came to comfort him or give him a word of solace in his bereavement. Since his father passed away so suddenly and received burial at once, hardly anyone knew of it. And those who knew were busy preparing for Passover (which requires an immense amount of toil to prepare for it religiously).

As this man later recalled, this is what happened afterward: "A very few hours before the holy *yom tov* began, Reb Aryeh came knocking on the door. In that stormy beating rain he had trudged on foot all the way to the Katamon section, from his neighborhood of Mishk'noth, to visit me in my time of sorrow. He was the only man who came to bring me consolation that day. I can never forget this act of sheer kindness; nor will I ever forget the words of solace he spoke then to comfort and hearten me, just a few hours before Passover began for us all, while I was utterly alone in my grief."

the daughter who blamed herself

When a certain man in Jerusalem became ill from heart disease, his daughter, an only child, left her own home and came to take care of him. But he saw that she was taking too much trouble over him, spending far more time and energy than she could afford, and he pleaded with her to go back to her own home, where she was needed. He insisted that he could look after himself. The daughter, however, refused to listen. Finally he said, "If you want to respect your father you must do as I say. Go back now to your home." Well, since it became a matter of respecting her father, a religious study that the Torah requires, she yielded and left to take care of her own family.

A few days afterward the man suffered a heart-attack and passed away. His poor daughter was so beside herself with grief that she was not to be comforted. She blamed herself for leaving her father, abandoning him when he was so ill. Convinced beyond argument that she was guilty of his death, she began to be emotionally ill herself.

Then Reb Aryeh came to talk to her: "Listen to me," he said gently. "Even if you remained by his bedside he would not have lived longer. A man's lifetime is fixed and set by a higher Power. And then, if you had remained and he died, you would have been twice as stricken with grief—because you did not fulfill your duty to honor and respect him. After all, he told you clearly to go back home. You would have been sure that by refusing to leave him you caused him anguish—and *that* hastened your father's death while he suffered with his heart."

He went on talking in the same vein, on and on, until the truth of his words struck home, and she was comforted.

with a grief of his own

When a noted woman, the Israeli jurist Dr. Gitta Gneḥovsky passed away, Reb Aryeh did not hesitate to travel to B'ney B'rak to comfort her husband during his seven days of mourning. The pious rabbi came to the man's home and sat; and suddenly feeling the full impact of the family's loss he burst into tears. For a long while he could not control himself and stop weeping. Not a word of comfort or solace could he utter. And when the sorrowing husband saw this he himself began to cry bitterly.

Realizing that he was only darkening and deepening the gloom, and doing nothing to console any mourners, Reb Aryeh arose and left the house. He returned in about an hour, and sat once more with the bereaved family, forcing himself now to show a cheerful face and say kind words of comfort. No one noticed that only his face was cheerful and optimistic, but his eyes still bore his pain.

the time to visit widows

During *ḥol ha-moʿéd* (the intermediate days) of the festival of Sukkoth, a certain rabbi met Reb Aryeh walking about near his home. "What are you doing in my neighborhood?" he asked. "I am going to visit Mrs. Bengis, Reb Aryeh replied. (She was the widow of the noted scholar R. Zelig Reuven Bengis, head of the *beth din,* the rabbinic court of the *eyda ḥareydith,* the Orthodox community.) "Do me a favor," Reb Aryeh continued, "and come with me."

"For what reason?" asked the other man.

"It is a custom of mine," answered Reb Aryeh, "to visit the widows of worthy rabbis on the days of *ḥol ha-moʿéd*. The whole year everyone is busy and burdened with his work, and a widow does not feel her loneliness. On these intermediate days of the *yom tov,* however, it is different. Now people in this city are at leisure on these holy days, and such a woman surely thinks back to the good old days when her prominent, respected husband was alive, and all the eminent, worthy citizens of Jerusalem came to visit him. She must remember how her house filled with visitors, and the atmosphere was happy and cheerful. And now, what a contrast: she sits alone, forsaken; and the days of the *yom tov* turn into a time of pain. How much she must suffer. For this reason I make it a point, no matter what, to visit these widows specifically in the days of *ḥol ha-moʿéd*—to cheer them and bring a little happiness into their mournful hearts."

the purpose of tears

Bitterly unhappy, a woman once came to Reb Aryeh's home. "Let me sit in your house," she pleaded, "and cry and weep before you."

"You may surely sit," he replied, "and even cry and weep—but not before me. Direct your tears to the Holy, Blessed One who listens to weeping and hears the outcries of His human beings."

Taking a seat, the woman simply began a lament without end, unable to stop. In between her tears she managed to sob out her story of woe, about her husband who was mortally sick.

"Do not cry so," said Reb Aryeh. "The Holy, Blessed One will surely have mercy and grant a cure." But alas, a few days later the woman returned to tell him that her husband had passed away. And she wept anew with bitter tears.

Reb Aryeh did his best to comfort her, seeking words that would touch her heart. Finally, with some spirit she answered, "Look: I will accept your solace and stop my lament—but only if you tell me what became of the thousands of tears I shed over the *t'hillim,* the Book of Psalms, when I said its words of prayer to the Master of the world, imploring Him to cure my husband when he lay ill. It was all for nothing, wasn't it?"

"I will tell you," said Reb Aryeh gently, "When your life on earth ends and you come before the court of justice in heaven, you will find out how many severe and harsh decrees against the Jewish people were torn up, made null and void, because of those precious holy tears you shed for your husband. Not one teardrop goes to waste. The Holy, Blessed One counts them like pearls, and treasures them."

At that the woman burst into weeping again, but now with tears of happiness (that all her suffering and prayer were truly not in vain). Some time later she came back: "Tell me again, dear rabbi, those beautiful words: What happened with those tears of mine that I wept?"

writing and weeping

Once his student Yaakov David Perlin came to him, and found him bent over his table writing a letter, while he wept bitterly. What happened? his student asked. What made him grieve?

Reb Aryeh answered: He was writing a letter of consolation to a known family that had suffered for years in the Soviet Union, since its members had insisted on speaking Hebrew at home, in a land that considered "Zionism" a major crime. Just a while ago, however, they succeeded in getting out and migrating to Israel—and now the parents lost their only son: He served as a medical doctor on the submarine Dakar, which was lost in the depths of the sea, with no survivors....

to comfort an army chief

The time came when Arik Sharon (who became famous more recently for his daring military leadership in the Yom Kippur War) lost his son in a tragic accident. A mutual friend went to Reb Aryeh and asked him to invite Sharon to his home, to try to comfort and console him. For this was the second tragedy that struck him since he had lost his first wife and their child in a road accident.

Under no circumstances would Reb Aryeh consider having the griefstricken man come to his home. "Heaven forfend," he exclaimed. "It is I who have an obligation to go to him, to his home, to keep the mitzvah of comforting mourners."

Reb Aryeh was severely ill at the time, but that did not deter him. Determined, he simply stood up and went. And he found Arik Sharon a broken, stricken man. The pious rabbi spoke with him, striving to make comfort and hope reach him. Then, once back home in Jerusalem, Reb Aryeh bought *mezuzoth* in silver cases and sent them to Sharon as a present. (A *mezuza* is a piece of parchment with two paragraphs of the Hebrew Bible written on it, rolled up and enclosed in a case; it is attached to every right doorpost in a Jewish home, to serve as a reminder of God's presence and to earn His protection.) During his visit the sharp eye of Reb Aryeh had noticed that these sacred objects were missing in Sharon's home.

The military leader never forgot this act of kindness. Reb Aryeh was then so ill that he had to remain for a time in the Hadassah hospital; and Sharon made a special trip to Jerusalem to see him.

Reb Aryeh was profoundly moved by the visit. Here was a man come to see him who commmanded the defenders of Israel, the soldiers for whom

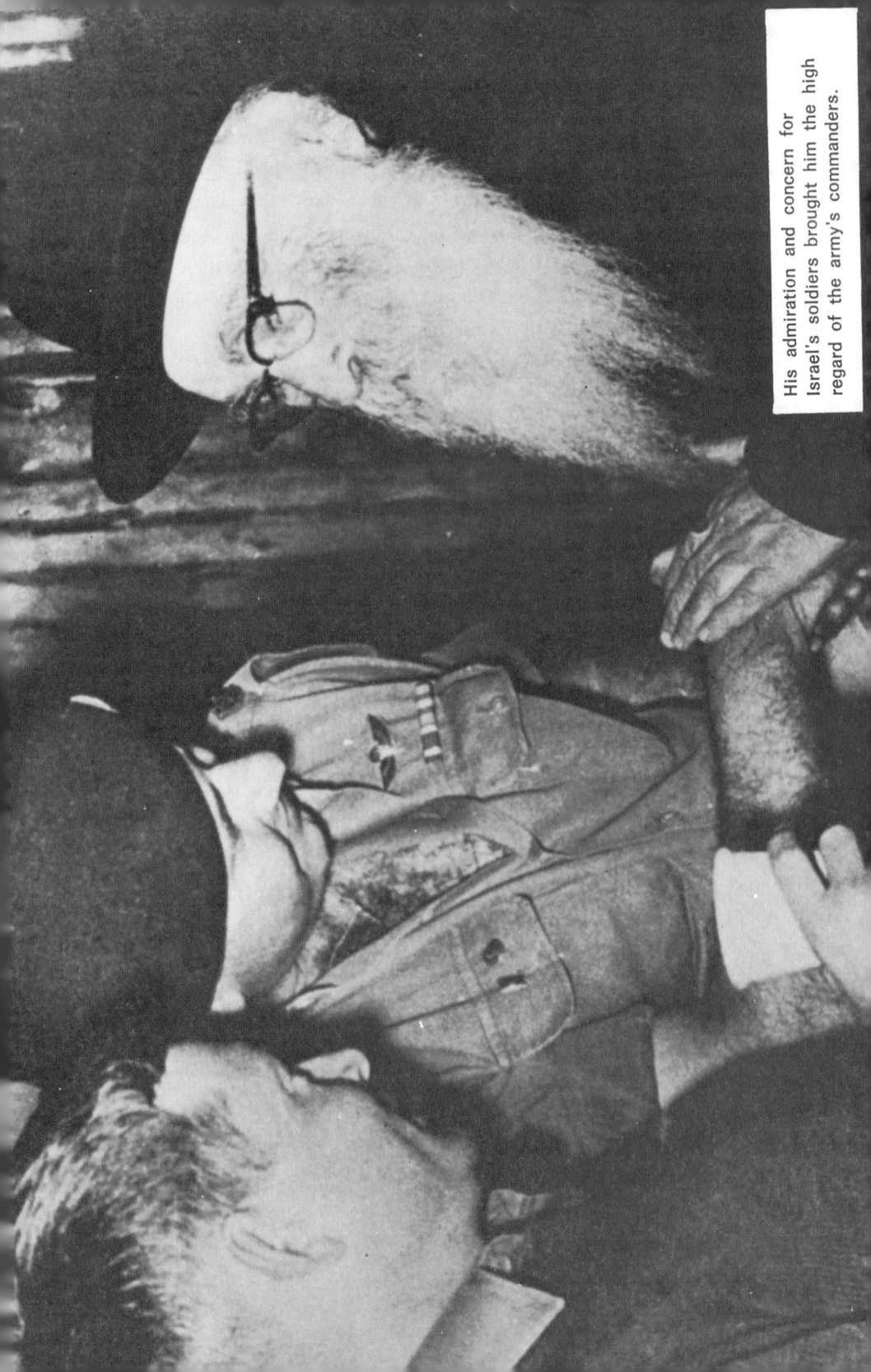

His admiration and concern for Israel's soldiers brought him the high regard of the army's commanders.

Reb Aryeh always prayed. "They are angels," he used to whisper. "Not one of us knows how to appreciate or value them properly."

Excited and pleased to see this visitor, Reb Aryeh did not merely shake hands. The two embraced warmly. Then Reb Aryeh thought: 'Now, what am I to tell him?' As the part of the Hebrew Bible to be read in the synagogue on the next Sabbath was *sidrah* (the portion) *yithro,* he decided to tell Sharon about a sentence in it:

"The part of the Torah that we read this week is the *sidrah yithro*. It begins: Now, Jethro... Moses' father-in-law, heard of all that God had done for Moses and for Israel His people (Exodus 18:1). The commentary of Rashi asks: What report did Jethro hear that made him come? It answers: He heard about the division of the Red Sea, and the battle between the Israelites and Amalek.

"Well now, why was it not enough for Jethro to hear about the Red Sea, to make him come? It was a wonderful miracle: Just when the Egyptians wanted to recapture the Israelites, the sea divided in two. The Israelites crossed on dry land; and when the Egyptians went after them the waters returned and drowned them. Was this not unique, without parallel in human history? When did anything like that ever happen again?

"Still (Reb Aryeh continued) it seems that it was not enough. For when Jethro heard about it he thought: It was a miracle, that the Almighty wrought; but a miracle is something extraordinary, unusual; it happens once only. From a miracle you cannot tell what the future of the Israelites will be. Will they always have miracles if they need them?

"But now, when he heard about the battle with Amalek—a real, actual battle, which the Israelites fought with courage and bravery—so that this miracle happened through plain warfare—Jethro understood that this is a unique kind of people. Then he was convinced that it was necessary and worthwhile for him to come and get to know this people at first hand." Reb Aryeh paused a moment, and added, "Well, what happened once will happen again!"

the comforter comforted

During the Six-Day War a fine young Torah scholar fell in the battle for Jerusalem, leaving behind a young widow with small children. In their days of mourning, Reb Aryeh went to visit them, to offer his consolation. When he arrived at the house, however, his spirit failed him. He did not have the heart, the spiritual strength to enter. So he went home and returned the next day. But the second day too he was utterly unable to open the door. However, the young widow heard some slight sound of movement, and she came into the hallway.

Once Reb Aryeh saw her he burst into tears, simply unable to restrain himself. So the young woman comforted *him*: "Reb Aryeh, if it was decreed in heaven that I should be a widow and my children orphans, what greater merit could we have been given than this—that my husband fell fighting for Jerusalem?"

Thus the one who came to give consolation was himself given it. A long time later, when he told this to someone and repeated the young woman's words, tears still choked up his voice.

when neither could speak

How ready he was to comfort people in their bereavement, perhaps the Herzog family knew best of all. When Rabbi Isaac Herzog, Israel's noted chief rabbi, was suffering from the serious illness that was to end his life, late one night a rumor spread that he had passed away. It was well past midnight when the rumor reached Reb Aryeh, and by then it was being told almost as fact. About two in the morning he came walking up and rang the doorbell of Rabbi Herzog's home. When Mrs Herzog opened the door, he was unable to say a word, but stood there speechless, waiting for her to tell him the worst. She in turn stood silent, utterly bewildered by his visit. And so they stood for several minutes, dumbfounded, till at last the good rabbi was able to speak, and it was all cleared up.

15
Giving heart and courage

when he refused to move

During the War of Independence (1948) when Jerusalem was under siege, his neighborhood (Mishk'noth) was shelled, as it was in range of the enemy's guns. Nor was he spared: His home was hit and severely damaged. The members of *le-ḥee* (Fighters for Israel's Freedom) then came and begged him to move to lodgings further away from the wall where the enemy guns were stationed, to one of the southern neighborhoods that they had liberated.

Reb Aryeh would not agree: "I should move, and the others who live in the neighborhood should remain?"

He was not dismissed

When Israel went through a depression people everywhere were dismissed from their work in the name of "efficiency." One day a government clerk came to see him, with anxiety written all over his face. "I am deeply worried for my livelihood," he confided in Reb Aryeh. "Perhaps I will be among those fired from their jobs." The poor clerk continued pouring out his uncertainty and anxiety—and Reb Aryeh remained calm. "*Nu*," he said, "I am not worried at all."

"But why?" asked the other. "Can't you feel something of what I am going through?"

"I will tell you: If you came and told me that the Holy, Blessed One was being discharged from His position, there would certainly be reason for very great concern and fear. But the Holy One is remaining at His job. He is not resigning; no one is dismissing Him. Then why all the worry?"

esteem has value

A certain minor government official had a fairly respectable position, but the salary was not particularly high, and neither were the conditions of his work very much to his liking. He therefore debated with himself whether he ought to change to some other position—until he decided to ask Reb Aryeh's advice. He went to see him and told the pious rabbi all the details that entered into the problem.

Reb Aryeh thought the man should remain in his present position; and he began listing all the advantages he had in his present place of employment. Among other things, he said, "And then, in this post you enjoy esteem and honor."

So the good rabbi who ran from honor all his life knew well enough that honor and esteem *was* something of value.

helping the helper

One Sabbath day, as he was walking in the street, he met Dr Gumpertz, a religious Jew who specialized in ailments of the ear, nose and throat. Carrying his small bag of instruments, the doctor was on his way, a bit wearily, to visit a patient. Brooking no refusal, Reb Aryeh took the bag from his hand and carried it for him as they walked together. "You see," said the rabbi with his usual smile, "I cannot do any healing. Let me at least have a share in your mitzvah of curing the sick, by carrying this."

An answering smile appeared on the doctor's face. "Do you know?" he said. "I always feel a bit resentful when I have to visit a patient on the Sabbath. I mind having my Sabbath rest broken. Now I feel much better about it."

the sacred task

On the Sabbath, his holy day of rest, he never failed to visit the people in prison, whether they were criminals or political prisoners, to cheer them up and raise their spirits. As he wrote in his last will and testament, "...never was I stopped by rain or snow, cold or heat, no matter how much self-sacrifice it required."

Neither did he mind that in those hours that he spent visiting he was unable to study the Torah he loved so dearly, although studying Torah is the most important mitzvah of all. About this he used to tell a little story that he once heard from R. Ben-tziyon Zisling, a much older colleague:

A good many years ago R. Zisling went to spend a Sabbath with the renowned hassidic rabbi, R. Nahum of Hurodna. On Friday evening after the prayers, R. Nahum was quite late in returning home. For there were Jewish soldiers of the Russian army who came to spend the Sabbath in the town and rest a bit from their harsh army life; and R. Nahum busied himself finding homes that would take them in. He would not go home till he made sure that every soldier had a place to go, where he would receive Sabbath meals and find a place to sleep.

Several hours passed before R. Nahum came home, his task completed; and as soon as he entered he stood and chanted the *kiddush* over a cup of wine (the blessing to declare the Sabbath day holy). It pained the pious hassidic rabbi, though, that his guest had been forced to wait so long because of him, before starting the festive Sabbath meal.

To prevent any bad feeling in his guest, R. Nahum began speaking: "Listen now, I pray you, to what I will tell you: This is what the great tzaddik R. Alexander Ziskind (of blessed memory) used to do: On Friday he would go to the *mikvah* (a body of water for immersion that cleanses spiritually), then put on his Sabbath clothes and go to the synagogue. In his hand he carried a parchment scroll with *shir ha-shirim,* the Song of Songs, written in the same script as a *séfer torah.* He himself had written it, with the same holiness that a scribe invokes in writing a *séfer torah.*

"In the synagogue he would chant the words of the scroll slowly, with immense sweetness, great fervor and awesome devoutness. It is told that the angels on high would then stop uttering their own Divine song, and come to stand and listen to his *shir ha-shirim* (as you know, its inner meaning is the most intense holiness in all the Bible). For that chanting of his would split and pierce the heavens.

"All that, however, was in earlier generations, when they did not have the burden of putting up Jewish soldiers from the Russian army of the czar, always to make sure that they receive meals and have a place to sleep. In our generation, though, I am quite certain that R. Alexander Ziskind would not have hesitated a moment to break off his exquisite, mellifluous chanting of *shir ha-shirim* and hasten about to save the life of a Jewish soldier in need of rest on the holy Sabbath to revive his spirit."

Well (Reb Aryeh concluded) I accepted it as a firm principle that going on the Sabbath to those who 'sit in darkness and the shadow of death, prisoners in affliction and irons' (Psalms 107:10) to take care of their physical and spiritual needs, is a sacred task. I rated it above the lovely Sabbath meal, even when it is accompanied by the sweet hymns of *z'miroth*.

a royal crown

Benjamin Kaplan was a member of the Irgun (*irgun tz'va'i le'umi*, "National Military Organization," one of the two underground movements that fought the British rule till 1948) who eventually fell in the successful battle for Ramle. In his earlier years he was seized by the British and sentenced to life-imprisonment. Afterward he used to say, "When I found myself behind bars, sentenced for life, it was only thanks to our good rabbi that my spirit was not broken and I didn't lose all hope. Whenever he came to see me he would say, 'You have an advantage over your brethren. In the Almighty's eyes you wear a royal crown, because you are imprisoned for life.' Because he said this in all sincerity and utter certainty, it gave me a sense of pride; it just heartened and strengthened me."

the true door to open

On one Sabbath that came in the middle of Passover he went to the prison for his usual visit; but this time he was curious to know how the prisoners had managed with their *seder* (the ritual celebration on the first night of Passover—in the Diaspora, the first two nights—which includes reciting the *haggadah,* drinking four cups of wine, eating matzah and bitter herbs, and having a festive meal).

One prisoner answered him with a smile, "We had a wonderful time, in high spirits. We observed the *seder* quite properly, with all the details. There was only one difficulty: When we said *sh'foch hamath'cha* we could not open the door..." (After the seder meal the leader recites *sh'foch ḥamath'cha,* "Pour out Thy wrath against the nations that do not know Thee, and on the kingdoms that do not call on Thy name..." It is a custom to open wide the door while this is said, to show that when He protects us we fear no one. But of course the prisoners did not have the key to their door.)

"You know," said Reb Aryeh, "you are making a mistake. Every man is put in a prison of his own self. He cannot leave it by going out of the door of his house, but only through the door of the heart. And to make an opening for himself in his own heart—that anyone can do, even a prisoner behind bars. And then he will be truly free—in spiritual freedom."

a matter of life and death

The year 1937 brought bloody uprisings and riots in the land of Israel; and in the course of events five Jews were killed near Motza (on the outskirts of Jerusalem).

In those times Yeḥezkel Altman was a guard who had to defend Jewish convoys (buses, trucks, etc.) on their way up to Jerusalem. In doing his duty he shot at Arabs who tried to ambush the Jewish passengers. With their usual "even-handed" or "impartial" justice (that turned a blind eye to anything the Arabs did) the British arrested Yeḥezkel and put him on trial for his life, in February 1938.

With its customary "one-way mind" the British court of justice would not accept his argument that he had only defended the Jewish passengers in the convoy. Nor were the arguments of his defense attorney of any use. He was sentenced to death by hanging.

Yeḥezkel Altman accepted the sentence calmly, with a quiet courage that amazed the judges and all those present in the courtroom. But when the terrible news reached his mother in far-off Kishinev, in the Soviet Union, she veritably went out of her mind with the grief and anguish, and it was feared that her state of health might be permanently affected. For she thought that the verdict had already been carried out and the truth was being kept from her.

A short while afterward, however, the condemned young man's life was spared, when General Wavell, commander of the British armed forces in the Middle East, commuted his sentence to life-imprisonment.

It was close to the beginning of the Sabbath (Friday toward sunset) when Reb Aryeh learned of this. At once he hastened off to the prison and implored the warden to let the young man write a few words to his mother, to tell her the wonderful news that his life was spared. The warden refused: "You can write a few words yourself," he argued, "to tell his mother."

Reb Aryeh explained patiently: "First of all, the Sabbath is about to begin, and it is improper for me to write." (It was already past the time for lighting the Sabbath candles.) "Secondly, if she gets a letter written by anyone else, she will not believe it." (Reb Aryeh knew what efforts had been made to convince her that her son was still alive—to no avail.)

"But look here," the warden objected. "Even if I allow the prisoner to write a short message, the letter has a long distance to travel before it reaches his mother. Then why all the rush?"

"What you say is true. Yet still do me this favor and grant my request." And the warden gave way. (For Reb Aryeh knew that the condition of the young prisoner's mother was critical, and the letter he wanted was the key to her recovery. For this reason he did not hesitate to have Yeḥezkel write the note at a time when the observant Jew already desists from any activity forbidden on the Sabbath.)

Once the letter reached his mother, she quickly recovered and became her old calm self again.

the price of a hasty temper

This is something that his son R. Simḥa Sh'lomo Levin recalled:

Once I accompanied my father when he went visiting the prisons in the land. On the way we stopped off at the prison in Ramle. Joining us to take us around, the warden said, "Look: in that cell over there is a man who murdered his neighbor on the day before Yom Kippur (the Day of Atonement), after an angry quarrel with him over some garbage cans. He was sentenced to life-imprisonment; and I cannot understand what has happened to him. He was always a quiet man by nature, tranquil and refined. Yet now he is in the grip of a strong gloomy depression, and we fear for his mental health."

Without further ado my father went over to the prisoner to talk with him, and asked how he was. "I am not fit for you to talk to me," answered the man. "I am a murderer. I hate myself, because I could not control my evil impulses and my terrible anger. If only one of the people around me during the quarrel would have seized my hands and said, *Stop! what are you doing?*—if only someone would have stopped me—he would have prevented bloodshed. That man I killed would be alive today. What I did is unforgivable!" And with that he burst into tears and tore his hair in grief.

My father saw that in his depression this man was losing all faith in himself and giving way to despair, with not a shred of self-esteem left in him. So my father went to work to rebuild something of his shattered self within him:

"Look, you are not a murderous type at all. You did not lose all faith and hope in your fellow-man, to decide to kill in cold blood. You have only one defect: that you cannot control yourself. Well, that is what you have to work on while you are in prison. This is your life's task now, to repair and correct that defect." Then my father added, "Believe me, all is not over and lost for you. Struggle and strive to repair and improve your character, and after you have paid your debt to society for your sin of heedless haste, you will be fit to live among people again."

For a while the two sat together, silent and thoughtful. Then my father spoke again: "You know: in the Torah there is something puzzling. When our father Jacob (the Patriarch) lay on his deathbed and gave his twelve sons his final blessings, he said to Reuben, his eldest son, *Unstable as water, you shall not have pre-eminence* (Genesis 49:4). Our Sages explain that it means Reuben was punished; he lost his rights as the eldest son (firstborn)—because he interfered in his father's marital life after Rachel died. Yet the Talmud states, 'Whoever says that Reuben sinned is only making an error' (*Shabbath* 58b). Now, how can that be?

"The answer is that Reuben had a bad trait, a defect in his character: he was 'unstable as water.' He was not bad in his nature or personality; he just had the one unfortunate trait, that he was terrribly quick-tempered. Well, as the eldest son he should have had certain privileges. He should have been the ancestor of the kings of Israel, not his brother Judah. But because of the defect in his character he lost all that. So this is really what Jacob told him: Reuben my son, it is not that you are a sinner or a criminal; but your problematic character trait has prevented you from fulfilling the tasks and enjoying the privileges that were destined for you; and for this reason they have been given to your brother."

From the time he heard this, the prisoner's mind was calmed.

the key that unlocked hope

One evening, Abraham Ber Weisfish, an upstanding member of Jerusalem's religious community, met him walking in the Bukharan quarter of the holy city. "Rabbi," he asked, "what brings you here?"

"Come with me," said Reb Aryeh, with his infectious smile, "and you will see." The two walked on together, and soon entered a wedding hall. People were gathered there for a wedding celebration, but the marriage ceremony had not yet taken place. When the bridegroom saw the good rabbi, his face beamed with happiness. He called Reb Aryeh to his side, put his arm around his shoulders, and called the gathering to attention, demanding silence. Then the bridegroom spoke:

Under the British mandate, he said, he had joined the ranks of the red-clothed "élite" in the Jerusalem prison: He had been sentenced to death. As he sat in his cell brooding over his fate, he found himself broken in spirit and plunged into the blackest melancholy. All he could see ahead was his imminent end.

Came the first Saturday after his sentence, and Reb Aryeh appeared at his cell. The good rabbi talked long and earnestly with him, trying to imbue him with courage and hope—but to no avail. The young man could see before him nothing but the gallows. Finally Reb Aryeh said, "Promise me that you will invite me to your wedding!"

"What?" asked the young man. "What was that?" It was the last thing

Reb Aryeh participating happily at a wedding of Sephardic Jews, beside one of their noted rabbis.

he had ever expected to hear. He was not even very friendly with any particular girl. Yet Reb Aryeh repeated his request with the utmost confidence, as though it were the most natural request in the world.

Well, said the bridegroom, that did it. The wrinkled face of the dear rabbi, half worried, half smiling as he asked this of him, was more than he could resist. He gave his promise, as against his will, a sunlight of hope began shining in his heart.

The good rabbi's hope and cheer stayed with him till he found his sentence commuted, and the end of the mandate brought his release. And now, the happy bridegroom concluded, he had kept his promise....

it had to happen this way

The Israeli poet Miriam Yellin-Shtekelis once related: My father was an eldest son who came from a long line of eldest sons, going back many generations. It was the special privilege of every eldest son in turn to keep a precious *séfer torah* in his possession that was written by R. Feivush the son of R. Sh'muel of Brisk, the head of the Jewish community in Cracow, who died in 1604. At the risk of his life (because the Soviet Union punished all religious observance and confiscated such objects) my grandfather R. Baruch Z'ev Wilensky took it out of Russia; but he died on the way to the land of Israel, and it was my father who brought the precious scroll here. For safekeeping he entrusted it to the large (main) synagogue in Tel Aviv.

In the summer of 1935 my father was not in the best of health, and the doctors advised him to go abroad for a long vacation. Before setting off he came to Jerusalem and told me, "Come with me to Tel Aviv, to have a look at our *séfer torah*. I have a feeling that the velvet covering is very worn and threadbare. You take the measurements and order a new covering made here in Jerusalem. When I come back I will give the scroll to a scribe to check the script and fix it where it might be necessary. I also plan to have a little silver plate made to decorate it, with the name of R. Feivush on it—that he wrote the scroll—and our family name."

I felt very happy to hear this. Never in my life had I seen the Torah scroll, our family heirloom. So off I rode with my father to the large synagogue in Tel Aviv, and for the first time in my life I held it in my hands, to take the measurements for the covering. The appearance of that *séfer torah* etched itself into my memory: The covering was of reddish-purple velvet; the *rimmonim* (ornaments around the top parts of the poles about which the parchment scroll was wound) were of silver darkened with age; and the letters of the Torah itself were incredibly beautiful. It was a small scroll, with a unique charm of its own.

Once back in Jerusalem I hastened to buy velvet of the same color, reddish-purple; and a few days later I ordered a covering made from it at a workshop.

My father returned from his trip a sick man, in need of surgery, and he entered the Hadassah hospital immediately. The operation was successful; but alas, the night afterward his heart stopped beating.

There were family problems and burdens after that, as well as a trip abroad that I had to take. And so for a while the family Torah scroll went completely out of my thoughts. It was only three months later, when I returned to Israel, that I rode with my husband to Tel Aviv, to the large synagogue. But a jolting surprise awaited us there: The *séfer torah* was gone!

It is hard to say what exactly happened to it. The custodians told me that for the high holy days (Rosh haShana and Yom Kippur) they always lend out Torah scrolls to all kinds of small synagogues and temporary congregations that form just for the holy days. Apparently someone borrowed the *séfer torah* and forgot to bring it back.

We demanded that the custodians of the large synagogue should help us look for it. But they argued that as unpaid keepers they were free of any obligation in the matter, and would hardly lift a finger. We scurried about as best we could, looking for that Torah endlessly—and could not find it. Once we rode back to the large synagogue, and it suddenly occurred to me to ask one of the custodians, "Is there perhaps another *aron kodesh*, another holy ark where Torah scrolls are kept, except this large one?"

The custodian let out a shout of joy and ran—and we after him. We descended to a large basement, and there, at the bottom of another *aron kodesh*, I found the two *rimmonim*, the silver ornaments darkened with age, and another decoration of tiny bells—but nothing more. At that point we stopped looking for the Torah; in my heart, however, the grief did not stop, nor my feeling of blame and accusation toward those custodians.

I have kept the two *rimmonim* and the small decoration with me since then, safe and sound. Yet more than once I asked myself: Perhaps I ought to arrange some better, more distinguished place for them to be kept safe?

One evening I happened to be sitting with Reb Aryeh Levin in his home, and suddenly I felt a need to tell him the whole story. In his usual way he listened patiently till I was done. Then he said, "*Nu*, what is the great value of the *rimmonim*? They are just a bit of silver; and how much is silver worth? What else is there to consider?—the *séfer torah*. So what are the possibilities? Either it is being used somewhere in a synagogue, and then all is well; or Heaven forbid, it is not being used. *Nu*, perhaps a number of letters in it became spoiled, and it is not fit to be used in a synagogue, to read from it? Who knows?"

The pious rabbi sat there lost in his thoughts, and we were both silent. Then he continued, "Why do you grieve and suffer so much over it? Why do you agonize and inflict pain on yourself? That is forbidden—plainly forbidden! Stop making yourself suffer.... Look: let us assume that someone took the *séfer torah* deliberately; he stole it. Suppose you had been able to have the new covering finished and put it on the scroll. Then he would far more certainly have taken it."

Again he sat there quiet, thinking. And finally he added, "But in any case, what do we know? What does a human being ever know? Perhaps it had to happen this way."

I mulled over those last words of his, "Perhaps it had to happen this way." They were simple words, that he said with such conviction, with sincerity and inner peace. For me they were a healing, soothing balm.

The worry and pain that had ravaged my heart faded and melted away, as though they had never been. For in the voice of Reb Aryeh it seemed to me I heard the overtones and echoes of the voices of my forefathers, all the people who had kept and guarded the *séfer torah* through so many generations—all whispering to me, "Perhaps it had to happen this way."

the intuitive response

One member of the family, Rabbi Kugel, heads an organization (*t'nua l'hafatzath torah*) that sets up Torah centers (synagogues, schools, etc.) in far-flung communities throughout Israel. He took the time one day to visit a wealthy person who, he had reason to believe, would give generous assistance. To his dismay, however, Rabbi Kugel came up against a blank wall. Talk as he would, he could not prevail on the man to give a penny. At last he left, weary and dejected; and as he was nearby, he came to Reb Aryeh's home to rest a bit.

The good rabbi looked at his relative sitting there in a cloud of silence, and suddenly he said, "I thought of an interesting point in the meaning of a passage in Scripture: *It is better to take refuge in the Lord than to trust in man. It is better to take refuge in the Lord than to trust in* n'divim (Psalms 118:8-9). Why does Scripture repeat the thought? The second time it speaks of *n'divim,* generous men who give *n'davoth,* donations. Even if you have reason to put confidence (*livto-ah*) in them, because they gave you a *havtaha,* a promise (to contribute support), it is yet better to trust in the Lord."

Rabbi Kugel found solace in these heartfelt words, that applied so accurately to his own unpleasant experience. To this day, though, he does not know what made Reb Aryeh say this to him just then.

the Scriptures left no doubt

The Blondheims in Jerusalem had been close friends of his (and of his family) for years, and when Mrs Blondheim found herself in a quandary, it seemed only natural to turn to Reb Aryeh.

The phone message from New York had been brief, but enough to leave her hardly able to think clearly. A member of the family had called to inform her that her father was dead, and the funeral was to be at two in the afternoon the next day; and she should please try to fly over.

But should she? In 1962 she was the mother of four young children. Did she have the right to leave her husband (a professor of nutrition at the Hadassah Medical Center) and some odd assorted neighbors burdened with the little children, while she went flying off in her grief? And what if she decided to fly and plane connections were bad, and she arrived too late for the funeral? There was no point in going post-haste merely to join her mother in New York for *shiv'ah,* the seven days of mourning. She could observe the period of mourning just as well in her own home.... What to do?

Without hesitation, Dr Blondheim sent his wife to see Reb Aryeh—who told her to weigh two factors and decide which she found more important: her mother's wish to have all her children with her at the burial, or her sense of duty not to burden her husband and neighbors with the four little children. (Of course, he added, from the point of view of Jewish law, it would have been better if the family in America had not informed her of the death immediately. Had she learned of it after thirty days, she would have had no need to observe any formal acts of mourning).

She could only reply that her mother would not have allowed anyone in the family to call her unless she really wanted her to be with her.... And yet she could not decide.

Now Reb Aryeh had but one answer: It was time to "cast the Scriptures". He would use the method (described above on page 165) by which he had identified twelve soldiers slain in the battle for Gush Etzyon, in the 1948 War of Independence. He took out the precious Hebrew Bible printed in Amsterdam 1701 (picture on page 166) and opened it at random. Seven times he turned the yellowing pages haphazardly, this way and that, his mind completely a blank. Then he followed the rest of the procedure which, according to tradition, R. Elijah the Gaon of Vilna had originally used, and he arrived at Genesis 42:16, *Send one of you*...

For Reb Aryeh there was no more doubt. The Scriptures told her to go. Yet, she now thought, with the funeral scheduled for two o'clock the next day in New York, would she ever get there on time? Heaven only knew.... She returned home, and set off at once with her husband for the American consulate, located then (1962) in the Jordanian sector of Jerusalem, to get her passport renewed. Then they rushed back to a small local travel agent, only to hit an impasse: They explained the urgent need for her to get to New York without delay. But the travel agent could find no regular flights to New York scheduled out of the Lod airport that day or night. They urged the agent to keep searching and hunting; and at last he came up with something: At about one or two in the morning a plane was coming in from Japan, Bangkok and Teheran, which would fly on to Paris. If Mrs Blondheim's luck held, she could catch a plane there to New York and arrive approximately in the nick of time.

At one in the morning, Dr and Mrs Blondheim were at the Lod airport, her bit of luggage checked through and her ticket bought; and she flew out on the plane from the Far East. In Paris there were further mix-ups and problems, whose memory has grown dim with time; but eventually she was on the plane from there to New York's Kennedy airport. If the arrival would be on schedule, she could arrive in good order for the funeral.

Alas, as happens all too often, the plane was delayed, and Mrs Blondheim arrived not too calmly. It was definitely too late for her to get to the funeral services in Manhattan. To her relief, however, she found a member of the family waiting for her with a car, and he drove her directly to the cemetery. They met the funeral procession arriving from Manhattan — and Mrs Blondheim's mother found her earnest wish fulfilled: to have all her children with her when the beloved head of their family was brought to his eternal rest.

As soon as she reasonably could, Mrs Blondheim called her husband by transatlantic telephone and told him how everything had turned out, after all those hectic hours. Heaving a vast sigh of relief, the doctor hurried off to tell Reb Aryeh. As the saying goes, the good rabbi never batted an eyelash as he listened to the tale of all the tension and uncertainty that Mrs Blondheim had experienced.

"But of course," said the good rabbi, with his little smile. "It had to work out. How could there ever have been any doubt? When we cast the Scriptures, it said she should go!"

he was sure to be there

To one member of *le-ḥee* (*loḥamey ḥéruth yisra'el,* "Fighters for the Freedom of Israel," one of the underground movements under the British mandate) a son was born on the first of Adar, the very day that two others of the underground movement, Meir Feinstein and Moshe Barzani, having been condemned to death by the British, blew themselves up in the prison rather than let the British hangman touch them.

One week later, on the eighth day of his life, it was time for the newborn child to be circumcised, to be entered into the "Covenant of Abraham." The infant's father came by car to take Reb Aryeh and the aged father of Moshe Barzani to the happy event. On the way, Mr. Barzani (still immersed in grief over the death of his son) asked, "Is Tz'vi Shohami coming?" A fellow-member of *le-ḥee,* Tz'vi Shohami had been a very close friend of his son. "I don't think so," the infant's father replied.

At that, Reb Aryeh noticed that the old man seemed stricken with added sorrow. "On the other hand," said the rabbi, "Elijah the prophet is very certain to come. We don't see him, but he is present in spirit at every circumcision." The aged grieving father smiled and felt more content.

he readily agreed

Until his untimely death Yaakov Herzog (son of Israel's former chief rabbi) was the director-general of the prime minister's office. Once he told me: "Reb Aryeh was not an ordinary person. He was an angel. His wondrous, magical effect on all those around him was immense and extraordinary.

"You know: in the days of the mandate the British authorities turned one day to my father (then chief rabbi) and asked him to use his influence with Reb Aryeh and persuade him to visit the Arab prisoners as well (when he made his regular visits to the prison camps). Why?—because they realized that his cheerful, radiant face and clear optimistic look were a heartening and soothing balm. But they were afraid that if they asked Reb Aryeh directly he would refuse. So for humanitarian reasons they were taking the liberty to ask the chief rabbi to kindly give his help in the matter.

"Well, my father went and made the request to Reb Aryeh—and he agreed readily and willingly. After all, said he, they were also human beings, formed in the image of God."

a practical sense

A senior civil servant (in the government's employ) received an offer to take a respectable position with a private commercial firm. So he turned the matter over in his mind, whether he should accept the offer or not. At last he decided to ask Reb Aryeh's advice. For not only was Reb Aryeh a profound tzaddik, but he also had an unusual practical sense.

There was only one thing that made the man hesitate: How could he explain to Reb Aryeh that to him it was a very important consideration that the new position offered a salary amounting to some 2,000 Israeli pounds a month? He knew very well that Reb Aryeh managed on a monthly salary of about 100 pounds! How would the tzaddik ever respond to his problem?

Nevertheless, he decided to go ahead and talk openly with the pious rabbi. Forcing himself to overcome embarrassment, he told Reb Aryeh all. "Well," said the good rabbi, "and how much do you earn now?" Still fighting embarrassment, the man replied, "about 1200 pounds."

"Is that gross or net?" asked the good rabbi (before or after deductions —which in Israel can be dismayingly large). "Gross," answered his visitor. "Then it is certainly not enough for you," said Reb Aryeh simply.

The Talmud tells of one Sage (R. Ḥanina) who lived on a small measure of carob from one week to the next, yet his great merit in heaven brought sustenance to the whole world (Taanith 24b). Beyond any doubt Reb Aryeh was somewhat akin to him. Whatever was enough for himself, he understood and accepted how others lived.

a fit companion for the rebbe

One of the great, renowned ḥassidic leaders in Jerusalem, a *rebbe* descended from a long line of distinguished ḥassidic leaders, used to come regularly to visit Reb Aryeh at his home, and the two used to sit alone for long hours, talking in absolute privacy.

This famed *rebbe* would himself sustain tens of thousands of his followers with advice and words of encouragement and cheer. When he needed a companion with whom to sit and talk over matters of importance, he went to see Reb Aryeh....

as long as there is someone like him in the world

Among Jerusalem's myriad citizens there was one man who had escaped alive from the Warsaw ghetto and then survived the Nazi hell in Auschwitz. Once he said: "When my entire family perished in the Nazi holocaust, I thought: What desire have I to live? What for? I even wanted to take my own life. But once I came to know Reb Aryeh my viewpoint changed. I said: If there is someone like him in the world, then the world is again a pure, good place. On his account alone it is worth living. So it was he who gave me new life and spirit."

the Hereafter is also a fine world

A young man had business interests that took him from Israel to the United States. There, however, he contracted a serious illness for which medical science had no cure. The truth could not be kept from him; and as might be expected, it threw him into a deep melancholy. Knowing that he had not much longer to live and not wanting his life to end abroad, he returned to Jerusalem.

There he went to see Reb Aryeh, who would surely listen patiently to his heart's woe. Well, Reb Aryeh quickly realized that there was no room here for idle optimism or the encouragement of vain hopes. Reality had to be faced and accepted.

To the young man's surprise, the pious rabbi began speaking about *olam ha-ba,* the "world-to-come" where, as the Oral Torah firmly and unshakably teaches, all human beings find eternal life according to their merit, when death makes them leave the physical body behind on earth. Simply and clearly Reb Aryeh explained that this "world of truth" which lies ahead for us all is also a full, complete world, a universe in its own right—and most certainly there is life after death. To this great principle of our faith he firmly directed the young man's thoughts.

From one heart to another went his words, and the young man left with a new inner peace.

the apology

After Israel's noted chief rabbi, Isaac Herzog, died Reb Aryeh made it a habit for many years to visit his widow every Monday without fail, to ask how she was and keep up her good spirits. It was a custom he kept faithfully, till a short time before his last illness, from which he did not recover.

The day before Rosh haShana, the solemn festival that would begin a new Jewish year, and only a few months before his own life was to end, he telephoned Mrs Herzog and apologized for not coming any longer to visit her, because his physical condition made it impossible....

"out of the depths"

On one of his visits to the Hadassah hospital in Jerusalem, he learned that my aunt was there—Rachel Kook, the wife of the rabbi of Tiberias, R. Raphael Kook—awaiting an operation. He went to her at once, to visit, talk, and give her some needed courage.

"May you be blessed for coming here," said my aunt. "I feel so depressed and miserable, knowing that I am going to the operating table soon—and only last night I dreamed that I was worsening and collapsing, and falling down, down into an abyss..."

"But on the contrary," Reb Aryeh rejoined, "that is a reason to be happy. It is a good omen for you, because we read in the Book of Psalms, *Out of the depths I have called to Thee, Lord. O Lord, hearken to my voice* (Psalms 130:1-2). The dream shows that your prayer is reaching Heaven."

"don't be angry with me"

There is an incident that Abraham Krinitzi (former mayor of Ramat Gan) recalled:

I once succeeded in persuading Reb Aryeh to come to Ramat Gan and take a rest from all his wearying labors. I argued, I urged and I pleaded;

and with great reluctance he finally agreed, so that I should not feel chagrined at his refusal. On a bright sunny day he arrived and entered a convalescent home in Ramat Gan that was specifically for rabbis—a quiet, charming retreat.

Something most amazing happened, however. He found no rest in the rest home. He became dispirited and went about looking miserable. With great difficulty I managed to get him to explain. "What am I doing here?" he asked. "I sit and I eat and I drink." (Don't ask how little food he took.) "No one comes to pour his heart out to me. I don't have the opportunity to do a single thing for anyone, to help a single human being. At this very moment, someone is quite likely coming to my home to talk out his troubles with me—and the door is shut. He will wonder: why is the door of my home suddenly shut? And he will leave with nothing for his troubles.... No, dear Abraham. Don't be angry with me, but I cannot go on staying here...."

He left the convalescent home and returned to his dwelling in the Mishk'noth section of Jerusalem, his simple room or two with the furniture that dated back to his wedding days, more than fifty years before—the modest home that was always sparkling clean, because he cleaned it with his own hands, not wishing to have anyone serve him.

Indeed, Abraham Axelrod, who knew him very well, once wrote: Reb Aryeh had a philosophy of life all his own. As he saw it, life's main purpose is to help others. If a few days went by and he found no opportunity to help someone with a bit of advice, a kind word, or simply with a little chat to make a person feel better, he began to wonder if he was perhaps superfluous in the world, and the Almighty had no further use for him on earth. And when people crossed his threshold from early in the morning till late at night to ask advice, guidance and all kinds of personal help, Reb Aryeh felt they owed him nothing. On the contrary, he was so greatly indebted to them, because they gave him the blessed opportunity to do mitzvoth.

16
Within the prison walls

the "congregation" he chose

It was not widely known that Reb Aryeh began his activity as a rabbi at the central prison in Jerusalem, when he took to visiting regularly the Jewish convicts there.

Except for two individuals and a few members of the Palestine Communist Party, there were no Jewish political prisoners interned there at the time. They began arriving only in 1931. Till that year the prison held only a few Jews occasionally, sentenced to longer or shorter terms of detention for their acts as thieves, rapists, robbers, and even murderers.

This was the "congregation" that Reb Aryeh wanted to serve as rabbi. As a rule, throughout Jewry, the congregation chooses the rabbi. Here it was the other way around.

The British authorities under the mandate were most particular to be objective, fair, and even-handed. So they realized that just as there was a kadi (Moslem religious head) who visited the Moslem convicts, and nuns who visited the Christian "residents," so they had to provide a man of religion for the Jewish inmates.

The authorities of the British mandate turned to the office of the chief rabbinate and asked for an ordained minister to be sent to the prison on regular weekly visits, every Saturday. There was no rabbi to be found, however, willing to give up his Sabbath rest and spiritual ease and delight, to go every single Saturday morning, as well as on the days of *yom tov* (festivals), to say his morning prayers with a bunch of criminals.

Unable to find even one Jewish minister for the task, the chief of all the Israeli (Palestinian) rabbis, R. Abraham Isaac Kook, then suggested that Reb Aryeh should be asked. For he knew well this pious man's nature.

Devoted as he was then to activities of charity and kindness, Reb Aryeh responded favorably to the request of the chief rabbi's office, and undertook the task—with no thought whatever of receiving anything in return. And so he began visiting the people whose horizon ended at iron bars and concrete walls.

If the truth must be told, though, the first convicts who came to the prison synagogue room (chapel) to join him in prayer on Saturday morning, would sit there smoking openly, brazenly, in heedless violation of the holy Sabbath. For them it was only a social gathering, a chance to sit and chat. Reb Aryeh chided them about their behavior, gently but firmly, as he greeted them with a friendly "Good Sabbath" and asked them to join him in the prayers as a congregation.

In the course of time, however, he developed his own special bond of friendship with them—to such an extent that he aroused jealousy in the Moslem convicts. Why?—because inside the prison walls nothing could be hidden from the eyes of the inmates, Jewish or Moslem. And the Moslems saw only too clearly the difference between the kadi, their own precious religious leader, and the gentle pious rabbi. When the kadi came, in his great kindness he deigned to put out his hand and let the prisoners kiss it. Reb Aryeh, following his lifelong habit, would take a prisoner's hand in his and pat it absent-mindedly while he spoke words of encouragement to cheer the man's spirits.

"You certainly have good fortune," the Moslem convicts would tell the Jews, "to have a rabbi like that. Just go take a look at that kadi of ours, so tall and stately, blown up with his pride. He murmurs words of prayer for us; but did you ever see him sit down and talk with us? We never hear a sociable word out of his mouth. Just think: only now he went to see the Arab inmates sentenced to death. He left them without saying a thing to them. Nothing. Not a muscle ever moved in him. He never wants to meet or know our families.... Now, your rabbi is a small man, not tall; but he does big things..."

The jealousy soon turned to hostility. When the kadi came they would open wide the great doors of the prison, and he entered in his precious hauteur. For Reb Aryeh they opened only the wicket, the little door set into the main ones, and he had to bend down to go through. (No one ever noticed that he minded, though—because he didn't.)

In the beginning of the thirties, as the British started bringing political prisoners there, the relationship of the authorities to Reb Aryeh had to start changing too. These new prisoners were no ordinary criminals but solid citizens of the *yishuv* (the Jewish settlement) fighting for Jewish rights and fair treatment under the mandate. Soon enough they were complaining of the clear discrimination in the treatment of the kadi and Reb Aryeh on their regular visits—and the order was given to accord the pious rabbi the same respect as the haughty Moslem visitor. This was in fact the first battle in Israel to change the attitude of the British authorities toward a Jewish man of religion.

From 1939 on the "Jewish population" in the prison increased considerably, as the British stepped up their "arresting" activities (this was their way of dealing with Arab-Jewish conflicts and Arab uprisings). Then Reb Aryeh started a battle of his own—to get the Jewish inmates separated from the Arabs and kept in a ward of their own. The reason?—he discovered that the Arabs, given to sodomy, would victimize Jewish youngsters who were arrested for "illegal entry" into the land (a major crime in the eyes of the British, when in Europe Hitler was beginning his extermination work in earnest) and placed in the cells of the Arabs.

Reb Aryeh sent off an impassioned letter to Captain Worsely, the warden of the prison, who had served as a Christian army chaplain in the First World War. In the letter he wrote, "To my great sorrow I am not versed in your English language. I have therefore asked a good friend to write in my name. But I pray you: accept these words as though they were carved from my heart."

In addition to the letter, Reb Aryeh tried to influence an officer named Steele, in command at the prison, through his close Jewish friend Dr Ephraim Voschitz (an attorney). But when Steele learned what Reb Aryeh wanted, he answered his friend (with perhaps the typical crust of the colonial officer), "The moment that the Jewish prisoners will have separate quarters, I shall no longer be in command of this prison. The Jews themselves will then be in charge." Which meant that as long as he was there Reb Aryeh could hope for nothing.

The pious rabbi persevered, though, and at last his efforts bore fruit. In the main building of the central prison in Jerusalem, a room was assigned—to be known ever after as Ward 23—for all Jewish prisoners, criminal or political. All were lumped together, as "one happy family."

When Reb Aryeh saw his impassioned request finally granted, he sent off his next letter to Colonel Scott of Britain's CID (criminal investigation department) in Palestine, who had authority over the prisons in the land. What did the pious rabbi want now?—that a kosher kitchen should be set up for the Jewish inmates, complete with two sets of dishes (one for meat meals and one for dairy). With the British sense of justice and fair play, Colonel Scott answered Reb Aryeh that he understood the need for *sheḥittah,* kosher (ritual) slaying of fowl and animals to provide kosher meat; but why the need for different dishes, cooking pots and utensils? What was the basis or authority for that? Moreover, Reb Aryeh asked in his letter that the milk supplied the prisoners should be gotten only from Jewish farmers. "Where," the colonel wanted to know, "is it written that it is necessary to supply Jewish prisoners with Jewish milk?"

He asked for sources in authoritative Jewish religious law. And he did not have to wait long for his answer. Reb Aryeh went to work, poring over the large volumes of religious law and practice, finding and citing chapter and verse. And true to his sense of justice and fair play, Colonel Scott accepted the request. Thenceforth, he informed Reb Aryeh, milk for the Jewish prisoners would be ordered from T'nuvah, the national Jewish cooperative that marketed (and markets) dairy products, fruits and vegetables. In addition, he dismissed the Arab slaughterer of fowl and animals, and appointed one of the political prisoners in his stead, who was a qualified *shoḥet,* trained in the ritual slaughter of animals.

This was in effect the second battle for the rights of the Jewish inmate. Political prisoners and not ordinary criminals, the new "residents" in the house of detention regarded this as a matter of principle, apart from the requirements of religious law and practice. And it was a battle that Reb Aryeh had to wage alone, backed only by the strong will and demand of

203

the inmates themselves. For at this time the prisoners, with Reb Aryeh at their head, could get no help from the office of the chief rabbinate or from other national institutions.

when they wanted to replace him

As more and more political prisoners were given "residence" in the central prison of Jerusalem, it did not take the intelligence officers long in the British CID (criminal investigation department) in Israel, to discover that a special warm and close relationship formed between Reb Aryeh and these inmates, who were interned only because they could not accept the British "even-handed" treatment of the Jewish settlement. And the intelligence officers did not like it. They feared that this strong bond of friendship could be a source of trouble.

Plans began to be hatched to end Reb Aryeh's tenure in the position. It was concluded in the CID offices that he had held the post long enough. It was time to relieve him of his duties and find a replacement. But try as they would, he was not to be kept out of the prison. He had been in the post too many years, and he showed no inclination to retire.

Ordinarily Reb Aryeh was most humble; he shunned positions of importance and authority. But this was one position he wanted, with all his heart and energy. When it became British policy to deport prisoners to camps in Kenya and the Sudan, he strongly wanted to go with them; but various official forces were brought to bear to prevent him.

The time came when Colonel Scott, in command of the central prison in Jerusalem, wanted to sign a document formally appointing him the rabbi (chaplain) of the prison. But "someone" (evidently at intelligence headquarters) intervened and cancelled the plan—just as difficulties were placed in his path when he wanted to visit the political prisoners in Acco in the far north of Israel. This frustration pained him greatly, as we can see from his letter to Abba Ahimeyer (a professional journalist, when he was not in prison himself for his political views):

".... And now, dear friend, take a few moments off from your tasks, and give your kind attention to these words that I write you: Over two weeks ago, on my way to visit the prison on Sabbath morning, I met the [Sephardic] chief rabbi, Ben-zion Uzziel, as he was going to his morning prayer. He asked me if I would like to accompany him when he went to visit the prison in Acco—if the trip would not be too much for me. I thanked him cordially for his invitation, and told him that where people deprived of their freedom were concerned, nothing was an obstacle to me. I accepted his offer gratefully.

Incidentally, last Friday evening I met Dr Reuven Katznelson at the home of the [Ashkenazic] chief rabbi, Isaac Herzog. R. Herzog introduced me to him, and he was most happy to make my acquaintance, because his son Sh'muel had written him about me, telling him of the impression that my visit to the prison made. Dr Katznelson invited me to come to his office after the Sabbath, and to read his son's letter for myself. I did so on one of my trips on foot in the city, and read the charming words of his son, which moved me greatly. I then told Dr Katznelson that I was invited by Chief Rabbi Uzziel to go along with him to Acco. He telephoned R. Uzziel, thanked him for his visit to the prison in Latrun, and wished him success on his journey to Acco with me. The trip was set for the next day, the last day of the month of Sivan.

Today, however, I received word by telephone from the honored chief rabbi that no permit was received for me, but only for another rabbi. For me there was nothing at all, to allow me to accompany the chief rabbi.

Perhaps those people are right who believe that it is not worthwhile and not to their liking that anyone else but they should have any influence in such matters. Well, whatever the merciful God does is always for the good. But at least my intention and my wish were good."

One setback, though, did not daunt the pious rabbi. His visits between grey, dark prison walls continued, with his own brand of happiness, willingness and dedication. Time after time he came to bring comfort and cheer, to strengthen and lift up sagging spirits. And in due course, slowly and reluctantly his esteem in the eyes of the British prison authorities rose too. One thing at least was an absolute miracle: Never once was any search made in Reb Aryeh's clothing. The written messages he always carried in his deep pockets (and seams) could have caused him serious trouble.

As soon as they realized that he was approaching, the British sentries would spring to attention and open the prison doors wide for him—with an alacrity and despatch that they showed only for the chief warden.

But this period of activity came to its own natural end. In 1948 the State of Israel was proclaimed; the British left; and all political prisoners were set free. Reb Aryeh, however, did not retire. He had begun by visiting ordinary convicts and criminals; and now he resumed this "career" of his. In many of these prisoners he was able to kindle a light of faith in goodness, decency and honesty, as he continued his work in the position he had chosen for himself.

Only old age retired him, when after many years his strength failed him. But by then he was replaced by an official, recognized, salaried prison chaplain.

"the only vessel"

When he was asked to make a written record of the events in his life, he described his work as spiritual supervisor in the elementary Torah school Etz Ḥayyim, in Jerusalem; then he added: "On the Sabbath and festival days (*yom tov*) as well as weekdays, visited his brethren, despised and castigated human beings hidden away in prisons and interned in detention camps—for half a century, with no remuneration."

The year 1929 brought bloody riots, when Arabs attacked Jews in the holy land. One Jewish policeman, Simḥa Hinkes (a member of the then-illegal Haganah) went off on his own to take retaliatory action. Promptly and efficiently the British authorities arrested him, put him on trial, and sentenced him to death. Finally, though, his life was spared.

During the harrowing weeks that he spent between his arrest and the news at last that he would not be marching to the gallows, he came to know Reb Aryeh very well. One day he wrote a letter to R. Abraham Isaac Kook, then the chief rabbi of the land, telling him simply that Reb Aryeh was "the only vessel into which the tears of the wronged and oppressed can pour."

He never tired of collecting these tears, from the "despised and castigated human beings." And when he met people imprisoned for the sake of the Jewish homeland, the tears would come flowing back out of his eyes, directly into their sorrowing hearts. Fighters in the underground movement actually used to say that as soon as Reb Aryeh entered their prison cell, "we suddenly felt a moisture in our eyes."

never a prison rabbi, or even an assistant

One member of Israel's *k'nesseth* (parliament) expressed it this way: "Reb Aryeh was never a prison rabbi (chaplain). He was simply the rabbi of the prisoners (in every sense of the word). Once I turned to the man in authority over such matters and asked him to appoint Reb Aryeh—not the prison rabbi, Heaven forbid; this tzaddik would never hear of that—but at least the assistant prison rabbi, so that he could have some official standing and receive a proper salary. Nothing came of it. And actually, those who hesitated to give him an official position and title in the prison, were right. He was not suited for that. He was far above that. He simply was not a prison rabbi, but only and ever the rabbi of the prisoners.

"I will never forget the first time I met Reb Aryeh in the prison in Jerusalem, shortly before Ḥanukkah in 1946; nor the other times I saw him there, and in the Latrun prison. This I will say: In those moments when I looked at the rabbi's eyes, when I saw how he worshipped God, and I felt how much he loved people—I knew then that he was a true example of what the Bible calls a man of God."

And another person who knew him in the days of British internment added, "He was neither the rabbi of the prisoners nor the father of the inmates. Reb Aryeh was simply the *prisoner* of the prisoners. That, I think, is the title that fits our rabbi"—for he felt himself bound and sentenced by Heaven to serve and help them.

the ultimatum

Convinced that it was a holy cause, many devout, religious young men joined the underground movement, against the stifling rule of the British. Among them was a grandson of the noted Rabbi of Sochatchov (of blessed memory). Unfortunately, though, he was caught and taken to prison.

As soon as the boy's father learned of this, he rushed to Reb Aryeh, the only pious Jew and friend who had entrée into the prison, "Reb

Aryeh," he pleaded, "you must go to my son. He does not even have his *t'fillin* (phylacteries) with him. In the morning he won't be able to say the prayers without them, and he will be in anguish.... Here are his t'fillin; *please* go to him, I beg you."

Gently but firmly the good rabbi replied, "If you bring me food for him, I will go."

"Why worry about food? He will surely get something to eat there. But the t'fillin..."

"Oh, the t'fillin are important. But he has to eat also, and most of the food there he won't touch, because he will not consider it reliably kosher. If you bring me something for him to eat, I will go."

side-effect

As he became throughly involved in helping the prisoners from the battle of the underground movement against the British rule, there were sometimes unexpected side-effects. During the week, of course, he continued his regular work as "spiritual supervisor" at the Etz Ḥayyim elementary school. When one of the instructors learned of the good rabbi's devoted

The dolorous building of the central prison in Jerusalem, located in the "Russian compound." Here the British herded the many fighters in the underground movements whom they caught; and here Reb Aryeh came faithfully every Saturday morning to bring cheer, transmit messages, and lead the men in prayer.

help to those prisoners, he was greatly disturbed. He was a member of the religious camp that roundly condemned such an underground organization as *étzel* (*irgun tz'va'i le'umi*), to which many of Reb Aryeh's "customers" belonged. After reflection, this instructor decided that either Reb Aryeh must be dismissed from Etz Ḥayyim, or he himself must leave.

In his dilemma the man went to B'ney Brak to ask the *Ḥazon Ish* (the world-renowned scholar R. Abraham Isaiah Karelitz, of blessed memory). As he unfolded his problem, the Ḥazon Ish answered curtly, "Let Reb Aryeh be. He is a tzaddik." At that the instructor asked if perhaps *he* should leave. "Why, what are you afraid of?" asked the Ḥazon Ish, "that he will make an *étzel-nik* out of you?"

"do me a favor"

This is something that one of Jerusalem's scholars of the Hebrew language remembered:

On a Sabbath morning in 1937 I was going my way down Reḥov haN'vi'im (the Street of the Prophets). It was winter, and one of Jerusalem's rare snowfalls covered the city's streets. Not a soul was to be seen.

Suddenly I noticed a man, well wrapped, approaching me. When he came closer I saw it was a man of distinguished appearance (though rather short) wearing a *shtreim'l* (a flat hat with a black velvet center surrounded by a thick ring of fur, worn by the very devout on the Sabbath). He came over to me and greeted me with a cheerful "Good *Shabbos*"; then he asked me, "Perhaps you can help me?" Without any idea of who he was, I replied, "In what way, dear rabbi?"

"Well," said Reb Aryeh, "I am now on my way back from my visit to the prison, and there I promised to bring greetings and messages to twenty-five families in Jerusalem, from their sons who are confined there. I usually deliver these messages on the same day, during the Sabbath. But today, on account of the heavy snow, I am afraid I will not be able to visit all the families; and I fear that I may forget some of the names and addresses. Perhaps you would be prepared to memorize the names and addresses of five families, and after the Sabbath I will come to you to get them?"

Naturally I agreed. Do you know what my reward was? The time came when the British arrested *me* and threw me into a prison in the Old City, and my wife, parents and father-in-law had no idea in the world where I had disappeared. When I arrived at the prison I found about another hundred Jews there. In his usual way Reb Aryeh soon came to visit us. I went over to shake his hand. He looked at me a moment, then exclaimed, "Aren't you the man whom I once asked to memorize some names and addresses of prisoners' families for me?"

Hardly a half-hour passed before Reb Aryeh was on his way, as fast as his legs would carry him, to tell my parents and family where I was. And my parents came quickly in turn, to bring me a *tallith* (prayer-cape) and *t'fillin* (phylacteries).

When the British mandate ended I was at the prison in Latrun, and from there I was set free. From the bus into Jerusalem I got off at the neighborhood of Maḥaneh Yehuda, to visit Reb Aryeh at his home nearby and bless him for all he had done. When he saw me he embraced me warmly. "But do me one favor," he said: "I beg you: let me have the privilege to go tell your family that you have been let out."

the occasion of happiness

This is what Yaakov Kotik recalls:

The British military court sentenced me to death (for what I did to defend our homeland). Dressed in red prison clothes I was taken to the special cell for condemned men. Well, the very first Sabbath after the verdict was given, Reb Aryeh came to see me in my isolation, in the condemned men's cell. He just came in, took my hand between the two of his, and said, "They will not succeed in hanging a Jew in Jerusalem!" After praying with me, he put a *t'hillim* (Book of Psalms) in my hands. "Recite this," he told me; "say the words constantly, and have absolute faith that you will not go to the gallows."

"Dear rabbi," I answered, "at some time in his life everyone must go—sooner or later."

"No," he exclaimed. "You have to believe that you will not hang!"

He spoke quietly, but with so much faith that he infused me with the belief that I would remain alive. A sense of relief came over me, and my life alone in that condemned cell became easier; it no longer oppressed me.

Well, a week after the verdict was given, the warden informed me that the military commander had commuted my sentence to life-imprisonment. My red prison garb was exchanged for the usual brown clothes, and I was taken back to the regular prison ward. The very next Sabbath after the good rabbi had visited me, I was privileged to greet and welcome him together with the other Jewish inmates.

I do not have the literary gift or power to describe his sheer happiness. He kissed me; for a very long time he would not let my hand out from his; and he said with me the blessing of *ha-gomél,* that people recite when they come safely through a danger to their life: "Blessed art Thou, Lord our God, King of the universe, who dost bestow favor on the undeserving, that Thou hast done me every good."

When the British left and I was set free, it was a Sabbath day. I went to the home of Moshe Segal, where my ordinary clothes were kept, washed myself about a bit, and changed into them. Then I hurried off with Moshe to visit our good rabbi. We reached his home toward evening, and found him in the midst of *shalosh se'udoth,* the third meal of the Sabbath. He sprang up toward me and kissed me on the forehead, with tears in his eyes; and I cried a bit too.

Then he took out a bottle of wine. "Look," he said. "This bottle I bought on the day that your death-sentence was commuted. I bought a second bottle when the same verdict against Yeḥezkel Altman was similarly changed. I made a resolution to drink this the day of your release. The other bottle we will drink, if God wills it, on the day of Altman's release."

Between one thing and another it was soon time for the evening prayer-service (*ma'ariv*). We went out to go to the synagogue; and whomever the good rabbi met, he stopped him to tell him, "Share in my happiness!" The handshakes and congratulations were endless.

Ever since then I used to visit him on every possible occasion; and he would invite me to the happy events in his family. When his daughter was married I brought a small present; the rabbi, however, refused to accept it. "But dear rabbi," I told him, "this is not really a present. It is just the custom."

"*Nu,*" he replied, "if it is only the custom, very well."

A TZADDIK IN OUR TIME

one of the thirty-six

On the thirteenth of Adar 1938, Dr Abba Ahimeyer (a noted journalist) was freed from British imprisonment. The next day (Purim) he sat down and wrote to Reb Aryeh: "Yesterday I was released, and this morning I hasten to write to my dear, esteemed rabbi. Words fail me, my pen is inadequate to express my emotions, or even a thousandth part of what I feel in regard to my dear, cherished rabbi.... I do not know all the thirty-six hidden tzaddikim of our time (whose great piety and goodness sustains the world); but one of them I surely recognize. It has been my heaven-sent privilege to come to know him..."

they marked time by him

Once, within the prison walls, Yehezkel Altman asked a fellow-inmate, "What time is it?" The other prisoner laughed, a trifle sardonically: "What difference can it make to you? You, my dear friend, are sentenced to life-imprisonment. Why do you need to know what time it is? It would hardly mean anything to you to know the day of the week or the month."

"Of course you're right," said Yehezkel with a rueful grin. "I simply wanted to know how much longer it will be till Reb Aryeh arrives."

As another man who served his time under the British remembers, "We counted our days in prison according to Reb Aryeh's visits. On Sunday, Monday and Tuesday we used to say: He was just here yesterday or the day before to see us. From Wednesday on we would say: Tomorrow or the day after he will be coming to visit us again.... And every Sabbath day, when he finally came to be with us in the prison synagogue, it would have seemed to any outside observer that Reb Aryeh was the prisoner, and all the inmates around him were only visitors from the free world, coming to shake his hand."

when the British officer was convinced

On one of his many walks through the holy city Reb Aryeh crossed Chancellor Street one afternoon, only to find a police sergeant hurrying toward him. "Oh, I am sorry," said Reb Aryeh. "I broke the law and did not cross the street at a proper crossing. But I am ready to pay the fine, whatever amount you say."

"That," said the man, "is not why I hurried over to speak with you."

"Oh, no? Then why?"

"I have been waiting years for a chance to tell you of an incident that happened: In the time of the British mandate I was stationed as a sentry at the entrance of the 'Russian compound' in Jerusalem (where the prison was located). One day you came up and asked to be let through the gate, as usual, to make your weekly visit. But the British officer of the guard, standing next to me, informed you that this time no visitors were allowed inside, including those who had permit-cards for regular visits. He was therefore unable to let you in.

"You then began pleading with us. 'What will be with my children?' you asked. 'Will I be unable to see them at all?' So I answered you in Hebrew, to make sure the officer of the guard would not understand: 'It is possible to get into the prison through the wicket, the little door set into the eastern entrance to the Russian compound, near the city park. There the guard is not so strict; and those who hold permanent entry-permits are allowed inside. But take care. Riots have been going on inside, and your life can be in danger there, from the rioting, rebellious Arab prisoners. They have organized themselves into a band. If you want my advice, skip your visit today.' Your answer was, 'People on their way to do a mitzvah go unharmed'; and off you went on your way.

"Well, I explained to that officer of the guard how much it hurt you that you were unable to get into the prison. In his cold British manner he replied, 'I am certain he is doing it for the salary. He ought to look out for another position, that's all.'

"The next day, however, that officer came over to me and said, 'Do you know? I saw the rabbi inside the prison yesterday, after all. He must have succeeded in getting in through the side entrance—and the man just never paid any attention to the danger to his life. Well, I'm convinced: That rabbi is not doing this for the money. Just for a salary he would never put himself in danger like that.'

"There," the police sergeant finished; "that is the little incident that I have wanted to tell you for a long time. This is why I hurried over to talk to you."

Passover, the festival of freedom

Ever so often the British arrested and interned the "illegal immigrants" who came to Israel from Europe to escape Hitler's inferno, but without an official permit from London. Reb Aryeh worked day and night then to arrange for their release. Speed was essential, because the British gave each illegal immigrant exactly six days to have someone come forward and provide surety for him, a guarantee that he would be taken care of. If no one came forward to provide surety in six days, the immigrant was sent out of Israel—to the alternative of returning to Hitler's inferno.

So Reb Aryeh worked feverishly to find good uncles or big brothers (*et al.*)—people willing to go to police headquarters and sign a document of surety and responsibility, guaranteeing that their newly-arrived "relatives" would appear there at the proper time (as the law required).

This is how Yeḥezkel Altman recalled one related incident:

It was the very day before Passover, 1939. In just a few hours it would be time for the *séder*. The British caught sixty illegal immigrants who came from Iran. Having no other place to "lodge" them, the authorities put them into our cells, with us.

Well, the *séder* went off all right. We had special food packages from the community council, complete with matzah, *maror* ("bitter herbs"), wine, etc. We numbered then about forty political prisoners, and we simply shared everything with our "guests." But worry hung like a dark cloud over our hearts. Four days had already passed since these newcomers arrived, and no one seemed particularly concerned to find sureties for them to get them released.

The next day, when Reb Aryeh came to visit us and join in our prayer-service for the festival (*yom tov*) of freedom, we told him of the worry that was gnawing us. "Never you worry," he replied. "There is a great and mighty God in heaven." But we were reluctant to accept his assurance: How would he ever round up sixty families in such a short time, all willing to stand surety and ask for the release of their "relatives"?

Still, we put our worries aside for a while, as best we could, and joined him in the melodious festival prayers.

Noontime came, and we were stunned: Several hundred people were gathered in the prison courtyard. We could not understand it. Where did they all come from in just two hours (from the time we finished our prayer-service)? But there was not a soul we could ask. We could only watch in happy amazement as one after another of our sixty new arrivals went out, free.

The very next Sabbath Reb Aryeh came for his weekly visit, and we flocked around him burning with curiosity, asking questions. He kept quiet, however. So we pleaded with him to tell us what had happened; and at last he spoke: "As soon as I left you I headed for the Yeshiva Etz Hayyim (where, as you know, I have my permanent position). I asked all the older Talmud students there (fine youths) to spread out through the city and go to every synagogue of the community of Bukharim (the Jews from Bukharia). There they should speak from the pulpits and tell the people about the sixty new arrivals under arrest, and then plead with them to go to the prison at once to see their 'relatives' and demand their release under surety. (I needed Bukharian Jews because those sixty newcomers come from the same part of the world. I could not expect the police to believe that they are related to Ashkenazim.) That is all."

to the last house

In the years under the British mandate when Jews from all over the world, in desperation, had no choice but to make every effort to enter Israel illegally, a great number of them were caught and imprisoned. In the thirties it was the official British policy, however, that if any of them had close friends or relations in the land, they could get their imprisoned friend or relative released on their responsibility, and he was given a permit to stay.

This turned Reb Aryeh into a one-man "immigrant aid society": From such new prisoners he learned (and memorized) the names and addresses of appropriate people in Israel; and then off he went to get them to come and take the newcomers home with them.

One Saturday morning, on his regular weekly visit to the Jerusalem prison, he found a rabbi from Aleppo, Syria, who had discovered to his surprise that the British considered it illegal for him to enter on foot into his ancestral homeland. Gently Reb Aryeh asked: did he have any relatives or close friends in Jerusalem? Yes, said the Syrian rabbi: an old pupil of his was now a merchant in Jerusalem; the man lived in the Geula section. And he gave Reb Aryeh the man's exact name and address.

The prayer-service with the prisoners finished, his individual talks and warm handshakes with them all ended, Reb Aryeh left the prison and heard its gates shut behind him. He decided to go at once to Geula and find the Syrian rabbi's former pupil. And suddenly he stopped in his tracks: He had completely forgotten the man's name and address! For the first time that he could remember, his mental "filing system" had failed him.

What to do? He knew the British authorities would never open the doors and let him re-enter, to speak again with the rabbi from Aleppo. He was entitled to one morning visit, and that was that. Should he wait a week till the next Sabbath? The Torah's law demands that captives must be gotten out free as soon as possible.

Without another thought he set off for the Geula section and began trudging through the streets systematically, block by block, asking at every door for the former pupil of a rabbi from Aleppo. At last he found him— in the very last house in Geula!

behind bars

In the years of the underground movement against the British authorities, there was a "courier" or "contact-man" between the political prisoners and their families on the "outside": This was Yitzḥak Gorion, who as far as the British authorities knew, was an employee in the office of Max Zeligman, the attorney of the prisoners from the underground movement.

This is a fragment from his reminiscences:

On a burning, stifling summer day I had to travel in the prisoners' van (wagon) with half a dozen Arab prisoners, from the Serafin (Sarafand) internment camp to the central prison in Jerusalem. For once I myself was to spend time inside, as an inmate, since some of my activities had displeased the British.

Well, there was one prison officer of the Jewish faith there, in the Jerusalem prison, who could not realize that I was coming this time as a plain ordinary inmate. He knew me quite well from a previous term of duty in the Acco fortress prison, and then from his more recent turn of duty here. And he knew that whenever I came to visit, it meant a liberal "tip" that "crossed his palm with silver" (paper money, actually), to let me do my work smoothly. So he came over, as usual, ready to serve me with a cordiality that bordered on obsequiousness. There was nothing he was not ready to do for me. And since, as it happened, Max Zeligman the attorney was himself also "inside" then, for a six-month term, for helping in an operation to bring in Jews illegally—this underground officer was convinced that I had simply come to see Mr Zeligman, my employer.

So he blandly turned to the prison guard and told him to inform Mr Zeligman that there was a visitor to see him. Then he brought me a chair; and he said in a sad tone of apology, "Reb Aryeh is now in the prison synagogue with the Jewish inmates, and none of them will be willing to come out for a visitor as long as he is there." In his effusive friendliness he then suggested that I go to the nearby cafe for a cup of coffee, and come back in about half an hour.

Had it been four or five years later, I would not have hesitated to take full advantage of this Jewish officer's gorgeous mistake and walk off nonchalantly and disappear. It would have caused me no pain or strain if on account of his cordial friendliness he lost the single star that he wore on his epaulet. But in 1939 I was far from prepared for an anonymous life hidden in the underground movement.

Well, in only a few moments I saw Reb Aryeh coming from the corridor of the prison cells in his slow steady walk, accompanied by Zeligman. They perceived what my situation was, and did not make the same mistake as the Jewish prison officer. When he (poor fellow) now realized his error, Reb Aryeh smiled his usual spirit-lifting smile, but Zeligman burst into a guffaw of laughter. And behind the officer's back a fellow-prisoner whispered with appropriate clowning gestures, "All is prepared for your eminence. Welcome, and be you blessed, for honoring us with the distinction of your company." But most important: I saw the clear, radiant blue eyes of Reb Aryeh conveying solace and comfort straight into my heart, as I was about to cross the threshold into this little world of purgatory.

I still thank the God of Israel that as the door of Cell 48 opened to lead me into an unknown future, into life behind prison bars, in His kindness He sent me this good angel of His. As I bent down to go through the opening, Reb Aryeh gave me his comforting radiant smile. And something of his spirit stayed with me.

My memory leaps ahead now to Yom Kippur (the Day of Atonement) in 1939. Cell 29 was converted into the temporary synagogue of the central prison. We were all there, close together. Yet at the same time, how far apart one inmate was from another. Here was a man who had murdered his wife in cold blood and could not understand why they were bringing him to trial. "She was my own wife," he expostulated simply. There stood a man sentenced to fifteen years' imprisonment for the death he had caused. After years within these walls he still tried to convince every newcomer to our ranks that he was completely innocent. On the other side there was a group of hashish-smokers. In their cell you could still sense the sweetish fragrance of the drug. And over there was the "business group"; merchants and shopkeepers who went bankrupt (evidently by some sharp calculation) and were brought to the central prison the very day before Yom Kippur.

Side by side with the murderers and criminals of various kinds stood some of the finest sons of the Jewish people, who risked every danger (as fighters in the underground movement) to free their homeland from crippling foreign rule.... Over there stood a group of three students who invented a special kind of explosive for the *irgun tz'va'i le'umi* (*étzel*, the "National Military Organization"); and nearby, two who faced the gallows until their sentences were commuted to life imprisonment; Yeḥezkel Altman (Ben-Ḥur) and Yaakov Kotik....

Only one thing united this strange, motley crowd into a congregation of worshippers: the deep respect, even reverence that they bore for the kindly man, short in stature, who blended his voice with the sweet chant of the *ḥazzan* (reader), Max Zeligman, both the night before, when the solemn prayer of *kol nidrey* was heard, and again in the prayers of the day. Zeligman was worlds apart from the man who had murdered his wife. Yet they shared one thing in common: Both would speak with Reb Aryeh with a quiver of mingled affection and reverence.

While Reb Aryeh was chanting aloud from the Torah scroll, there was a whispered conference in one corner; and it was decided to make an earnest suggestion to our dear rabbi: that for the final prayer-service of Yom Kippur, *ne'ilah* (held shortly before evening) he should return homeward and join a congregation close to home—so that when the long and difficult day of fasting ended, he would not have to make the long wearying trip on foot from the "Russian compound" to his neighborhood of Mishk'noth. As soon as he finished his prayers he could go home and break his fast. (After all, he was no youngster.)

I used all my powers of persuasion to make him accept the proposal; and Zeligman and Moshe Segal agreed wholeheartedly. But Reb Aryeh only listened patiently and smiled: "By now I have established a tradition to be the *ḥazzan* (reader) here for *neʿilah*. I will not give that up." And there the discussion ended.

Later, alone with me for a moment, he whispered, "We will quite certainly have 'guests' tonight." He had no need to explain. By a ruling of the British mandatory authorities it was forbidden to sound the shofar (ram's horn) at the *kothel maʿaravi* (Western Wall) at any time—because "it disturbed the sensibilities of the Moslems." The Arabs learned early the value of screaming in hysterical protest when there was something they wanted; predictably, the British with their sense of fair play would "compromise," leaning over always a bit more toward the Arab side. Yet just as predictably, when Yom Kippur came and the greatest possible number of Jewish worshippers squeezed into the alleyway before the Western Wall, at least one dedicated militant spirit smuggled in a shofar—and at the precise moment Yom Kippur ended, its clear beautiful call was heard.

As we prisoners had forgotten but Reb Aryeh remembered, the rest of the "scenario" was just as predictable: The conscientious British police always seized the man (although, as in elegant football play, the shofar was instantly passed from hand to hand to someone quite far away); and shortly after Yom Kippur he would duly arrive at the prison in the Russian compound.

As usual, it was a member of *Betar* (B'rith Trumpeldor) who was brought to us. He did not recognize any of us, however, and his lips remained sealed. Then Reb Aryeh sat down by his side, took the young lad's hand in his, and began talking.... In a few moments the secret was out: We were privileged to have with us the shofar-blower of the *kothel* for 1939.

Now Reb Aryeh hastened to say goodbye and leave. The boy's family had to be told of his whereabouts, and legal counsel for him had to be arranged.

So ended a day when we could all see his profound love of fellow-Jews at work. It was a palpable force as deep as the abyss and wide as the sea, that radiated from his twinkling blue eyes, to enter and take possession of your heart.

a key of gold

This is how Herzl Rosenblum, who knew him well, once praised Reb Aryeh when he was no longer among us:

A people is fortunate indeed when it has, at the necessary moment, a rabbi of its own, a man with the power to reach all the hearts about him and merge them into one heart.

You can hardly find any two people in this country who would agree about one individual that he is extraordinary in his excellence—an individual in the government, in a settlement, in a political party. No two will ever agree.

Yet he was such a man. He kindled a flame of affection and harmony in our people's hearts. I was shaken and moved to see the vast multitude that would press around this "wonder rabbi": All were there—the indifferent and the inflammable, the deeply embittered and the sublimely hopeful, the cynical and the believing, the Litvaks and the Galitzianer; the Yemenites, Iraqis and Bulgarians; the Germans in their buttoned coats and the Siberians with their open chests. All milled about him yearning to catch his glance, ready to undertake any task, bear any burden if it would bring him pleasure. When you see this with your own eyes, how can you help being caught up and warmed by the atmosphere? All your reserves melt, and before you know it, you too are his *ḥassid*.

With him among us Israel was not bereft and abandoned. A miracle like him could still occur for our people. And this fact is enough to give courage and heart to every member of our nation. As we need air to breathe so do we need leaders in the image of Reb Aryeh Levin, who hold in their hands a key of gold to a person's heart.

"only to share in your plight"

He firmly rejected the praises that were heaped on him. When some spoke of him as "our rabbi" he retorted, "I am not a rabbi. I only went with you to share in your plight, to be with you." Once Israel Eldad, one of the founders of the underground movement *le-ḥee* (Fighters for Israel's Freedom), related:

He would take seven insults and seventy-seven rebuffs (from officials of every stripe) till he received a permit to visit an internment camp. True, he was the permanent rabbi of the prisoners in Jerusalem. But it was also true that he was never satisfied to stop short, to bound himself. He was indeed "imperialistic," seeking always new "territories" to conquer and make his own: the areas of suffering of Israel's youth—the general suffering of all, and the individual pain of a prisoner alone in his cell; but above all, their aching longing for Israel's freedom.

If you never saw a camp of prisoners receive Reb Aryeh and give him welcome, you cannot know the power of love and faith. And more: you cannot perceive that no Jew is ever a complete heretic, no member of our people ever loses and denies entirely his religious belief. Every member of Jewry truly has a potential share in the world-to-come, a place in the Hereafter—because in every Jew there is always one small corner hidden deep in his spirit, which the *shechina,* the Divine Presence, still illuminates, where faith still lives. It is only that outer layers upon layers cover it. When are the layers cast aside to let it be revealed?—when a tzaddik comes along and evokes it.

I have seen a youth strolling nonchalantly about a synagogue while the worshippers within were immersed in their Sabbath morning prayers, as he smoked a cigarette in fine careless style, in open defiance of the holiness of the Sabbath. And suddenly that same youth went dashing off madly into a nearby building in search of a *kippah,* a little skull-cap, so that with his head symbolically covered in reverence, he could make his way to Reb Aryeh and give him a friendly greeting, to be able to look at the rabbi's benevolent face and gaze a moment at his kindly eyes. If he had a heretic "philosophy," a "system of thought" that denied the God of Israel, he would be slightly embarrassed, and would rationalize his strange emotions: "Well, I am not revering Reb Aryeh as a religious man but as a human being." Needless to say, his heart would pay scant attention to what his mouth was saying. With Reb Aryeh a distinction like that was irrelevant....

The detention camp knew no happier days than those when Reb Aryeh came on a visit. Even the blind could perceive the *shechina,* the Divine Presence entering with him. No bodyguard or secretary came with him. He came only with his heart, ready to move others and be moved. How happy he was to see us—like a child that finds its mother.

He came laden with love, and left laden with love sevenfold, as everyone reciprocated and returned the affection he gave. He came laden with greetings, messages and news (from the inmates' families and friends), and left laden sevenfold with greetings, messages, and news. There was information that we would not have revealed to our nearest relatives, yet we entrusted Reb Aryeh with it. Addresses, names, dates—he had his own mnemonic devices and ways to remember.

Of a sudden he might begin calling out names of inmates (as though reading from a mental list), "Where is So-and-so? And what has become of So-and-so? Why is he not here?" Then away went some of us to find them. For at times he came unexpectedly, and the inmates were scattered about in the camp. But Reb Aryeh had to see everyone....

On a cold stormy day, when he himself came in a very thin frock-coat, he once rubbed my hands and asked anxiously, "Why have you come out like this without a proper overcoat? You are likely to catch cold!" For a brief moment I had the sensation that my mother and father were standing at my cradle, covering me warmly and fondling me with affection.

He would gather us into a congregation and lead us in *minḥa,* the ordinary afternoon prayer-service that so many ignore and treat with disrespect. Following the usual procedure we said *sh'moneh esré* (the "eighteen benedictions") silently, standing, and then Reb Aryeh repeated it aloud. Yet what was this? Why were there suddenly tears in one's eyes? Why did a lump suddenly form in the throat?

Reb Aryeh was simply saying the benedictions of the *sh'moneh esré.* "Restore our judges as at the beginning," he prayed to the Almighty. And it was as though you heard the prayer for the very first time. Only now the meaning of it dawned on you—here, in this British internment camp in the land of Israel, you realized in full the impact of those good plain words: "Restore our judges as at the beginning."

So it was with one benediction after another. Every word went simply from his heart, and our hearts responded, rising and falling like waves in the small building that served as our synagogue. This was the prayer of Reb Aryeh, like a seafaring vessel, rising and falling on waves of emotion.

After the prayer Reb Aryeh addressed us. Other rabbis spoke better than he did, in measured tones and cultured voice, with techniques of rhetoric. He had none of the speaker's gifts. In fact, his Hebrew had half an Ashkenazic accent (from the Eastern Europe of his youth) and many, accustomed to the Sephardic pronunciation current in Israel, could hardly follow him. Yet the people stood and listened, drinking in his words with parched spirits. For Reb Aryeh spoke from his heart, and he expressed the thoughts of our own hearts. In every talk he gave he managed to allude to the topics of the day that were of burning interest in the world of the inmates—a new decree by the British authorities, an armed clash or attack, brethren of ours who fell under fire, or condemned men who were executed.

Reb Aryeh lived with these happenings. He knew and shared our feelings.

I don't know how or why I deserved his attention, but from time to time he would tell me, individually, some thought or point to be found in the words of the Torah—apart from the Torah thoughts and lessons that he conveyed to all the camp prisoners. I felt myself unworthy of this honor. With very many others I retain a sense of my own worth and standing. In his presence I felt myself an empty vessel, gratefully receiving what he gave.

When the time came to depart, he found it hard to leave us. "I envy you," he would tell us. "I truly do." Again and again he assured us: "Here you have this immense opportunity to bear suffering actually for all the Jewish people. But as for me, what am I? I can only share somewhat in this suffering. Your merit before God is far greater than mine." We all knew he spoke the truth he felt. We believed him: indeed he envied us.

At last he walked toward the camp entrance. Yet again and again he would look back. Again and again he would shake someone's hand, cover it with both of his, and whisper once more the old Jewish saying, "God's rescuing help comes in the twinkling of an eye, in the twinkling of an eye."

Long after he left, the warmth of his visit remained with us, in the eyes that had seen him, in the hands he had held. The words of his prayer still vibrated and coursed through the heart. Our emotions overflowed and swirled about, to meet at one focus, one simple thought: It is good to be a Jew when there are Jews like that.

the young visitor

Once a week every prisoner was entitled to a visit by relatives and family. As a rule the relatives would bring packages of food and sweets that lasted a whole week. The family visit was a major event in the desultory camp life of the prisoners that bored them to distraction. A day or two before, they began looking forward to it in eager anticipation, and the effect of the pleasant experience lingered on till the next visit.

One man, however, received no visitors. Yaakov Becker lost his entire family in the Nazi holocaust. Alone he remained alive, and came to Israel. Enraged at the rule of the British that excluded other survivors of the Nazi nightmare, he threw himself into the underground movement with a furious intensity. But in time he was arrested, brought to trial, and sentenced to death. His sentence was commuted afterward, however, to life-imprisonment. And thus he was another inmate in the prison—but with one difference: When visiting day came around there was not a soul in the world to see him. All were called to come to the visitors' room to greet their relatives. He alone was left in his cell, with nothing to disturb his gloom and misery.

One day, though, lo and behold: he too was called to come to the visitors' room. It took him by surprise, and he couldn't understand it. Oh well, he thought as he walked to the room, it must be some mistake. But it was not. A young lad was standing in the room, waiting specifically for him. "Hello," said the youngster with a smile. "My father sent me to visit you and give you this package of food and sweets."

"What? Who in the world is your father?"

"Didn't you know? Reb Aryeh!"

Ever since then the youngster came faithfully every week on visitors' day, to ask if there was anything he needed or wanted, to chat with him generally and cheer him up, and of course to bring him a food package.

the hunger-strike

In 1939 the ninety prisoners in the Serafin detention camp declared a hunger-strike. Baruch Duvdevani, one of the ninety, described the event as follows:

Notable personages and men of distinction came to the camp to talk with us, to persuade us to give up the hunger-strike—because people were becoming alarmed. We had maintained it for ten days in a row, without a break. We listened to these important visitors—and continued fasting. It was a political battle we were waging against the foreign rule of our homeland, and we were steeled in our determination to continue this strike until they met our demands and released us from prison.

But then Reb Aryeh came. He wept like a child, and pleaded with us as a father might plead with his children. In a voice choked with emotion he said, "You know well that my life-spirit is bound up with yours. There is no way I can survive if you continue this strike!"

At one fell blow our resistance was broken. There was simply no heart left in us to go on with the hunger-strike. We could not bear to see him suffering so, and we yielded.

It would be hard to describe the utter happiness that wreathed his face when we agreed to take food at last.

he wrote nothing down

The year 1944 brought bitter fighting between the underground ranks and the British in the land. Many who fell were buried in secret and anonymously; only "Abraham the son of Abraham" (the appellation given to a convert to Judaism, when he must take a new name) was marked on their graves, to keep any possibly useful information from the British. Others were captured and taken to detention camps.

As one of the prisoners (later a member of Israel's *k'nesseth*) recalls, on the day before the festival of Shavuoth the Sephardic chief rabbi Ben-zion Uzziel came in the afternoon to visit them, accompanied by Reb Aryeh.

The chief rabbi addressed the prisoners, exhorting them to accept their ordeal cheerfully, since it is a principle of the Talmud that "the law of the ruling authority is binding." On the other hand, Reb Aryeh spoke on the theme that the Torah was given at Sinai (at the time of the Shavuoth festival) amid thunder and lightning. (He left it to the men to draw the possible conclusion that perhaps the Jewish people were to recover their homeland somewhat similarly, with the "sound and fury" of conflict.)

But Reb Aryeh never came primarily to preach sermons. After his talk he launched into the main purpose of his visit. He went to every one of the prisoners in turn to ask what he wanted or needed, what he might wish to have done for him, etc. One asked that a message of greeting be brought to his children. Another wished that his family might send him certain textbooks, so that he could continue his education. A third asked to be informed how his sister-in-law was faring. She had recently undergone surgery.

Reb Aryeh listened patiently, recording everything in his mind. Never once did he produce paper and pencil to write anything down. Where the prisoners were concerned, a phenomenal memory seemed to operate automatically. Names, addresses, facts, details—nothing was forgotten until the messages were delivered.

Only one man there began showing signs of growing impatience. Soon enough Chief Rabbi Uzziel approached Reb Aryeh: It was growing late; at sunset the festival of Shavuoth would begin, and travel would then be forbidden. They had better leave.... Unmoved, Reb Aryeh held his ground, speaking with every prisoner in turn, as though he were his own son.

the visit in the heat

Abraham Axelrod recalled: One day Reb Aryeh came to visit us in the prison camp of Latrun. It was an extremely hot day, and we had been going about dressed almost like Tarzan in the jungle. Suddenly we caught sight of Reb Aryeh approaching the camp, and we scampered to our quarters to get dressed properly, in shirts, trousers and of course hats or *kippoth* (skull caps, so that we should not appear irreverently before him). His sharp eye however, saw enough signs of our scurry and flurry, and he understood all. First he led us in *minha*, the afternoon prayer-service. Then he gave each and every one of us personal messages of greeting from families and dear ones. After that he began addressing us in his gentle voice that never chided:

"Today it is very hot, and you were going about dressed comfortably. If you changed your way of dressing because of me, that was not good. Perhaps my visits impose a burden on you."

Not another word did he say about it. He himself was dressed in his usual black coat and hat, and the temperature was surely higher for him than for us. And probably he would have liked to see us clothed according to his own ideas of proper dress (like his own children, for example). Yet he was unique in his capacity to understand us, and he accepted us as we were. This was the very main reason why we always had such a boundless love and admiration for him.

what his visit meant

This is perhaps the best description of all, written by a man who spent time in detention, of what a visit by Reb Aryeh meant to the men within the prison walls:

When the Sabbath came, the joy of this holy day of rest was embodied for us in the prison, strange as it may seem, by a human being of flesh and blood. He was an ordinary, everyday Jew that we would call ultra-orthodox—definitely old-fashioned. Like all very devout Jews he wore a long black coat, and on his head a black broad-brimmed hat, which he replaced on the Sabbath and festival days (*yomim tovim*) with the traditional *shtreim'l*.

About this Jew there was always a wondrous aura. It was as if the rays of some splendid holy light had been captured or absorbed somewhere in the far past, and now they were shining and streaming forth, returning, from the depths of the spirit that was embodied in this simple "old-fashioned" Jew. An intense luminosity flowed from that inner spirit to the man's countenance, and from his face on outward to the world about him, to serve the needs of human beings. Like the fire of the sun this luminosity would burst into our room within the prison walls, to assure those who lived in its darkness that there are lights and radiances in the world which will never be extinguished. So there would ever be hope for them too, who dwelt in the darkness with their freedom in chains.

All expectancy and anticipation in the prison came to converge at one focal point of radiance: the Sabbath. And its central figure was Rabbi Aryeh Levin—or "the rabbi," as the prisoners called him. How he ever took to making these visits, none of us knew. We only knew when they began: in 1925. Since then he never missed a single Sabbath or day of *yom tov*—literally, not once since 1925. In the wintertime, when the streets of Jerusalem turned into raging streams and torrents of rain, he would come stricken with cold and thoroughly wet, from his *shtreim'l* to his shoes that oozed rivulets of water. In the great heat of the Middle Eastern summer he would arrive perspiring and breathing heavily. Sick or well, he was there.

Only once in the course of the dozens of years, he left the prayer-service on a Sabbath morning about a half-hour before it ended. There was a reason for it, to which I was a witness: Someone came to tell him that his daughter had been stricken by paralysis. Yet one week later he arrived punctually on time, and he left the prison after the prayer-service, as usual.

Every Sabbath morning at eight o'clock the Jewish prisoners would gather in one of the largest cells. The cots were taken out into the hall. From the storage-room an *aron kodesh* (holy ark) containing a Torah scroll was brought, as well as a table and a number of benches (in the cells there were usually no tables, benches or chairs). At half past eight "the rabbi" stood in the doorway of the cell; so every inmate remembered clearly.

In the doorway he would stand a few seconds, scanning the faces in the room—looking for "new guests." When there were any he went to them first. He took a new inmate's hand between both of his and caressed it on the back, as though seeking to caress, calm and reassure the spirit of the man. Difficult as it may be to believe or explain, his face, lined with wrinkles and adorned with a silvery beard and curling sidelocks (*peyoth*), radiated a boundless benevolence, a feeling of goodness. Never before did I see the face of so good-hearted a man. His eyebrows were sprinkled with a multitude of dots that formed all kinds of lines and tiny, mi-

WITHIN THE PRISON WALLS

croscopic geometric patterns. And in the eyes beneath the complex brows, joy and sorrow formed a harmonious mixture.

Out of those eyes, in addition to the blend of joy with sorrow, shone a certain wonder, a kind of almost childlike amazement at the world about him. Standing or sitting he would sway his head and shoulders; and it seemed as though he were constantly amazed at the wonders of the Almighty, the Creator of light and darkness, who adds shadow to every brightness. In the view of the rabbi, in his vision of light and dark you could find his whole wisdom of life, his entire philosophy: Life is neither gladness nor grief. It is a blend of the two.

On the strength of this life-wisdom he came to the prison, to recall to the inmates by his very presence that besides the darkness there is also light in this world of the blessed Lord; and the light can be formed in the very intensity of deathly darkness.

A week of prison life would end with a Sabbath filled with light. The week was a unit of shadow-time, behind walls, in a world shut off from the world. The rabbi brought the inmates a perception of hope: that just as the week of shadow-time ended in the Sabbath, so they would yet reach a Sabbath in their lifetime, a period of light when the shadow-time would finally end. For life is neither gladness nor gloom, neither light nor darkness, but a long chain of days and a long chain of weeks. At the end of every day comes night; yet with the dawning of a new day, the last traces of night disappear. And at the end of every week comes the Sabbath: a day of rest, a time of holiness.

I have yet to see a radiance like his in the visage of any Jewish man of piety or holy gentile. I have yet to find it in the Jewish faces rendered by such artists as Rubens, El Greco and Rembrandt.

Through him I understood that the Sabbath is ours alone to treasure. Through him I understood the reason for our ordeal, for the plight we had to bear in the fearful weekday-despair.

It was all the burden of preparation for our Sabbath.

irrefusable prayer

When the festival of Sukkoth (Tabernacles) came in 1939, Reb Aryeh arrived at the central prison in Jerusalem carrying the "four species":

lulav (palm branch), *ethrog* (citron), myrtle leaves and willow branches —so that each inmate could hold them in turn and say the benediction over them. As usual, he joined the prisoners in the morning prayer-service, with himself as the *ḥazzan* (reader) and the reader of the Torah.

When the service was concluded he told the men, "A great privilege was granted me: to pray together with you. For you see, I am absolutely certain that it is your entreaties that are accepted in heaven. Scripture states: *Out of the constraint (imprisonment) I called to the Lord; He answered me...* (Psalms 118:5); *Out of the depths I called to Thee, O Lord* (Psalms 130:1)."

so many sons

Whenever he took the bus to the Latrun prison to visit the inmates, it was his custom to recite in a whisper the prayerful chapters of *t'hillim*, the Book of Psalms, as an entreaty to Heaven for the prisoners.

Once he became so moved by the pertinent meaning of some of the words that he began weeping like a child. The driver of the vehicle looked at him thoughtfully. "Tell me," he asked. "Do you have a relative in the prison?"

"Yes," said Reb Aryeh. The driver nodded. "I see that you are all upset. Is it a son of yours who is a prisoner?"

"Oh," said Reb Aryeh, "I have not one son there, but many."

The driver gave him a most puzzled glance.

he was never searched

Ever so often British army men would stop a bus that he was riding and search the passengers for concealed weapons, etc. (a very serious crime then). Reb Aryeh's long black coat had many special pockets—his dear wife Hannah used to sit up whole nights sewing them in—filled with written messages for the prisoners from families and friends. Many of the notes were from members of the underground to their buddies, and were far more than innocent good wishes and chatty news. They were definitely not for the eyes of British army officers. In the searches, however, by some minor miracle they always passed him by, as not worth troubling about.

Whenever he spoke of it, he insisted it was through the great merit of his "many sons" and of two outstanding mentors of his: Rabbi Ḥayyim Berlin and Chief Rabbi Kook.

"I am grateful to you"

There was a time when the Sephardic chief rabbi, Ben-zion Uzziel, accompanied him on a trip to see the political prisoners in Latrun. He had a reason: The prisoners were maintaining a hunger-strike, and he meant to convince them to give it up.

Rabbi Uzziel spoke long and earnestly to the men, doing his best to prevail on them. He went so far as to order them to stop their fasting. Yet it was all to no avail. When Reb Aryeh saw the men growing hot under the collar—restless and aggressive—he announced, "Look: in the meantime let us say the afternoon prayers (*minḥa*)." He promptly became the reader, and the inmates joined in. With the prayer-service over, the good rabbi began speaking to the men, trying to bring *his* influence to bear to make them give up their hunger-strike and take food. But he too met with an adamant refusal.

Realizing what the situation was, he said at last, "Very well. You are determined to continue. Then I want to join you and take part in your struggle. So now let us make a 'deal': You have already done your share, by being here behind bars. I, however, am a free man; and so I will fast and maintain the hunger-strike for you, in your behalf. And whether you agree or not, as long as you continue fasting I intend to do so with you."

No one doubted Reb Aryeh's determination to keep his word. There and then, with a few glances, whispers and shrugs among themselves, the men decided that their hunger-strike was over. They simply could not let their rabbi suffer the pangs of hunger.

At the end of the visit, in all sincerity, Reb Aryeh went over to Chief Rabbi Uzziel. "I am grateful to you," he said, "that you were able to persuade the men to give it up." (He was convinced that the chief rabbi's words had turned the tide.)

WITHIN THE PRISON WALLS

in the wake of the black Sabbath

One Saturday under the British mandate became known as "the black Sabbath": Circumstances brought the conflict between the mandatory authorities and the leaders of the Jewish population to such a pitch that many of the leaders (including future members of the Israel government) were placed under arrest and taken to the prison in Latrun. The very next day Reb Aryeh was there, happy at the thought that at least so large a congregation, including such prominent personages, were gathered for him to lead them in the afternoon prayer-service. Whatever else might happen, he considered that a fine thing.

This is how one of the new inmates in Latrun (Dr Joseph Paamoni) remembered his experience:

It was three days after my imprisonment that I met for the first time

The infamous "Black Sabbath" brought to the prison in Latrun the heads of the **yishuv**, the Jewish settlement in Palestine under the mandate—including such notables as Dov Joseph (second from left) and Moshe Shertok, later Moshe Sharett, Israel's foreign minister.

the man who was to become a spiritual father to me, the man who was revered and beloved by all who came in contact with him. Of course I had heard quite a lot about him, including stories that were almost legends. But I had never managed to see him until then, my third day of detention in Latrun.

He came to us that day carrying a Torah scroll, to use in the prayer-service in the impromptu synagogue that my fellow-inmates began to set up in one of the shacks. Then he distributed *kippoth* among us (small black skull-caps, to cover the head in reverence before the Almighty) and prayer-books. He had a great many "clients" in the prison, yet he remembered everyone by name. His handshake was an affectionate caress; and from his shining twinkling eyes radiated affection for each and every one of us. (Many years later I visited him with my daughter Yael, who was thirteen then. She asked me afterward, "Father, did you see the rays of light shining from his eyes?")

He invited us all to join him in the afternoon prayer-service (*minḥa*), and we followed him dutifully into the shack that was designated to serve as our synagogue.

On his first visit to us some British officers came with him, accompanied by an Arab in the uniform of a special guard. We were told that the task of the Arab was to serve as interpreter between Reb Aryeh and the officers. It was obvious, though, that this was no "escort of honor" for the good rabbi, but only a means of strict precaution taken against him and against us. They feared that he might be bringing secret messages in from the outside, or he might carry messages out.

As we entered the synagogue the officers remained respectfully outside; but the Arab came in with us. At that Israel Rokéaḥ (later to serve as a mayor in the State of Israel) turned to him and asked point-blank if he was Jewish. When the man replied that he was a Moslem, Rokéaḥ informed him that he had no business being in a place of Jewish worship. To this the Arab rejoined that he was only doing his job. Suddenly Israel Rokéaḥ the suave, cultured official vanished, and Israel Rokéaḥ the "sabra" stood in his place. In pure Arabic he ordered the man brusquely out. When the man still refused to budge, Rokéaḥ took hold of him bodily and threw him out, to the accompaniment of some rich and pungent Arabic epithets.

Needless to say, the Moslem ran at once to the British officers to complain. But the head of the inmates (who served as their spokesman) came up directly to explain that Rokéaḥ had been motivated only by the principles of the Jewish faith, which (supposedly) forbid a gentile to enter a place of worship during prayer.

Heaven knows if his explanation satisfied the officers or they only gave the appearance of understanding. But the incident went no further. And the next time that Reb Aryeh came, and the times after that, he no longer had any "escort of honor" or "interpreter."

the midnight visit

It was about midnight when Reb Aryeh came once knocking on the door of Sh'muel Tamir (today a prominent member of Israel's *k'nesseth*), to bring him friendly greetings from his cousin, imprisoned then in Latrun, with the assurance that the young man was alive and well.

"Rabbi," Tamir asked in amazement, "what made you trouble yourself to come now, in the middle of the night, just to bring us this greeting? Surely it could have waited till the morning!"

Reb Aryeh shook his head: "Good news must not be delayed. It has to be delivered immediately."

This was indeed his rule, never to hold back any message of greeting or good news that would make people happy. Once he gave an explanation for it: "The prophet Jeremiah complained about his people: *They are wise men for doing evil, but for doing good they know not* (Jeremiah (4:22). When something evil has been done, something bad has happened to people, then I am a 'wise man' for them: they come and pour out their pain and tale of woe to me. On the other hand, *for doing good,* when something good and wonderful happens and their situation improves, *they know not*: Then they do not know me any more, and do not let me share their happiness. Yet you see: while I prayed and implored Heaven for them, I suffered with their anguish. When they tell me nothing afterward of the help and rescue that came to them, the pain and anguish remain with me."

Hence his happy eagerness to bring good news to people without delay, to share their joy.

"we have full confidence in him"

At the head of the State of Israel, the late Yitzhak ben-Zvi was destined to serve as the second president. Under the British mandate he was the chairman of the *vaad le'umi* (National Committee), the political regulating body of the Jewish settlement. One day Reb Aryeh came to the central prison in Jerusalem for one of his numerous visits, and to his amazement he found Yitzhak ben-Zvi waiting at the entrance.

"My dear sir," the good rabbi exclaimed. "Whatever are you doing here?"

Ben-Zvi smiled. "I came to see some of the underground fighters imprisoned here. But under no circumstances will the sentry admit me. He says that he recognizes neither me nor my name, nor has he heard of the *vaad le'umi*. I was quite astounded and voiced my complaint. But he had only one suggestion to offer. Wait a bit, he said: At any moment Reb Aryeh Levin is due to arrive. We know him and have full confidence in him. If he will identify you and give his approval, I will gladly let you in!"

Purim under curfew

This is an incident that Reb Aryeh once recounted from his vast memory: In the period before the birth of the State of Israel, the authorities of the British mandate decided one day to declare a curfew in Jerusalem for the night: From sunset till the following sunrise no one would be allowed on the streets of Jerusalem. It may or may not have been coincidence that at sundown, with the advent of night, Purim would begin—the evening and day when Jews celebrate the ancient rescue of their people from the schemes of the wicked Haman. In the evening (and again in the morning) there is a religious obligation to hear the *megilla,* the Hebrew Book of Esther, read from a parchment scroll in the synagogue.

When Reb Aryeh learned of the impending curfew he took his parchment *megilla* under his arm and set off for the central prison in broad daylight, to be sure to reach it before the curfew went into effect. He went there every Saturday morning to lead the prisoners in the prayer-service; and he intended to read the Hebrew Book of Esther for them that evening, in the cell that was always converted into a temporary synagogue. He realized that he would not be able to return home afterward, as the curfew would forbid it. And so he planned to stay the night at the prison, in company with his "congregation."

At the prison, however, he met with an unexpected impasse: The prison supervisor came to tell him that in his calendar he had a list of all the Jewish holidays and festivals—and Purim was not listed there as a holiday. Under the circumstances, said the supervisor, he could not permit the prisoners to assemble in their place of worship to hear the *megilla*.

Reb Aryeh was stunned. In vain he argued and pleaded, trying to convince the official that his calendar was simply "misinformed." The supervisor would not yield.

Left with no choice, Reb Aryeh prepared to leave. He would have to hurry now to reach a synagogue in time, so that he himself might at least hear the *megilla* read. But he set off on his way with a heavy heart.

Meanwhile, however, either by prison grapevine or by intuition the inmates, gathered then in the prison courtyard, came to know what happened. Instantly they decided to stage a protest and refuse to return to their cells....

Several hours later a police van drew up before Reb Aryeh's home. A British policeman came out, knocked on his door, and asked him if he would kindly come to the prison with them without delay. The heaviness in his heart gave way immediately to a radiant joy. He took his parchment *megilla*, and "under police escort" returned with them to the prison courtyard. There he went directly to the supervisor and began thanking him most cordially that he had finally granted his kind permission, in response to Reb Aryeh's pleading, to let the men hold their prayer-service and hear the *megilla* read.

"Oh no, no, no!" said the supervisor. "That's not at all why I've had you brought here. You must not misunderstand me. You see, the inmates refuse to return to their cells. As I don't want to use force, I have sent for you to ask you to persuade them. I know well your influence with them."

Reb Aryeh was crestfallen. He realized that he would probably never understand the British official mind. But to spare the men any suffering or injury he stepped forward willingly and explained the situation to them, after which he asked them to obey the rules and go back to their cells. "It simply seems," he concluded, "that by Heaven's decree you are not to hear the *megilla* this Purim, and you won't be able to make a happy din whenever Haman is mentioned in the reading of the *megilla*."

Suddenly a voice sounded over the courtyard: "Fellows, Reb Aryeh orders us back to the cells. We have to go. Everyone, march!"

For the next year, apparently Reb Aryeh made sure it would not happen again. In the file of Chief Rabbi Kook this letter was found:

> To the administration of the local prison, the warden:
> I herewith respectfully request that permission be granted my emissary Rabbi Aryeh Levin to enter the prison this day—now, at night, and tomorrow morning, to read the *megilla* for the prisoners, as the custom is every year.
> Most respectfully yours / Abraham Isaac

his pleasure

This is a passage in a book of reminiscences by a *kibbutznik* of Givat Brenner who served in the Haganah (the Jewish defense force that the British declared illegal) and spent time in prison:

Reb Aryeh would come every single Sabbath and festival day. When he appeared with his light step and radiant face that never darkened, some kind of glow was kindled in our hearts too. He went over to each and every one and greeted him warmly; and his kindly reassuring eyes spoke too, communicating with your heart in their honesty and truth. Whoever didn't experience his unique handshake would not understand its essence. One hand shook yours in greeting, and the other patted it in affection, as he spoke with you in his calm assuring way.

He never asked any probing or dismaying questions. He never demanded anything sternly of anyone. He never preached morality or religious observance. We joined him for the prayer-services only on account of our profound human relationship with him (since we were not, in the main, religious). From his rich and benevolent spirit a flow of loving-kindness radiated outward to us all.

Summer and winter, in heat, rain and snow he always came. It was unthinkable that the "father of the prisoners" should fail to appear even once. There was one Sabbath, though, when a heavy snow fell over Jerusalem. It was cold enough to freeze one's skin and bones, and a fearful wind blew and shrieked outside. Added to that, we knew that "the rabbi" (as we called him) was not in the best of health. We thought that this time he would not come. After all, said we, there are limits....

At the appointed time the door opened, and the rabbi entered, just barely alive. He was thoroughly chilled and frozen, totally drenched, barely dragging his feet—but his eyes were smiling in their kindness just as always.

We came rushing toward him then, all of us: "Rabbi! How could you come in this weather, and in your state of health? You were putting your life in danger to walk here today!"

For a moment he was still. Then he smiled with his old charm and said, "Well, indeed, my children: Were you able to come to me, I would not have to go to you."

Another ex-prisoner recalled: I remember a different Sabbath day when there was a heavy snowfall. Then too it was fearfully cold, and the rabbi nevertheless arrived as usual. Of course the men remonstrated with him that he should not have come in such foul weather. With a smile he answered, "You know, every man has his own hobby and his own pleasures. My great delight is to see my children. Do you know anyone who would willingly give up his supreme pleasure?"

a role for his children

Yaakov Eliav was the commander of a fighting unit in the underground movement of *le-ḥee* (Fighters for the Freedom of Israel). His activities earned him a sentence of life-imprisonment by the British authorities, that was later commuted to a term of ten years. This is an experience that he recalled:

On December 23, 1943 Moshe bar-Giora (may he rest in peace) and I escaped from the central prison in Jerusalem, while we were acting as "volunteer electricians" to arrange the wiring for the Christmas lights in the quarters of the warden. We had been planning the break-out for over a year. It was the first successful escape ever made from Jerusalem's central place of detention for political prisoners.

Our plan was that my friend and I were to flee in different directions, and at eight o'clock at night we would meet at the Berman bakery, located then in the Meya She'arim neighborhood. If we were unable to meet then we would try again to get together at midnight, at the same rendezvous.

The escape went off most successfully; but unfortunately, while I was in flight a patrol caught sight of me, pursued me and shot at me. Without going into lengthy details let me merely relate that by a miracle I remained safe; but it was out of the question for me to try to keep our rendezvous at eight o'clock. Unobtrusively I made my way along a most roundabout route, through side streets, alleys and courtyards, till I reached the house of Moshe Segal, who held high rank in the underground movement. He provided me with the clothing of a member of the devout Jewish community (the old *yishuv*). Suitably outfitted in a long black coat, etc. so that I looked like a young adult student of the Talmud, I went out into the streets again, to make my way to the Berman bakery and wait there for the second agreed time to meet my friend.

As I walked along, though, I noticed the pious Jews of Meya She'arim staring at me strangely and giving me peculiar glances. I was puzzled and alarmed: Could they detect perhaps that I was in disguise? It was a most uncomfortable time that I spent walking those streets to Berman's bakery. Only after the incident was long past I understood the reason for all those glances: In my great haste and confusion I had put a *shtreim'l* on my head—the traditional flat hat with the thick ring of fur. But the good pious Jews of the old yishuv wear a *shtreim'l* only on the Sabbath and festival days; and there was I sporting mine on an ordinary Wednesday!

Later I discovered too what happened with my friend and partner in the escape. Moshe bar-Giora heard the patrol shooting at me; and when eight o'clock came and was long past, and there was no sign of me, he feared the worst. There he was (as far as he knew) left all alone and helpless, not knowing which way to turn to find safety. At last, unable to think of anything better, he decided, "I will go see Reb Aryeh."

The good Reb Aryeh was astounded to see him. While Moshe stayed safely in his home, the rabbi went running through the streets of the city trying to find some suitable place of refuge for him. For a good long while he went swiftly hither and thither—and found nothing. When he returned home in dejection, Moshe told him of his agreement with me, that we were to try a second time to meet, about midnight. He was afraid, however, to walk through Jerusalem's streets, since an alert had been declared and the British police were out searching for the escaped men.

Reb Aryeh stood up and did something utterly unexpected. His daughter Ethel was then engaged to be married. He called her and asked her for a favor: to go with a brother of hers to accompany Moshe bar-Giora to his rendezvous. The police scouring the city would pay scant attention to three religious young persons out for a pleasant stroll through the streets, on their way perhaps to a *sheva b'rachoth*, a festive meal in the wake of a wedding.

Without hesitation Reb Aryeh's son and daughter agreed to the plan, although they knew the great risk involved: Had they been caught, helping an escaped political prisoner, they could have expected a sentence of imprisonment for life.

(Fate, however, added its own tragic postscript to the story: Some three years afterward on the second of November 1946, Moshe bar-Giora's life ended. As he was working to blow up the oil refineries in Haifa, one of the bombs went off in his hand and he was instantly blown to bits.)

the death-sentence

In July 1944 the Jewish homeland was in the throes of a mighty uproar. Matithyahu Shmuelevitz, a member of the underground movement, had been arrested by the British police in the streets of Tel Aviv while carrying arms. He was brought to trial, and at last his verdict was pronounced with solemnity by a British judge: "You shall be taken from this court to the house of detention, and from there to a certain place where the sentence of the court shall be carried out upon you and you shall be hung from the gallows. And may God have mercy on your soul."

Matithyahu received the verdict calmly. When the presiding judge of the court finished reading it, everyone present in the courtroom rose to his feet as Matithyahu sang *ha-tikvah,* the national anthem of the Jewish homeland.

Not since the hanging of Sh'lomo ben Yosef had there been so stormy an uproar in the land following a death-sentence for a Jew. The heads of the Jewish settlement and the chief rabbinate set to work to make every effort to save his life.

This is what the focus of the storm, Matithyahu Shmuelevitz himself, later recalled from this period of his life:

On Saturday the rabbi came to see me. Yet before the trial my friends had told me a great deal about Reb Aryeh Levin. They were absolutely captivated by his personality, and with the passage of time I became just as captivated. Never before had I known anyone so decent and kindhearted; he was goodness itself. For the past twenty years he had come every single Sabbath to the prison. He treated every prisoner as if he were his own son. He knew the family of every inmate, and served as the go-between, the contact-man between the prisoners and their folk. More than once the official agencies offered him a salary for his service as the rabbi or chaplain of the prison. Invariably he refused it. And he put himself in danger for our sake: He served as a courier, bringing in written messages and taking others out in turn. He knew well enough that it was forbidden, and if discovered he would stay in the prison for some time. Yet he risked that to help us.

Well, as I said, he came to see me on the Sabbath, his face all gloom and worry. When I held out my hands through the bars of my cell-door he shook them warmly. But I could sense that he found it hard to utter a word.

"How are you, rabbi?" I asked, to make him feel at ease. He only continued holding my hand, and with deep emotion he whispered, "Matithyahu, Matithyahu..." just as if I were his son. Finally he recovered from his emotion a bit. "The Lord will guard you," he said. "God will protect you. Recite the chapters of *t'hillim,* the Book of Psalms. Pray..."

"If God wants me as a sacrifice," I replied, "I am willing to give myself to Him."

"But you have no right to throw your life away," retorted Reb Aryeh with spirit. "I hear that you are refusing to sign a plea for a pardon. You must never do that!"

"You have heard correctly: I refuse to sign it. Nor is this all. I want to ask you, dear rabbi, to inform the chief rabbis that I have no wish for them to write any plea for mercy on my behalf. I don't want the leading rabbis of Israel to abase themselves before those gentiles."

"But why?" he cried. "Why make sure that your life must end? You must not do that. It is a grave sin." And tears stood in his eyes.

"Rabbi," said I, holding my ground, "this is what I ask of you."

"Never! Impossible! If you yourself will not ask for mercy, at least you must not prevent others from doing so."

The tears began streaming down his cheeks. He was so imbued with a fatherly affection that against my will I was shaken by it, seeing his devotion. "Matithyahu, Matithyahu," he continued, "it is a great sin to bring on your own end. Have compassion on me. I cannot commit this crime, to let you die without a chance. You did your duty as you saw it. But you still must live. Our people still need you. Do not be obstinate! Give way for my sake!"

"Rabbi," I answered, "I can't!"

"Do not write anything yourself, but don't prevent others from writing."

"Dear rabbi, can't you understand that I'm not able to give my consent that Israel's chief rabbis should abase themselves before those gentiles? Don't you see? I know what they'll write. I know how they'll phrase it: They will write that I was led astray, into ways of error. They will write that they, the British, are entirely right and just, and I acted criminally—and the rabbinate implores mercy for me. It's degrading, and it helps not one bit. Those pleas have no effect on their decisions."

"But it is necessary," Reb Aryeh persisted. "Chief Rabbi Herzog can go and speak with them..."

"That's also superfluous, absolutely unnecessary."

"No, oh no. Do not say that. What do you wish—to die? It is forbidden for you to want that."

Resolute as I was, it was hard for me to withstand his tears. "At least," I said at last, relenting a bit, "if I could only be sure that they would write a proud, firm letter..."

"What would you want them to write?" he asked promptly.

"Let them write without any servile self-humiliation, but with strength: that they demand that the death verdict be changed to a term of imprisonment, because it is neither just nor ethical to send to the gallows a man who risked his life for his people."

"Good, very good. I will tell this to Chief Rabbi Herzog. I myself will read the letter before he sends it off."

"I should also like to see it," I responded.

"But that is not possible. When could I bring it?—only on the next Sabbath; and it must be sent sooner than that. Don't you trust me?"

"Yes," I truthfully admitted, "I rely on you." And suddenly I felt tired and weary. Regaining a bit of his strength, the good rabbi told me how everyone in the land was concerned and anxious over my fate. Then he asked for details about my relatives, whom he recognized waiting at the gates for a chance to visit me. Finally he showed me which chapters in the *t'hillim,* the Book of Psalms, to say in prayer, and he left with his blessing.

Matithyahu Shmuelevitz received his pardon. His sentence was changed from death at the gallows to life-imprisonment. When he learned of this, Matithyahu wrote to Reb Aryeh:

With the Lord's help / 18 Tammuz 1944

Rabbi:

When they came to the isolation cell for condemned men, where I was kept, and informed me that I had been pardoned, they were quite enraged that I did not say "Thank you very much." Well, I didn't curse them when they sentenced me to death, and I didn't bless them when they gave me their pardon. For I think this wasn't *their* kindness. My life wasn't put in their power, but in the hands of a higher power.

But I do want to convey my thanks hereby to those Jews who toiled and worked on my behalf, being concerned for my welfare. Then please convey my gratitude, dear rabbi, to the Chief Rabbis Isaac Herzog and Ben-zion Uzziel. My profound thanks to the Jews about whom you told me, who did not rest or relax in these days of suspense, and to all the people whose names I don't know, but whose closeness and care I sensed and whose whispered prayers I heard in those hours which I expected to be the last of my life.

Yet there is one person in particular to whom I remain grateful first and foremost: a dear, precious Jew about whom you told me nothing; but it was he who stormed heaven and earth for me; and more important—it was he who brought me closer to my Maker in these fateful days. I believe that although we were not aware of it, every one of us who serves our people faithfully, ready to give his life to sanctify God's name and redeem and rescue our people— every one of us is worthy and esteemed in the sight of God and is close to Him, whether or not he is careful to observe the specific mitzvoth (religious commandments) of the Torah.

This dear, precious Jew, however, whom I will not name but who is so beloved by all the prisoners for Israel's sake, has made that closeness of us all to God something clear and obvious. If I pray with this man and together we say the supplication to the "merciful Father who dwells on high" asking Him to "remember in compassion those pious, worthy, blameless souls... who gave their lives to sanctify the Divine name"; if I see his own profound love for Jews and his own dedication—I cannot help but feel both a reverence and a love for our Creator.

Before all else I thank that precious man for being a pillar of support for my spirit in the days when I stood before heaven's court of justice, just as my political convictions and my friends were a source of strength to me when I faced the court of justice here on earth.

How can I bless this man of wonder? There is only one great blessing truly suitable for him: May he merit soon to see the final, complete Messianic redemption of our people and our land; and then may he say the morning prayers every Sabbath in the perfect place of prayer—the forecourt of our rebuilt Temple—there to sing our psalms of celebration. May it truly be rebuilt soon in our time.

Be you blessed and blessed again, rabbi.

Yours with all my heart,
Matithyahu Shmuelevitz

the "authorization"

His affectionate handshake, his heartening fatherly smile—what remains of them in the spirit of those who knew him, when today everyone is pushed and thrust toward some unknown destination and shrouded fate, when you find yourself dragged along the murderously rushing stream and you cannot hold back?

If I stop but a moment and reflect, I feel instantly amid this frightening emptiness of the present world, where I move always relentlessly with dizzying speed, how utterly I miss the hands of Reb Aryeh, stretched out instantly to take my hand and hold it, like a rescuer at the edge of a yawning abyss.

I recall what another man who knew him once said:

The years went by, and his prayers were answered: Jerusalem became a whole, united city once more, set free from alien powers. To him it was natural—as natural as any miracle of redemption and rescue: A man prays, and his entreaty is answered.

Once (the man continued) I went to visit him shortly before Israel's Independence Day was to begin. For a good long while I sat listening to his stories and anecdotes. They were as strange and extraordinary as the liberation of Jerusalem itself, yet so natural and commonplace in the world of Reb Aryeh. This is one striking tale that he related:

On a Sabbath morning (said Reb Aryeh) I was on my way for my usual visit to you inmates in the prison [Jerusalem's central place of detention, located in the "Russian compound"]. Suddenly I realized that the street was utterly empty. Not a soul was out walking. Only a group of British soldiers were patrolling about. It could mean but one thing: A curfew had been imposed on the city, and it was forbidden to be out walking. I continued going steadily, however. God's purposes were more important to me than curfews by an alien authority.

I was still quite a distance from the prison when I heard a shout: "Halt!" A British officer ordered me to come to him, and of course, I was placed under arrest for violating the curfew. In a moment I was in the detention room of a police-station, that was already quite full with others who were arrested for violating the curfew. Well, I could not sit still. I simply paced through the room, filled with distress. I myself had already said *shaḥarith* (the first part of the Sabbath morning prayer-service) with a congregation near my home, in the early hours of the day. But what of all the prisoners who were waiting for me to have them start their prayer-service? They would just keep waiting till kingdom come!

Suddenly a man in civilian clothing came over and asked me if I was the one who came to visit the inmates of the prison every Saturday. When I answered that indeed I was, he left me and returned with a folded note in his hand. "Take this," he said, "and go directly to the prison"—just like that.

I took the folded sheet and marched straight out, never looking right or left. So I made my way to Jaffa Street and on toward the Russian compound. As I walked I heard kind fellow-Jews calling a warning from their windows: "Sir, where are you going? There is a curfew in the city. Go inside a building!" I paid no attention to these voices, but merely kept walking, secure in the power of the note I carried. There were many units of British guards posted along the way; but I passed them by, never once being stopped and questioned. At last I went through the prison gates and was soon with my "congregation."

They were utterly amazed to see me. How did I ever manage to get to them? they wanted to know. Through the prison grapevine they had learned that on the day before, several Britishers had been killed by members of the Jewish underground movement. So they knew that a curfew would be imposed. Well, I blithely showed the men my folded note—my official authorization. We opened the sheet to read it—and it was absolutely blank. Not a word was written on it!

Some of the prisoners began to laugh. But I felt that it was some kind of sign or talisman from heaven, with an ability of its own to get me through the streets in safety. And I was right. With it I had arrived at the prison in perfect order. And with it I returned home with equal ease. When my visit with the inmates was over (with the prayer-service completed, of course) I returned as I had come, the folded sheet held firmly in my hand. [Jerusalem has always had an *éruv*, a technical arrrangement that makes it permissible under religious law to carry objects in the street on the Sabbath.] Again I passed by the numerous British guards posted on the way. And again not even one stopped me for questioning.

That sheet of paper (Reb Aryeh concluded) is still in my possession. I have kept it safe to this day.

"they will all know"

One rule that he would not break was never to take a penny from any parent or relative for his help to the prisoners. Once, however (as he told Sh'lomo Nakdimon, a journalist), he was tempted. The only son of a very wealthy man came to spend some time behind bars, at the "invitation" of the British authorities, and the father came to see the good rabbi, no doubt believing that for a generous donation the rabbi would give his son better attention.

"Look, rabbi," he said. "I know you take no money; but since you know to whom to give money (charity for the poor), I ask you please to take this and distribute it."

"Well," said Reb Aryeh as he recounted the incident years later, "I asked my wife, may she rest in peace, if I should take it or not. And she answered: Aryeh, don't you dare. This is worse than taking money for yourself. If you take for yourself, no one else will know; but if you take money for others, they will all know."

What would they know, all who received a share of the money?— that Reb Aryeh was "selling" his service to the prisoners. This was enough to make up his dear wife's mind for her. So he never took a penny for this work of his, either for himself or for others.

when illness struck

By his activities he accumulated a source of constant, unfailing satisfaction in his life: to remember and recount the gratitude that the imprisoned men expressed for his visits. This is an incident of which he once told me:

On a certain Sabbath morning he was in the central prison of Jerusalem for his regular weekly visit. As usual, he had the prisoners join in the morning prayer-service; and as usual, when the time came, he began chanting the weekly portion (the *sidrah*) from the Torah scroll.

As he was reading aloud, one of the Arab guards approached and asked him to come outside, as there were people waiting for him. The good rabbi, however, had no wish to interrupt the reading of the weekly

The corridor in Jerusalem's central prison

portion, and he motioned to the guard to be so good as to wait till he was finished.

A few minutes passed by, and the guard came back, to ask Reb Aryeh again to accompany him outside. Once more, though, the rabbi motioned to him to kindly wait till the end of the Torah-reading. But then the captain of the guards himself came, and asked Reb Aryeh to come with him. There could be no further doubt: something serious indeed was afoot. Reb Aryeh asked one of the inmates to continue the reading of the Torah, and he left with the captain of the guards.

Once outside, he saw his son-in-law waiting for him at the prison entrance. In his heart he knew at once that some accident had occurred. But not a word did he say, to ask his son-in-law for an explanation. In many situations he had the wise man's gift of silence, when he knew that was best.

The two went off together, the son-in-law in the lead and Reb Aryeh right behind him, walking steadily till they reached the Jerusalem neighborhood of Shaarey Hessed, where his married daughter lived with this young man and the many children she had borne. As they reached the young man's home, Reb Aryeh saw members of the family and medical doctors gathered there. And then he learned the news: His daughter had been stricken by paralysis. The only comfort that the doctors could give him was their estimate that in time the total incapacitation was quite likely to become a partial paralysis; and there was a likelihood that after a few years she would recover completely. Still in silence, Reb Aryeh went to see his daughter, lying absolutely motionless on the bed; and he burst into tears. In a few moments, though, he recovered his composure, and he firmly reminded the members of the family that "the rescuing help of the Lord can come in the twinkling of an eye."

That night, when the Sabbath was over, Reb Aryeh had a visitor at his home: the Arab prison guard who had come during his Torah-reading to tell him he was wanted outside. Why did he come now? The Jewish inmates had realized in the morning that something drastic must have occurred in the private life of their beloved rabbi. Dying with curiosity, they crossed the Arab guard's palm liberally with silver and sent him immediately after the Sabbath to Reb Aryeh's home to get the facts. The rabbi told him what had occurred, then asked the guard to tell the Jewish inmates not to worry or grieve excessively. He firmly believed that the Lord's rescuing help would come.

The next Sabbath morning the rabbi went to the prison as usual. As soon as he appeared, the prisoners flocked around him and asked how his daughter was. With an effort he mastered his emotions and said briefly that she was as well as might be expected. Then he sternly bid them start the morning prayers, and he chanted the Torah portion as always.

Now, the weekly Torah portion is divided into seven parts. For each part one of the worshippers is called to the Torah, and he says a benediction before the part is read, and another benediction after it. The usual practice is for the reader then to recite *mi she-bérach,* a prayer asking the Lord to bless and protect the man just called to the Torah. In the *mi she-bérach* he can insert, at the request of the man called to the Torah, any pledge to charity that the man wishes to make (which becomes an additional reason for the Lord to bless and protect him).

As Reb Aryeh duly recited the *mi she-bérach* for the first prisoner called to the Torah, he was taken by surprise to hear the man announce that he was pledging a day of his life for the recovery of the good rabbi's daughter. When the time came for the *mi she-bérach* for the second man called, he announced that he forfeited a week of his life for the sake of the sick young woman. The third man called pledged a month of his lifespan; and so it went. At last it was the turn of the seventh man. (He was Dov Tamari, who was to become a professor at the Haifa Technion in later life.) "What is our life in prison worth," he cried, "compared to our rabbi's anguish? I pledge all the remaining days of my life for the complete recovery of our rabbi's daughter!"

Reb Aryeh looked at the man (then a young student, at the beginning of his adult life), and as he realized what this inmate had said he simply wept uncontrollably. He was moved beyond words to see how devoted the men were to him and how much affection they bore him. Unable to continue with the prayer-service, he shook hands warmly with every single one of the inmates and went straight home.

The men he visited remained bound to him for life, in affection and reverence. Typical was Dr Israel Eldad, a founder of the underground fighting movement called **le-ḥee** (loḥamey ḥéruth yisrael, "Fighters for the Freedom of Israel").

Incredible as it may sound, that very evening, after the Sabbath, members of his family came to tell him that his daughter was beginning to show signs of recovery: She had started to move some limbs. A few days went by, and her health returned completely, in utter contradiction of the medical prognosis, which looked forward to a long period of illness.

act of gratitude

All his years he kept well away from honor. Yet a splendid opportunity came at last for those who had suffered detention for their homeland's sake, to pay tribute as they wished to their rabbi, who had brought them spiritual strength and comfort in the dark days of their lives. In the intermediate days (*ḥol ha-moʻéd*) of Passover 1955 they celebrated with him his seventieth birthday.

A committee of those who revered and cherished the "father of the imprisoned" arranged for a mass reunion of all former inmates of the British prisons and detention camps. To the courtyard of the former central prison in Jerusalem (in the Russian compound) came some 1500 men: members of all the underground fighting movements in the years of the mandate, who had been imprisoned in the land of Israel or in the detention camps in the Sudan, Kenya or Eritrea.

(If anyone thought, though, that he came easily or eagerly, he was mistaken. Before the event he went to ask advice from two notable authorities in religious law. They told him to go, because primarily he would not be taking pleasure and tribute from the gathering but would strengthen their link with authentic Judaism. And indeed, both there and at later occasions when he was publicly honored, in his addresses he invariably made the point that "the only true thanks you can give me is to live in the age-old way of the Jewish faith.")

The first to speak was Aryeh ben Eliezer, who had served as the "supervisor" of the men arrested and deported to Eritrea. He said in part: "Dear rabbi and teacher, we have come to bless you on this day. For we remember your great kindness in coming to us in our places of darkness. We remember every word you uttered, every tear you shed, every prayer you said for the imprisoned and the fallen, for the bereaved parents and families. We filled the prisons in the land, Latrun, Acco and Bethlehem,

WITHIN THE PRISON WALLS

and the detention camps abroad, in the Sudan, Kenya and Eritrea—because we plowed a furrow of freedom and liberation, so that a free state and a free people might arise. And you, dear rabbi, watered that furrow with your tears and your prayers."

Then the former prisoners and inmates arranged themselves in rows in the courtyard. At the head of each row stood a man with a placard that bore the name of a prison or detention camp—indicating that all the men in that row had "done time" in that particular place. One placard, however, read simply, "Condemned to death." Behind it were ranged eighteen persons with the distinction that the British courts in Israel had sentenced them to the gallows and their verdicts had been subsequently commuted.

There was a group of women too, behind the placard "Bethlehem," since the British had maintained their women's prison there. And the group

Reb Aryeh holding the scroll presented to him in celebration of his seventieth birthday.

included at least one member of Israel's parliament, the *k'nesseth*. Relatively young men stood side by side with older men, whose lined faces showed the effects of years of detention. Quite a few of them had become well-known since they returned to freedom.

A trumpet sounded, and Reb Aryeh was escorted into the courtyard by an "honor guard" headed by Menaḥem Begin. Four of the eighteen "condemned to death" then stepped forward and handed the rabbi the "Scroll of the Prisoners"—a long roll of parchment that bore the names of them all, the thousands who had lost their freedom for a while by fighting for their homeland. It was a unique document out of the years of struggle for the homeland. A fifth member of the "élite" group of the condemned, Matithyahu Shmuelevitz, stepped forward and took the parchment roll, and unfurled it to read it aloud:

"This is the scroll given by those imprisoned for Zion in the days of the battle for freedom, into the hands of their rabbi and source of solace, R. Aryeh Levin, at the completion of seventy years of his life and fifty years since his arrival in the holy land. So may the God who dwells in Zion grant him and increase for him many more days and years.

We who are signed to this are your sons and daughters who honor and love you, being bound to you from our days as captives of the oppressor. We ever thirsted behind the bars to see your countenance. We became prisoners of your heart, and we imprisoned you in our hearts. Now we bless you for all the kindness you bestowed on us, when we were privileged to soar with you out of our cells, on the pulsing eagles' wings of your earnest prayers. Between the walls of cold stone we were privileged to have your warm hands hold ours, and in their veins we sensed the warmth of all the generations of our historic people. In our darkness we were privileged to see the radiance of your eyes, the light of faith and the love of holiness.

Even so may you be privileged, dear rabbi and source of our consolation, to go up with us and with the whole Jewish people, freed from all the incarcerations in the world, to the Temple Mount, to see the rebuilt Sanctuary, the House of our God. Even so may you merit to hold the hands of the Messiah, the ultimate king of Israel who will rescue all the prisoners for Zion throughout the reaches of the Diaspora. Even so may you merit to light a holy menorah that will cast its illumination over the entire Jewish people in pure faith and abounding love."

After this the good rabbi was presented with a medallion of pure silver to commemorate the occasion. In relief it showed the Western (Wailing) Wall, with chains at its two sides; and it bore the legend (in Hebrew): "For the freedom of Jerusalem / the assembly of the imprisoned, for the seventieth birthday of Reb Aryeh Levin."

In a voice choking with emotion, he gave his blessing to the gathering: "My brothers and sisters, it is difficult for me to express what is in my heart. My heart simply flows with a boundless love for you. We bear witness now that all of you were ready to give your lives for our people and our land. And therefore we say a benediction here today: Blessed be

לזכר בית אלקינו שיבנה בב"א

וזאת המגלה אשר נותנים אסירי ציון מימי מלחמת החרות על ידיו של רבם - מעודדם הרב ר' **ארי' לוין** שליט"א. במלאות לו שמונים שנה, וששים שנה לעליתו לארץ הקודש. כן יתן וכן יוסיף לו אלקים השוכן בציון ימים ושנים בבריאות הגוף ושמחת הנפש:

רבינו - מחזקנו, בבואך בגבורות
הבאנו לך היום תשורות - תשורות
את מלוא נפשותינו, כי לך מסורות

שהיית עמנו בימי מחרות
עיניך מחשכי הצינוק מאירות
ידיך מרככות על ידינו שרשרות
רוח נשפת בלוחמי גבורות

הפכת למקדש תאי - כלא ובורות
לנו גשר היית אלי קדם דורות
וקשר תפילה לאלקי הגבורות

ובזכות אהבתך אותנו בצרות
עוד תזכה לבשרנו במהרה בשורות
להדליק על הרי ירושלים מדורות
לקראת משיח בן - דוד ישיבוא לגבורות

the One who wrought a miracle at this place, not for our glory but for Heaven's honor.

"The inner thoughts of your hearts, I know. For I was close to you all, and from afar I felt your plight. *Come, let us go up to the House of our God.* This is my blessing from the depths of my heart. May I have the merit to ascend together with you to the rebuilt Sanctuary of our God, and there we will sanctify the name of Israel and its Divine Redeemer. That would be my truest happiness."

With the ceremony at the Russian compound ended, the assembled people went toward the synagogue called Aḥduth Yisrael ("the Unity of Israel"), as masses of onlookers watched from sidewalks and rooftops. No musicians played at the head of the procession. No impressive vehicles cleared the road for them. No review stands were erected in honor of their parade. No distinguished government officials awaited them to give greetings. But masses of Jews clapped their hands in applause as they came walking by.

At the Aḥduth Yisrael synagogue the program began with the afternoon prayer-service (*minḥa*) in festive spirit, with Reb Aryeh as the *ḥazzan*, the reader of the immense "congregation." This was followed by a series of short addresses by the mayor of Jerusalem, the son-in-law of Rabbi Abraham Isaac Kook (the holy land's first chief rabbi), and a rabbi of the old religious yishuv.

Then a woman spoke—one of the former inmates of the women's prison in Bethlehem. No Israeli planes flew overhead in formation, she declared, to join in their parade and honor their gathering, and perhaps send a message of greeting floating down to them. But in place of them, the great spirit that motivated Sarah Aaronson, one of the martyrs in Israel's battle for freedom, was certainly with this gathering, together with the spirit that animated every one of the women who fought for the liberation of the homeland.

Israel Eldad spoke next, expressing the thought that in Reb Aryeh the former prisoners for Zion had always seen and still saw the living embodiment of the *t'hillim,* the Book of Psalms. He was a boundless source of immortal prayer for Jewry and its land.... Reb Aryeh was then presented with a tablet of olive-wood bearing the Hebrew legend, "I perceive the Lord before me always." Such a tablet is generally to be found in the traditional synagogue, placed to face the *ḥazzan* (reader of the congregation), to inspire him to devotion; and this particular tablet was the handiwork of some of the former prisoners.

The next speaker avowed that "the dedication of Reb Aryeh and his love for us drew us powerfully out of our feelings of isolation in the dark recesses of our cells." Since half of Jerusalem was then in foreign hands, he ended with the blessing that all might be privileged to walk through a united holy city, together with their "father of the imprisoned." Finally, on behalf of the Jabotinsky Institute Reb Aryeh was presented with an album of photographs taken in the various British prisons in the land and in the detention camps abroad—as a memento and a commemoration.

The next day, after a night of sleep and reflection, he wrote a letter of thanks:

> "... As a man of seventy, 'hoary old age,' who has been privileged to take part in this great gathering, I consider it an honor to express a very small bit of the holy emotions that were aroused in every part of my being at this assembly that was arranged for the glory of the Almighty. That majestic sight was unforgettable. It will never leave my memory.
>
> I learned so vividly from this how far the quality of gratitude and appreciation can go (even toward someone who does not deserve it). And if it is so on the part of human beings, how much stronger must the quality be on the part of the blessed Almighty God.
>
> I remain in prayer to the blessed Lord, Israel's Rock of strength and Rescuer, that I may be privileged together with all of you to go up to Zion, to the House of our God, there to fulfill our obligation to sanctify the name of the Holy One of Israel, and to become one with our sacred Torah to be able to prepare with its force the road to our final, complete redemption."

a postscript

It should have been a day of pride and great satisfaction. With thousands gathered to honor him on his seventieth birthday, he should have sat back and basked in the splendid tribute.

Actually, he did nothing of the sort. Tovia Preschel was there, and he took part in the celebration. When he moved afterward to America, he went to visit Reb Aryeh's oldest son, R. Ḥayyim Yaakov, who was then serving as rabbi in Jersey City, and he described it all to him.

"Yes," said R. Ḥayyim Yaakov Levin, "you saw my father walking at the head of all those former prisoners—and it looked splendid. But did you also know what was going on in his heart? He prayed that day, and ordered the members of the family to say *t'hillim* for him (prayers from the Book of Psalms), for fear that the honor might harm him spiritually!"

The central prison in Jerusalem, as it looks today. A handsome sign over the door proclaims it as **héchal ha-g'vura,** the Hall of Heroism—a museum commemorating the grim past.

17

For the partners in the struggle
at the women's prison

the melody of silence

Not only men fought in the underground movements to free the land of Israel from the yoke of the British mandate when it became blindly oppressive. There were women enough who joined them, and in consequence a good number were given enforced "vacations" in the women's prison at Bethlehem. Among them was Geula Cohen, who served as the broadcaster of the secret radio station of *le-ḥee* (the Fighters for the Freedom of Israel).

During her prison stay she came to know Reb Aryeh in the course of his visits, as he included this place of detention in the round of his activities. Later she wrote of him:

"We couldn't understand his words, since his voice was choked with tears.... Reb Aryeh came in quietly, as though he had taken off his shoes in the doorway. We prisoners sat about the large table and he took his place at its head, closing the circle as it were. And uncannily, I felt as though a flash of fire went through me.

"There he sat facing us, his white beard quivering. Every hair in it seemed to quiver with the pulsing of his heart's blood. In his eyes two teardrops seemed to stand constantly: one tear at his first innocent wonder at the utter beauty of the world; and another, final tear at the abysmal pain and suffering in the world. With these two constant drops in his eyes the rabbi seemed to come to us weeping.

"And between the tears he conveyed his words and thoughts about such heroines of the Bible as Yael and Deborah, about Israel's struggles and heroism in ancient times, about holy wars and the sanctification of God's name. We couldn't follow every word: the tears got in the way. But it didn't really matter. The words went straight to the heart of us and became a melody of prayer. And that melody we understood.

"He left, and we remained in the prison. He couldn't take us with him out into the free world. But instead, he always brought the outside world in to us."

the long roads that were shortcuts

Another prisoner in Bethlehem was Celia Amidror. She recalled:

It was an extra holiday for us whenever the pious Reb Aryeh came—a man whose personality became a living legend. He could come to visit our prison only in the weekdays (since it meant traveling by car, and on a Sabbath or *yom tov* that was out of the question for this devout Jew). But then any weekday when he appeared became a most happy holiday for us inmates, both in the prison proper and in the adjacent detention camp. He had a gift of imbuing us all with fervor and faith. With his eyes that brimmed with goodness and kindness, with his warm, affectionate heart, this pious faith-filled Jew instilled comfort and consolation in our hearts.

Every word he spoke found a place to lodge within us. He was so happy when he was able to do something, anything, for the imprisoned women. Always he pleaded with us: "What can I do for you to help you? to make things a little better for you?" He was an old man already then, with a natural dignity; and we were innately constrained and reluctant to burden him with small, petty requests. Yet he asked and pleaded insistently: "Let me help you; let me be of service"—till not one of us dared refuse him what he asked.

Any word of greetings or message that he was asked to give a prisoner's family, he would deliver the very same day. It never mattered to him what distance he had to travel. In his eyes all the roads and distances seemed short and easy, as long as he was of help to the imprisoned women. And when he brought a message of greeting, he gave it with a warmth and heartiness that the family sensed immediately.

with a child's innocence

Here is a fragment of memory from a woman who was sentenced by the British to a term of fifteen years:

With me in the Bethlehem women's prison were inmates who had only just been arrested, on their entry into the land without the official consent of the British. They found it hard to understand Reb Aryeh when he came visiting and spoke to us. They were Sephardic, and he (bless him) used his good old Ashkenazic pronunciation that he brought with him from Eastern Europe. If that were not enough, he spoke in a rather faint voice mingled with the intermittent sounds of his weeping. Yet these new inmates would always sit right opposite him, drinking in his words.

So I asked them, "Did you understand what he said?"

"Not a word," they replied. "But we come to contemplate his pure clear eyes. Such an absolute childlike innocence looks out from them. And his glance gives us affection and courage..."

so hard to leave

When he visited the women's prison in Bethlehem, the most difficult moment for him was when he had to leave. He simply could not tear himself away from his "daughters." The inmates sat facing him, their glances focused on him and his glance focused on them. They couldn't control their tears, and neither could he stop his.

After the Six-Day War there was a happy reunion at the Bethlehem women's prison.

At last, with an effort, he stood up. Yet such was his admiration for these prisoners that he could not turn his back to them. He always left the room facing them and walking backwards, like a loyal subject taking leave of his king.

Long after he was gone they still remembered his words: "Daughters of Israel in captivity? held captive by Edom and Ishmael? Heaven forbid! Perish the thought. It must not and cannot continue. So do not lose hope. God's kindness is very great. Now, on my way back, I will stop off at the tomb of our Mother Rachel and say prayers for you."

the treasured letter

Among the letters that he kept and treasured, there was this:

The Woman's Prison, Bethlehem
With Heaven's aid, 8 Nissan 1947

To our dear father, boundless peace:

We received last week your letter of 22 Adar, and were greatly distressed that we had no chance to answer it immediately.... Our words are too poor to express our gratitude for your great worry over us. We have not yet had the chance to convey our feelings of appreciation for your visit. It was a wonderful, precious hour for us. We were happy to become acquainted with the dear man who has earned such immense gratitude and love from hundreds of young men and women. We are still talking today about that hour.

We will be most happy and appreciative, dear rabbi, if you will honor us with another visit. Actually, we have already been promised it by Rabbi Goldman, and we hope that our dear father will not refuse.

Please do not worry. Thank God, we are in good health; and we hope to the Lord that He will gather our cast-off people from the four corners of the earth and will lead us all, with heads lifted high, into our land; *amen!*

With great admiration and love,
your daughters

"this was our rabbi"

Malka Heppner's situation was quite different, as she related it:

Since I was a wounded prisoner, there were many occasions when I had to stay at the government hospital in the Russian compound, in Jerusalem. So it was my privilege to get to know Reb Aryeh before he ever came to visit the women's prison in Bethlehem.

My first meeting with him was so moving and emotional that I remember every gesture and word from those few moments that I spent in his presence.

It was a Saturday, before noon. All the other patients in my hospital room were Arab women. At my bed an Arab policewoman was posted, since I was primarily a prisoner and secondarily a patient. At the door of the room British officers were posted. (Obviously they considered me more dangerous than I considered myself.) Visitors were never allowed in this room, and I lay there utterly alone, resigned to my isolation and never expecting a soul.

Suddenly a man of dignified appearance entered, slightly stooped, with a full white beard, wearing a long black coat. I had no idea who he was, and I was simply astounded: What was this pious Jew doing in those surroundings? How had he ever wandered into this unfamiliar milieu?

Without hesitation he came directly toward me (accompanied, of course, by a British officer; remember: I was a dangerous criminal). He looked at me with his kindly eyes, and before any word was said I could sense his feelings: If he but had the means, he would get me out of there. What was a Jewish girl doing in that hostile environment, under guard? His eyes blazed as he blessed me in his soft voice and asked how I was. Then, to start the conversation, he told me that he had come directly from the central prison, where he had joined the "boys" in the morning prayer-service—and he had greetings and regards for me. He named several friends of mine and gave me their messages of encouragement.

In age and life-style he was certainly far apart from us. There was little that we youngsters had in common with the pious Jews in the old yishuv, with their oldstyle clothing and oldstyle ways (or at least so we believed in our defiant certainty). Yet this man always knew and understood what interested us and what was important to us. After asking me about everything and telling me all that he had to relate, he wanted my name and the address of my parents, so that he could convey greetings and messages back and forth. As it was the Sabbath, the rabbi would do no writing on the holy day of rest. So he memorized the details I gave him; and in the evening, when the Sabbath was over, he contacted my parents (who lived in Tel Aviv) to tell them how I was coming along.

To people today, living under normal conditions, this might seem an ordinary or trivial matter. A telephone call is made and a message is given. Our situation then was quite different, though. Our parents were allowed to visit us once in two months. We were permitted to receive a letter just once a month. So what Reb Aryeh did was tremendously important.

A number of years after the State of Israel was proclaimed, when I was no longer a militant young girl but the mother of two small children, I was walking down the street when I saw Reb Aryeh in the distance, coming toward me. I was not sure if he would recognize me; but after a moment's

At the reunion in the former women's prison in Bethlehem, held after the Six-Day War (when Jews could get to Bethlehem again), the Arab women who had served as prison guards also insisted on flocking about Reb Aryeh.

hesitation I went to greet him. To my surprise and delight he looked at me and cried, "Malka? Is it you?"

"It certainly is," I answered; and I could feel his happiness. He asked after my welfare and how large a family I now had; and then with a slight tremble he asked how I was managing, and if the housework was not too hard for me. Did I have adequate help, he wanted to know.... For you see, in my fighting career in the underground movement I was severely wounded in the spine, and it left its effects. And of course Reb Aryeh made it his business to know that.

This, you see, was our rabbi.

18

In the sphere of martyrdom

when all hope was gone

As a rule, when political prisoners were sentenced by the British courts to the gallows and the shadow of death was not to be thrust aside by a pardon, they had one last request: to have Rabbi Aryeh Levin with them in their final moments on earth. He used to say, "None of us has any idea how high is the spiritual rank of these martyrs." Often, though, his own spirit failed him when he spoke with them, and it was they who had to comfort him.

If he had an abounding love for the underground fighters for Israel's freedom, it was not because he had concurring political views or any philosophy that affirmed the use of violence. Far from it. In his last will and testament he bade his sons belong to no political party in Israel, because the party system splinters the unity of the people and tries to channel one's love for the people and the land to this group or that. He once told me that he grew close to the imprisoned members of *étzel* (Irgun Tz'va'i Le'umi: National Military Organization) and *le-ḥee* (Lohamey Ḥéruth Yisrael: Fighters for Israel's Freedom) only because they were persecuted and driven, and the Hebrew Bible states, "God seeks him who is driven" (Ecclesiastes 3:15).

He was profoundly affected by their dedication to their cause, their readiness to make any sacrifice willingly and happily for the sake of our people and our God-given land. In his later years, looking back on his activities, he would say to their veterans, "Who am I, what good fortune have I, that you should bless me and give me honor? You gave me ten times as much as ever I gave you. You see: I had the privilege to enter the sphere of martyrs, hallowed and purified by their fate to shine with the radiance of heaven above, exalted to a spiritual rank by their lot where even the highest ministering angels cannot approach them. You were refined and purified in the furnace of agony, pain and suffering. You have become a spiritual élite. Who am I and what is my lowly rank compared to you?"

Writing of the Jewish victims of the British gallows in the holy land, one man related:

The Sabbath is a happy, festive day for every Jewish inmate in the Jerusalem prison. For on the Sabbath Rabbi Aryeh Levin visits them, and they wait for him with great anticipation. He puts new life into them, even though he uses few words. It is his heart that gives them new strength. His very presence instills in them a faith in the God of Israel. "God's rescuing help comes in the twinkling of an eye!" This is the phrase that he is forever saying and repeating with utter sincerity and absolute faith, until his belief and enthusiasm infects everyone about him.

More than once the prisoners would sit down and discuss and debate among themselves, trying to probe and discover the secret, the essence of their rabbi's "sorcery." Why has he become so beloved to them since the first day that they met him? What is the source of the strong bond of affection that has been forged between them? Why does everyone call him "the father of the prisoners"? How was he able to infuse them with confidence and inner strength to bear all that they have to suffer, physically and spiritually, in the suffocating conditions of the prison?

All realize and agree immediately that his face is radiant, and with his own inner luminosity he kindles a flame of faith in a human being. His beaming, radiant face bears witness to a joy of life, a sworn optimism in the world of the Almighty, and a profound faith in man's future. It is easy for the thirty-six tzaddikim, the great holy persons who uphold the world with their merit. They hide in their fabled anonymity. Even when they walk among their fellow-men no one knows them. No one points them out; no one subjects them to any searching inspection by the physical or the spiritual eye.

Reb Aryeh, however, mingles constantly with people. They look at him and measure him by his ordinary everyday deeds. Yet his stature never diminishes. On the contrary, his esteem in their eyes doubles and redoubles.

He was particularly moved by the gratitude they showed him, and the affection that the men condemned to death bore him in response to his deep love for them. The noted author Hayyim Hazaz once wrote this description of an encounter between Reb Aryeh and the men awaiting the gallows:

... The outer doors of the corridor opened and the rabbi came in.

"Rabbi!" exclaimed Menahem, leaping to the door of his isolation-cell. "A good Sabbath to you. You've brought me back to life, rabbi."

The pious man stood sedately at the door of the isolation-cell, dressed in the long black coat that reached to his ankles, and the *shtreim'l,* the standard Sabbath hat of the pious. In his face with its full white beard and in his bodily stature there was something of the tranquility and holiness of the Sabbath mingled with a thread of melancholy, evoking the mood of the Sabbath before the ninth of Av, the national historic day of mourning.

He began by speaking to them of their families, bringing each one news from home. In his usual way he was sparing with his words. Everything he uttered had the air of an apology or a plea for their grace. Between one sentence and another he would make a pause, laden by a burden of silence, which reached the heart like something heard. Eliyahu and the rabbi became enmeshed in a host of questions and answers: What is my father doing? How is my mother? How are the little children coming along? Is the family managing? ... and so forth—basic subjects standard in content and meaning.

Menahem stood there (at his door) contemplating the rabbi; he seemed to be wondering and pondering: Perhaps the rabbi really exists, and perhaps not. Maybe he is not even of this generation, and his face attained its appearance generations ago. And perhaps his soft, still voice is an echo from ancient times. But his silence is weighty and dignified, well suited to the long black coat and the full white beard. But his silence is apt and fitting, deriving from his knowledge of the bitter truth. The stillness is indeed at the very center of his knowledge of the truth....

the hand of fate

In 1946 the activities of the underground organizations were at their height, and at Sarafand (Serafin) the British maintained their largest military camp in the land. For some time *étzel* (one of the main underground groups) had been thinking of a way of breaking into the camp, to acquire vital supplies.

On March 6 the raid of the camp was carried out, but two men were wounded and caught: Yoséf Simḥon and Michael Ashbel (God rest their souls). Two months afterward they were brought to trial before the British military court, with Lieutenant-Colonel Pell as presiding judge and two others as associate justices. Lieutenant-Colonel Campbell was the prosecuting attorney, while Max Kritchman appeared for the prisoners. The thirteenth of June was celebrated as a holiday that year, as it was the birthday of the king of England. Jerusalem saw the day celebrated by a colorful military parade. And in many a heart fluttered the hope that perhaps under the influence of the birthday-holiday mood, the verdict in the trial of the two men, due to be given that very day, might be lenient.

During their stay in prison the two men studied the laws of the British authorities; and so they learned that when they decide on a sentence of death, British justices put on a black cap. This time, though, the judges entered in haste. Two were bare-headed, while the presiding judge wore the cap. There was silence in the courtroom as the presiding judge read the sentence calmly, without undue emotion. The verdict was death.

Now the prisoners were taken to the condemned men's cell, next to the room with the gallows, and given the "red clothing" of the condemned. In the diary that Michael Ashbel kept, this entry was later found:

> Today is the holy Sabbath; we await the visit of our rabbi. Although our spirit is strong as iron, we want to hear what this wise man who regards every prisoner as his son will say. We always speak with

him through the bars of the door. His face, adorned with a silvery beard, is pale. Tears always appear in his eyes, and he has to wipe his spectacles many times.

He asks of us to hope for God's mercy and to pray. In addition he begs us to ask for a pardon from the military British commander and not refuse obstinately. The rabbi reminds us about Matithyahu Shmuelevitz—that he sat in this very same cell—as if to prove to us that there is a way out other than the gallows. He tells us of the fast he is observing, and how ill he is, in his concern for us. I assure the rabbi that I lack for nothing and our spirit is implacably strong, and I ask him to be courageous and gather his strength. We promise him faithfully to pray. He has brought us *t'fillin* (phylacteries) and a prayer-book for each of us. It is amazing how he thinks of every detail. He brought an Ashkenazic prayer-book for me, and a Sephardic one for my friend (so that each of us can pray in his accustomed rite).

The rabbi leaves us, the prison director going with him. After his visit we are quiet. Each of us feels the suffering of this precious Jew, and we share in his grief. We didn't voice any complaints to him. He doesn't have to know how bad our situation is for us here. He is suffering enough."

Once the death-sentence was announced, *étzel* assigned one of its best men to kidnap British officers as "hostages" (to be able to promise to take "a life for a life"). The mission was carried out successfully, but a few days afterward the two condemned men received a pardon, as the British high commissioner commuted their sentences to life-imprisonment.

Fate, however, had its own verdict. In March 1948 Yoséf Simḥon escaped from the Jerusalem prison, only to die in 1955 in the Negev from an accident at work. Michael Ashbel died on the fourteenth of Iyar (May) 1947, in an attempt to break out of the prison in Acco.

a share in a mitzvah

From the reminiscences of Max Kritchman, one of the defense attorneys of the underground fighters, comes this account:

One of the most difficult battles to save a condemned man from the gallows occurred in connection with Dov Groner (God rest his soul). He took part in an attack by *étzel* on the police-station in Ramat Gan, and was caught and brought to trial at a military court. He denied the court's authority, and was sentenced to death.

The verdict was given secretly and was not publicly announced (so as not to produce a violent reaction). As soon as I learned of the verdict I rushed to the prison—it was on a Sabbath—and I found Groner already dressed in the red clothes worn by condemned men. I felt a profound need burgeoning in me to go out and shout and scream, to arouse the population to a mighty response, so as to save this young man from the hangman's noose. For in those days death-sentences were carried out very soon after they were given.

Dov Groner

As I went to visit Groner I met Reb Aryeh coming as usual for his visit to the prison on Sabbath morning. I told him of the frightful verdict and of my determination to raise a great hue and cry. "Whatever you do," said Reb Aryeh, "please take me with you. I want to have a share in the mitzvah of saving a human life."

That very Sabbath day we went to see Yitzhak ben-Zvi, the chairman of the *vaad le'umi* (National Committee, the political head of the Jewish population, and later Israel's second president), and from his house on to Chief Rabbi Isaac Herzog. We wanted to lose no time in getting our campaign started.

For Reb Aryeh, however, even this was not enough. Having trudged along with me to Yitzhak ben-Zvi and Chief Rabbi Herzog, he then asked the chief rabbi to go with him to the office of the Chief Secretary of the British mandatory government and the High Commissioner, outside the city limits, to plead with them to spare the condemned man's life.

To our great sorrow all these efforts proved of no avail.

IN THE SPHERE OF MARTYRDOM

the message of escape

At least once, though, Reb Aryeh was able to intervene most directly and most effectively.

On a side street in the Maḥaneh Yehuda section of Jerusalem there is a candy and sweets shop run by a man who answers to the name of Moshe. His hair has turned silver and he is a grandfather; but if you find him when there are no customers to claim his attention, and you press him a bit, his mind goes back to 1935 and 1936, when he was young

The letter Reb Aryeh wrote the British High Commissioner, in an effort to save Dov Groner: "...It is my privilege to implore your excellency with every possible kind of plea, to beseech with every possible kind of entreaty, on behalf of Dov Groner, who stands on the threshold of death (Heaven forbid). The fate of this unfortunate man, whether he is to live or die, depends now on your excellency. He is broken and wretched, oppressed by miseries. None knows this better than I myself: I have palpably felt his fearful suffering while under arrest and imprisonment. He is the only son of parents who were destroyed by the despotic Nazis—a brand plucked from the fire. I pray you: have mercy and compassion on this unfortunate soul. His hallowed martyred parents will then stand before the Divine throne of glory and pray for your excellency's welfare and the welfare of the entire British government. And thus a source of shame will be removed from our holy city. For in all the years of my service [at the prison] no death has ever been imposed on any of my fellow-Jews.

"From your humble servant who writes amid tears, with his heart's blood, hoping for mercy,   Aryeh Levin"

273

and militant, and quite determined to help rid the Jewish homeland of the oppressive British rule.

He joined an underground movement, and in time found himself in the Jerusalem central prison, where of course he came to know Reb Aryeh on the good rabbi's Sabbath morning visits. Moshe is not a religious observant Jew, but when he speaks of Reb Aryeh a note of reverence comes into his voice. "He was a tzaddik," he murmurs; "he was a tzaddik."

If the British assumed that imprisonment would be a corrective educational experience for Moshe, they were mistaken. Released eventually

> Government of Palestine.
>
> In replying to this letter please quote the date and reference number.
> C.S. 755/6.
>
> Chief Secretary's Office,
> Jerusalem
>
> 16- April 1947.
>
> Sir,
>
> I am directed by the High Commissioner to acknowledge the receipt of your letter of the 3rd February, 1947, in which you appeal for the exercise of clemency in the case of Dov Groner and to inform you that His Excellency has carefully considered your petition, but regrets that he is unable to intervene.
>
> I am,
> Sir,
> Your obedient servant,
>
> CHIEF SECRETARY.
>
> Rabbi Aril Lewin,
> Mishkenoth,
> JERUSALEM.

The reply Reb Aryeh received about Dov Groner

from the Jerusalem prison, he went back into the underground fighting with renewed fervor—only to find himself in one of the other prisons in Israel. There he was forced to carry water in a bucket that weighed more than the liquid it held; and as he and his fellow-sufferers trudged with their buckets over the long hot dusty road, there was always a British guard prodding their backs with his short stick, goading them with his cry, "Go on, go on!"

Free again, with more reason than ever to hate the British, Moshe resumed his underground activities—and was caught carrying a loaded weapon. This was an offense punishable by death, and Moshe soon found himself in the Acco prison, in the isolation ward for condemned prisoners, wearing the red prison garb of a prisoner awaiting execution.

For lunch, however, he was allowed to join the other prisoners; and that was the time when Reb Aryeh could occasionally come for a visit. After their meal, before they had to return to their cells, the good rabbi had a chance to speak with the inmates, giving messages from their families and recording their new messages in his mind to take back. For Moshe, however, he had a most startling message one day. "Look over here," Reb Aryeh whispered, indicating a large circular disk set in the floor, in an unobserved corner of the kitchen. "That is a trap door leading to the drainage system of the prison. It won't be pleasant to walk through it, with all the dirty water and waste matter about your feet; but it can be done. And it leads out to the shore of the Mediterranean Sea. Get your friends to help you and go down through it tomorrow at this very time, after lunch. When you come out near the ocean, you will find other friends waiting for you."

Moshe couldn't believe his ears. True, the good rabbi knew the right prayers to say to implore Heaven's mercy. And in his humility he tended to cast his eyes downward rather than haughtily upward, so that he was likely to notice that disk in the floor much sooner than other people. But how could the good rabbi know about the drainage and sewage system? Most likely, Moshe decided, the underground movement devised the plan, and Reb Aryeh simply brought one more message among many.

But Moshe had to be certain. In the short time left before he would have to return to his cell, he joined a few close friends among the prisoners and whispered to them. There and then they managed to send one of them down the sewage system to investigate. Fifteen minutes later he was back. Reb Aryeh, said he, was absolutely right.

Just how they were able to keep the guards from noticing, Moshe never knew; for he was the first to go. Evidently prisoners with short sentences (for whom it was not worth risking escape) kept the guards away and distracted. In all, some fifty men escaped. And as Reb Aryeh promised, where the sewage conduit ended, the underground movement had transport waiting to spirit them all away to safety, till the ensuing hue and cry died down and the intensive search for them was given up.

In the years after the mandate, with the British gone, Moshe could make a free normal life for himself; and his bond of friendship with Reb Aryeh continued. Every morning, on his way from home to the Etz Ḥayyim school (where he worked, supervising the progress of the children) Reb Aryeh stopped at Moshe's shop and bought a bag of candies, as standard equipment for his day's work with the children. If he came too early, he would wait till Moshe appeared.

A favorite topic of conversation between them was the *kothel ma'aravi* (the Western or Wailing Wall), then in Jordan's hands. With some stubborn conviction or streak of intuition, Moshe kept assuring the good rabbi through the years, "Some day I will take you to the *kothel*. You will see." At last the Six-Day War came, and the Western Wall became part of the land of Israel again. Directly after, on the Thursday morning before the festival of Shavuoth, 1967, Reb Aryeh appeared at the candy shop all wreathed in smiles. "Come, Moshe," said he, "the time has come for us to go to the *kothel*."

death at their own hands

The traditional seven days of mourning were not yet over for Dov Groner and three others, executed in April 1947, when death sentences were announced against another two: Meir Feinstein and Moshe Barzani. These condemned men, however, were determined to die a hero's death, at their own hand, giving the British no chance to end their lives. They therefore pleaded with their good friends to smuggle a hand-grenade into their cell, and at a time of their own choosing they would blow themselves up.

Well, their wish was granted them. Within the very walls of the prison in Jerusalem two inmates prepared a primitive grenade, enclosed it in orange-peel, and smuggled it into the condemned men's cell.

Moshe Barzani

Meir Feinstein

It was twenty years since Reb Aryeh began visiting the prison. Never had he failed to come as expected or as needed, even during riots and curfews in the city, even when he felt ill or unwell. Yet this time, when he was called by the British authorities to go to the condemned men on the night before their hanging, to say with them the confession of sins and to pray with them, he felt his strength fail him. He was brokenhearted to see that all his efforts to have them spared were fruitless.

"What sins did my children commit?" he asked the British officials who came to take him to the prison. "To what sins should they confess? Is there anyone in the world who ranks higher in heaven than they, if tomorrow morning they go to the gallows to sanctify God's name and Israel?" He could not and would not budge.

So it was that Rabbi Yaakov Goldman, appointed by the *vaad le'umi* as rabbinic supervisor of the prisons, was with the condemned young men during some of their last hours. After he left them they decided it was time to follow the heroic example of King Saul, Elazar ben Ya'ir and the brave men and women of Massada, all of whom had chosen in ancient times to die by their own hand sooner than give any gentile the privilege and exultation of putting them to death. The two embraced each other, holding the grenade between their hearts. They shut their eyes, and with intense concentration recited the holy words that every martyr has uttered before his death, since time immemorial: *Hear O Israel: the Lord is our*

God, the Lord is one! At the word "one" they lit the match and touched it to the fuse. There was a tremendous explosion, and the two young men lived no more.

As soon as their act became known a heavy curfew was put on the city. Only members of the immediate families received special permits to attend the funeral, and Reb Aryeh was invited to join them. Under heavy military escort (since the British were fearful of what the underground movement might try to do) the two martyrs were brought to burial in the old cemetery on the Mount of Olives. By the order of Chief Rabbi Herzog their graves were dug in the part of the cemetery where the martyred victims of the Arab riots of 1929, 1936 and 1939 lay buried—the part which looks out toward Mount Moriah, the Temple Mount, where before Israel's history began, Abraham had bound his son Isaac on the altar.

It was Reb Aryeh who eulogized these two hallowed "sons" of his, praising them justly and humbly. He recited the psalm of the day (it was a Wednesday), which begins, "O Lord, God of vengeance, Thou God of vengeance, shine forth!" (Psalms 94:1). Perhaps it was just as well that the members of the military escort didn't understand Hebrew. Then he said *kaddish* (the mourner's prayer) for them, and other supplications.

The burial completed, he refused to return to the city by car. He insisted on trudging back on foot, all the way to his home in the Mishk'noth neighborhood, as a mark of his grief over them. Then he observed *shiv'ah*, seven traditional days of mourning, as though they were his children.

A few years after the State of Israel arose, a part of the central prison in Jerusalem was converted into a "Museum of Heroism." At its dedication there was an assembly of former prisoners in the courtyard, with the rabbi and father of these prisoners of Zion in their lead, his head now bent and his shoulders slightly stooping. A journalist described the event:

In the courtyard gathered the former members of the two underground organizations, with their bold commanders, among them the former inmates of such places of detention as Latrun, Acco and Bethlehem—the women's prison where the women in detention remained proud in their isolation and suffering. Included too were some of the last to be condemned to death, as well as people who were exiled to the detention camps of Kenya and Eritrea and people who escaped from there. With them came their rabbi, who had been with so many of them in their time of suffering—a man unique in his generation, who would sit with them in their prison cells to listen to their whispered confessions and problems, and to give them courage.

Now the aged rabbi went up on the rostrum and asked permission to speak, to offer a confession of his own: "In the middle of the night before the heavy curfew was imposed, I was sitting on the upper floor of my home in Mishk'noth, when the regional commander of *étzel* [Irgun Tz'va'i Le'umi, one of the two underground organizations] arrived to speak with me. As always, my dear wife (of blessed memory) listened and kept silent. There he sat, and told me the secret (that Meir Feinstein and Moshe Barzani were planning to take their own lives). And he wanted my consent; no more than that; no deed, no act, but only a sign that I gave my approval....

"I began to weep. 'How can you ask it?' I told him. 'God's rescuing help comes in the twinkling of an eye. We did not give ourselves our life, and we ought not to end it. Let the Holy One who gave it to us take it as He pleases, and let no one destroy himself.' I could not give my consent.... But all that night I lay awake. In the morning, when the curfew was already in effect, British officers came and invited me to take part in the funeral of these two hallowed men of courage. With me went only their immediate families and members of the burial society, and a heavy British military escort.

"There, at the burial ground on the heights of the Mount of Olives, I let my emotions speak for them. I let myself recognize their worth, their bravery and courage; in my eulogy I gave them the admiration they deserved."

Some time later (the journalist continued) I visited him at his home. Bidding me wait, he took the tractate *Avoda Zara* out of his bookcase, from the set of Talmud in reduced size that he owned. He turned the pages, and his fingers stopped at page 18b, in the first chapter. From those small letters of timeless wisdom he read to me in full the passage about the death of Rabbi Ḥanina ben T'radyon, one of the ten Talmudic sages who were cruelly executed by the ancient Romans. In Jewish history they have remained perhaps our most noble and illustrious martyrs, who

In the presence of their close relatives, Reb Aryeh offered prayers for the two martyrs, in the prison building, converted into the "Hall of Heroism."

died because they would not cease teaching the Torah to their people, despite the Roman ban.

"Rabbi Ḥanina ben T'radyon (Reb Aryeh read aloud the words of the Talmud) would sit and engage in Torah study, and he would assemble large public gatherings with the Torah scroll in his lap [to teach them its contents]. They [the Romans] took him and wrapped the Torah scroll about him. All about him they piled bunches of twigs, which they set on fire. Then they brought spongy masses of wool, soaked them in water, and placed them on his heart, so that his life should not expire swiftly [but he should suffer long-drawn-out torture]. 'Rabbi,' his students asked him, 'what do you see?' He replied, 'The sheets of parchment [of the Torah]

IN THE SPHERE OF MARTYRDOM

are burning, and the letters go soaring!' [Then they asked] 'Why do you not open your mouth wide and let the flames get inside your body?' [to die instantly and end the pain]. Said he, 'It is better that He who gave it [our life to us] should take it, and one should not destroy himself.' "

There was silence in the room when Reb Aryeh finished, and I pondered our people's long history of martyrdom, of brave Jews who accepted death for the causes sacred to them and to Jewry: from a Talmudic sage under the rule of ancient Rome to two underground fighters in a Jerusalem prison a few years ago, under British rule.

"Do you see?" said Reb Aryeh. "From this account I had to conclude that when a person is willing to give his life for a holy cause, he may still not bring on his death himself, directly. It was the only answer I could give the commander of *étzel* who came to ask my consent."

"go to your father Abraham"

Three others who could not be saved from their death-sentence under the British mandate were Avshalom Ḥaviv, Yaakov Weiss and Meir Nekker. Of them Reb Aryeh himself wrote:

I could be with them only on a few Sabbaths (during my weekly visits to the Jerusalem prison); but during these visits I formed a vital bond with them; and it was difficult each time to leave them. When they were transferred to the prison in Acco I spared no effort to visit them, along with the other inmates. I asked them how their morale was. "Rabbi," they replied, "we remember what you told us when we were imprisoned

| Avshalom Ḥaviv | Yaakov Weiss | Meir Nekker |

in Jerusalem. You spoke of the innate holiness and purity of Rabbi Akiva, when the ancient Romans were stripping his flesh from his body with iron combs and he simply submitted in Divine love to the yoke of the kingship of Heaven. His disciples asked him, 'Our rabbi and teacher, even so?' [Even to this extent you will not turn your mind away from your faith and fall prey to your torture? However did you reach so exalted a state that you have lost all fear of death and suffering?]

"He answered them, 'All my life I would suffer over the words of the Torah to love the Lord our God with all our soul—meaning even if He takes your soul, your life.' All my years I imagined myself giving up my life willingly to sanctify His name. In my mind I rehearsed it and experienced it as though it were actually happening. 'Now that I have the chance to fulfill this command of the Torah, shall I forego it and fail?'

"Even if we three haven't reached this noble spiritual state and never will reach it, we are training ourselves, however, to give up our lives with dignity for our people and the land of our God. Those sacred words of Rabbi Akiva echo down from generation to generation. They penetrate into the lives of our people, till they reach their proper place and time. Our people will never lack such heroes, who have suffered bitter, painful forms of death in silent acceptance. You, dear rabbi, know them well."

I asked them then if the love of their homeland was so precious to them that they were really willing to die for it like this. Surely they should also have thought of their home as well as their homeland—the parents, who suffered as a result.

"Rabbi," they answered, "you must certainly remember what you told our fellow-fighters in Jerusalem: that in 1492, when Spain issued its terrible decrees against its Jewish population, the gentiles slew two sweet, precious children right in their mother's lap, and that courageous mother cried out: 'Master of the world, until now I loved Thee, but not completely, not with all my heart. I also had two children to love. Now, however, my heart is entirely freed and emptied to be a vessel solely for love for Thee.' We are ready to leave room in our parents' heart to love the land and the people of our God in our place."

I looked at them in silence. What was I to say to them? "My dear sons," I said at last, "go to your father Abraham." Their life-spirits would surely rise to the sphere of our Patriarchs when they left this world.

At the burial service of David Raziel, another victim of British "justice," Reb Aryeh stood between the martyr's sister (now a member of the Knesset) and the Sephardic chief rabbi.

his life was spared

How deeply he cared for those condemned to death by the British (not because he agreed with their policy of violence, which he did not, but simply because acting by their lights in a noble cause, they found themselves ruthlessly and stupidly persecuted), how far he was ready to go in his efforts to save them, is shown by this story (told by Reb Aryeh to Yitzḥak Agassi of Israel's Ministry of the Interior):

One of the underground fighters, a young man of Jerusalem, was caught by the British and sentenced to death. Time was short, and as he generally did in such cases, Reb Aryeh made his way to the official quarters of the British high commissioner, the supreme officer in the holy land, to plead with him to spare the boy's life. The sentries at the gate, however, would not let the gentle rabbi in. After all, he had no official appointment.

What to do? Reb Aryeh thought, and reached a decision. He went a good distance down the road and waited. How long he waited no one knows, but at last his patience was rewarded. He saw the high commissioner come out of his residence and get into his limousine, to be driven off by his chauffeur, with an escort of attendants. Instantly Reb Aryeh went into the middle of the road, and in plain view of the chauffeur he stretched out full length in the limousine's path.

The chauffeur's reflexes were good, and as he applied his brakes instantly, the large car screeched to a halt barely in time. In great excitement, the high commissioner and his entourage came out of their vehicle. "What happened?" they asked. "Is anything the matter with you, rabbi? Were you hurt? Are you unwell?"

Recovering his aplomb, he told the high commissioner (with the aid of a translator) of his cold reception by the sentries and his desperate need to see the high commissioner and plead for the young man who was to lose his life so soon.

That very day the high commissioner issued an order sparing the boy's life.

their words at the end

In 1952 Joseph Nedava wrote a book called *oley ha-gardom* ("Those who mounted the gallows"), and he asked the good rabbi to write something as an introduction. This is the reply he received:

I have been honored by the request to write a few words in your estimable book commemorating our martyred brethren...whose misery I witnessed myself...those whom I cannot forget, who will never vanish from my memory.

My dear friend, with all my heart I want to fulfill your wish, which is even more *my* wish. Yet I am no man of words; and who can evaluate the true worth of our hallowed brethren who dared to die a hero's death for our people and our holy land? They took no pity on themselves, but stuck out and exposed their necks, and stood firm through the ordeal while the terror of death cast its pall over them for days and weeks... and their spirit never broke within them. Too poor is my pen now to write any [proper] words, as I lack the disposition.... Nevertheless, let me set down a few things that inscribed themselves in my memory—words that I heard from our holy martyred brethren when I was alone with them for the last time:

"For one must not give way in a day of trouble, but must particularly show courage at the appointed time to go.... Now is the most fitting time to really see that there is no reason to worry or quaver before the fear... but to give up our lives for our people and our holy land. For the readiness for self-sacrifice has always been necessary and vital for the Jewish people, especially during their exile at a time of religious coercion and persecution, to give up their lives for the sanctification of God's name.

"Had they become accustomed to hold dear their temporal, ephemeral earthly life, they would have also given up their faith so as to hold on to their life. However, like people marching to the fife they went forward to meet their fate with a peal of happiness, singing *adon olam,* the hymn of praise to the Lord of the world, and *ani maamin,* the affirmation of their unquenchable faith. So we have the right and the obligation to follow in their footsteps and give up our lives for our people and our land. Were we to keep still at a time like this, who could estimate the catastrophe that would befall our people in the Diaspora (without a homeland)? We have had our fill of Isaacs bound and sacrificed on the altar."

Then I would say perhaps, "The moments have already come when we must separate, my dear children. Yet I remain in prayer to the blessed Lord to be able to share in your happiness—God's rescuing help comes in the twinkling of an eye." They would ask me, "Rabbi, where is that maxim written?" "Oh," I replied, "it must certainly be in the holy writings. I looked for it and could not find it; but the words are right and true. Fortunate are you, wise men shining like the firmament, since the calamity of our people [in Hitler's inferno] has touched your very heart and soul. For everyone has to reach the level of making himself part of the whole of our people, so that his times of rejoicing and sorrow should always fit with the situation of all, to the point that if he comes across something saddening and grievous, it should remind him of the general situation of his people.

"The Midrash (Echah Rabbah 1) tells: It happened that a certain woman lived in Rabban Gamliel's neighborhood, and she had a son just grown to manhood, when he died. She would weep for him in the night; and Rabban Gamliel used to hear her voice and be reminded of the destruction of the holy Temple, whereupon he would weep with her, until his eyelashes began falling out."

The souls of all the holy martyrs will find no rest until the Lord avenges the spilled blood of His servants, and His land will atone for His people. Then we will be privileged to have the complete redemption and the true rescue, when Zion will be told, "Your God has become sovereign."

Signed in trepidation at this hallowed memory,

Aryeh Levin

how he gave them courage

Afterward, when the long nightmare of British "justice" was over, Abraham Axelrod once asked the good rabbi point blank, "When those boys finally had to go to the gallows, how did you give them courage and heart? What did you say to them in the last moments of their lives?"

With his own childlike simplicity he answered, "What I said to them? How I gave them courage? I used to enter their prison cells. My heart would burst within me and be torn to shreds; my eyes would begin pouring tears; and they would come around me and begin comforting me and bolstering my spirit. At the very most we used to say a few paragraphs of *t'hillim* (Psalms) together. I used to look into their sorrowing eyes that were filled with trust in God, and so I went out encouraged by them."

Of course, those who "lived to tell the tale" because they were pardoned, told a different story: His deep silences, the tears that came of themselves, and his prayers gave them new spirit and strength, imbuing them with new spirit and trust.

And one journalist who always saw him in the corridor, waiting for the end to come for them, testified that in a sense Reb Aryeh went to their doom with each and every one. Some part of him felt their death with them, and felt the agony of every mother and father left desolated by the executions. His palpitating heart went with them all.

the reunion

On February 18, 1969 the veterans of Irgun Tz'va'i Le'umi held a reunion in *binyaney ha'uma,* the large assembly building in Jerusalem, to celebrate the twentieth anniversary of the State of Israel. Reb Aryeh wanted to attend, but could not, confined to bed as he then was by illness in his last months. Instead, he sent a letter:

"To our dear brethren and sisters [he often used the plural in his letters when referring to himself]:

With the help of the blessed Lord, Healer of the sick among His people Israel / Tuesday the first of Adar (a month of increased happiness in the Jewish calendar) 1969 / in the united holy city of Jerusalem:

From the hills of Jerusalem and the depths of the heart of a brother who has not been forgotten but lies tied to his sickbed—I am yet bound to you with the bond of dozens of years of pure affection without any ulterior motive, which shall remain a lasting hallmark for us all, enduring for all generations.

Although it is hard for me to concentrate in my writing, I retain in my memory what I wrote on this day of the year seventeen years ago, when our dear brethren asked me to send some impressions and reminiscences of my visits through the dozens of years that I served as a reservoir for the tears of my oppressed and persecuted brothers and sisters and their families. They were a humiliated and despoiled people, hidden away in the prisons, stowed away in the detention camps. Certainly it would be worthwhile and fitting to make the world recognize them as true prisoners for Zion, heroes of the spirit, precious sons and gentle daughters of Zion, children of our father Abraham who guarded their dignity and honor to a wondrous degree. Some were exiled from their homes; others, from our land to such places as Kenya. Among them were scholars, writers and poets, learned of the Lord, in the prisons of Latrun and Bethlehem, and finally of Atlith. May they all be blessed with great peace.

There were those who managed to taste the bitter experience of four exiles, and then they could not manage to find their homes, because their homes had been despoiled and emptied of everything they cherished and treasured. May the Almighty have compassion and repair their broken hearts.

In all my visits, every time, I felt that my dear brothers and sisters sensed that I shared their suffering and pain. They always wished to hearten me, to show me a cheerful face. And every time we broke out in tears, overwhelmed by emotion.

During my last visit to the prison in Acco we stood still, none of us saying a word, until I calmed myself and my dear brothers, the spirited heroes who were there with me. In those moments too they hid their pain from me. There was laughter on their faces as they reminded me of all the thoughts and sayings that they had heard from me when they were in the Jerusalem prison. There was but one request they had, one thing to beg of me: that I should promise them not to feel sorrow or suffer at all on their account.

In the isolation cell of the condemned, Dov Rosenblum told me cheerfully in Yiddish, "Let us talk of happier matters" (when I wanted to speak about his impending fate). Then, offhand, he asked me that if by chance I could not be with them in their last moments of earthly life—although the prison officials had assured them that I would be there (and as it turned out, this was a prophetic flash of intuition)—what holy words could they say, from our Hebrew Bible or prayer-book, if some small bit of time was left them after they said *sh'ma yisrael* ("Hear O Israel, the Lord is our God, the Lord is one").

The question caught me unawares, and I remained still as a stone. We kissed each other's hands, until the hands became wet and we both wept.... I could only murmur the teaching of the Talmud: Even if a sharp sword is placed on his neck, let a man not lose hope of Heaven's compassion.

Who is there to describe the great spirit of these courageous men and noble souls who submitted in purest faith to their verdict. Once the ten martyrs among our Talmudic sages received a message from the Divinity, "It is My decree; accept it," they did. And so did our precious sons in our time. Gracious God, look down from the highest heavens and see how the blood of tzaddikim was spilled. Let the outpouring of their blood appear on Thy curtain, and may Thou cleanse the stains—Thou, God the king who reigns from the throne of compassion.

We do not have the writer who can describe the greatness and reach of the spirit of these brethren of ours. From the faint echo that they heard in their lifetime they sensed from afar the agonies of our brethren in distant lands [of Europe] and became imbued with a holy spirit to dedicate body and soul for our people and our land, determined to descend to the depths of the sea if need be. They became inspired and intoxicated by the aura of holy martyrs burnt at the stake, the most exalted part of our people, whose spiritual level no ordinary mortal can reach. Now all these martyrs are united in the holiness of the Supreme One who gives life to every living spirit.

It is a great meritorious privilege for you and us to join and be as one in memorializing their immortal spirits and recalling the miracles that occurred for those who survived in safety. With your actions you did a great kindness for both the living and the dead. And it is a signal privilege I enjoy that you have not forgotten me even afterward. It is an act of Providence for me that through these many years you have not put me out of mind.

May you then relate even to the last generation that "once there was an ordinary man without any official position who loved your forefathers and felt the pain and suffering of your families; and the love remained in my heart like a blaze of fire." I most earnestly beg of you to let the bond of affection remain through all the generations as a permanent tie in this world and the next [in the Hereafter], as you know well that this is my desire.

With the Lord's help, may we merit to see the rescue of Israel come in the twinkling of an eye. Let help for the righteous come from the Lord, and let the children return within their borders.

Yet will we merit to see one another.

Your brother, bound to you heart and soul,
Aryeh Levin

19

The gateways of piety and decency

"Did you forget, perhaps?"

On a day just before Passover, in the afternoon, a neighbor came knocking on Reb Aryeh's door. "I've caught sight of a thief," he told Reb Aryeh, "here in the neighborhood, breaking into one of the stores. But I simply don't have the courage to raise a hue and cry: He may turn on me and attack me."

"Show me the shop where he broke in," said Reb Aryeh; and the two set off swiftly. Without any hesitation the good rabbi entered and spoke softly to the thief: "My son, did you forget perhaps that it is written in the Torah, *You shall not steal?*"

For a full moment the thief stared at Reb Aryeh. Then he dropped his gaze, put down the merchandise he had gathered, and left without a word.

the telling answer

When a certain man committed a very serious crime, the result was that he was sentenced to life-imprisonment. With most of her life still ahead of her, his young wife asked him for a divorce, dreading the thought of being condemned to a life alone. Through some quirk, however, he turned obstinate and absolutely refused to grant her any divorce, unless he was given some impossibly large sum of money. Members of the chief rabbinate spoke with him at length, using every possible kind of argument and persuasion. The prison authorities talked to him till they were blue in the face. Over and over they asked him what possible good he could derive from wealth while spending his entire life in prison. The man seemed to have turned into a mule, and a deaf mule to boot.

Finally appeals were made to Reb Aryeh: Would he please draw the prisoner into conversation and see if he could budge the man from his obstinacy?

Within two minutes Reb Aryeh knew that he was talking to a seasoned, hardened criminal whom nothing could shake. He was well beyond the reach of ordinary human considerations. Reb Aryeh continued chatting with him pleasantly though. Then, without warning, he changed his tone:

"Look here: I don't know why you need a great amount of money while you spend your life in prison. You are not going to get it, however, because there is no one to give it to you. Then it is your choice to refuse to give your wife a divorce. But if you do that, you are only punishing yourself. Do you think you have some kind of hold over your wife? Who is going to give you any guarantee or assurance that she will remain faithful to you as long as you do not divorce her? You are simply going to lie here night and day eaten by doubts, gnawed by jealousy. You will always be wondering: Is she being unfaithful to you now?... where?... with whom?"

The prisoner looked at Reb Aryeh thunderstruck. This was the last thing in the world he had ever expected to hear from the short rabbi with the long white beard and those old-fashioned clothes....

Their conversation went on for several hours. When it ended, the man gave his consent; and that very night, members of the chief rabbi's staff came, including a scribe and proper witnesses. The divorce was written, signed and sealed.

the effect of his presence

Whoever knew Reb Aryeh remembers most vividly his unique, affectionate handshake: He would hold the other person's hand and pat it—and it felt as though electric currents passed through the person's body, carrying the pure affection of the rabbi to every fiber of his spirit.

One Sabbath morning, as Reb Aryeh was chatting as usual with the inmates of the central prison in Jerusalem during his regular weekly visit, one prisoner came over to him. "Rabbi," he said, "I want you to know that I have taken an oath never to smoke cigarettes again on the Sabbath."

When Reb Aryeh asked what the reason was, the man continued, "This morning, when you came over to me to wish me a good Sabbath (in greeting), you took my hand and patted it, as usual, in your own gentle affectionate way, with that heartening smile on your face. Dear rabbi, at that moment my other hand held a lighted cigarette hidden behind my back, where you couldn't see it. I know well enough that our religious law forbids smoking on the Sabbath, but that never meant anything to me. At that moment, though, I wanted most intensely that you should know nothing of my burning cigarette. Yet all at once I felt as if that cigarette were giving me blisters all over my body. One thought burned in my heart: Is it right that while the rabbi is holding my hand and giving new life to my spirit, my other hand should hold a lighted cigarette in direct violation of the Sabbath? At that moment, in my heart, I took an oath never again to smoke on the Sabbath."

One of the officers of *étzel*, the underground fighting movement, who spent time in the prison under the British mandate, witnessed another incident: On a Sabbath morning a young inmate was standing off at the side, smoking a cigarette and watching a game of soccer that was going on in the courtyard. He became so engrossed in the game that he failed to hear the others in the room calling out, "The rabbi is coming; the rabbi is coming!"

All of a sudden the young man looked up, and there was Reb Aryeh coming directly toward him to greet him. Unable to bear letting the good rabbi see the cigarette, because it would hurt him cruelly, the young man just took it and swallowed it!

Such incidents happened not only within the prison walls. In the funeral procession, when tens of thousands marched to pay the good rabbi his last honor on earth, a son of Reb Aryeh noticed a young Sephardic Jew who was obviously not observant or devout; and for a moment he stared at him in curiosity. The young man came over to him. "Do you wonder why I am here?" he asked. "Your father once saw me smoking a cigarette on a Saturday, late in the afternoon. He took my hand and patted it, and he murmured: 'It is still the Sabbath you know. It is still the Sabbath.' Since then I don't smoke on Saturday."

the dilemma

Late one Friday afternoon, after the Sabbath candles had been lit, Reb Aryeh went his way sedately to the synagogue, for the prayer-service that would usher in the holy day of rest. With him went his young son Simḥa Sh'lomo.

On the way, a Jew stopped Reb Aryeh; and as a burning cigarette dangled from his lips he asked the good rabbi to kindly show him the way to a certain hotel.

Now Reb Aryeh was in a dilemma: How could he walk through the streets of Jerusalem side by side with a Jew smoking a cigarette when the Sabbath was approaching so imminently? Yet on the other hand, the man was obviously a stranger in the holy city, looking for the place that would give him food and lodging. How could he just leave the man to go wandering about aimlessly?

The good rabbi reached his decision: to take the man to his hotel. So they went together, the short man with the white beard in his Sabbath clothes, and the tall man without a trace of religion about him. True to habit, Reb Aryeh held one hand of his affectionately and engaged the man gently in conversation, asking how he was and hoping that he would enjoy his stay in the holy city. With a mild, unobtrusive insistence, however, the good rabbi kept interspersing comments on the imminent approach of the holy Sabbath, when (he added) smoking was forbidden by religious law. To these remarks, though, the man responded with a stolid, studied indifference.

Try as he would, however, the man could not help but feel what a peculiar, if not ridiculous, figure he cut, walking beside this dignified rabbi through Jerusalem's streets and retaining his cigarette with a rather obvious obstinacy. When they reached the hotel, the two looked at each other—and the man threw his cigarette away. "Rabbi," he said in a voice somewhat husky with emotion, "I am not religious, and I am quite obstinate. In all my life I have yielded to no one. Yet somehow you have broken my resistance. How can I remain disrespectful before you? Here you see, I have thrown that confounded cigarette away; and I solemnly pledge never again to smoke on the Sabbath."

a discerning eye, an unerring instinct

His son R. Simḥa Sh'lomo recalls one Sabbath that Reb Aryeh and he spent not at home but in Tel Aviv. The good rabbi's wife was ill and in the hospital, and he knew his presence would be welcome at two ceremonies of circumcision, to be held in Tel Aviv that Saturday.

The first *b'rith* (circumcision ceremony) was an affair quite after his own heart. The "hero" of the occasion was the infant son of Uri Tz'vi Greenberg, a noted Israeli poet, who in his adult years had returned in full to the age-old Jewish faith. It was a traditional ceremony in every respect, attended by people whose company Reb Aryeh enjoyed.

The second ceremony, however, was an entirely different matter. The father of the infant had formed a warm bond of friendship with Reb Aryeh in his years as a fighter in the underground movement; but he had never been observant of the Jewish faith, and was not now. The people gathered for the ceremony were a motley company of bare-headed non-religious Jews mingled with a sprinkling of Arabs.

When Reb Aryeh appeared in their midst, accompanied by his son, a few put on *kippoth* (skull caps) in deference, but most simply ignored him. He, however, moved among them with aplomb, smiling slightly as usual, as he made his way to the infant's father to convey his good wishes and blessings. The rest of the gathering tended to take precious little notice of him.

Suddenly, though, as he stood off at the side with his son, his eyes alighted on one young bare-headed man whom he knew. In a moment he had the young man's hand between both his palms, and he drew him aside to talk privately. Although his son Simḥa Sh'lomo stayed nearby, he caught little of the conversation. He could only gather that his father was berating the young man, in his usual gentle way, for having descended to such a state of irreligiosity. Apparently the good rabbi had known the young man's late father well, and he dwelt a great deal on that man's piety and devotion to the Jewish faith. "You know the life your father lived," said Reb Aryeh. "Then how could you come to this?"

Eventually, Reb Aryeh and his son learned, the young man left the non-religious neighborhood of K'far Saba and moved to B'ney B'rak, so that his young children would be able to receive a good Torah education and grow into their heritage of faith.

the test of temptation

On Friday afternoons as the Sabbath approached, it was Reb Aryeh's habit to make his way to the synagogue early, so that he could pass by the various stores and shops and alert their owners to be sure to close up before the Sabbath arrived.

One Friday afternoon, in the midst of the blazing summer heat, the good rabbi noticed a long chain of customers lined up before a store that sold ice cream. Inside he could see the shopkeeper busy serving one person after another, utterly unaware of the time, with no thought of closing.

Reb Aryeh stood still, debating in his mind. "If I were that shopkeeper," he thought, "and all those people were in my store, could I withstand the temptation? Would I drive them all away and close up because the Sabbath was approaching?" He was not at all certain of the answer. "Still," he then mused, "the Sabbath will be here very soon. The man must be urged to finish his work."

There and then he entered the ice cream store, put his *shtreiml* (his flat circular fur hat) carefully on a chair, and sat down calmly at a table. When he noticed him, the startled shopkeeper came over. "What can I say to you?" Reb Aryeh asked. "You are certainly facing a great trial and temptation. Nevertheless the Sabbath is the Sabbath." Not a word more did he say, but rose from his seat, put on his *shtreiml* and left the store. When he was a bit of a distance away, he turned around and looked back; and he saw the line of customers dissolving: people were dispersing and going off, while the shopkeeper was putting up his shutters and locking the place.

Some time later the shopkeeper happened to meet the good rabbi. "Do you know?" he said, "those few words of yours struck home, to the depths of my heart. I realized that you knew and felt just what I was thinking and feeling, and yet you felt pain for the sake of the Sabbath. Then I thought in my heart: A Jew like that must not be made to suffer pain. So I withstood the test; I overcame the temptation and sent all those people away."

Reb Aryeh chuckled. "I believe you are greater than I am. If I were in your situation, who knows if I would have withstood the test..." Those words of honest admiration were reward enough for the storekeeper.

the communist and the skull cap

As indicated earlier, the inmates of the Jerusalem prison all adored and respected Reb Aryeh greatly. Although many of them were not observant Jews, they waited with impatience every Saturday morning for the rabbi's weekly visit, so as to draw their spiritual strength from his unique warm and affectionate handshake.

Yehezkel Altman was one of the "distinguished" prisoners, since he was sentenced to death. (Later, though, his sentence was commuted; and ultimately he was freed.) These are his recollections:

In those gruelling days when I wore the red prisoner's garb of a condemned man and lived under the shadow of the gallows, Reb Aryeh used to come to visit me very frequently. For this reason I always kept a *kippah* (a skull cap) in my pocket; and when I saw Reb Aryeh from afar, I would put it on my head immediately. (It is a scrupulously observed religious custom among observant Jews not to go bareheaded, so as not to show irreverence toward the Creator.)

Well, in those days there were many communists imprisoned there with me... including one young fellow named Yaakov. He was most insolent and rather nasty, and he kept trying to make Reb Aryeh lose his temper. Thus, for example, whenever he saw Reb Aryeh arriving on Saturday morning to join us in our makeshift synagogue in the prison courtyard, he would light a cigarette before Reb Aryeh's very eyes in order to get him angry; and then he himself would be most irritated because he failed to ruffle the rabbi's calm. You just could not make Reb Aryeh lose his temper. It was his firm habit to greet everyone with the blessing of a good Sabbath.

Well, one day Reb Aryeh was surprised to see this young communist, Yaakov, waiting for him at the entrance to our makeshift synagogue. As the good rabbi reached the entrance, the young fellow snapped out, "Why do you deal with liars and cheats?"

"My son," Reb Aryeh replied, "why do you defame and slander human beings?"

"Do you think those prisoners are religious, because they come here Saturday morning and join you in the prayer-service? I live with them in this prison. I see how they eat and drink with nothing to cover their heads in reverence; and they never say a word of blessing or grace to God for their food. Look at that Yeḥezkel Altman. When he sees you coming from afar, he hurries to put a skull cap on his head, so that he can appear religious and reverent to you!"

"You call those people liars and cheats?" Reb Aryeh chided him. "How foolish and wrong you are. Believe me: I never so much as glance at their heads to see if they are wearing any head-covering or not. I focus my thought on their hearts. To me their hearts are open and revealed—and those hearts are aglow with human warmth!"

The upshot was that a short while afterward, this Yaakov, who had been so critical of Reb Aryeh, began himself to hurry to put a skull cap on his head at Reb Aryeh's approach, and he became one of the regular visitors in the synagogue.

in response to the Holocaust

One inmate recalled years afterward how the good rabbi would sit with the men after the Sabbath prayer-service and teach them a chapter or so of the Mishnah. Then he would expound on some interesting passage from the Talmud or Midrash, ending with his wish that by the next Sabbath they should have gone "from bondage to freedom." He knew it was hard to wait years in patience for the precious release; but he kept reminding them that "the rescuing help of the Lord comes in the twinkling of an eye"; and he made them set their hope always on the week ahead, till the next Sabbath.

One time, however (as this inmate recalled), he gave no lesson in the Mishnah after the prayer-service, and no blessing. More than the words he spoke, the tears that stood in his eyes and the sorrow that marked his face conveyed the full impact of the news that had finally reached the land of Israel: the enormous extent and nature of the Nazi holocaust.

In his simple words the good rabbi told the harrowing tale, characterizing the six million victims as martyrs of supreme holiness, who sanctified the name of God. For a while he sat sunk in thought. "And therefore," he suddenly continued his thought aloud, "in the heart of each and every one of us, the love of Jews and Jewry must be aroused with greater zeal. Everyone must help his brother, so that we should not fall, Heaven forbid; so that we should not be decimated further. For we have become so very few in number, and who knows when that vicious hand of malice will be cut down. We have to keep the flame (of our Jewish spirit) alive everywhere, so that it should not go out, Heaven forbid. It can swiftly turn into a new blazing fire, to cast a great light.

"This is why," he continued, "you are so much more precious to me today than always. There is no other replacement for our slain and fallen, but only those who remain alive, becoming outstanding in their love for fellow-Jews and strong in their faith in the God of vengeance."

Words like these strengthened the belief in the God of Israel among the religious prisoners, and kindled the beginnings of faith in others.

the cherished gift

During a session of the City Council of Jerusalem an argument broke out among its members about the exact wording of a sentence (a verse) in Scripture, in the Book of Psalms. At that, Abraham Axelrod, a deputy mayor, took a very small edition of *t'hillim*, the Book of Psalms, from his pocket, found the sentence in question, and showed that he had quoted it correctly.

A colleague on the Council admired the small, attractive edition and asked Axelrod if he might perhaps let him have it as a gift.

"What?" asked Axelrod, "this Book of Psalms? This small booklet I will never let out of my possession. I guard it like a jewel and carry it with me constantly."

"But why?" asked his colleague. "What is the reason?"

"It was given me as a present by Reb Aryeh. When I was in the depths of despair and life lost all meaning for me, that rabbi gave me back my zest for living in this world; and I suspect that he also brought me a share of life in the Hereafter. This little *t'hillim* remains my link with him."

It remains to be added that in his last will and testament, addressed to his sons, Abraham Axelrod noted that it was Reb Aryeh "who brought me back to observant Judaism. Thanks to his good influence I began putting on *t'fillin* (phylacteries) every single day, to say the morning prayers; and I began going to the synagogue to attend his daily lesson in the Talmud."

for the sake of the Almighty

Till the age of thirteen, R. Ḥayyim Yaakov Levin was Reb Aryeh's only son. These are his words:

Since I was his only son during those years, he took me everywhere with him. It was then I absorbed my father's simple whole-hearted dedication, his love for every wretched, miserable victim of suffering, his readiness to help another person simply because the other was a human being. All those experiences remain with me, unforgettable: the prayer with my father in the synagogue every morning at sunrise; his vibrant stories; his encounters with noted rabbis and men of Torah on the one hand, and with imprisoned Jews on the other hand.

Above all, I remember his uncompromising stand in his constant conflict with the members of the old yishuv, the religious settlement in Jerusalem, who did not look with a kindly eye on his close-knit relations with the irreligious Zionists, although they knew well that he acted solely for the sake of Heaven, in the service of the Almighty.

Once two *ḥalutzim*, pioneers of the new Jewish settlement, happened to come to my father's synagogue in the Mishk'noth section of Jerusalem, for the solemn prayer-service of Rosh haShana, the festival that begins the Jewish year. Without proper hats, their heads covered only with handkerchiefs, they stood self-consciously at the side—till my father went over to them, shook hands warmly with them, and invited them home for a meal after the prayers.

At another time my father became involved in a debate or a harangue with a leader of the extremists in the old yishuv, regarding my father's "Zionist connections." As the two stood thus engaged, in one of Jerusalem's side streets, a stranger happened to come along; and when he saw my father his face lit up. It was one of the two mentioned above, who had come by chance to our synagogue for the Rosh haShana prayers.

"I have been looking for you," said the man to my father, his face beaming. "I simply want to thank you. Thanks to my meeting you in that synagogue and getting to know you, and as a result of all you told me and explained to me about our religion—my kibbutz (collective farm settlement) in the Valley of Jezreel now keeps a kosher kitchen. I just wanted you to know."

With a sigh of relief my father turned to his opponent from the old yishuv who had been debating and arguing with him. "There," he said. "Do you see? Do you see?"

the reason for a hat

One day Dr Abba Ahimeyer (the late prominent Israeli journalist) prepared to leave his home, and he settled a hat firmly on his head. "Since when," asked his wife Sonia, "have you taken to wearing a hat?"

"I will tell you," he replied. "I am going into Jerusalem, and it is very likely that I will meet Reb Aryeh on the street somewhere. I won't have any peace of mind if Reb Aryeh ever sees me walking about bareheaded."

At another time Reb Aryeh came to Ramat Gan, and he visited Abba Ahimeyer at his home. The rabbi noticed that a number of *m'zuzoth* were lacking on doorposts in the home. To his host he said not a word; but after returning to Jerusalem he took pains to send Ahimeyer a package of *m'zuzoth*. To make certain that the man would not take offense, he sent along a note: "Let me gain the merit of observing this mitzvah (this religious good deed), and do not refuse to accept these *m'zuzoth*."

Laden as he was with mitzvoth to his credit, Reb Aryeh now had another one.

in the innocence of childhood

In Netanya, Shulamith Katznelson managed an *ulpan,* a school that taught new settlers to understand and speak Hebrew. Once she made a confession to Reb Aryeh: "At times my conscience troubles me. About the time of Purim we have a practice at our ulpan to dramatize and act out the stories in Scripture. We dress up in costume and make-up to play the parts of Abraham, Sarah, and so forth. Is it right to do that? We take the sacred narratives of our Written Torah and make a kind of children's plaything out of them, saying: Let the children play!"

"On the contrary," Reb Aryeh replied. "If you wish to draw close to our Torah people who are distant from it; if you want to induce adults to cherish our Hebrew Bible when they know so little of it—it is very good to draw them to it initially when they are in a state of childlike innocence. Then they can truly experience the incidents recounted in our Bible, in all their intensity of meaning. Yet how can adults reach such a condition?—only when they dress up in costumes and see themselves in the biblical roles. Then they return a while to the purity of childhood; and then they are able to identify with those admirable archetypes of our early history."

he insisted on paying

This is the recollection of David Shimon Rudnitzki:

During the War of Independence (in 1948), as a soldier in Israel's army, it was my custom to rise early in order to say the morning prayers before my military duties began. Thus I used to put on my *tallith* (prayer-robe) and *t'fillin* (phylacteries), and take up my prayer-book.

In the tent with me was a non-religious soldier who had only recently come to Israel from abroad. As I prayed silently, he formed the habit of watching me with curiosity. One day he told me, "If you get me a tallith and t'fillin, I will pray with you. I'm afraid, though, that I won't have enough money to pay for them." And with that he took out a few pounds from his pocket and gave them to me.

At the first opportunity I had, I went to a shop of religious articles in Jerusalem whose owner I knew, and I asked him for a tallith and a pair of t'fillin. As I examined them I saw the price tags; and there I stood racking my brains for a way to buy what was so hopelessly beyond my very limited means. Tentatively I began broaching the problem to the shopkeeper, to ask if he might let me have something acceptable for a very reduced price.

Suddenly the door opened and Reb Aryeh came in; and there he stood listening to my hesitant attempts to bargain with the owner. Without any warning, Reb Aryeh interrupted: "Please give this soldier a very fine pair of t'fillin, and add on a handsome prayer-book. And I would ask you also to give him a good velvet bag for the tallith and t'fillin."

I looked at the rabbi in amazement. How was I ever to pay for those fine, handsome items? The money I had would not even cover the t'fillin alone. Then I heard Reb Aryeh talking further to the shopkeeper: "If a person wants to keep our mitzvoth, we have to help him and give him of the best. As for the price, there is no need to worry. I will pay."

I began arguing with him and protesting; but he was not to be budged. "Look," he said. "You are a soldier; so the price for these articles is equal to a full month's salary of yours. It is enough that you are doing so much to help your friend observe a mitzvah." Nothing I could say was of any use. Reb Aryeh paid in full.

hashish

There was a Jew in Jerusalem who developed a liking for liquor and became quite addicted to it. Some time later a friend of his met him on the street. "Well," he asked in the course of their conversation, "have you given up your drinking habits?"

"Oh yes," the man replied, "but I've developed another addiction: hashish."

"What? Hashish?"

"Yes, sir. Reb Aryeh is my hashish. I began visiting him, and I've become so attached to the man that I'm simply compelled to go see him every single day."

advice for a kohen

The Torah has special laws for a *kohen*, a direct descendant (in the male line) of Moses' brother Aaron. When the holy Temple stood in ancient Jerusalem, only a kohen was permitted to serve and minister there; hence the special laws, to keep him on a higher level of holiness.

One of these laws forbids a kohen to marry a divorced woman and live with her as her husband. Since human nature is not flawless, however, it happened that a kohen in Israel fell in love with a divorced woman, and he was determined to marry her despite the religious law. Since he knew, though, that Reb Aryeh listened to the troubles of human beings and tried to help, he asked a good friend to visit the rabbi and ask him to find some way for him to marry the woman within the law; for otherwise he would simply make her his wife in violation of the ban.

The good friend carried out his mission faithfully and gave Reb Aryeh all the pertinent facts and details, even describing fully the kohen and the divorced woman.

Reb Aryeh listened patiently, never interrupting with a word. When the good friend was done speaking, the rabbi simply said, "You must forgive me, but now I have to go to the synagogue and give my daily lesson in the Talmud. Please wait here for me till I return. While I go I will think the matter over." He asked his wife to serve the man tea and cake, and left.

When he returned, Reb Aryeh began without preamble: "Please go and tell your friend in my name that the personality and character of this woman, as I perceive her, leads me to one conclusion: He must flee from her and save himself as from a blazing fire." For a full moment there was silence, as the visitor looked at Reb Aryeh in amazement. Then the rabbi added, "Tell him, too, that I say this only from humane considerations, as one human being to another, without giving any consideration to the aspects of religious law that the matter involves."

The good friend went and gave the kohen Reb Aryeh's answer verbatim. "Well," said the kohen, "had he simply forbidden me to marrry her on account of the law, I doubt very much if I would have listened to him. Now that he tells me to leave her just for personal reasons—because it won't be a happy marriage—I think I had better listen to him. That

THE GATEWAYS OF PIETY AND DECENCY

rabbi is a wise man; he knows human nature; and he always gives trustworthy advice."

Reb Aryeh the pied piper

Sometimes, indeed, the advice that he gave bordered on the uncanny. There was the time when an acquaintance came to see him, looking quite haggard and distraught. "Reb Aryeh," said he, "I simply don't know what to do. I am at my wits' end. Recently I bought a warehouse for grain and wheat. It is a good, profitable business, as many farmers and millers store their produce there. Now, however, I am facing utter ruin. The place has become infested with mice. Every night they come and do damage to the sacks of wheat and grain."

"Was the previous owner ever troubled by mice?" asked Reb Aryeh.

"Definitely not," the man replied. "I checked carefully before I bought the warehouse. If word of this ever leaks out, I'm a ruined man. Soon enough the authorities may close it down as a health hazard. What am I to do?"

With closed eyes Reb Aryeh sat a moment in thoughtful silence. In all the Talmud and the great volumes of religious law he would find no direct answer for this. Then he asked, "Tell me this: the money you used to pay for the warehouse when you bought it—was it all kosher and above-board? Was it all honestly come by?"

"Of course," said the man. "How can you even ask?"

"Don't be in a hurry to answer. Go home and give the matter some thought, and come back tomorrow."

The next day the man returned a bit more crestfallen. "How did you ever know to ask that?" he wondered. "At night, before I went to sleep, I suddenly remembered something that I have completely forgotten for years. Many years ago an aged rabbi came here from America. He was retired from his rabbinic position in the United States, and wished to spend his last years in Jerusalem. My wife and I took him into our home, gave him room and board, and looked after him generally. As time went on he grew a bit senile, and became rather vague about what was going on around him. Letters always arrived from old friends and members of his congregation in America, but he often paid them scant attention.

305

"One day a very large check arrived in the mail, a gift from some old friend in his congregation. There it lay on the aged rabbi's desk, and he was quite unaware of its existence. The temptation was simply too much for me. The man did not need the money; he had more than enough for the rest of his life. I pocketed the check and later put it into my bank account as part of my savings. Now, when I went to purchase the warehouse, having forgotten the matter completely I used that money as part of the amount I paid."

Reb Aryeh nodded slowly. "Well," he said, "you will simply have to give that money back."

"How can I? The rabbi is long since dead."

"You will have to find an heir and turn the money over to him. You must advertise in the newspapers."

This the man did. One relative of the American rabbi turned up in Jerusalem, and replies from several others came from abroad. As the one in Jerusalem proved to be the nearest of kin, he received the amount in question.

Some time later Reb Aryeh met the man on the street. "*Nu*," he asked, "how is the situation with the mice?"

"It is utterly amazing: They've disappeared!"

away went his indifference

As often mentioned, on his weekly visits to the central Jerusalem prison every Saturday morning, Reb Aryeh always organized the inmates into a congregation and led them in the Sabbath morning prayers. First, though, it was his practice to greet every single prisoner there, squeeze and caress his hand, and ask how he was and if there was anything he wished or needed. Then he gave each prisoner greetings and messages from relatives in the free world outside. Only when this was done did he go to stand at the lectern, his back to his "congregation," to begin the prayer-service.

If no one could understand how he had such a phenomenal memory, neither could anyone doubt it. He remembered the names of all the prisoners and their relatives (and particularly their children, for whom he bore an especial fondness), as well as their wishes and requests. It was no wonder then that no prisoner would ever willingly miss the prayer-service, even if he was totally irreligious and had never entered a synagogue outside the prison walls. Just about all crowded into the room that was used as a synagogue; for none could resist the powerful inducement or compensation of a weekly personal chat with the good rabbi.

Still, to every rule there is an exception; and among the political prisoners there was one who refused on principle to join in any prayers. He was a dyed-in-the-wool communist, who was indeed imprisoned on account of his communist activities. At every opportunity he would announce, "I'm a non-believer! I'm a confirmed atheist!" and so forth. (After all, according to the "canonic" writings of Karl Marx, "religion is the opium of the masses.")

Soon enough Reb Aryeh learned of this one Jewish inmate who refused to ever enter the synagogue; and it troubled him. He made his way to the prison commander, Captain Steele (who respected the good rabbi greatly and saluted him whenever he saw him) and asked permission to visit this man in his prison cell. The permission was granted, and Reb Aryeh went with Moshe Segal, the *muchtar* (head) of the prisoners.

Once inside the cell, in his usual way Reb Aryeh went directly to the prisoner, took his hand to squeeze and caress it in his own affectionate way, and asked the man how he felt. The prisoner answered with deliberate indifference bordering on disdain. "What is your name?" asked the rabbi. "Lipkin," the man replied, his cold indifference unchanged. "Lipkin?" exclaimed the startled rabbi with emotional force. "Are you perhaps a great-grandson of the famed Rabbi Israel Salanter, the founder of the teaching of mussar? His family name was also Lipkin."

"Yes," said the man with a shrug, "he was my great-grandfather. Well, what does that matter?"

"Why," said Reb Aryeh, "I feel such a great reverence toward you. You are a descendant of a renowned, distinguished tzaddik who taught mussar, ethics and piety to our people. Please tell me: is there anything I can do for you?"

In an instant the mask of indifference melted and disappeared. In a new tone of voice the man replied, "I am bound to admit: at this very moment you have already done much for me. This meeting here with you is helping me greatly."

From that day on this communist prisoner was always the first, every Saturday morning, among those who stood at the entrance of the prison synagogue waiting for Reb Aryeh.

to make him happy

This is a fragment of memory by Matithyahu Shmuelevitz, one of those condemned to death by the British authorities who was later spared and eventually released:

I had never prayed in my life. Even in my childhood, at the age of bar-mitzvah, I had never put on t'fillin. Then came the first Sabbath after my death-sentence was commuted to life-imprisonment. Through the bars of my cell I saw Reb Aryeh coming swiftly toward me. He stopped before me, tears of happiness in his eyes because my life had been spared. In a whisper he told me, "Here: I have brought you a present—a pair of t'fillin."

In spite of myself I was deeply moved. Later I learned from friends who were familiar with the ways of the Jewish religion that ordinarily, observant Jews will not touch or handle t'fillin on the Sabbath, since they are not to be worn on the holy day of rest. Reb Aryeh knew my emotional condition, however, and he knew that during the week he would not be allowed to visit me. Hence he was willing to overlook a rabbinic ruling for my sake.

Later I asked a good friend who was imprisoned there with me, "Do me a favor: Next Saturday mention to Reb Aryeh that I'm putting on every morning the t'fillin that he gave me. I want him to be pleased and happy."

"It's impossible to lie to the rabbi," my friend answered. "He senses it at once if you aren't speaking the truth. I won't tell him any such thing."

"Look," I retorted. "If you promise to tell it to the rabbi, then I really will put on the t'fillin every morning—as long as it will give the rabbi satisfaction."

It was the very first time in my life that I put on t'fillin every day, and I continued over a fairly long period of time. It was worth it, though. If only you could have seen the twinkle of pure happiness in Reb Aryeh's eyes when my friend whispered to him, "Matithyahu puts on the t'fillin, regularly."

the spark in the cinders

It was the policy of the British authorities, when they governed the Jewish homeland under the mandate, to lodge political prisoners together with convicted criminals. Thus it happened that in a cell intended for twenty people, forty were placed, among them murderers, rapists and thieves, mixed liberally with fighters for the liberation of the homeland. In every cell there was one prisoner, chosen by the authorities, who served as *muchtar,* the head or chief.

When Reb Aryeh came on his weekly visit, however, he made no distinction among the inmates, but squeezed everyone's hand equally in turn, with the same acceptance and affection.

Well, among the prisoners in one cell there was Yona M., sentenced to life-imprisonment because in broad daylight, with his own hands, he had murdered his wife when she was out walking with their child through the streets of Jerusalem. The *muchtar* of the cell was Moshe Segal (indeed, he was the overall *muchtar,* of all the Jewish prisoners), and this is his recollection of events:

One Sabbath morning in 1939 I saw our rabbi with Yona M., squeezing that man's hand in his usual affectionate way, asking him how he was and listening to his talk. The man was quite coarse and crude; it was hard to conceive that he was created at all in the Divine image. I was stunned to see our rabbi just chatting with him like that, and began to have doubts and misgivings about him. This was going a bit too far, I thought, to give his affection so very generously and freely, with no limit or boundary whatever—even to a wife-murderer. For me it was simply too much.

The next morning, as usual, I finished my prayers and began to wrap up my t'fillin and put them away. To my surprise, this prisoner, Yona M., came over and asked me to kindly lend him my t'fillin. He wanted to put them on, if I would not mind.

I looked at him and hesitated. Was it right and proper for a man whose hands were stained with innocent human blood to wrap himself in a tallith and t'fillin, in the trappings of religion and piety? He pleaded with me, however, and at last I yielded. Off he went to a corner of the room, put on my tallith and t'fillin, and began murmuring words from the prayer-book I gave him.

Unobtrusive though he wanted to be, his action was like a blazing red beacon. Several *convicted criminals* who were lodged in the same cell came over and asked my permission (since I was the *muchtar,* the head of the prisoners) to punish that avowed killer for making a travesty of objects and values sacred to Jewry. "Since when," asked one of them, "does that boor put on t'fillin and say prayers? His only purpose can be to mock and ridicule the truly religious people in the cell. And look—here is the proof: He deliberately went and put the t'fillin on his right hand, when everyone knows they must be put on the left (unless a person is left-handed, which he is not)." I might add that the criminal convicts among us were generally intolerant toward others. They only asked my permission now, instead of taking matters immediately into their own hands, because in relations among the prisoners the muchtar's word was law.

Well, those criminals were no gentle lambs, and I knew that I was dealing here with a bit of dynamite. I told them that I would investigate the matter and then give them my decision, but in the meanwhile they were to do nothing. Without delay I took Yona M., the murderer in tallith and t'fillin, off to a private corner, and between the two of us I demanded to know why he put the t'fillin on incorrectly, in disagreement with the religious law. His reply was laden with emotion: "You understand—after Reb Aryeh spoke with me I kept thinking all day of what I had done; and I felt so sorry for the terrible crime I committed. Then I just felt a mighty need to pray, properly, wrapped in tallith and t'fillin. Yet then I thought: But how can I put holy t'fillin on my vile, unclean hand that killed a human being? You see, though, I found an answer: It was the left hand that did the murder. The right hand is still pure and clean..."

Only then did I begin to understand the full strength and way of our rabbi's approach. In any human spirit he would find the holy sparks buried in the cinders, and those he would bring to life.

compelled to steal again

The day came when a messenger from Yitzḥak ben-Zvi, the second president of Israel, knocked on Reb Aryeh's door. The president would like the rabbi to kindly pay him a visit that evening, at such-and-such an hour. Reb Aryeh sent back word (in writing) that at this particular time in the evening he always taught a daily lesson in the Talmud to those who prayed with him in his neighborhood synagogue. If, however, it was a matter involving the public welfare, he was ready to forego his sacred Torah study period.

Soon the messenger was back: The president, said he, merely wished to tell Reb Aryeh of something that had made a deep impression on him. The rabbi could come the next morning, if he pleased, at such-and-such a time. At the appointed hour Reb Aryeh was at the Israeli president's office; and this is what Yitzḥak ben-Zvi told him:

This week a member of the supreme court of the United States came to pay me a visit. As we sat talking he asked me to tell him about you. Taken quite by surprise, I asked him the reason for his curiosity, and indeed how he had come to hear of you. He answered that he had been present in the central prison of Jerusalem when the authorities were interviewing inmates who were due to be released early, with one third of their sentences removed as a reward for good behavior in the prison.

"Well," said this American judge, "in came a seasoned veteran thief whose behavior in prison had been exemplary, quite perfect, so that it was decided to reduce his term by a third. We asked him if he felt morally strong enough now to follow the straight and narrow path of honesty and do no more stealing. His reply was, 'In my heart there is no doubt whatever that I have returned to the proper way of life and I will never again go back to a life of crime.' He prepared to leave, but before he reached the door he turned around and said, 'Gentlemen, I will be honest with you. I feel that I will have to commit one more theft.' As the judges looked at him in wonder he added, 'I just feel an inner need to steal a gold watch, in order to give it to Reb Aryeh Levin, because he brought me back to the good and decent path.'"

20
Of children and grandchildren

a glance and a caress

Reb Aryeh was especially known for his overflowing affection toward young and tender children. Once some visitors went wandering through the alleys and side streets near the Maḥaneh Yehuda section of Jerusalem, trying to find the good rabbi's home. A little girl noticed them, and with complete certainty in her voice she said, "Oh, you must be looking for Reb Aryeh!" Without another word she led them straight to his home and ran swiftly up the stone steps to his room. The door was open, but no one was within. Undaunted, the little girl told the people, "Come with me. I'll show you where he is"; and she took them to his *beth midrash,* his place of Torah study.

Reb Aryeh received his visitors with warmth and affection, as he received everyone. First, though, he patted the child on the head and thanked her cheerfully for bringing the people to him.

The children in the street knew how grateful the good rabbi was in such instances, and they always ran to bring visitors to him, in order to earn his warm loving glance and his affectionate caress—for in all his relations with children he was without affectation, being simply moved by a great love for them.

the children of Israel

A noted personage in the religious Zionist movement once came to see Reb Aryeh. When the visit was over, the rabbi went to accompany the man a short distance on his way (as his custom was). As they left the house, there were children of the neighborhood playing near the threshold, engrossed in their games. Reb Aryeh stooped down and patted their faces with fatherly (or grandfatherly) affection; and he murmured, "If it is a mitzvah to have a compassionate love for the stones and earth of the land of Israel—as Scripture says, *Thy servants hold her stones dear, and compassionately treasure her dust* (Psalms 102:15)—how much more should we love the children of the land!"

"buy her a candy"

Once I was waiting for the bus with my daughter, about three years old, and we were standing near a candy store (sweets shop). Reb Aryeh happened to come along, and he asked how I was and began patting the child's head. Suddenly he said, "Do me a favor and buy the child a candy. Little children love sweets so much."

the mystic and the practical

One year, when the high holy days (Rosh haShana and Yom Kippur) arrived, Reb Aryeh invited Rabbi Abraham Isaac Kook (the renowned chief rabbi) and his devoted students to use the small synagogue in the Etz Ḥayyim elementary school for the solemn prayer-service of those days of awe. Rabbi Kook and the students close to him wished to pray by themselves, as a small congregation, without the distracting influence of a large group of worshippers.

When the time came to hear the blasts of the shofar (ram's horn), the man calling out the instructions for the sounds (*t'ki'ah, t'ru'ah,* etc.) was Rabbi David Cohen, a mystic who spent the latter part of his life under the vow of a *nazir*, thus forbidden by the Torah to cut his hair, drink wine, or become ritually defiled. Rabbi Kook himself blew the shofar; and the *ḥazzan* or reader, who led the small congregation in the prayers, was Reb Aryeh. He chanted the prayers in utter simplicity, like a child confessing to his father. The students who were there afterward said that this entreaty of crystal purity was an unforgettable religious experience.

On Yom Kippur, the solemn Day of Atonement, when everyone over thirteen fasted, it was at an advanced hour of the day when the *musaf* prayer-service ended. Reb Aryeh went over to his wife, in the women's section, and implored her not to forget to take Rabbi David Cohen's boy home with her. This was She'ar-yashuv Cohen, today the chief rabbi of Haifa, but then only six years old. "On a sacred day like this," said Reb Aryeh, "his father's mind is in the rarefied world of mysticism, and he knows nothing of hunger and food. The boy is very young, though, and you had better make sure he gets something to eat."

the alternative to divorce

One day a man and his wife came to see him. Sadly they told him that they had decided on a divorce, and asked for his consent. What was the trouble? he asked. Were they unable to get along amicably? Oh no, was the reply; they loved each other dearly. But they had been married well over ten years, and no children had been born to them. And the Jewish law advised married couples to divorce in such a case.

Nonsense, said Reb Aryeh; and he gave them his "prescription": Let them each go over to a doorpost in their home, put a hand on the *m'zuza* attached to it, and thus let them pour out their heart in prayer. There is a Father in heaven, he added, who always listens when a child of His weeps in distress. So let them make sure to have a good cry, holding nothing back....

Then, whatever mitzvoth they observed, they should solemnly undertake to keep with greater devotion. They should serve their God wholeheartedly. Let them give more charity; the man should devote more time to Torah study; and so on....

Within a year they had a child.

the reward for prayer

One day Reb Aryeh was on a visit to the cemetery on the Mount of Olives, when he met an acquaintance, a former librarian of the Hebrew

OF CHILDREN AND GRANDCHILDREN

Reb Aryeh on one of many visits to the **nazir,** R. David Cohen (of blessed memory), participating in a learned discussion on preparing a rabbinic document.

Three typical students at the Etz Ḥayyim elementary school, who received his affectionate attention and care.

University. "Whatever are you doing here, among these graves?" asked the good rabbi.

"For many years," the man replied, "my wife and I have failed to have any children. The Almighty has not granted us a son who will say *kaddish,* the mourner's memorial prayer for us when we are gone. Hence I thought I had better come up here and choose a good grave-site for myself (a plot of burial ground). If I don't make the preparations, there will be no one to do it for me."

"Oh, don't be silly," said Reb Aryeh; and he took him by the hand and led him to the grave of Rabbi Sh'lomo Elyashav, a noted mystic who was related to Reb Aryeh by the marriage of their children. There the good rabbi and his acquaintance took to praying to the Creator most earnestly, tears flowing from their eyes, that the man might be granted a son. When they were done, Reb Aryeh blessed him that the Almighty should answer his prayer.

Reb Aryeh participating (as a **sandek**) at a **b'rith**, something he did innumerable times in his lifetime.

About a year later the man's wife bore a son, who was named Hillel. A few more years went by, and the man departed this world. In time Hillel grew to manhood, married, and became the father of a boy. He came and invited Reb Aryeh to be the *sandek,* the godfather who would hold the child on his lap for the circumcision.

to be blessed with children

One of the most notable rabbis in Jerusalem reached a state of distress because his daughter, married for twelve years, had borne no children as yet. His suffering became known to Reb Aryeh; and at the end of Yom Kippur, after the last prayer-service of the day (*ne'ilah*) was ended, the good rabbi gathered a few fine and worthy Jews, headed by Rabbi

Abraham Shapira, chief of the rabbinic court of Jerusalem. Under his direction they formed themselves into a *beth din,* a religious court, and declared in unison: "We, a beth din below (on earth), decree that So-and-so and his wife shall be granted healthy, viable progeny; and as the beth din below has decreed, so may it be fulfilled by the beth din above (in heaven)."

That year a child was born to the couple.

three things

There was a wise saying of his grandmother (whose wisdom he would always mention) that the good rabbi was given to quoting: It is good to do three things early: to get up in the morning; because then you have the whole wide day before you; to go to a trade fair, because then you can get the best merchandise; and to marry, for then you can live to see your grandchildren and great-grandchildren."

he noticed

Reb Aryeh had a sharp, discerning eye, although few realized it. Elimelech bar-Sha'ul (of blessed memory) became the rabbi of Reḥovoth as an adult; as a child he was a pupil at the Etz Ḥayyim elementary school, where Reb Aryeh was the "spiritual supervisor." Once Elimelech bar-Sha'ul recounted:

Our home was extremely poor, and I simply went hungry—literally. The pangs of hunger always tortured me, and it was hard for me to focus my thoughts. In my studies I could concentrate somewhat, for in the company of others, studying together with them, my plight was easier to bear. Under no circumstances could I say the prayers, however. It was too difficult for me to listen to what I was uttering.

Well, no one really paid attention to me. I was just one little boy among hundreds, and my condition did not trouble anyone greatly. From time to time, though, Reb Aryeh would cast his sharp, shrewd glance at me—and he guessed (or perhaps he knew for certain). One day he came over to me and thrust some money into my hand. "Here," he said. "I've gotten this money from a good Jew. Now go and get yourself three meals a day. Do you understand?"

All the years I spent at that elementary school of Torah, he kept me supplied with money for meals... and the light of Torah shone in me.

It should be added that in time the Etz Ḥayyim yeshiva took to providing lunch for its pupils. As its kitchen was, however, not exactly up to the standards of a Hilton hotel (as we might say), there were always children who preferred to forego the school meal. They never escaped Reb Aryeh's sharp eye, though, and he always saw to it they had something to eat, at the very least a *pitta* with *falafel*.

"we wept with him"

This is a reminiscence by another former student of the Etz Ḥayyim elementary school:

About thirty-six years ago, when I was a pupil there, in Jerusalem, a number of children became embroiled in an argument and fight right at the entrance to the school. Well, as soon as Reb Aryeh caught sight of this he called the boys to him and took them into his room. From the bookcase he took down a volume of the Talmud and opened it to the tractate Yoma, page 86a, and began reading to them the words of the Sages on how serious a sin it is to profane and insult the name of God. (There was no need for him to add that when pupils of the school, who were expected to set an example of religious behavior, fought and wrangled out in the open, for all to see, the name of God was profaned and degraded. This we understood ourselves.)

As he read the words and unfolded their meaning, the rabbi was seized by emotion, and he began weeping. "I," he said, "I would rather be taken from this world than cause any insult or degradation of God's name!"

I need hardly add that his words had a profound effect on us, and we wept with him.

OF CHILDREN AND GRANDCHILDREN

the skilled peacemaker

It was not only the quarrels of children that he settled at the Etz Hayyim school. Once, his son recalled, he saw two Jewish laborers at the school engaged in a violent argument, with raised voices and raised fists. Instantly the good rabbi went and separated them, bidding each remain in a place that he assigned, so that one could not see the other. Then he spoke to each separately. What he said to them, his son never discovered; but the next thing he saw was the two going and embracing each other in brotherly affection!

what he was looking at

When the time came in the morning for the young children to enter the classrooms for their daily lessons, Reb Aryeh would stand at the doorway or at a window, and he would study each small boy—to the puzzlement of the children, who could not understand his reason.

One day his own son asked him, "Why do you always stand at the entrance waiting for the pupils, and then you look at them so closely as they enter?"

"I'll tell you what," said the rabbi. "You come and stand with me and take a close look at them. What do you see? What do you observe?"

"It is quite interesting to watch them going in," his son replied. "You can see how eager they are to study the Torah. There I saw a boy pushing ahead of another. He has a zest for learning. That one over there, though, is not at all anxious to enter. His mind is still on the games he was playing."

"Yet I look at different things altogether," said Reb Aryeh. "That child's trousers are torn. This one's shoes are quite tattered and worn. That boy over there is definitely hungry; how will he ever be able to study?"

"More than once," his son later recounted, "my father would take money from his pocket and give it to children so that they could ride home on the bus in the cold winter nights and would not have to trudge through the wet muddy (unpaved) streets."

through two generations

There is at least one Jerusalemite who can bear this out. A man named Meir Skol remembers how the good rabbi would particularly notice which children, who lived far from the school, had torn shoes; and to them (including Meir) he would give half a piastre each, on rain-sodden nights, to ride home on the bus. To the poor children, however, half a piastre was an undreamed-of treasure, which could buy fabulous goodies at the candy store. So they pocketed the money and continued trudging home in the wet and the cold.

Reb Aryeh soon learned of their stratagem, however, and he devised a "home-made" type of bus-ticket (no proper ones were printed then), which the bus-drivers would honor, and he gave the little pupils these instead.

When Meir Skol grew up and married, he had a boy whom in turn he sent to the Etz Hayyim school. Once, at the beginning of a school year, there was a complete rearrangement of the classes, and by some oversight or misunderstanding Meir's son found himself one grade lower than his proper level. Afraid to speak up to anyone in authority at the school, the boy was equally afraid to go home and tell the doleful tale. Meir, the boy's father, tended to be strict and short with him, and the boy was certain that he would be blamed (and punished) for having done poorly in his studies in the previous school-year, and having thus brought his own fate upon himself.

Not knowing what to do, the child took to walking the streets of the city—till by chance Reb Aryeh spied him. He called the boy to him, and with his kindly, compassionate approach he soon had the whole story pouring out, accompanied by a few unsuppressible sobs. There and then he took the boy to the principal of the school and spoke up for the small pupil, until the problem was untangled and he was moved to his proper grade. Then the lad went home.

like a junior Rothschild

In Reb Aryeh's neighborhood the head of a family passed away, and his poor widow had to place her son in an orphan home. There all the children wore the same standard clothing, and when the boy came home to visit, he felt a sense of shame that all could know from his clothes that he was an orphan. With his uncanny sensitivity, Reb Aryeh divined the boy's feelings.

One day, not before Passover, he called the boy to him. "Go with your mother," he told him, "to this-and-this tailor (he gave him the name and address) and have yourself measured for a suit for Passover." (Custom-made clothing was also known then, but better suits were made to measure.) The boy could hardly believe his ears, and Reb Aryeh had to repeat his instructions. Of course, he had previously contacted the tailor and told him that he would pay for the suit (out of the money for charity that people kept entrusting to him).

For the rest of his life that orphan remembered the dream-like feeling he enjoyed as he went with his mother to the tailor. No junior member of the Rothschild family, he was certain, could have felt more lordly, more in the lap of luxury, at being measured for a suit....

the prize

Once he noticed a small student at the school going in very tattered shoes. Clearly the boy needed a new pair without delay; but Reb Aryeh knew that the lad's father was a tight-fisted gentleman who would take offense if the good rabbi simply bought him a pair. During the morning recess, while the youngsters were playing in the courtyard, Reb Aryeh called the lad to his room, because, said he, it was time to test the boy on his Talmudic learning. The questions he asked were well within the boy's grasp, and he answered them all. "Splendid," said the good rabbi, beaming; "that was just splendid. For this you deserve a prize." And there and then he gave the boy a note to a local shoemaker to give the boy some good footgear, for which Reb Aryeh would pay. When the lad went home after school, he took with him another note from the good rabbi, to his father, explaining aobut the "prize" he had won.

sweeping the dark away

In 1943 the father of a small pupil at the Etz Ḥayyim school asked Reb Aryeh, as the "spiritual supervisor," to speak to the boy and motivate and encourage him to improve in his studies. The rabbi called the lad into his little room and began talking with him. The boy explained that he was simply unable to concentrate on his studies. He had tried all kinds of ways to overcome his difficulty, but nothing helped.

Reb Aryeh gave his usual smile. "I will tell you," he said. "A wise man once passed by a house and noticed a man inside sweeping the floor very conscientiously with a great big broom. The puzzling thing, though, was that the floor was perfectly clean. 'Why are you working so hard to do all that sweeping?' he asked the man. 'Oh,' the man replied, 'I am sweeping out the darkness. I want to have light in the house.' The wise man laughed. 'What kind of a fool are you?' he asked. 'Open that shade just a little bit, and the house will be quite light. A little bit of light, you know, drives away a great amount of darkness.'

"Well, young fellow," Reb Aryeh concluded, "it is the same with you. Don't try to drive away the snags and difficulties that prevent you from

The historic Etz Ḥayyim Yeshiva in Jerusalem, where Reb Aryeh was employed.

learning. There is so much great light in the Torah. All you have to do is to sit and learn Torah. Its illumination will automatically chase away whatever blocks or disturbs you."

the afterglow

In another instance the good rabbi had a simple way to encourage a pupil to improve in his studies; and it was without any conscious intention. The boy's name was Sha'ul Yitzḥak, but everyone knew him as *Itchalle*. One day Reb Aryeh stopped him in the school courtyard, patted him on the cheek, and asked, "Are you the Itchalle who did so well in the little oral test that I gave your class the other day?" Sha'ul Yitzḥak had quite forgotten the test, and when he thought of it he did not remember having done particularly well in it. But the bit of attention and praise left an afterglow, and for a good while he applied himself with extra zeal to his studies.

the special offer

In the memory of another former pupil of Etz Ḥayyim, the days of the First World War stand out clearly. The pious Jews of Jerusalem depended greatly on financial support from abroad, and when the conditions of war disrupted the lines of communication, famine came to the holy city. People collapsed right in the streets and died of hunger and epidemic disease; and this particular pupil became an orphan when the ravages of death took his father and mother too.

One day Reb Aryeh came to the synagogue where the little boy always went for the daily prayers, and he noticed the youngster saying *kaddish*, the mourner's prayer. No one had to explain to the rabbi why he was saying this prayer. Once the service was over, he went over to the child and asked him, "Would you be willing to study with me for a half hour every afternoon at the school?"

As this boy recalled when he was a grown man, "Of course I agreed; it gave me great prestige among my playmates. 'Do you know with whom I'm going to be studying?' I asked them—'with Reb Aryeh himself!' They looked at me with awe and envy.... Thanks to that extra attention and extra prestige, I did quite well and finally became one of the teachers at the Etz Ḥayyim school."

"perhaps it was the accent"

Early one morning Reb Aryeh made his way through a part of the Meya She'arim section of Jerusalem known as *ba-tey ungarin* ("houses of Hungary"), a subsection allocated originally for settlers in the old (religious) yishuv who came from Hungary.

"What are you doing here, in my neighborhood?" asked an acquaintance.

"Yesterday I tested a boy from this neighborhood, when he came to the Etz Ḥayyim school wanting to be admitted as a pupil; and I found that he did not know his Torah studies properly. Before I went to sleep, though, it occurred to me that perhaps the trouble was that he has always learned his Torah with a Hungarian accent, and I speak Yiddish with a Lithuanian accent. Who knows? It could be that he knows his studies well but my pronunciation confused him. Perhaps I rejected him unjustly. I am going now to find out and perhaps apologize."

correcting his oversight

Early one evening, when yet a small child, Sh'muel Avidor saw him walking sedately in the section of Jerusalem where Sh'muel lived. As he asked to be taken to the home of one particular boy, a whole group of children gathered happily around him to lead him there. At the doorway of the boy's home he dismissed them with his smile and entered alone.

After he finished his visit and left, the children were dying with curiosity to know why he had come; but the boy's parents forbade him to tell. Years later, when both were grown, Avidor met him in an army camp, and recalling the incident, he asked him why the good rabbi had come to see him that evening.

The reason was simple: In the afternoon the boy had gone to Reb Aryeh's cubicle to see him about something. The good rabbi was busy, however, and he asked the boy to wait outside till he would call him. Yet he remained so occupied and distracted that he forgot about the boy and never called him. In the evening, home after his wearying day's work,

At the funeral of a great Torah scholar, Reb Aryeh gathered his charges about the coffin (lower left) to explain what a loss his departure meant.

the good rabbi remembered—and he set off at once to find the boy and ask what he wanted. Who knew? Perhaps it was something important, and the boy was in distress because of the oversight....

his "angry rebuke"

Sh'muel Avidor attended Etz Ḥayyim as a child. One winter day, during the recess, while all the children were playing in the courtyard, he happened to be with Reb Aryeh in his cubicle. Suddenly it began raining strongly. The children were so happy at their play, however, that they took no notice of the raindrops and continued romping and running. Looking through his little window, the good rabbi became excited. "What is this? They can catch cold! They need a good scolding!"

In the way of children, the boy Sh'muel looked forward in glee to seeing the good rabbi berate the children strongly—"lace it into them." Instead, however, he went to the doorway, and standing placidly, he called the youngsters to him. "Dear children," said he, "I beg you: Do me a favor and go into the big hall. You are likely to catch cold."

So great was their love and regard for him that they trotted in like lambs.

profit and loss

For a time he taught a class of young children at the Etz Ḥayyim school. Then he impressed on his small pupils how important it was not to miss any sleep at night. "If you go to bed an hour earlier," he would tell them, "you lose one hour, but you gain a whole day—because the next day you are fresh and alert. If, however, you go to sleep an hour late, do not imagine that you have gained an hour for yourselves; for you then lose a whole day, because the next day you will be dizzy; your head will go spinning around."

This, though, was only advice for his tender pupils. For himself three to four hours of sleep a night were enough; and he never stopped envying the great Talmudic scholars of whom it was told that they managed with less.

the enviable privilege

Officiating at a wedding, R. Simḥa Sh'lomo Levin asked a distinguished-looking guest to serve as one of the two witnesses. Named Shwadron, he was a member of a distinguished family in Israel. As they began talking and he discovered that R. Simḥa Sh'lomo's father was Reb Aryeh, the man exclaimed, "There is a story I must tell you":

Teaching Talmud to an advanced class, in his early years at Etz Ḥayyim. A good number of these students became notable rabbis and scholars in their adult years.

Reb Aryeh addressing his young charges at a special occasion.

He himself, said the man, escaped alive from Europe in the Second World War, by way of Siberia; and shortly afterward he came with his family to Israel. Some time later, when he had a thirteen-year-old son with him, he met Reb Aryeh at a small festive gathering; and in his usual way the good rabbi shook hands with him, greeted him warmly, and began chatting in friendly fashion, learning in the course of the conversation that he, Mr Shwadron, was a kohen, a direct descendant of Moses' brother Aaron.

Then the good rabbi turned his attention to Mr Shwadron's son. "Do you know what a tremendous privilege you have?" he asked the boy. "You are a kohen. You have the God-given right to go up every day before the ark and give the blessing of the kohanim!" (Outside the land of Israel, this benediction, often called the "priestly blessing," is given by kohanim only on festival days—*yomim tovim*. In Israel it is generally given every morning in the prayer-service.) "How I envy you," Reb Aryeh continued. "You are already bar mitzvah, over thirteen. Every single day you can give Jews this wonderful blessing out of God's love. Through you the Almighty gives the people His blessing, and so you become blessed in turn. How I wish I could give a benediction like that every day. But here I am, just a plain Israelite." So he continued, till the boy was smiling happily.

"To this day," said Mr Shwadron to R. Simḥa Sh'lomo Levin, "I do not know what prompted your father to talk to my son about this blessing of the kohen. Since my son turned thirteen, it had been a bone of contention between us. I tried in every way I could to prevail on him to go up every morning with me before the holy ark, and give the blessing. And he kept obstinately refusing. He would go up only on Saturdays;

weekdays he would walk out of the synagogue when the time came. From the time your father spoke to him, however, he just changed. Since then he went up before the ark faithfully every morning...."

he was grateful for the transcript

Yeshiva Merkaz haRav, a noteworthy Torah academy in Jerusalem under the guiding influence of the first chief rabbi, Abraham Isaac Kook, began its high-school division with a fine group of first-year students. During the month of Elul, as the high holy days were approaching, the youngsters expressed a wish to have Reb Aryeh address them on *mussar,* the proper rules and ways for learning ethical behavior—as it was the custom for yeshiva students to hear such instruction during Elul.

A mutual acquaintance, who knew both the students and Reb Aryeh, agreed to arrange it; and when he came to the rabbi's house and broached the subject, the rabbi agreed readily and set a specific time for his talk to the youngsters. On the appointed day the man came again to Reb Aryeh's house, to remind him in case he had forgotten; and he found the good rabbi on the upper floor, where Reb Aryeh maintained a small yeshiva for students of his own. The good rabbi was arranging the benches, so that the visiting students would find everything in order when they came.

When his young visitors arrived and took their places, Reb Aryeh began: "You have come to hear words of Torah from me, and your intention is praiseworthy indeed. Yet what does a man like myself know that would be of value to you? It would be far better for you to teach me, since you spend your days in pure Torah study. Tell me what you learned today..." In a few moments they were engaged in a lively discussion with him about the topics of Talmud and ethics that they had studied that day. It went on for a considerable time, and when at last it drew to a close, and they prepared to leave, Reb Aryeh said, "I beg you: do a kindness for an old man like me, since I have so little time to study the Written or the Oral Torah properly, and come visit me frequently so that you can tell me what you have studied in your *beth midrash."*

To his own students in his yeshiva, though, Reb Aryeh had to give talks on mussar, putting aside his usual modesty. To one of these talks a lawyer who knew him well came to listen, enjoying it immensely. When it was over, the lawyer went home and put it down in writing, so that it should not fade from his memory. Some time later, when the man had occasion to visit him, he took the written copy along to show Reb Aryeh.

"Thank you so much for letting me see this," said the good rabbi. "You see, these talks on mussar that I give, I really mean for myself alone, for my benefit. Only, I say everything aloud so that my students too can listen. Now that I have a written copy, I will be able to review the contents thoroughly and work on myself with zeal to improve myself. I really must thank you for this."

he broke the strike

Several decades ago the funds of the Etz Ḥayyim elementary school allowed it to give only a most meager salary to the teaching staff. The instructors found it quite hard to eke out a living.

One day (as a student of that time later recounted from memory) the instructors reached a state of desperation and declared a strike. They stood in the halls and the courtyard, and refused to enter their classrooms.

When Reb Aryeh learned of this he went into the school courtyard, wrung his hands, and cried out, *"bittul torah, bittul torah!"* (an almost untranslatable phrase, meaning that the precious time for Torah study was being squandered); and with that he burst into tears. When the children watching through the windows saw that, they burst out weeping with him... and when the instructors heard that they hurried back into their classrooms to resume their daily activities....

the vanished stranger

One day a very small child of his was resting in a cradle in the back yard of his home, quite near the well from which his wife drew the water. At the doorway of the home sat Reb Aryeh's wife, silently reciting the chapters of *t'hillim*, the Book of Psalms, as it was her custom to do.

Suddenly she looked up and saw a stranger, a man she had never seen before. "Could you please give me a glass of water?" he asked her. She went into the house at once to get a cup and fill it at the well. Then she saw that her child had managed to get out of the cradle, and there he was, lying close to the well. A shudder went through her. In an instant she scooped up the little child; and as she held him safely she filled the cup for the stranger. When she returned to the doorway, however, he was gone—nowhere to be seen.

Perhaps it was because he had completed his heaven-sent mission. Reb Aryeh's wife was convinced, though, that in this way she was rewarded for the mitzvah of giving a stranger water (which she prepared to do, even if she was unable to complete the good deed).

the addition to the family

It was mentioned in an earlier chapter that along with their own children his wife and he always had other youngsters in their one-room dwelling. If there was no room for them to sleep there, at least they took their meals there and were assured of clean clothing. When the time came for them to marry, Reb Aryeh and his wife would sometimes act as their parents, arranging a match, providing expenses for an apartment, etc.

One of these youngsters was Sh'muel Aharon Yudelevitch. During the First World War his father was deported to Damascus by the Turks, as a foreign national, and there the man died. When his widow married a farmer in a distant settlement, the boy (not yet thirteen) remained in Jerusalem to be able to learn Torah. So he slept at night on a solid bench in a little synagogue, and took his three meals a day at Reb Aryeh's home.

One day a certain man took a very great liking to young Sh'muel Aharon, and having no children of his own, he strongly wished to take the youngster into his home and raise him. When he broached the idea to Reb Aryeh, the good rabbi replied, "It would be hard for me to give up such a rare privilege, of raising a fine youngster like that. But I will tell you: I can only give him simple food every day—bread and vegetables. If you could give him meat every day, then for his sake I would give up my mitzvah."

The man readily agreed, and young Sh'muel Aharon Yudelevitch moved into his home, to sleep in a proper bed and eat (relatively) lavish meals. After two days, however, he was back at Reb Aryeh's home. Somehow, he said, the simple food at the good rabbi's dwelling tasted better ... and there he stayed.

When the lad was sixteen and an outstanding Talmudic scholar, Reb Aryeh took him for a walk and asked, "Would you like to be my son-in-law?" With a touch of shyness he replied, "Where could I find a better father-in-law?"

Throughout his adult life, following the ways of R. Elijah the Gaon of Vilna, he would go to no cemeteries or graves (although he is not a kohen) so as not to become ritually unclean. However, after his mother-in-law, Reb Aryeh's dear wife, passed away, he always made an exception and visited her grave, citing the Talmudic teaching that very righteous persons can cause no ritual uncleanness after their death.

expecting the Messiah

Every observant Jew generally says each morning, after the prayer-service, among the thirteen principles of our religion formulated by Rambam (Maimonides), that he believes with perfect faith in the coming of the Messiah. To Reb Aryeh this was no routine formula to be said by rote while his mind was on something else. To him it was a palpable reality, an utter truth.

One day he showed a friend of his a letter he had received from his son R. Hayyim Yaakov, who was serving then as the rabbi of a congregation in New Jersey, in the United States of America. In the letter his son invited him to come and stay with him for a month. Reb Aryeh loved this oldest son of his; he was outstanding in Torah learning and in qualities of character; and in the United States he maintained a home that could have fitted perfectly into the religious community of Jerusalem. "*Nu*," asked his friend, "then why don't you go and visit him?"

"How can I make a journey like that?" replied Reb Aryeh. "Perhaps *he* will come in the meantime."

"Who will come?"

"What do you mean, who?—the Messiah, of course. I don't want to be away from Jerusalem then."

the quiet cleaner and his daughter

On the upper floor of his home the good rabbi maintained a small yeshiva (Torah academy) for a handful of fine advanced Talmudic students. It was called quite simply *béth aryeh* (the house of Aryeh).

One day he posted a note on the door of the study-room requesting the students to be very careful not to throw any cigarette ash on the floor. He was not in the best of health (the note continued) and it was hard for him to lift up the benches while cleaning the floor (which he would have to do if there was cigarette ash).

Few of the students knew it, but Reb Aryeh himself cleaned the room regularly, standing the benches up against the wall in order to get at the floor properly, He always had to move the benches very quietly, for otherwise his married daughter, who lived close nearby, caught the sound, and she came over immediately to stop him.

In his note on the door Reb Aryeh went on to ask the students to give his daughter the reward due her for all her toil and effort on behalf of the yeshiva. What payment did she want?—that when they said their afternoon and evening prayers every day (as a small congregation) they should pray in a loud, clear voice. Then she would be able to answer *amen* (and so on) to their benedictions and entreaties to Heaven....

the call to return

As mentioned above, Reb Aryeh's oldest son was appointed the rabbi of a congregation in New Jersey, on the shores of America. One day Reb Aryeh, who loved him dearly, wrote him this in a letter:

> "One thing I ask of you, my dear son: Do not lose hope when things go ill with you; do not give way to despair because you find yourself drowning in troubles. No immunity (of any kind) lasts forever (Proverbs 27:24), but neither is any trouble or distress eternal. When your situation is good do not grow proud-hearted; in a time of anguish do not lose heart. Let your eyes always be turned toward your land. Look for ways to return to your native soil. Let your heart not sway you to seek refuge and safety in a foreign land and search for your success and good fortune among a people you knew neither

yesterday nor the day before. Who can find a true friend among strangers? You will seek in vain for a brother among aliens. Only amid the heritage of your fathers will you find your place; there is your fortune hidden."

The son took his father's advice and returned to Israel, where he became the rabbi of Pardes-Hanna.

when his grandson was arrested

This is an incident recalled by an attorney named Simha Mandelbaum:

Once in 1959 my telephone rang, and when I answered, the operator told me it was a long-distance call from America. The caller was a Mr Gurevitz, who told me that his son had been arrested by the police of Jerusalem for demonstrating in the streets against the flagrant violation of the Sabbath in the holy city. The man implored me to make every effort to have his son released on bail.

Well, I went to the police station in the Russian compound, and in the courtyard there were about twenty boys, all under arrest for the same reason. I found the Gurevitz boy and began talking with him, and told him that I had come at his father's request to try to get him released. In the course of our talk he told me that in the group under arrest there was a grandson of Reb Aryeh.

As I left the police station, whom should I meet but Reb Aryeh himself. "Where are you going?" I asked him. "I am going as usual," he replied, "to make my visit at the prison." Then I told him that he would find a grandson of his there, under arrest.

At this he was taken aback. "If my grandson is there too," he mused, "I think I will break my long habit and cancel my visit this time. I don't want them to say that I have come on account of the boy..."

So moved was I by his words that I turned right around and went back to the police station. An officer named Elazar Shiloni was there, and I went over to him: "Look here: Reb Aryeh always gets people out of prison. Are you going to put his grandson into prison?"

He gave a meaningful smile and replied, "You're right!" (So I obtained the release of one boy right there, although not the one about whom I had come.)

the grandson could run faster

One year, when he was of advanced age, the good rabbi set off for the synagogue accompanied by a grandson, as the approaching sunset was about to usher in the beloved festival of Passover. As the two walked sedately, an elderly neighbor came rushing over: "Reb Aryeh, what shall I do? I forgot to take off *hallah* from my matzos!" (Whenever bread or matzah is baked from a sufficiently large batch of dough, a portion, called *hallah,* has to be taken off and burned, in commemoration of the religious obligation to give such a portion to a kohen in ancient Temple times. When the baking is done at a factory, the portion is generally taken off right there. The pious Jews of Jerusalem, however, use hand-baked matzos from small local hearths, and each must separate *hallah* from his matzos himself. If one forgets, it is a serious and difficult question in law if he may use the matzos at the seder.)

Instantly Reb Aryeh told his grandson, "Run to this man's home and take off *hallah* from his matzos." As the teen-ager sped away, the good rabbi told his neighbor, "He can run faster than the both of us; so he can still do it before sunset."

The next year, as Passover approached, he set out for the synagogue with the same grandson. "Come," said he, "let us go by the same route as last time. Perhaps we will meet a neighbor again who forgot to take off *hallah,* and you will have a chance to do the mitzvah again."

21
The world of dreams

the call in the dream

Reb Aryeh was prone to having dreams of significance, but he would never speak much of them unless there was something in a night vision which affected another person. Here is the tale of one astonishing dream:

Abraham Stavsky was a young member of the Jabotinsky (Revisionist) movement who had come to Israel from Poland. When Hayyim Arlozorov was assassinated in 1933 on the seashore of Tel Aviv, Stavsky was condemned for the murder, and he lived for a while under the shadow of the hangman's noose—until his innocence was established and he was set free, thanks in no small measure to the storm of protest that the chief rabbi of the land, Abraham Isaac Kook, aroused.

Abraham Stavsky

With Rabbi Kook, his close friend and disciple Reb Aryeh believed as strongly in Abraham Stavsky's innocence, that he had never committed the foul murder. As a result of the entire episode, Stavsky and Reb Aryeh became firm friends for years afterward.

In 1948, during the War of Independence, Stavsky was killed trying to land a ship (the *Altalena*) laden with ammunition. A few years later Reb Aryeh saw him in a dream, standing dressed completely in linen shrouds, both pleading and speaking harshly at the same time. "Reb Aryeh," he said, "are you going to stand by and be still? Heaven forbid!

The burning ship **Altalena**, laden with ammunition, was set afire from ashore; on it Abraham Stavsky lost his life.

You should know, Reb Aryeh, that there is a living brother of mine who survived me; and here is my wife, with whom I was never worthy enough to have any children, about to marry again—and she has received no ḥalitzah from my brother."

(By the law of the Torah, if a man dies and his marriage has been childless, if he has any surviving brothers, his widow may not remarry until a brother of his releases her by the ceremony of ḥalitzah.)

In the dream the figure of Abraham Stavsky continued, "Get up, dear rabbi, and take action. Please find my wife, please find my brother, and arrange it between them that she should receive ḥalitzah from him. She is not allowed to remarry till then. I simply will have no peace as long as this isn't done."

THE WORLD OF DREAMS

Morning came, and Reb Aryeh awoke in considerable agitation. He told the dream to his pious good wife; and she in her usual way tried to calm and soothe him: "Dreams are always worthless nonsense"—although in the privacy of her own heart she quivered too with apprehension. In his uncertainty Reb Aryeh took no action.

A few weeks went by, however, and the dream returned to him. Once again he saw Abraham Stavsky standing before him in white shrouds, imploring the good rabbi to save him in the world of the Hereafter and save his wife and brother in this mundane world. "Look," he pleaded, "here I am turning from side to side in my grave, unable to lie at rest at all."

Reb Aryeh decided to write to Sh'muel Tamir, an attorney (today a member of the *k'nesseth*, Israel's parliament) who was a close friend of the Stavsky family. In his letter the rabbi related the dream in full. Then he added, "It may well be that the whole thing is only stuff and nonsense. It is quite likely that there is no living brother of Abraham's; and very possibly his widow is not preparing to remarry. I am merely writing you the burden of my thoughts and visions, and you do as you think best."

Reb Aryeh's eyes widened in surprise, however, when he read Sh'muel Tamir's reply: Abraham's widow was in the United States, and she was getting ready to marry again.

Shortly afterward Reb Aryeh had another vivid dream; and the next day he wrote again to Sh'muel Tamir:

"...and now, my dear good friend, let me tell you of my distress, that I may find relief. This is the third time. On the seventh night of Passover I fell asleep after midnight; and in my dream I saw the martyred Abraham Stavsky giving me a letter sealed with wax and entreating me to open it and read it. I told him that since it was now *yom tov* (a festival day) it was forbidden to tear or cut open a letter. He retorted that it was a matter of life and death, and I was therefore permitted to open it. I begged him, though, to tell me, verbally, what it was all about. At that he asked me if it was permitted to weep on *yom tov*. I answered that it was most certainly forbidden, and on the contrary, it is a mitzvah to be joyous on a festival day. He took the letter from the table and read it.

Then he asked me, 'Is the ceremony of *halitzah* permitted on yom tov?' Definitely not, I told him. 'Is it permitted,' he asked, 'on the day before yom tov if the matter is urgent?' I replied that I would have to look for the answer in the volumes of religious law. Then he asked me, 'Why have you aged so much since the time I visited you, when the writing of a Torah scroll was completed at the *kothel ma'aravi* (the Western Wall)? ... Oh, I beg your pardon: I forgot that we are not permitted to go to the *kothel*. Tell me then: When is *yizkor* said—the memorial prayer for the dead?'

I did not know how to answer him, and I awoke. This is the third time I have had this kind of dream, although it varies from one time to the next. What shall I say to you, dear good friend? Here am I, so utterly confused. Perhaps I failed in my duty because I did not go to his parents and prevail on them to find some way to persuade his widow somehow that she must undergo *halitzah* with his brother. For you see, not only is she forbidden to remarry without *halitzah*, and the consequences of disobeying the law are very serious, but it is certainly most unpleasant for the departed spirit of the martyred Abraham. It is written in our holy volumes that in such an instance she remains bound to him.

Believe me, dear true friend, my hands are trembling as I write this; and weary and all too brief are my words. Every time I have seen him in a dream it has left a profound effect on my waking hours—for each time he comes to me with a complaint and a demand. May the blessed God have mercy and inspire Abraham's parents to make every possible effort to have the matter end in a way that will bring their son spiritual peace and satisfaction in the upper realm."

Helpless though he felt, Reb Aryeh's letters were evidently not without effect. Apparently they moved some person or persons to write Abraham's widow in the United States. For she returned briefly to Israel, underwent *halitzah* with her brother-in-law, and only afterward she returned to America to marry her second husband.

So all ended well, in full accord with religious law; and Reb Aryeh's happiness knew no bounds. He beamed with pure pleasure. "Such a mitzvah," he murmured. "What made me worthy to have so great a mitzvah happen specifically through me?"

the report from beyond

If he ever needed to learn how significant a dream can be, he surely learned it in his early years in Israel, before he married. He was then very attached to the renowned Talmud scholar Rabbi Hayyim Berlin (of all the Torah luminaries with whom he formed strong links of friendship, he was closest to Rabbi Berlin); and this sage in turn had a firm bond of friendship with a colleague of his named R. Yitzhak Blaser.

Once, in Reb Aryeh's presence, the two aged scholars made a solemn agreement that whoever of the two died first, he was to visit the other in a dream and tell him of his experience in passing over to the world beyond this mundane life. As it happened, it was Rabbi Blaser (better known as R. Itzalleh Peterburger) who passed on first. His close friend observed seven days of mourning for him, but saw no sign of the departed sage in his dreams. A few days afterward, though, his late friend appeared to him clearly as he slept. "Well," asked Rabbi Berlin, "what has it been like?"

The reply was: "The profundity of the Divine judgment is immeasurable. The sins of the tongue are the worst of all. But those who are humble and lowly, forbearing and forgiving, receive special consideration!"

the empty place

The War of Independence brought a frightful period of bloody fighting on the outskirts of Jerusalem, when Israeli soldiers battled fiercely to open a road into the holy city. One dreadful night during this period, Reb Aryeh had a most disturbing dream: Before him stood a young soldier who had died in this brutal fighting, the son of a renowned great Torah scholar. "Rabbi," said the young man, "you should know that the grave dug for me by the road through the hills about Jerusalem, is not my burial-place at all. My name is nicely inscribed on the marker, but it was not my body that was buried there. I was laid to rest somewhere else."

The next night, the young man appeared again in the rabbi's dream. "Reb Aryeh," he said, "I want you to know that I have not yet been given proper Jewish burial. Now the high holy days are approaching. I want to come to your synagogue and pray. Please leave a place for me."

When Reb Aryeh awoke, his brow was covered with cold sweat; and that day he spared no effort. He contacted all individuals and groups concerned with the burial of fallen soldiers, and put them on their mettle. He demanded in no uncertain terms to know the truth about this boy's burial. He knew well enough of instances in the past when fellow-soldiers under fire couldn't find the body of a fallen friend; it had simply disappeared somewhere, somehow. In the dark of night they would dig a grave and put a marker on it with their fallen buddy's name on it. Then the next day they would show his stricken, grieving family, "Here your dear son was brought to his final rest"; and the bereaved family would be somewhat comforted by that.

In the next few days Reb Aryeh gave himself no rest. He continued searching, investigating and asking, until the true grave of the young man was found. Over that the marker with his name was now placed.

When Yom Kippur came, Reb Aryeh made certain to have an empty seat near his own in the synagogue. Before the seat he placed a small stand (lectern, *shtender*), and on it a prayer-book. It was Reb Aryeh's custom to stand the entire solemn day of fasting and worship. As he now stood he kept turning the pages of the prayer-book before the empty seat next to his, so that it was always open at the proper page. This he did till the sound of the shofar marked the end of the last prayer-service of the holy day, when it had become quite dark outside.

the source of his saying

He once told me that when he went visiting the prisoners condemned to death (by the British under the mandate) it was his custom to take his leave from them with the proverbial saying, "God's rescuing help comes in the twinkling of an eye." At times they would ask him, "Where is that written?" and he had to answer, "I don't know; but it must certainly be somewhere in our holy writings."

"Well," the good rabbi told me, "when I returned home once I looked and searched for the source of the saying, and I was unable to find it."

A few years later a three-volume collection of proverbs and apothegms drawn from rabbinic lore and similar olden sources, was published in Jerusalem. Leafing through it, I found Reb Aryeh's well-loved saying; and the source was given as one of the liturgical poems found in the prayers of the high holy days. Losing no time, I wrote a postcard to the good rabbi to give him this information. His letter of reply was almost incredible: Toward morning (he wrote) he had dreamt that he was taking his leave of me, and he told me, "Simḥa, God's rescuing help comes in the twinkling of an eye." A few hours later the postman brought him my card, with the source of the saying!

"the snare is broken"

This is what Reb Aryeh himself once recounted:

At one time I went to see Rabbi Abraham Isaac Kook (of blessed memory) and told him of a very distressing dream that I had experienced, and I asked him if he thought I should fast the entire day, thus to implore God's mercy to change it from an evil omen to a happy augury. The difficulty was, though, that the day was *rosh ḥodesh,* the beginning of a new Jewish month—a semi-holiday, when generally a person should not fast.

Without a word Rabbi Kook stood up and put the palms of his two hands on my head, and he blessed me with *birkath kohanim* (the "priestly blessing"—Rabbi Kook was a *kohen*). I left his room to return home, and suddenly, somehow, my glasses fell from my nose and broke in pieces. Well, Rabbi Kook came out to see what the trouble was; and as soon as he realized what had happened, he quoted Scripture with a smile on his face, "The snare is broken, and we have escaped (Psalms 124:7). You know it is *rosh ḥodesh* today. Go and eat your food in happiness" (Ecclesiastes 9:7). He took it for granted that whatever ill the dream boded, it had already happened—to the glasses.

the feelings of a youngster

In an early chapter it was told how Reb Aryeh left home at a young age in his longing to study Torah; and eventually he managed to gain admission into the noted Yeshiva of Volozhin. One particular youth in the yeshiva was appointed librarian; and as luck would have it, he developed a dislike toward the young Aryeh Levin. To the best of his ability he made life difficult, even miserable, for the boy. Whenever the young Aryeh wished to borrow a volume of Talmudic learning he would treat him with disdain, mockingly fobbing him off with some excuse, so that the boy had to return again and again.

One night before going to sleep, the young Aryeh began musing: "Why has this fate befallen me? For what reason is he so hostile to me when I have done him no harm?" In his misery he wept, and thus he fell asleep. As he slept he dreamt of his childhood years, of a time when grown Talmud students came to his small town to study, and in accordance with the general practice each was assigned to have his meals with seven well-to-do families, one day at each house. (This was known as "eating days," *essen teg*.)

Well, the children—including him, Aryeh Levin—had the task to wait on the Talmud students and serve them their food. One day one of the children struck one of the youths and offended him deeply. Thinking the young Aryeh had done it, the Talmud student beat him soundly. Aryeh wept bitterly and cried, "You're hitting me unjustly. I never did you any harm!" The youth, however, paid no heed.

Later, when this student left the *beth midrash* (house of study), the young Aryeh mocked and ridiculed him before the other children, in retaliation for the undeserved thrashing he had given him, until he had all the children laughing at the student in high glee and mocking him in turn.

All this came back to Aryeh Levin now in his dream. He awoke and thought: "Who can know the ways of heaven? Perhaps I deserve the anguish that this young librarian is giving me because I caused that young Talmud student anguish then, in my home town."

With alacrity he leaped out of bed, washed his hands, and went to the *aron kodesh,* the holy ark in the main study hall of the Yeshiva of Volozhin. Opening the *aron kodesh,* he exclaimed, tears running down his cheeks, "Master of the world, how can I atone and make good for what I did as a child? If I knew just who that Talmud student was whom I held up to ridicule, and where he lives, I would run there, however long the distance, to beg him to forgive me. If, however, the suffering that I now bear in my loneliness and misery can count as an atonement, to make up for the pain I caused another human being—then, O holy, blessed One, I am ready to go on suffering as much and more..."

The next day, the young librarian came over to him and began apologizing and begging his pardon for having treated him so abominably all along.

To Reb Aryeh it was a clear sign that his childhood misdeed had been forgiven him in his heavenly account.

the spirit that attended

In 1936, a year after our first chief rabbi, Abraham Isaac Kook, had departed this world, an uncle of mine saw him in a dream, dressed in his holiday clothes, walking-stick in hand, about to leave his house. "I am in a hurry to get to a *b'rith* (ceremony of circumcision)," Rabbi Kook told my uncle, "It is scheduled for ten o'clock, and there is not much time."

In the morning my uncle asked his wife to call the late chief rabbi's family and ask if they were having a b'rith. Rabbi Kook's widow answered the call. "There is no b'rith in our family, but there is one in the family of a very good friend of ours, who is dearer to us than our own kith and kin. A grandson was born to Reb Aryeh, and the b'rith is to take place at ten this morning. We are rushing now to get there."

To my uncle there was now no doubt that the spirit of the chief rabbi (of blessed memory) would be present and hovering at this joyous mitzvah; so he too hurried off to attend. With Reb Aryeh very much in attendance as the proud grandfather, the child was named Abraham Isaac—the first in Israel to be named for the late chief rabbi.

information by telepathy

On the right doorpost of his home, an observant Jew always has a *m'zuzah* affixed, in keeping with a law of the Torah. It is a case containing a rolled piece of parchment, on which the two first paragraphs of *Sh'ma yisra'el* (Deuteronomy 6:4-9, 11:13-21) were written by a scribe. If the paragraphs were written correctly, every letter clear, every word properly spelled, Judaism teaches that it brings Divine protection to the home. If anything is wrong, or if even a single letter becomes obliterated, the *m'zuzah* is disqualified (*pasul*) and utterly worthless for its purpose.

One night Reb Aryeh dreamed that the *m'zuza* at the house of Uri Tz'vi Greenberg, one of Israel's notable poets, was flawed and unfit. The good rabbi awoke and returned to sleep, only to dream the same thing again. In the morning he knew what he had to do. He bought a kosher (perfectly

Reb Aryeh in conversation with his devoted friend Uri Tz'vi Greenberg, the noted religious Israel poet.

good) *m'zuzah* and sent it off to Greenberg with a letter recounting his dream.

Quite to his surprise, Reb Aryeh received word soon afterward that upon receiving his letter, Uri Tz'vi Greenberg began examining the *m'zuzoth* on all the doors of his apartment. Within the house he found all in order, but when he went to the front door and began examining the *m'zuzah*, he was taken aback to find that it was an empty case. There was no parchment at all within. Without delay he took Reb Aryeh's gift and attached it to the door post.

the white notes

A year before his death, when he was already stricken with the illness from which he was not to recover, the good rabbi told of a dream he had: In the dream his bed began rising from the floor, with the head higher than the foot, and he knew that thus he was about to depart from the world. His life was to end. Suddenly, though, hundreds of white notes (folded sheets of paper) began falling from heaven. They were the notes that (at the risk of his own imprisonment) he had carried, concealed in his clothing, in and out of the prisons on his innumerable visits to the many Jews detained and imprisoned by the British under the mandate. They were the notes that had carried greetings and messages between the prisoners and their families and close friends.

Now (in the dream) the notes came falling like white snowflakes, until they began accumulating and piling up on his bed as it pointed heavenward. Thanks to their weight, at last the bed began moving back to earth and settling firmly.

(At about that time, alarmed by his illness, his oldest son, R. Ḥayyim Yaakov, had come on a flying visit from America. The doctors at Hadassah told him gravely that they did not expect the good rabbi to last more than a week. He lived another year.)

R. Ḥayyim Yaakov Levin at his father's bedside, during Reb Aryeh's illness.

the dream that ended a doubt

Even with his death, the relationship between Reb Aryeh and the world of dreams did not end: He has appeared in the dreams of others.

In his later years, the good rabbi accepted a request to teach *Pirkey Avoth* (Ethics of the Fathers) every Sabbath afternoon in a Jerusalem synagogue called *Aḥduth Yisrael* ("the Unity of Israel"). Its members were largely of a certain political party (headed by Menaḥem Begin), whose ranks came in great measure from the underground fighting movement of the years of the British mandate. Thus a good number of the synagogue members had been imprisoned by the British during those years, and had formed a strong attachment to Reb Aryeh, the "rabbi of the prisoners." Hence their invitation to him—to renew the link. And he, welcoming a chance to teach some of his beloved Torah, accepted without hesitation.

Unfortunately, such was the political controversy and rancor in the land that an advertisement appeared in the newspapers accusing Reb Aryeh of having decided to lend prestige to Begin's party, by teaching at that synagogue. Two close friends of his took advertisements in the papers to refute the scurrilous charge; but the matter remained under a cloud.

The good rabbi was born the sixth of Nissan and died the ninth of Nissan, shortly before Passover. A year after his departure, during the intermediate days of Passover (*hol ha-mo'éd*) the heads of the synagogue made a strong request to have one of Reb Aryeh's sons come and speak there, in honor of his memory, on the last day of the festival, before *yizkor,* the memorial prayers for the dead.

One son in Jerusalem, Raphael Binyomin, passed the task on to the other son, Simḥa Sh'lomo, on the grounds that he had no ability at all to speak in public. Simḥa Sh'lomo too was determined to decline, as he also was not given to public speaking, and there was not enough time to prepare. He reckoned without his father, however.

The night before the final day of Passover, as he slept, he saw his father in a dream, and the good rabbi told him, "If they have called you, go. I shall be with you." Simḥa Sh'lomo awoke, and was unable to go back to sleep.

At the synagogue he related the dream; and he added: "At the time, there was controversy about the lessons in *Pirkey Avoth* that my father of blessed memory gave at this synagogue. Now he is in the world of truth, where nothing can be distorted or misrepresented. If he told me to come here and speak, it is proof that Heaven approved of his teaching here."

the reassurance

As one member of the family heads an organization for the establishment of Torah centers in far-flung communities of Israel, he must travel occasionally to outlying districts and border towns. During a period when Arab infiltrators were extremely active and terrifyingly successful, the man had to make a trip to a rather dangerous area of Israel, and he was wondering if the risk might not be too great.

The night before the trip, he saw Reb Aryeh in a dream, dressed in soldier's uniform and carrying a rifle, and with his usual smile the good rabbi said, "You can go."

He made the trip and returned safely.

the gift of healing

Once a grandson of his became dangerously ill, and the doctor in attendance was considering sending the boy to the hospital for surgery. The night before the doctor was to make his decision, the boy's father, Reb Aryeh's son-in-law R. Sh'muel Aharon Yudelevitch, dreamed that he saw the good rabbi come to the sick boy and give him fragrant spices to smell.

In the morning the doctor found the boy considerably improved and out of danger, and there was no longer any question of surgery.

the happy visits

Four months after the good rabbi's death, his first great-great-grandchild was born, on a Tuesday night. The previous Friday night, as the child's father (the rabbi's oldest great-grandson) slept, he saw Reb Aryeh in a dream, performing the wedding ceremony of a young man who had been his (the prospective father's) classmate when both had been quite young. He had not seen this classmate since, but he remembered the boy clearly, a dejected and downhearted product of a broken home—the boy's parents had been separated.

"Reb Aryeh," his great-grandson asked him, "what are you doing here? I thought you had passed away."

"For the happy celebrations of forlorn and miserable people, I may still come down on earth."

"Will you come on account of the birth of my child?"

"O yes," replied the good rabbi. "You will have a son, and I shall be at the *b'rith*" (the ceremony of circumcision).

When his child was born, the new father went to the hospital—only to meet there the young man whom he had seen under the wedding canopy in his dream. And sure enough, the young man told him happily that he was about to be married, and invited him to the wedding.

the training of the great-grandson

During the very night of the first anniversary (*yortzeit*) of his death, the good rabbi appeared in a dream to the oldest of his great-grandsons. "Passover is coming soon, you know," he told the young man, "and it is an old tradition to give *ma'oth ḥittim* ('money for wheat')—charity to enable the needy to celebrate Passover. Here you have twenty *liroth*" (and in the dream he handed his great-grandson twenty Israeli pounds). "Give ten *liroth* to family A and ten to family B"—he named two specific families whom the great-grandson knew.

In the morning the young man remembered the dream vividly; but of course he found no twenty Israeli pounds lying about, and he put the matter out of his mind, as of no great significance. In the course of the day, however, he happened to visit his grandfather; and that gentleman suddenly took out twenty *liroth* from his wallet and handed them over. "Here," he said, "I have this money for *ma'oth ḥittim*. It is time you became accustomed to observing this mitzvah. So you take it and see that it gets to people who need it for Passover."

The dream came back to him in full force. Try as he might, he could not dismiss this as coincidence.... He went and told his father of the matter, and his father was astounded. "Imagine that," he said. "Mr A" (he named the head of the first family that Reb Aryeh had specified) "was here to see me this morning. He has just been dismissed from his place of employment, and he asked me to try to find him some other regular work. He was worried by the expenses that Passover would bring. Your great-grandfather certainly had a reason for naming *that* family."

The young man, however, did not rush off immediately and carry out Reb Aryeh's instructions. It was before Passover for him too, and he had recently become the father of his first child. He had a great deal to do in his own home to prepare for the festival (for which the home must be thoroughly cleaned and the dishes either changed or cleansed according to Jewish law). He postponed the matter until it began receding to the back of his mind. And as he shamefacedly admitted later, he might even have harbored the thought that he himself might be short of money for the holiday; and then perhaps he could give the twenty *liroth* to himself, on the principle that "charity begins at home."

It was some two or three days before Passover when his child was suddenly taken sick. A doctor was called, and the young parents did their best to cure the infant. Yet alas, the child's condition grew worse, until the doctor shook his head and said that if there was no change for the better, the infant would have to be taken to the hospital. After the doctor left, the young mother sat by the crib racked by worry. Suddenly she looked up at her husband and asked, "Isn't there a tradition in your family that when someone is sick, you give charity to help him get well?"

The young man stopped short and stared at her. Then, without a word, he left the house and headed for the two families that Reb Aryeh had named in the dream. He told each family of the good rabbi's instructions, as he left ten *liroth* with each.

To the two families, more important than the money they received was the realization that even in the heavenly realm, Reb Aryeh remembered them and knew their situation. The news of the dream made their holiday a happy one. And the rabbi's great-grandson found happiness too: When he came home, he found his infant child on the way to recovery!

22
Incidents and fragments

the "attendant"

It once became important to Reb Aryeh to prevail on Professor L. Halperin, one of the noted specialists at the Hadassah Medical Center, that he should deal very kindly with an acquaintance of the good rabbi who needed his professional help. In his intense humility the rabbi could not bring himself to importune or pressure Professor Halperin directly. Instead, he sent a letter to Dr Moshe Feinsod, the professor's son-in-law, asking him to verify if what he wanted could be achieved. This letter the rabbi gave to Sh'lomo Harari, secretary of the Jerusalem Manufacturers' Association, a close friend and frequent visitor of his, and asked him to deliver it to the professor's son-in-law.

Dr Feinsod read the sheet of paper carefully, then looked at Sh'lomo Harari, knowing quite well who he was. "Please tell me," the young doctor asked. "Just how are *you* involved in this?"

"Oh, I'm simply the attendant of Reb Aryeh."

"Now, how did Reb Aryeh merit to have such a distinguished attendant?"

"Excuse me," was the reply, "but I think you probably meant to ask: How did I ever become worthy enough to serve as Reb Aryeh's attendant?"

the honor of a student

When a student of his married, the young couple moved into a small apartment in Mishk'noth, the Jerusalem neighborhood where Reb Aryeh lived. Shortly afterward the student began frequenting the synagogue where the good rabbi, his master teacher, always went to pray; and he took a seat near the rabbi, quite close to the entrance, at the western end (the front of a synagogue is invariably at the east end).

When Reb Aryeh noticed him, he came over to the young man. "I am going to ask the *gabbai* (manager)," he said, "to please give you a seat as your honor deserves, in the front, not here."

healthy and unhealthy quarreling

In the thirties the religious members of the Jewish settlement became split and divided among themselves far more than ever before, with quarrels and contention on every side. One noted Talmudic scholar, the director of a major program of research and publication, once told Reb Aryeh of the pain this caused him, how bitterly he felt the abysmal lack of a great Torah personage whom all could acknowledge as a leader, to whom all would turn for guidance. "I very much fear," said the scholar, "that the result will be a spiritual stagnation and moral disintegration in our ranks—the rotten fruit of all this sterile, futile quarreling among us."

Reb Aryeh listened with his usual gentle patience, and replied, "Of course I am appalled by all the contention and strife. I am entirely in favor of unity, not only among religious Jewry but among our people generally, through all its levels and movements. Only by drawing together in friendship can our people be rebuilt in strength and find ways to reach those Jews who never budge from their non-Jewish positions in life, whatever the party or movement to which they belong.

"Yet on the other hand," continued Reb Aryeh with great emphasis, "I do not think the reason for the increase of quarrel and division among our people lies specifically in any incipient 'disease' of spiritual stagnation or disintegration. Nothing of the kind!

"To my mind," Reb Aryeh explained, "the causes of this divisiveness lie in nothing less than our spiritual superiority, the high levels of awareness in Torah that we attain, and our profound conceptions of Judaism. This strife and division testifies to a spiritual dynamism and vitality that is ready to yield to no one. The firm unflinching stand that every group among us takes, which inevitably leads to clashes and quarrels, has its basis only in an advanced spiritual vigilance that will not compromise by a hairsbreadth on matters of faith.

"Moreover," he continued, "the purpose of a difference of opinion is to lead to a clarification of views and thoughts—if care is taken not to let it turn into a personal (venomous) quarrel between individuals, but to keep it always focused only on issues. This is what the Sages mean by 'a quarrel for the sake of Heaven'—for example, the differences in rulings between Hillel and Shammai—which 'in the end endure' (Avoth v 17): Their views and opinions endure; to this day (in Talmudic study) we continue to ascertain and explain what was the School of Shammai's reasoning, and what was the School of Hillel's reasoning. This clarification of views goes on simply forever."

the rejected gloves

There was a woman who so admired him that she took pains to knit him a pair of woolen gloves. When she brought them to him, however, he refused to accept them. "How," Reb Aryeh explained, "will I be able to feel a person's hand when he holds it out to me in friendly greeting?"

they too wanted a blessing

Non-Jews would also make their way to his home, to ask him to bestow his blessing on them. Among them were Jacques Soustelle, a minister of the French government in his time, and General Pierre Koenig, head of the France-Israel Friendship League. Both learned about him from members of the underground resistance.

better than a curse

Once a Jewish tourist from America had what he thought was a brilliant idea. He wanted to put an end "once and for all" to the distressing dif-

Reb Aryeh with General Pierre Koenig, one of his non-Jewish admirers. A World-War hero of the Free French, the general was twice the French minister of national defense, and president of the Alliance France-Israel.

ficulties of the fledgling State of Israel, by removing Nasser (the hostile head of Egypt before Sadat) from the political scene. What did he do? He went to Reb Aryeh and proposed that the good rabbi should curse Nasser, roundly and properly. There was no doubt in his mind that as a direct result, the nefarious Egyptian enemy of Israel would be thoroughly *kaput*.

"I will tell you," said Reb Aryeh. "I have never cursed anyone in my life. That is a task for Balaam (Numbers 22–24). But do you know what? I can bless Nasser that he should be privileged to see the advent of the Messiah, the righteous redeemer of Israel. If that will come true for him, we will have no further need for curses."

the strap of the t'fillin

Among violins no name ranks higher than Stradivarius. Decades ago in Jerusalem, among t'fillin (phylacteries) no name ranked higher than that of Reb Nethanel Sofer (the Scribe). When he wrote the portions of Scripture on parchment to be placed within the leather boxes, it was known that he wrote every last letter and line in holiness and purity. Before writing the most holy name of God, he would go to a mikveh (ritualarium) for ritual immersion. And he himself prepared the boxes and straps for his t'fillin, working to the highest standards that the religious law could require.

It is told that the very first pair of t'fillin which Reb Nethanel Sofer ever made were bought by R. Israel Meir haKohen, known as the *Hafetz Hayyim*—probably the most pious Jew of his generation. The day he received them, he celebrated as a holiday. The second pair of t'fillin that Reb Nethanel Sofer made became the property of the noted Jerusalem kabbalist R. Sh'lomo Elyashav. A later pair by the same scribe was bought by R. Abraham Isaac Kook, the chief rabbi of the holy land.

It became a ruling passion of Reb Aryeh, almost (as one might say) a "craving of the evil impulse," to acquire a pair of t'fillin by this scribe for himself, to pray before his Maker every morning adorned in nothing less. In his typical altruism, he bought two pairs from Reb Nethanel, one for himself and one for the pious scholar R. Nathan Tz'vi Finkel (of blessed memory), known as the old sage of Slobodka.

In time Reb Nethanel Sofer passed away; and the t'fillin that he had produced with his own hands became precious, treasured rarities, kept as prized possessions.

One day Reb Aryeh was visiting his good friend R. Abraham Isaac Kook, when, in the course of the conversation, the chief rabbi told him, in great distress, that in the morning the strap of his "t'fillin of the hand" had torn off. These were the t'fillin that he had bought from Reb Nathanel while the scribe was alive, and now it anguished him to think that he would quite certainly be unable to get another strap for his "t'fillin of the hand," personally prepared by that noted scribe, since such things were now simply unavailable.

"But this is surely God's own work," exclaimed Reb Aryeh. "A short while ago the thought came to me: Let me pay a visit to the widow of Reb Nethanel Sofer, to cheer her up. I found her living in her home in such obvious poverty that I wanted to give her some money, to ease her plight. Since I had no wish to shame or embarrass her, however, I asked her, 'Perhaps you have something that you could sell...' and she replied, 'You know that I have no t'fillin by my husband left. All I have are two straps for the t'fillin of the hand.' I bought them from her at once, for a very good price, since she certainly deserves the help. So here is your new strap!"

Told and retold among the Jews of Jerusalem, the matter remained a "modern miracle tale."

Reb Aryeh speaking at the dedication of the new building of Yeshiva Merkaz ha-Rav, where the teachings of his lifelong friend R. Abraham Isaac Kook are studied.

the blessing of a good woman

This is an incident recalled by R. Sh'lomo Zalman Auerbach, the eminent Talmudic scholar who heads Jerusalem's Yeshiva Kol Torah:

I once met Reb Aryeh trudging at his usual pace through the streets of my neighborhood, the Shaarey Ḥessed section of Jerusalem, during the ten days of penitence (between Rosh haShana and Yom Kippur). "Where are you going?" I asked him. "Oh," he replied, "I am heading for the home of Dr Miriam Munin" (may she rest in peace). Anxiously I asked him, "Who is sick in the family?" His answer was, "Thank God, we are all well. But the holy day of Yom Kippur is approaching, and since Dr Munin is an outstanding physician who has treated people with kindness all her life, I am going to her to receive a blessing for the new year that has started for us."

the list of names

In the days of the British mandate, a semi-underground group called *B'rith Ḥashmona'im* was organized in Jerusalem. Members of the religious youth joined it who were allied in their thinking to the underground resistance movement, and the group disguised its underground activities under the cover of a lawful educational program.

The British intelligence service suspected, however, that the members of *B'rith Ḥashmona'im* were working closely with the underground, but found it difficult to establish proof.

One day, however, Moshe Segal was called to the British Intelligence office. He headed this group of Jewish youth, but his activities were well masked by his duties on the "community board." Now the commander of the Intelligence Service demanded that he furnish, within twenty-four hours, a list of all the members of the youth group.

Boldly Moshe Segal (who underwent imprisonment more than once) replied, "I am not an officer in the British Intelligence, and it is not my job to compile lists of persons..."

The British officer simply repeated his ultimatum, threatening Segal with a prison sentence as the alternative. Without a word Segal left, and went to see the two other leaders of *B'rith Ḥashmona'im,* to decide with them on what to do.

The decision they reached was to comply with the order of the British intelligence—for two reasons: (1) The Intelligence Service had the means to acquire the names in any case. (2) A refusal to comply could be interpreted as a sign of fear of the authorities, and thus an indication of illegal activities. This was the decision of his two colleagues. Moshe Segal, however, remained firm in his minority view: Even if logic supported their decision, he could not carry it out. Such a deed would go against his conscience. He would never be the one to surrender his friends to the British Intelligence.

They resolved to consult the chief rabbis and get a ruling according to the law of the Torah. They went first to the Sephardic chief rabbi,

Ben-zion Uzziel; his opinion was that if the intention was to avoid persecution, and those who were affected by the matter agreed to have their names submitted, by the Torah's law there could be no objection to it.

As the Ashkenazic chief rabbi, Isaac Herzog, was not in the city at the time, it was decided to consult Reb Aryeh instead. His answer was, "The matter is equally balanced. There is as much reason to decide one way as the other. It is therefore up to Moshe Segal to decide for himself, since this question is one of those things left for the heart to determine; and he is not to be compelled."

The next day, when the period of the ultimatum was over, Moshe Segal appeared before the commander of British Intelligence. "I am not going to give you the names of my friends. I am not your lackey, and I am quite ready to go to prison."

His firmness caught the British officer by surprise, and he did not arrest him.

payment for a favor

One of his students resolved to do a kindness for him, and he offered to plaster and paint the good rabbi's apartment (flat). All his life, though, Reb Aryeh refused any gifts or free favors, and he accepted this offer only on condition that he would pay for it. Forced to accede, the student stipulated a much lower price than the usual charge; and Reb Aryeh paid him in advance.

When the work was finished, the good rabbi insisted on paying him a second time. "But I have already received payment," the student objected. "Well, at first," said Reb Aryeh, "I paid you for your labor. Now I am giving you the money for the plaster and the paint." His smile was as genial as always, but utterly firm; and he would not let the student go till he agreed to take the additional payment.

the lottery

There was an employee of the post office in Jerusalem whose family once came to the good rabbi to pour out their trouble: The head of their family, a postal worker, spent about two-thirds of his salary every week on tickets in the national lottery. Besotted with the certainty that Lady Luck would have to favor him sooner or later, he let his family starve in the meantime.

Reb Aryeh invited the postal worker to visit him, and persuaded the man to buy no more than one lottery ticket a week from then on. "Look," said the rabbi. "If you are going to be lucky, one ticket is enough for you. And if your luck is bad, even if you buy dozens of lottery tickets it won't help you." Seeing the light, the man promised to abide by this rule faithfully; and the good rabbi blessed him to earn the Lord's help.

After a number of weeks the man returned to bring the rabbi the happy news that the blessing had been fulfilled: He had won a large sum in the lottery. How much he won, the rabbi did not wish to ask; but the fortunate fellow brought the rabbi a gift: a basket of fruit.

The same day, Dr Israel Eldad came to the rabbi's home on a visit. Knowing how frugally Reb Aryeh lived and how he shunned gifts, Dr Eldad asked in surprise, "What is the meaning of this fancy basket of fruit?" The good rabbi told him the whole story; and then he asked, "Do you buy any lottery tickets?"

"Oh no," his visitor replied, "because I am never going to win."

"I don't buy any either," said Reb Aryeh, "because I might win."

This reached the ears of a Jew in Jerusalem who was blessed with a large family but with no regular way of earning a living. He went to see the good rabbi. "My dear Reb Aryeh," said he, "I hear that you refuse to buy lottery tickets for fear that you may get a winning ticket and gain a huge fortune of money—and it is not to your liking to become rich. That is fine. But you should know, Reb Aryeh, that I have to marry off my daughter and it is imperative for me to provide her with an apartment (flat); and where am I going to get such a great amount of money? So please, Reb Aryeh: you buy a lottery ticket, and with the Almighty's help you will win; and then you can give me the money to buy a dwelling for my poor betrothed daughter."

"True indeed," Reb Aryeh replied, "there is no greater mitzvah than that." And there and then he put three Israeli pounds into the man's hand. "Go and buy yourself a lottery ticket, and may the good Lord help you!"

it is natural to cry "Fire!"

One Sabbath day, returning from the synagogue to his home, he happened to meet a group of zealots on the way, incensed pious Jews who were demonstrating heatedly against the flagrant violation of the Sabbath by irreligious Jews. Reb Aryeh stopped and joined the demonstrators. And there I found him.

"How do you come to be here?" I asked him. "It is not your way to join in open demonstrations."

"There are two reasons," he told me. "First, a man does not have the right to separate himself from the community and go his own way. When I come upon a group demonstrating in protest against the violation of the Sabbath, even if the method of the demonstration is not to my liking—because I prefer an approach of education and explanation in pleasant, congenial ways—I have no right to keep separate from the group. And furthermore, when you see a blazing conflagration, it is only natural to cry *Fire!*"

what's in a name?

Once an unprincipled scoundrel began sending letters to various notable people, appealing for funds on behalf of abandoned and neglected children from the new wave of *aliya* (immigration), and to the letters he signed Reb Aryeh's name.

Soon enough Henrietta Szold, the veteran Zionist worker who headed the Youth Aliya, learned of these letters, and she felt deeply aggrieved at the insult to her agency which the letters implied. She called Reb Aryeh and asked in accusation, "Whatever made you embark on such a campaign for funds?" Reb Aryeh, of course, was stunned by the accusation, having known nothing of the matter. "Not one letter like that," he assured her, "was ever written by me. Here is how you can tell: If the letters have my full name spelled in the usual way, you can be sure they are forgeries. I never write my first name with the last two letters together (אריה). Either I omit the last letter and make an abbreviation mark (ארי׳) or I separate the last two letters by a hyphen (ארי־ה)—because those two letters together form a name of God, which I am careful never to write."

Henrietta Szold examined the letters and saw that they were indeed not from Reb Aryeh's hand. She hastened to call him back and apologize.

"my name is Aryeh"

One day, when a heavy rain was falling in Jerusalem, Reb Aryeh was on his way back from the *kothel ma'aravi* (the Western Wall) when he saw a woman trying to protect her little child from the gusts of rain. He took his coat off at once and gave it to her, so that she could wrap her baby in it.

"But you need the coat yourself," the woman protested. "Just look at that rain."

"Oh, I'll surely find shelter till it is over."

"But how will I return the coat to you? I don't even know you."

"My name is Aryeh Levin. I live in the the neighborhood of Mishk'noth. When you happen to come there, you can return the coat to me...."

(As he discovered later, the woman was the wife of a former student at Etz Ḥayyim who is today a university professor of Jewish studies.)

for the immunization of a blessing

A friend once met him walking in the neighborhood of Shaarey Ḥessed. "Rabbi," he asked, "what brings you to our section of Jerusalem?"

"They are celebrating my jubilee today," replied Reb Aryeh, "the fifty years that I have been going to the poor Jews in prison. So I am going to the great rabbi of Tchebin, R. Dov-berish Weidenfeld of blessed memory to ask a blessing from him that this celebration—at which they are going to eulogize and praise me to the heavens, you know—should do me no harm spiritually, that I should not become all puffed up with pride at all the titles and tributes that do not fit me at all."

the power of prayer

His wife once became severely ill, and the doctors despaired of her life. Prof. Herman Zondek, who was treating her, recalled later: "I was very dubious of her chances to live, and very gently I made her condition clear to Reb Aryeh. When he understood, he went to stand in a corner of the room and began saying prayers from *t'hillim,* the Book of Psalms, in earnest supplication for her health, weeping like a child. Well, a few days went by and the rabbi's wife recovered from her illness.

"There," Prof. Zondek concluded, "you could see palpably the great power of pure, honest prayer."

no easy matter

One year, on the day before Purim, Shulamith Katznelson came to visit him. Half in jest, half in earnest, he told her, shaking his head, "This day of Purim is harder for me than Tish'a b'Av (the ninth of Av). On Tish'a b'Av we can weep easily, without any effort. How can you possibly not cry on that day of sadness? On Purim, though, we have a duty to be happy, and this business of happiness is no easy matter. How great are the needs of our people, how endless is their suffering."

the origin of the smile

"When I came to the holy land and arrived in Jerusalem," said Reb Aryeh once, in a reminiscent mood, "I was utterly alone and lonely (and quite hungry too). I went to the *kothel ma'aravi* (the Western Wall), put my hands firmly on the massive stones, and said, 'O Sovereign of the world, I am so lonesome here. Be Thou with me, I pray Thee.'

"At that moment," he continued, "I had a strong, clear feeling that the Lord was really with me; and I returned home with a smile on my face."

This smile never left his visage, it might be said, till his last day on earth.

when he asked for time

Not long after the good rabbi began serving as spiritual supervisor at the Etz Ḥayyim elementary school, his neighbor and former instructor in Torah, R. Isser Zalman Meltzer, became dean of the entire yeshiva; and people began speaking to him in criticism and condemnation of Reb Aryeh, because the good rabbi was so close a friend of Rabbi Kook.

Rabbi Meltzer called his former pupil to him, and began berating and rebuking him. Reb Aryeh knew, however, that R. Isser Zalman had no personal acquaintance whatever of Rabbi Kook. He therefore asked R. Isser Zalman to kindly wait three years. If after three years he still wished Reb Aryeh to give up his friendship with Rabbi Kook, he would do so.

Long before the three years were over, R. Isser Zalman Meltzer himself became a warm friend and admirer of the holy land's first chief rabbi.

the aura of tranquillity

This is what R. Eliezer Judah Finkel (of blessed memory), the head of the Yeshiva of Mir in Jerusalem, once related:

For Reb Aryeh every human being was an entire world, and an only child.

Once I asked him, "How do you manage to get so much done in a day? In the morning and evening you are involved in promoting the study of Torah. You make peace among people, you comfort persons mourning their dead, and you even have time to attend religious celebrations. How do you do it all?"

"Early in the morning," he replied, "when I finish my morning prayers, I set a schedule for the day in my mind—a specific time for every visit; and Heaven helps me carry it out."

Well, I tried to emulate him (R. Finkel continued), but it never worked out for me. When Reb Aryeh came to visit people, he would sit with them with an aura of tranquillity spread about him. He spoke his words in placidity, and all about him was calmness. All this he conveyed to those about him, as he devoted himself entirely to them. A few moments went by, and he would disappear silently and be gone.

I, alas, am not like that. Even if I want to remain a long while, from the moment I enter everyone senses that time is pressing upon me and I am counting the minutes....

his was a listening heart

In his writings, the Israeli author Ḥayyim Hazaz once described Reb Aryeh as "the one who consoled with words and comforted with a silence that communicates." Hazaz wrote:

His face was kindly in friendship, in its silence. There was a sort of generous light in it, bestowed on a narrow alley of life that grew sorrowful in a time that was neither day nor night. Even more, his eyes told you about him—eyes as blue as some evening hour, filled with a sadness soft as a plucked flower, yet smiling and attentive, conveying hidden truth from one heart to another.

His words were few, the sound of his voice gentle, almost a whisper. All sorts of people, men and women, would come to him to pour out the bitterness of their spirit. His was a listening heart, that could comfort people in their time of trouble. But more than he consoled them with words he comforted them with a silence that communicated, as it seemed, out of love and compassion; with the nodding of his head; by lifting his eyelashes, or lowering them.

People would leave him purified and consoled, as though he had relieved them of all their troubles. Yet he never allowed anyone to call him a tzaddik—because he was not a tzaddik, he said, and he had no idea what he ought to do in order to be a tzaddik, so that all those beliefs and opinions that people had about him should not be mere illusion.

One woman, who knew bitterness of heart and bitterness of spirit and who came often to see him, once answered these words of his properly: "*Nu*, maybe he is a tzaddik and maybe not, but when I left him there was a light shining in my soul!"

23
Jerusalem triumphant

they will have to come back

One of his students married and went to live in B'ney B'rak. On one occasion he returned for a visit, and Reb Aryeh told him, "There are extremely religious persons who abandon Jerusalem and prefer to enclose themselves in the holy atmosphere of B'ney B'rak. Yet one day in the future even they will be compelled to come up again to Jerusalem, so that they can eat here their *ma'asér shéni*" [the Second Tithe, taken from produce raised in Israel, which the owner has to eat in Jerusalem when the Sanctuary is in existence—and it is the firm belief of religious Jewry that the Sanctuary will one day be rebuilt].

when Jerusalem was reunited

After the Six-Day War he was as though reborn. He rejoiced like a little child and wept, overcome by emotion. He felt himself fortunate beyond measure to see Jerusalem rescued from alien domination and reunited, and the Western Wall returned to Israel's domain.

During the war itself, a grandson of his was there, from America, as a volunteer to help Israel. On the very Friday of the week of the war, when the Old City was a very very new "war prize," the good rabbi determined to visit the Wall. Accompanied by his grandson, he set off on foot, at his usual steady pace. For nineteen years he had been unable to see the *kothel ma'aravi,* and nothing was going to stop him now.

The closer he came to his destination, the faster he went, forgetting completely his eighty-two years of age—until at last, with the Wall in sight, he was fairly running, and he went leaping to the ground before it. When he overcame his deep emotion somewhat, he arose and said the benediction, "Blessed art Thou, Lord our God, King of the world, who has kept us alive, sustained us, and brought us to this time!"

Even in his time of illness, when he was in considerable pain, he would not stop visiting the Wall, the *kothel,* every single week.

Once one of the worshippers at the *kothel* went over to him and asked, "Reb Aryeh, until now, when we were prevented from going to the *kothel,* this Western Wall was the focus of all our yearning and longing. Now that we can come and visit it whenever we wish, when it is so firmly in our reach, is there not reason to fear that it may become something commonplace for us? that we will take it for granted and will stop sensing the great holiness of the *kothel?*"

Gently Reb Aryeh replied, "It is written in *t'hillim*: *my soul has thirsted for Thee, my flesh has longed for Thee, in a dry and weary land without water. So have I perceived Thee in the holiness, to behold Thy power and Thy glory* (Psalms 63:2-3). This is what the verses mean: It is self-understood that 'my soul thirsted for Thee, my flesh longed for Thee'—yearning and longing possessed us when we were 'in a dry land without water' (half of Jerusalem being captive to an Arab power). But we continue to entreat the Holy Blessed One, that now too, when we 'perceive Thee in the holiness' at this hallowed site, may we sense that great holiness and thus merit 'to behold Thy power and Thy glory'."

a clear, sober view

The day after the whole of Jerusalem was freed and reunited, two members of Israel's *k'nesset* (parliament) set out to visit the Western Wall. First, though, they decided to pay a social call on Reb Aryeh. The joy and exultation among them was very great. "*Mazal tov,*" they greeted him. "At last the *kothel* is in our hands."

When the ebullient rejoicing subsided, Reb Aryeh commented, "Now we have to pray for Heaven's mercy." This left the two visitors wondering: "Now, dear rabbi, when everyone is celebrating happily, you are filled with anxiety and worry? Why?"

In essence this was his answer: "The Bible tells us of a brilliant war that Abraham our Patriarch waged and won. Four kings had won a battle against five kings, and in the process had taken Abraham's nephew Lot captive (Genesis 14:12). With 318 men Abraham then attacked the four victorious kings and defeated them, and set his nephew free (*ibid.* 15–16). What do we read then? *After these things the word of the Lord came to Abram, saying: Do not fear, I am your shield* (*ibid.* 15:1). Why in Heaven's name did he need this assurance not before he went off to battle but after his stunning victory?

"The answer is simple: After so resounding and astounding a triumph in battle, Abraham was certain that the nations all about him would not take it quietly. They would be stirred to their roots and would probably unite against him to undo his victory. So he needed the Almighty's assurance. It is the same today.

"The nations will not accept Israel's victory calmly. They will not consent to have the holy sites remain in our custody. Now, like Abraham, we need Heaven's assurance."

True enough, a short time later the pressure on this point by the great powers of the world began. Later Sh'muel Tamir, one of the two visitors, noted: "Reb Aryeh had indeed a clearer, more sober view in political matters than we did. In his instinctive reaction the age-old profound wisdom of the Jew found expression. I dearly wish that our leaders could see matters as he did."

on Jewry and the Western Wall

This is a fragment of reminiscence by R. Moshe Tz'vi Neriya, the veteran head of Yeshiva B'ney Akiva in K'far haRo'eh:

A short time after we were privileged, by the help of the Lord who chose Zion, to see all of Jerusalem, our city of holiness and splendor, set free, it was my singular privilege early one morning to have a most moving encounter at the *kothel ma'aravi* with that wondrous man of

At the Western Wall, when it was regained by Israel

kindly piety, Reb Aryeh Levin (of blessed memory), a rare soul in his unswerving expectation of our final Redemption.

I pointed to the Western Wall and said, "If the Holy Blessed One was so gracious as to bestow so great a gift upon us, even though we are not worthy of it, He is certainly able to give far more..."

In his gentle voice Reb Aryeh responded, "We should not talk like that. Only an individual has the right to say about himself that he is not worthy; but when we speak of Jewry, we have to bear in mind that we do not know at all the merits and virtues of our people in entirety!" Then he added, "We have to pray and entreat Heaven that our heart should not grow proud with familiarity over this relic of our ancient Sanctuary; that the emotion we experienced in our heart then, when we would reach the *kothel* in those days (under the Turks and the British) in reverent fear, should continue to pulse in us now too, when we come to it in joy."

Four days before he expired I came up to Jerusalem to visit him; and I found him sleeping in his feeble condition. When he awoke and I went over to his bed, he gathered his strength and held out his hand to me—that warm, life-giving hand of Reb Aryeh—and asked how I was. Then he added softly, "The last time, we met at the *kothel ma'aravi.*"

a dream and its meaning

After the Six-Day War one of the deputy mayors of Jerusalem met him in the street. Reb Aryeh took his hand and murmured, "We were like those who dream, we were like those who dream" (the last part of the verse in Scripture, *When the Lord brought back those who returned to Zion, we were like those,* etc.—Psalms 126:1). "It is characteristic of a dream," Reb Aryeh continued, "that in a few brief moments a man can see events occurring over a long period. It is just so right now. This is the time of our redemption. Here lies the mystic root of the redemption. We have seen the events of the redemption, the hopes of generations, coming true before our eyes in this brief time of six days. This is what R. Judah haLévi meant when he said, 'The rescuing help of the Lord comes in the twinkling of an eye.'

"Yes, we have certainly been like those who dream."

When the **kothel** was ours again, he hastened there to lead his fellow-Jews in prayers of gratitude.

"it will give me strength"

Infirm and feeble as he was in those days, he pleaded with the people close to him to take him to Rachel's Tomb and the Cave of Machpélah (the Tomb of the Patriarchs) in Hebron. Now that these holy sites were Israel's, Jews could at last go there, and he yearned with all his heart to visit them. His friends, however, were concerned for his health, and they tried their best to dissuade him from making these visits—but to no avail. His passionate wish was not to be denied.

During the ride to Hebron he began pleading anew with the people who accompanied him: "Please take me to Gush Etzyon" (the religious settlement which had been wiped out in the 1948 War of Independence; with the return of the territory to Israel in the Six-Day War, it began quickly to be resettled). "I must see the new settlers there. I will bless them and take a blessing from them." Once again they tried to make him understand that such a visit could be injurious to his precarious health—once again to no avail. "On the contrary, on the contrary," he retorted. "This visit will only give me strength and energy. Blessed be the God who establishes the boundary of the widow" (meaning Zion, Israel, left forsaken for almost 1900 years by her people).

This strong wish of his also had to be granted.

literally on foot

On one of the pilgrimage festivals (Passover, Shavu'oth, Sukkoth) a friend met him returning from a visit to the Western Wall, breathing heavily and panting for breath as he climbed the steps leading from the Old City of Jerusalem to the New City.

"Dear rabbi," asked the man, "why do you not take the bus from the *kothel*? Why do you need to struggle and tire yourself out?"

Reb Aryeh replied, "For these festivals our Sages do not speak of *yerida l'regel*, going down for the holyday, but of *aliya l'regel*, going up for the holyday—literally going *up*, and on foot!"

natural miracles

Seeing him suffering from the infirmities of illness in old age, in those days, there was a man who sought to bolster his spirit by telling him, "Dear rabbi, you have merited to see what others have not merited to behold. You have seen Jerusalem and its holy places freed from the clutches of a bitter enemy."

"Not I alone have merited to see it," replied Reb Aryeh. "Our entire generation is meritorious—for it has beheld more than the generations before us ever witnessed—even the generation of Moses our Master. All the miracles that were wrought for Moses, and for the generations after him, were unnatural occurrences. The miracles in our generation happen for us in a perfectly 'natural' way...."

the third stage

A journalist who knew him well went to visit him in the hospital on the day before he passed away. He found him with his strength gone and his voice very weak. It was necessary to bend down and concentrate to be able to hear him. In his hand the good rabbi held a *t'hillim*, a Book of Psalms, opened to Psalm 69; and he pointed to the last two verses: "Here," he said, "here it is all written: *For God will save Zion and rebuild the cities of Judah...and those who love His name shall dwell in it.*

"First, He saved Zion (Reb Aryeh explained). Initially the early pioneers and settlers came, to reclaim the land; and afterward their heirs and followers. Now we are in the second stage: we have to rebuild the cities of Judah. Only then will the third stage come—the period of love of God's name. That period too will come!"

24

His last years

the source of his energy

Until he was taken to Hadassah Hospital, it was his custom for countless years to get up each morning before dawn, in order to teach a portion of *Shulḥan Aruch* (the code of religious law). Afterward he would say the morning prayers, like the very pious Jews in ancient Talmudic times, with the rising of the sun. Toward evening, between the afternoon and evening prayers, it was his practice again to teach a group—this time, the *daf yomi,* the daily lesson of two pages of the Talmud.

When his strength began to fail and he had to take to his bed, his family pleaded with his physician to persuade him to give up his practice of getting along on three or four hours of sleep a night. They begged him to order Reb Aryeh to rest and take proper care of himself.

To this the doctor replied, "Reb Aryeh defies all the rules of medicine. The source of his vitality is something beyond the forces of nature. From his endless activity, from his incessant running and going to and fro, from his tramping and trudging to the homes of all those downtrodden and wretched people—from all that he derives his energy. Do you think I can stand up to him? Do you think I can order him to remain cooped up in his home?"

After his heart attack, when he had to be confined to bed, his sons pleaded with him, "Set yourself fixed hours for rest and fixed hours for seeing people." To this, though, the good rabbi was vehemently opposed. "I am not a tzaddik," said he, "nor a hassidic rabbi who sets certain hours to be 'at home' to visitors. If someone knocks on my door, that is a sign that something is troubling him. How can I turn him away?"

When he reached the age of eighty and he was already quite weak, a festive assembly was arranged by the old veteran underground resistance fighters (under the British mandate), in the courtyard of the old central prison of Jerusalem, to pay him honor.

The good rabbi wanted no part of it, since he shunned honors and tributes. Yet he agreed to go to this assembly, to avoid causing his admirers any unhappiness, since they wanted so strongly to honor him; and he hoped to be able to sanctify the name of God at the gathering, by bringing the people closer to the traditional, age-old faith.

Among the words of tribute addressed to him, there was this: "Your eyes illuminated the darkness of our cells.... For us you were a bridge to the past generations, a link of prayer with Almighty God."

As evening fell during the assembly, after the speeches, the turn of Reb Aryeh came to say a few words. He looked up and saw that stars had already appeared. Rising to his feet, he said, "Let us say the evening prayers together, as a congregation—just as we used to pray together in the prison." The prayer-service ended, he returned to his seat. Yet again they asked him to say a few words.

The rabbi rose to his feet. "The importance of this assembly," said he, "is that it has brought friends together. Moreover, this good meeting is taking place on the *other* side of the prison bars.... And it is good that I have been privileged to serve as the excuse for this gathering of friends, now having reached the age of eighty. It particularly makes my heart glad to see also the families of the prisoners, especially the little children, since I have always loved small children."

Then he added, "I do not know if I shall be privileged to be with you again like this. All I ask of you is this: Tell your children: *There was an old Jew in Jerusalem who loved us so very much!*" With that the good rabbi burst into tears; and among the thousands of people there, not a dry eye was to be found.

not to become a burden

When friends blessed him and wished him a long life, he would answer, "My prayer is that the Almighty may grant me years as long as I do not become dependent on people for help. May the Lord grant me the number of years that have been allotted to me, but only as long as I do not become a burden to others, needing them to serve me and tend to my needs."

acceptance of pain

In his last year of life he was stricken with intense suffering. He had a heart ailment as well as lung cancer, which gradually spread through his whole body. While bedridden he suffered a fracture in his arm. Two days before his death he fell, and a bone in his forearm was fractured. From innumerable radiation treatments, injections and transfusions, his body was an agglomeration of wounds. Nevertheless, Reb Aryeh accepted all the pain in good spirit, certain that Heaven was just in its judgment that it meted out. He did not cry out or groan. It might have been in reference to him that the Talmud taught: Of those who act out of love [of God] and are cheerful about their afflictions, Scripture says, *those who love Him shall be as the sun when it goes forth in its might* (Judges 5:31).

When friends came to visit him he would tell them, "I go searching through my life-history, and I find no virtue in it for which I could ask the Almighty to lengthen my life." Then he would add with his smile, "I can only make the same plea as a certain rabbi who once fell ill. When people came to visit him and wished him that the great merit of his Torah learning should stand by him, he replied: Heaven forbid. By that I would only stir up accusation against me in the heavenly realm. All that you can ask of the Almighty is this: In our neighborhood Thou hast thirty healthy non-Jewish peasants. What would it matter to Thee if a Jew named thus-and-so were also healthy?"

to provide warmth

During his illness, while confined in Hadassah Hospital, he learned that the students in his yeshiva (Torah academy) were suffering from cold, as a severe winter had set in. He sent for an acquaintance of his, and put a letter into his hand (which it had cost Reb Aryeh enormous effort to write), appealing to good friends to buy two kerosene stoves for the students, so that they should not be distracted from their holy study by the cold....

the years without pleasure

His final, incurable illness kept him firmly bedridden, and he was unable to come and go, to visit the many people who needed him. This pained him greatly; and once he exclaimed, "If I cannot do anything for anyone while I am alive, of what use is my life for me?" About this doleful period of illness he would say, "This is the time that Scripture describes as *the years* that *draw near when you shall say: I have no pleasure in them*" (Ecclesiastes 12:1).

the last station

During the last weeks of his life he longed to be in his own home. Said he, "A man's last station in his life-journey should be at home." He had always been so careful to be no burden or trouble to anyone. Now it pained him greatly to find himself completely bedridden, needing the help of others, including members of his family. He tried his best not to trouble the nurses, and he would not call them even when he really needed them. His sons tended him devotedly, but he could not reconcile himself with the situation. In his last days he told me, "When I see my beloved sons compelled to serve me and watch me in this terrible condition, I think of Scripture's phrase, *more bitter than death*."

nothing borrowed

Before he entered the hospital he bought a bar of kosher soap, and this he carefully saved together with the flaxen material that was always wrapped about the *ethrog* he bought before every festival of Sukkoth. This material was to serve as a "wash-cloth" and was to be used with the soap for cleansing his body at the end of his life, in preparation for burial, in accordance with Jewish law. But why (someone asked him) did he need to prepare these things himself, beforehand? His answer was, "Even after my death I want to have no need of anything borrowed, that is not my own."

the home-cooked food

During his enforced stay in Hadassah Hospital, the members of his family brought him tasty home-cooked dishes of fish and chicken to have for his Sabbath meals. In the course of the Sabbath, though, Reb Aryeh took the dishes and gave them to the patient in the bed next to his. "Here," said he, "eat this. It is very tasty. My daughters cooked it themselves."

"Why don't you have it yourself?" the other asked. "Your daughters put in the effort for you. They brought this food here so that you should really enjoy your Sabbath meal."

"Yes," said Reb Aryeh, "but just look: All around us there are many other patients; and when they see that I am not eating the food prepared in the hospital kitchen, they will think that quite certainly I don't trust the arrangements here for preparing strictly kosher food. They will imagine that I consider the hospital's food non-kosher, and that is why I have my family bring me this. So those who have very strict standards will leave their meal over and go hungry...."

the thought he could not bear

As the weeks of his illness turned into months, it pained him to think that he was "squandering Jewish money." He told one visitor, "Five years ago I was very sick, and the Almighty added years to my life only because I never took any payment for what I do. And now I am receiving compensation for my activities."

"Why, what have you received?" asked the visitor.

"I have received money."

"What? You have received *money*?"

"Yes," answered Reb Aryeh firmly. And as they continued talking it transpired that he could not bear to think that Kupat Ḥolim, the health insurance system, was paying the hospital large sums for his protracted stay.

the "farewell march"

When his condition worsened gravely and it was clear that he could not last much longer, a "farewell march" began. A multitude of people made their way to Jerusalem, to visit him at his bedside and take their last leave of him. Army officers and decorated fighters appeared before him. Ordinary people, including the poor, appeared at his bedside. Heads of yeshivoth, who spent their lives studying and teaching Torah, took time off to come; so too did Zalman Shazar, the aged President of Israel; and the good Jews whom he had taught for years their daily lesson in the page or two of Talmud.

One noteworthy visitor was R. Isser Judah Unterman, then the chief rabbi of Israel, who was older than Reb Aryeh. When he took his leave, it was clear that Reb Aryeh was grieved. "Just see what I have come to," he said to the rabbi of the hospital who stood at his bedside, "that now I must trouble my rabbis to come here..."

to return in complete repentance

The members of his family tried to conceal from him the truth about his condition; but with his sharp perception the good rabbi soon sensed how matters stood. Yet he "played the game" with his family and close friends who knew that his condition was hopeless, keeping up with them the pretense that his prospects of recovery were good. Of his radiation treatments he spoke as "electro-therapy"—all this so as not to cause them grief. In spite of the severe bouts of pain that he suffered, there was even a smile on his face for every visitor who came.

To his very close friends, however, with whom he dropped the pretense, he said, "I am prepared to die; only, I have asked the Almighty to let me live one more year—so that I can make myself ready and return in complete repentance..."

the last blessing

There was a combat unit in Israel's army which lost a number of soldiers in the Six-Day War, some of whom were the only sons of their parents.

One day the unit commander received a letter from the father of one of these only sons—a most unusual letter by any standard. In most cases, when army officers went to comfort and cheer the parents of a fallen soldier, they found themselves being consoled and heartened by the stricken parents. This letter, though, was filled with bitter complaint against the army and the State of Israel. The bereaved father wrote, for example, that his son had always gone hungry in the defense forces and had not received any leaves of absence. The unit commander could not understand it. There had never been any hungry or starving soldiers in the army; there never were and never would be any. Everyone knew that. And in the defense forces there has always been an absolutely fair and even-handed policy in regard to leaves for the soldiers. Still, that was what the bereaved father had written, and signed his name to it.

In addition, the letter contained a postscript: "I wish you and your family that Fate may avenge itself upon you, and you may suffer all your lives as I am suffering today."

Well, there was an organization of bereaved parents, who had lost sons in Israel's defense forces. The unit commander turned the letter over to the organization committee, whereupon the committee members went to see the author of the letter and roundly berated him for it.

Still, the commander of the combat unit was unable to forget it. The spiteful, venomous words rankled.... One evening he went to stand for a while at the *kothel ma'aravi,* the Western Wall. Whenever he could go to the Wall, he always found his hours there a moving experience, that left him spiritually uplifted, and especially at night.

This time, as luck would have it, Simḥa Holtzberg (known as "the father of the wounded" for his devotion to Israel's wounded soldiers) came over to him. "Tell me, Dani," he said, "have you ever met a tzaddik, a really righteous precious good Jew?"

"Who could that be?" asked Dani the commander.

"Reb Aryeh Levin," he replied. "Come with me. It will be an extraordinary experience for you." And off they went. It was a few months before the end came for Reb Aryeh, and he was already completely bedridden. Holtzberg introduced Dani to him, and as the two took to talking, the army unit commander revealed that before 1948 he had been in Gush Etzyon, the religious settlement that was wiped out in the

War of Independence. At that Reb Aryeh responded, "What a great privilege was granted me, my small insignificant self, to be in the proximity of people like those settlers of Gush Etzyon!" Then he recounted how he had identified the bodies of some of the thirty-five victims of the brutal Arab attack that had wiped out the settlement—using the very method (said Reb Aryeh) by which the victims of pogroms and massacres used to be identified in the time of R. Elijah the Gaon of Vilna.

As the conversation continued, Simḥa Holtzberg spoke up: "Rabbi, this army commander received a terrible letter from the father of a fallen soldier, that troubled him greatly. Please bestow a blessing on him. After a letter like that he deserves to have you bless him." Reb Aryeh took Dani's hand between his two palms and blessed him. The commander could not recall afterward what the good rabbi said; but he remembers clearly that he felt like a small child.

A short time afterward, the commander conducted exercises marking the end of a training period for his combat unit. The exercises took place near the famous tree in Gush Etzyon, and Simḥa Holtzberg was there. When it was over, Simḥa told him, "Listen: Reb Aryeh is in very serious condition at the hospital. Come, let us go visit him."

"I am sorry," said Dani, "but I am in such a situation now that I simply cannot go. I haven't slept for three nights, and my wife is pregnant. Next week, on the day before Passover, I will be visiting wounded soldiers at Hadassah Hospital. I can look in on Reb Aryeh then."

"We cannot wait," Holtzberg insisted. "Next week is likely to be too late. Come with me now; you won't be sorry." Reluctantly he agreed.

When they reached the hospital they found the waiting-room filled with people saying prayers for Reb Aryeh. One of his daughters stopped the two at the doorway to tell them that his condition was critical. In his present state, she said, there was simply no point in going in to see him. Holtzberg pleaded and importuned, however, until at last she let them enter his room.

To their surprise, they found Reb Aryeh not in his bed but sitting in an easy chair, doubled up, until his chin almost reached his knees. Gently, Holtzberg tapped him a few times on the shoulder. "Reb Aryeh," he said, "do you know who is here? It is the army commander from Gush Etzyon who came once with me to see you."

All of a sudden Reb Aryeh roused himself and murmured, "Is that the commander who lost a finger?" Yes, said Holtzberg. Reb Aryeh took Dani's hand and squeezed it. Before Dani could take it back, he kissed it. Then he told Simḥa Holtzberg, "In that corner lies my *tallith-katan*" (the small four-cornered garment with a tassel of eight threads at each corner, that observant Jews always wear to keep them mindful of the Torah's laws). "Do me a favor and put it over my shoulders." And with that he blessed Dani and his wife and child. It was close to seven in the evening then.

Early in the morning, when Dani awoke from sleep, his wife told him with great emotion that the death of Reb Aryeh had been announced. He had passed on to his eternal rest during the night.

his innermost wish

Reb Aryeh had the good fortune to see Jerusalem set free and reunited, and the Western Wall back in Israel's hands. Week after week he went to the Wall, without interruption, even when he fell victim to the severe illness that brought him so much pain. As long as he could still walk, he went to the *kothel maʿaravi* to pour out his prayer.

The central thread in the tapestry of his religious outlook was his constant hope, hour by hour, for the complete Divine redemption and rescue of his people and his land, the coming of the Messiah, and the subsequent resurrection of the dead. In the events that he witnessed in the holy land, he felt with all his being the footsteps of the Messiah approaching ever closer.

"Indeed," Baruch Duvdevani (a leading member of Israel's National Religious Party) later recalled, "I was once thoroughly shaken when he suddenly revealed the hidden thoughts of his heart to me. It happened when I went to visit him two weeks before his death. He held my hand a long time and embarked on a long conversation filled with reminiscences.

"As he spoke, I felt that all the stories and anecdotes that he recounted were only a prelude to the main thing that he wished to relate. Finally he opened his heart to me and began telling of a very pious Sephardic rabbi in Jerusalem named Isaac Agassi, who used to walk about talking softly to himself. Once Reb Aryeh went close to him, to hear what the man was saying; and he heard, 'It is a troubled time for Jewry. I pray Thee, Holy Blessed One: If my sins are holding back the final rescue, I am prepared to be the atonement for the Jewish people and the carpet spread for their redemption.'

"At that very point in his tale Reb Aryeh began weeping silently, and he told me, 'This is my entreaty also to the Holy Blessed One: If my sins are preventing the final redemption of our people, I am ready to let my death be the atonement for Jewry, if only it will bring the final rescue.'

"He squeezed my hand and indicated that I should leave. Past any doubt, such were his thoughts and meditations at the end, when he returned his spirit in purity to his Maker on the last Friday before the festival of Passover.

"When Elijah the prophet went up to heaven in the whirlwind (Baruch Duvdevani concluded) his disciple Elisha stood and cried out, *My father, my father!* (II Kings 2:12). He did not exclaim, 'My rabbi, my rabbi!' He did not shout, 'My leader, my mentor!' He did not call out, 'My sovereign, my king!' He could only cry, *My father, my father.*

"For everyone else there can be a replacement. The king is dead—long live the king. A leader dies—another takes his place.... For a father there is no replacement. It is a final, irreparable loss. Reb Aryeh was our father."

his last wishes

A few days before he departed this life, the renowned hassidic Rabbi of Ger came to visit him. As they talked, Reb Aryeh expressed his wish to go home on Friday. "Well," said the Rabbi of Ger, "if a tzaddik decrees something, the Holy Blessed One must make it come true" (this is a maxim in the Talmud, Shabbath 59b). "Not I am the tzaddik," retorted Reb Aryeh, "but you..."

On Friday his wish was granted him. His body was taken to his physical home in the Mishk'noth section, to be prepared for burial; and his life-spirit went to his eternal home in the Afterlife.

In his last will he requested that there should be no eulogies at his funeral, no long speeches of lament and praise for him. It was on a Friday in the month of Nissan that his life expired, when no funeral orations may be given.

A TZADDIK IN OUR TIME

the agent of purification

The Friday that he died, his body was brought by private ambulance from the hospital to his home, so that it might be washed and cleansed according to religious law, in preparation for burial.

His son Raphael Binyomin then remembered that Reb Aryeh had once requested that when this day would finally arrive, he wished the aged Menaḥem Klein to be the one to attend to the cleansing of his body. What was his reason? Reb Aryeh had a clear memory of the time when the great Talmudic scholar R. Isser Zalman Meltzer had passed away. Menaḥem Klein attended to the cleansing of his body; and in the midst of it all, he burst into tears. "Reb Menahem," asked Reb Aryeh, who was there at the time, "you have been performing this holy duty for well over thirty years. Do you still become overwrought by the dead?"

"*Ai*," Menaḥem Klein sighed. "When I attend to a devout Torah scholar such as Reb Isser Zalman, my heart grieves."

"If so," replied Reb Aryeh, "I beg of you: when my turn comes, be you the one who does the washing and cleansing."

Friday morning, an immense crowd pressed into the narrow street about his home, where the funeral procession was to start. At the left stood President Shazar.

HIS LAST YEARS

The funeral procession getting under way. In the foreground: the late Yaakov Herzog (Chaim's brother), former Chief Rabbi Unterman, and President Shazar.

All this his son Raphael Binyomin recalled as the body was brought to the humble dwelling. Yet how was Menahem Klein to be found now? No one knew where he lived....

While the family was still talking about it, Menahem arrived. He never listened to the radio, and had heard no announcement of the good rabbi's death. Only, that day he sensed some impulse within him to go to Reb Aryeh's home, and he came as fast as he could.

the chosen grave

During his life he purchased a burial plot in the cemetery on Jerusalem's Mount of Olives. When his life on earth ended, however, his family was in doubt whether to bury him there, in the grave he had bought, or next to the grave of his dear wife Hannah (may she rest in peace) in the Sanhedria cemetery (in Jerusalem). Then one of his devoted students recalled that after the Six-Day War, when the Mount of Olives was again in Israel's possession, Reb Aryeh had told him that his true desire was to be interred near her, since she had been so pious and virtuous, and his love for her had remained constant and even grown stronger after her death. It was therefore decided to bury him beside her; and sure enough, when his last will came to light, it was found that in it he had written this very wish.

The funeral had to be held on Friday, the very day he died (since as a rule no lifeless body may be left overnight in the holy city). Friday morning the family asked the members of the burial society to hurry please with the digging of the grave in the Sanhedria cemetery, so that the burial could be completed in the hours before noon, leaving enough time for his multitude of friends and admirers who lived outside Jerusalem to return home before the approach of sunset would usher in the holy Sabbath.

The burial society, however, wished to delay the funeral for several hours, so that they would have enough time to dig the grave, since the ground was hard and stony. As they stood at the entrance of the cemetery debating the matter, the watchman of the graveyard came over, to tell a strange tale: A few years earlier, said he, Reb Aryeh came to him in privacy and asked him to prepare a grave next to the burial plot of his wife: to dig up the earth and turn it over, so that it would be all broken up and soft. "Why would you want me to do a peculiar thing like that?" the watchman had asked him. And the good rabbi had replied, "Who ever knows the timetable of a man's life? Perhaps I may depart this world on a Friday, and they will find difficulty in digging the grave, since the ground is so rocky and stony; and then the people attending the funeral will be unable to reach their homes before the Sabbath has begun. I pray you: do me this favor, and dig the grave as I have asked you. Let it be ready..."

Discreetly, without letting anyone catch sight of it, the watchman had fulfilled the good rabbi's request. This wish too was granted him—that those who came to pay him the last honor should be able to return home before the Sabbath.

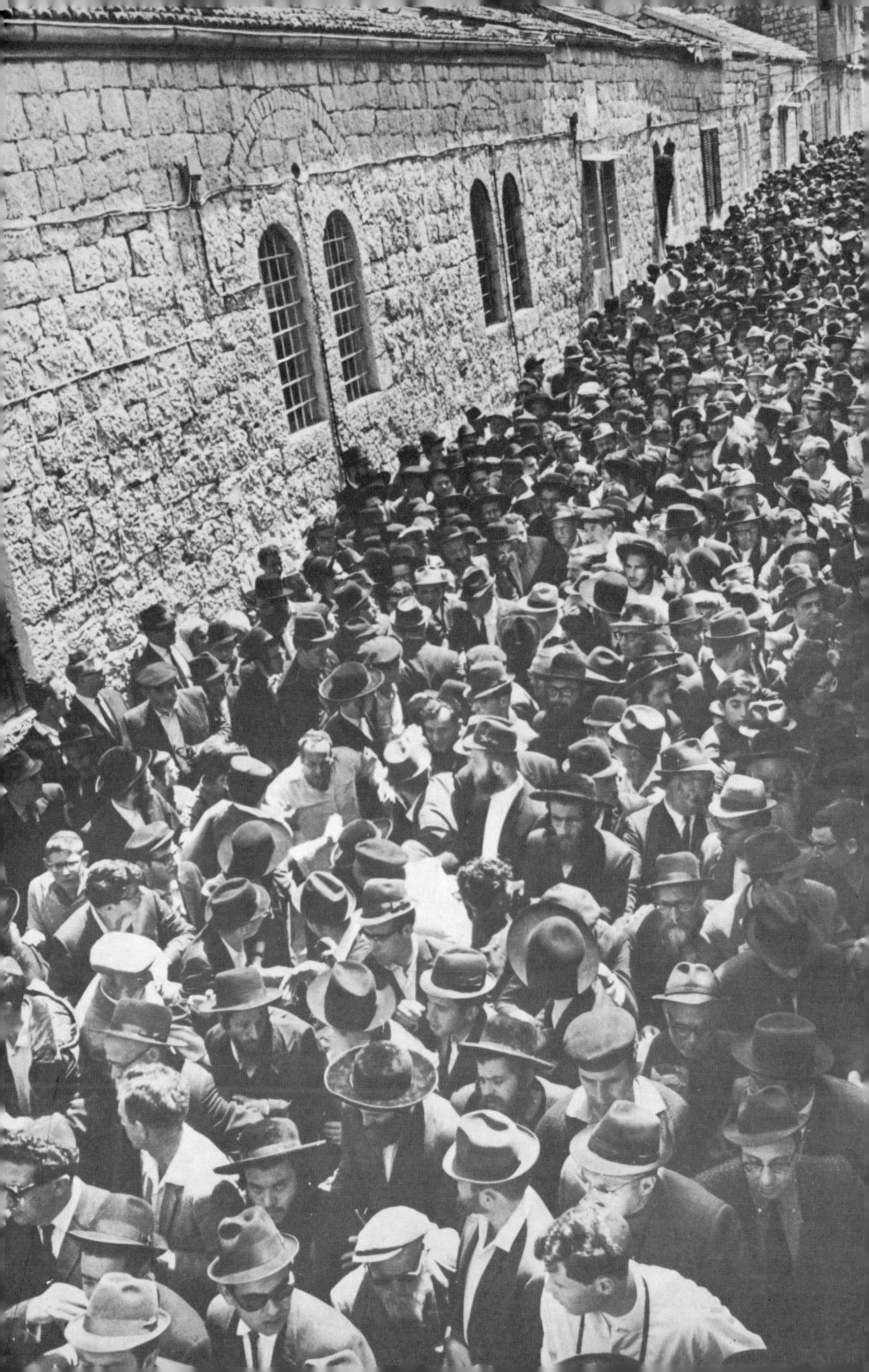

A TZADDIK IN OUR TIME

a source of peace and hope

On his tombstone these words were inscribed from his last will and testament: "I ask of everyone who comes to pray at my grave, to say wholeheartedly: I believe with perfect faith that there will be a revival of the dead at the time when it shall please the Creator, blessed be His name and exalted His remembrance for ever and ever."

At least one reason for this wish of his arose out of his knowledge that after his passing he would no longer be able to comfort or cheer any people in need of solace. Furthermore, persons who visit a grave in a cemetery tend to grow morose and melancholy at the thought of death, the fate that awaits all living beings. Hence he sought, in this way, to instill hope and courage even after his death, in all who came to his place of eternal rest.

Moreover, in at least one instance his grave has proved a source of healing. One noted rabbi in Jerusalem lost a son in the Six-day War. The young man had been engaged to a fine girl, who had already become like one of the family; and the blow of his death struck his mother, the rabbi's wife, a severe psychological blow. As a result, she has tended to suffer occasionally from moods of great emotional distress. Somehow the rabbi discovered that if he takes her to Reb Aryeh's grave, the visit invariably has a marked effect, soothing and calming her until she regains inner tranquility.

On the anniversary of his death, his son R. Simḥa Sh'lomo says prayers at the grave with some of his countless devoted admirers.

פ"נ
רבי ארי־ה לייב
ברבי בנימין בייניש ז"ל
המכונה
הרב אריה לוין
נולד ד' ניסן תרמ"ה
נפטר ערב שבת קודש
ט' ניסן תשכ"ט
והובא למנוחות בו ביום
דז׳ נ׳ צ׳ ב׳ ה׳

אני מבקש
מכל מי שיבוא להשתטח על קברי
שיאמר בפה מלא:
אני מאמין באמונה שלמה
שתהיה תחית המתים בעת
שתעלה רצון מאת הבורא
יתברך שמו ויתעלה זכרו
לעד ולנצח נצחים.
(מתוך הצוואה)

צור

The tombstone on his grave

נשיא מדינת ישראל

אני שמח כי נקלע מזמן להגיע לראית כמוסית ההתיחדות
אך כבר הצצק לפתי חולצא ורבית להכיר אישית
ר' אלון גני שמחתני היום כי יש פנינו קאול
המוקדצת לתורתו ולחקר חורשן של המסיב-רבית-אלכסנדריה,
שהיה מוקד התהבת אבא והנצחו לגל צרוק, אפיק
המסחרים ומוצב על נבכי ומריבג עוד להבי למקצע
ברתוגי רבים לגל חיי שפם רבה!. בטחים סגולות
נצמנית אחן, ורפורי אצלו ואהן הדין חדריך הבדרון,
ותחדריק של אשי הישוב הישו בארצן. ולרכו של
אושי זכרו משפ, חיל צדק נמצא חוקרים אבץ - עת
אל מאמו הקק ועולך אהכת ישראל, דעלה והשגות רבה.
                                           ישר כחך!

                                           ובי ברכה,
                                           זלמן שזר
טלט כסלו

the President's letter

Every year since his death, on its anniversary, a memorial meeting has been held by his lifetime friends and admirers, to refresh their recollections of him and to acquaint a new generation with the tzaddik who once lived in their midst. This letter, handwritten by the previous President of Israel in response to an invitation to the 1972 memorial meeting, gives a good indication of the esteem in which the departed rabbi continued to be held:

I regret that I will be unable to be present in person at the gathering devoted to the memory of the extraordinary, popular tzaddik, Rabbi Aryeh Levin of blessed memory, whom I was privileged to know personally. It has made me happy to learn that there is a nook somewhere in the land dedicated to his doctrine and to the study of the spiritual legacy of this *hassid,* this man of kindly piety, from a family line of *mithnaggedim* (non-*hassidim*) who was so imbued with love for humankind, and with concern for every wronged and deprived person; the 'father of the prisoners' who brought courage and cheer to every downtrodden, miserable person embittered in heart; this good man who did good, listening in compassion to all who suffered bitter misfortune.

A few times I had the chance to be with him. My visits with him are still luminous in my memory and make me think with fondness of the personages of the old *yishuv,* the old religious settlement in our land.

Blessed be all who preserve his memory and treasure the precious worth of his good deeds. The aura of his tender gaze still rests upon me, infused as it was with a love of Jewry, with humility, and with great simplicity.

More power to you.

Iyar 1972 *Zalman Shazar*

Zalman Shazar participating in a wedding ceremony, one of the occasions when he and Reb Aryeh met.

25

In the world of Torah

the promise was kept

To the Jews of Israel, the gentle undersized smiling rabbi was a phenomenon, with his boundless capacity to do favors and acts of kindness. Alone he took into the scope of his care and compassion every Jew imprisoned by the British for his struggle to make the land of Israel a haven for the persecuted Jewish people.

In the world of Torah learning he was equally a phenomenon—with his amazing ability to become bound in affection and friendship to the great scholars and authorities of Talmudic study. Thus, for example, as a young man recently arrived in Jerusalem, he found himself a neighbor of R. Isser Zalman Meltzer (of blessed memory), in whose Torah academy in Slutsk (Poland) he had studied in his youth. The two became so linked in friendship that in later years R. Isser Zalman's son testified that no one else was ever as close to his renowned father.

It was a trait that revealed itself early in his life. Before Slutsk, in his adolescent years, he studied at a yeshiva in Halusk with the famed R. Baruch Ber Lebowitz (who became revered afterward as the head of his yeshiva in Kamenitz). The two spent a set number of hours every day in Talmudic study, and R. Baruch Ber formed a strong tie to the youngster. For some reason, however, that he never revealed, the lad found it necessary to leave for another yeshiva (in another town). When he went to break the news to his dear tutor and take his leave from him, the great scholar was distressed, and paraphrasing a saying in the Talmud, he intoned, "Whoever parts from me parts from life!"

The youngster did his best to explain that he really had no choice, although he could not reveal the reason; then he promised that one day he would send a son of his to study with him; and with that R. Baruch Ber was mollified and allowed him to leave.

Many years later a youth named Ḥayyim Yaakov Levin (Reb Aryeh's oldest son) traveled from Jerusalem to the Yeshiva of Kamenitz. When he presented himself to the renowned Talmudic scholar, R. Baruch Ber asked, "Is your father Reb Aryeh Levin?" When the youth nodded, the sage's face lit up with a smile. The promise had been kept.

R. Baruch Ber Lebowitz   Ridbaz

the companion before sunrise

When Reb Aryeh was an adolescent student in Slutsk, the rabbi of the town was the noted scholar known as Ridbaz (from the initials of his Hebrew name: R. Yaakov David ben Z'ev), the author of a highly esteemed commentary on the Jerusalem Talmud. A strong, dominant personality, with a vast erudition, he was also an excellent speaker, who could hold his congregation spellbound.

A strong personality who brooked no interference, this noted rabbi once did the young lad a great favor without even knowing it. For his place of sleep, the young Aryeh had chosen a bench in the *shneider shul* ("the

Tailors' Synagogue"); other students used the other benches. One day the *gabbai* (head) of the synagogue decided that the young students were thus "ruining the furniture," and he went and put a stout lock on the door. A few days later, Ridbaz learned of this. Without further ado, he went and broke off the lock; and the young lad Aryeh and the others were able to return to their "lodgings." For two nights the boy had slept in some secluded spot on the street.

About midnight, having caught a few hours' sleep after the duties of the day, Ridbaz would come into the yeshiva, take a volume of the Talmud, and study diligently till the dawn came up. Yet even in those small hours of the morning he was not alone. The young Aryeh Levin was always there too, immersed in *his* study. A bench in the back was not conducive to long, luxurious sleep, and he had formed the habit of rising in the middle of the night to pursue his studies. So when dawn came, Ridbaz would take him along as a companion for his early-morning stroll.

At first the young student went willingly; but after a while he became reluctant. It would not do, he thought, for the rabbi of the town to be seen with a poor yeshiva student in tattered, hand-me-down clothes. Ridbaz, however, pooh-poohed his misgivings: "What are you concerned about?—that your appearance will reflect badly on me? It does not bother me in the least. And for you it can only be an honor, to be seen with the rabbi of Slutsk."

In later years both lived in Israel, and kept in touch by correspondence. In one letter Ridbaz wrote, "Your affection glows in my heart, and your assiduous zeal in Torah study still burns bright in my mind."

the Ḥafetz Ḥayyim

One desire that moved and impelled him through his adolescent years was his strong wish to see *gedoley ha-dor,* the great Torah luminaries of the generation. Amid his yeshiva studies he would give lessons to younger children and carefully save his earnings, to be able to travel and visit these fabled scholars.

Thus the time came when he rode to the town of Radun, Lithuania, to see R. Israel Meir haKohen, better known as the Ḥafetz Ḥayyim, as he had written a notable volume with that title. Since this volume deals with the sins of evil gossip and slander that people commit in their conversations, often without realizing it, the young Aryeh expected the Ḥafetz Ḥayyim to be a silent man, given to saying little. To his surprise he found the sage of Radun quite talkative; but he had so disciplined and trained himself that not a word of evil gossip or slander entered his conversation.

One incident remained in Reb Aryeh's mind particularly from that visit: A young man came to the sage and complained bitterly of all the dire troubles besetting him. His life had become a virtual nightmare, and he hardly knew which way to turn.

Calmly the Ḥafetz Ḥayyim replied: "Suppose you knew that Heaven decreed a certain period of suffering for you in your life, and you had a choice: You could undergo this suffering either in your youth or in your older years. Which would you prefer?"

"I would rather have it in my younger years," the man replied. "Then I have the strength to bear it; and when it is over I can look forward to a peaceful old age."

"Then why are you complaining if the Almighty has granted you your wish without asking you? And of this you may be sure: You will not receive one moment more of suffering than what Heaven has decreed for you."

the two scholars in Jerusalem

In his early years in Jerusalem, before his marriage, Reb Aryeh became very friendly with two outstanding sages of the religious community: R. Yitzḥak Blaser (called Peterburger) and R. Naftali Amsterdamer. R. Yitzḥak had been a major student of R. Israel Salanter, the founder of the *musar* movement (a new, chastening approach to the study of ethics, morality and piety). The young Reb Aryeh regularly attended R. Yitzḥak's *musar shmuessen* (talks or lectures in *musar*). In his later years, during the month of Elul, as the high holy days approached, he would always repeat these talks, out of his phenomenal memory, for the young adult students in his own yeshiva, that he maintained on the upper floor of his home.

Always seeking a way to draw close to great scholars, Reb Aryeh found it difficult to make R. Naftali Amsterdamer's acquaintance. But then he found a way. On Fridays the pious Jews went to a *mikveh* (ritualarium), which included a public bath-house. There they would wash thoroughly and then immerse themselves in the *mikveh* proper, to enter the Sabbath not only perfectly clean but in a higher state of holiness. One Friday, the young Reb Aryeh timed his trip to the *mikveh* so as to find R. Naftali there.

"Please, sir," he asked, "may I scrub your back?"

The noted sage looked at him a bit warily. "Are you a Talmudic scholar?" he asked. Should Reb Aryeh say yes, he would say no. He considered it disrespectful to the Torah to let any of its devoted students serve him in a menial capacity. Well, not wishing to lie, Reb Aryeh shrugged his shoulders. "I merely want to help," he said. So the sage granted his permission, and Reb Aryeh set to work. In the middle, another scholar, named Rabbi Epstein (a close kin of the authors of *Aruch ha-Shulḥan* and *Torah T'mimah*) came in. "How do you do it?" he asked Reb Aryeh. "How do you manage to get all the fine mitzvoth?"

At that R. Naftali Amsterdamer cast a beady eye at Reb Aryeh. "Young man," he grumbled, "this is the last time you scrub my back." For Reb Aryeh, however, it was enough. The two became firm friends.

the benediction over pure faith

Some time afterward Reb Aryeh went to visit R. Naftali, and he found him literally dancing for joy and clapping his hands as he recited aloud, with rapture, the benediction of *asher yatzar*. (This is the benediction said after one has been to the bathroom or lavatory to relieve himself, to thank the Almighty for this essential process in the maintenance of good health.)

The benediction finished, Reb Aryeh answered *amen,* and then asked for an explanation: Why all the joy?

Well, said R. Naftali, he suffered from a serious physical disability that made it impossible for him to pass water without the use of a catheter (a special glass tube). That morning, to his misfortune, the catheter broke; and he faced the prospect that before he could obtain another, he might well lose his life, or at least be taken seriously ill. At his wit's end, he decided to rely on pure faith: to set his mind on sheer trust in his Maker... and it was effective! He found himself able to go to the bathroom and relieve himself—and the danger to his life or health was over.

He took Reb Aryeh's hands in his, and made the young man join him in another little impromptu dance of joy and gratitude to the Almighty.

the message in the dream

Not long after he was married, Reb Aryeh dreamed that he was cleaning the fingernails of R. Naftali. In the morning he told his wife of it, and her reply was to go and see the aged scholar at once. Though neither said a word, both had the same thought: While a man is alive and well, he cleans his own fingernails. Only members of a *hevra kadisha*, a burial society, perform this service for someone else, when he has passed away and his body must be made thoroughly clean in preparation for burial.

Reb Aryeh went off without delay, and he found R. Naftali rapidly approaching the end of his life. He stood by the bedside as the aged scholar recited the sentence of *Sh'ma yisrael* ("Hear, O Israel: the Lord is our God, the Lord is one"); and then the sage expired.

Our tradition teaches that it is important to be with a person in his last minutes and not let him expire alone—for this eases his passage into the spiritual world beyond. Thus the dream called Reb Aryeh to this last mitzvah on behalf of a sage who had been a dear friend.

the private reason

The First World War upset many lives in the religious Jewish community. The Turks, who ruled the holy land, decided to deport all foreign nationals from Jerusalem; and thus they sent to an internment camp in Damascus Rabbi Michael Hurvitz, a man of vast erudition and fine character who was known as R. Michael Dayyan, because he served as the *dayyan* (the authority who decided and settled all questions in religious law) in a major part of the holy city. So this section of the holy city remained without a *dayyan*. Should a question arise whether a chicken was kosher, there was no one with the official duty to give an answer. It was an impossible situation that needed an immediate solution.

The community turned to R. Tz'vi Pesaḥ Frank, the rabbi of Jerusalem; and he sent for his brother-in-law, Reb Aryeh. Reb Aryeh was recognized as an official rabbi (or *ḥacham,* as they termed it) by the Turks in charge, and he had the official robes of a *ḥacham.* So R. Frank asked him to take the position of R. Michael Dayyan for the duration of the war.

Reb Aryeh asked for time to consider. The next day, he returned to R. Frank and accepted the position—for a private reason that, he said, he could not reveal. And so it was that he spent the war years in the "uniform" of a *ḥacham,* serving as *dayyan* in Jerusalem, answering, out of his considerable knowledge of religious law, the many questions and problems that arose.

With the return of peace (and the Turkish rule ended), R. Michael Dayyan returned. Once he learned, however, who had taken his place, he refused to resume his position. He considered Reb Aryeh eminently suitable and entitled to remain in his place. Reb Aryeh, though, would not hear of it. He almost used main force (so to speak) to make R. Michael return to his office.

Once that was done, Reb Aryeh revealed to R. Tz'vi Pesaḥ Frank and other intimates what his private, unrevealed reason had been for deciding to take the position temporarily. As it happened, there were many instances in the holy city in which people who had temporarily replaced others (who were deported) now refused to give up their positions when those others returned. In his perspicacity (with few illusions about the human capacity for unworthy behavior) Reb Aryeh had anticipated this from the start. When he was asked to take R. Michael Dayyan's place, his first reaction was to refuse, because he intensely disliked positions of title and lordship. Then he realized, however, that if he refused, another might accept who would keep the office tenaciously after the war. So he took the position—to hold it in trust for R. Michael Dayyan.

And never again did he hold a formal rabbinic position.

affection

As a son-in-law of his recalls, Reb Aryeh once went to a small religious celebration, where he met Rabbi Joseph Cahaneman (of blessed memory), the renowned head of the Yeshiva of Ponevezh (located in our time in B'ney B'rak). When Rabbi Cahaneman saw him, he joyfully rushed over to Reb Aryeh, shook his hand warmly in welcome, and kissed him on the cheek. "Forgive me," said he, beaming, "but when I see you I cannot restrain myself. I simply cherish you!"

"only with you"

R. Zelig Reuven Bengis, an outstanding Torah scholar and founder of a fine yeshiva that exists to this day in Jerusalem, once sat chatting with him. As they parted, Rabbi Bengis blessed him, "May you live long enough to see the Messiah."

"Very well," said Reb Aryeh, "but only with you!"

In learned conversation with R. Sh'lomo Yosef Zevin, the renowned Jerusalem scholar, editor-in-chief of the Encyclopedia Talmudit.

blessing

On a day before Yom Kippur (the Day of Atonement) Reb Aryeh once went to the illustrious Rabbi Joseph Hayyim Sonnenfeld, the spiritual head of the *éda harédith*, the very devout community in Jerusalem, and asked the venerable rabbi to bless him.

"On the contrary," said Rabbi Sonnenfeld; "let me beg you to bestow your blessing on me."

the amicable controversy

The impression remained with many that R. Joseph Ḥayyim Sonnenfeld and Chief Rabbi Kook were personal antagonists, because Rabbi Sonnenfeld was the spiritual head of the very devout community in Jerusalem which did not recognize Rabbi Kook's supreme authority. This was not true, thanks in some measure to Reb Aryeh. He was closely linked to both, and relations between the two remained harmonious.

Reb Aryeh's close bond with Rabbi Kook has been mentioned elsewhere in this book. Rabbi Sonnenfeld was given to saying that rearranged, the Hebrew letters of Reb Aryeh's given name (אריה) spelled יראה *yir'ah,* reverent fear (of God)—implying that he possessed this quality amply. And when Rabbi Sonnenfeld needed two colleagues to sit with him as a *beth din* (religious court) he very often called on Reb Aryeh to be one of the two.

Once Reb Aryeh provided an occasion for disagreement between Rabbi Sonnenfeld and Rabbi Kook, but it was altogether amicable. A son had been born to Reb Aryeh, and both renowned rabbis came to the *b'rith,* the ceremony of circumcision. Rabbi Kook was to serve as the *sandek,* holding the infant on his knees during the circumcision, and Rabbi Sonnenfeld was to have the honor of saying the benedictions.

The question arose: what to name the baby? A short while before, R. Sh'lomo Elyashav, the greatest scholar of his time in religious mysticism, had died. Related to him through the marriage of their children, Reb Aryeh had been very close to him, and he wished to name the child Sh'lomo, after him. Only hours before, however, R. Meir Simḥa of Dvinsk (Lithuania), indisputably the greatest Talmud scholar of the time, had also passed away, leaving no sons—and Rabbi Kook insisted that the child be named Simḥa, after him. Genially, Reb Aryeh acquiesced. A Jewish child can be given two personal names.

With the infant on the chief rabbi's knees, the *b'rith* proceeded, and Rabbi Sonnenfeld arose, cup of wine in hand, to say the benedictions. When he reached the point of announcing the child's name, Reb Aryeh whispered to him, "Sh'lomo Simḥa." Rabbi Kook overheard this, however, and instantly he sang out, "And may his name be called in Israel: Simḥa Sh'lomo son of Aryeh!" The deed was done; so the name remained.

Afterward the chief rabbi cited the Zohar to prove that a name which stands for the open, revealed Torah should precede a name signifying the mystic, hidden side of the Torah. R. Meir Simḥa had been a great Talmud scholar; R. Sh'lomo Elyashav, a profound scholar of mysticism....

true love for Jews

When the noted Rabbi of Lubavitch (one of the greatest leaders of observant Jewry today) wrote to Reb Aryeh, it was his habit to begin, "To the honorable rabbi, the tzaddik...who bears the Jewish people a true love."

Once a grandson of his went to see the Rabbi of Lubavitch, in Brooklyn, and the two began speaking of Reb Aryeh—about whom, the Rabbi of Lubavitch said, he had heard very much. At that, the grandson told the rabbi of Reb Aryeh's distress because certain members of the very devout community criticized and berated him for the great love and friendship that he showed toward personages and elements in the Jewish homeland who were unacceptable to them.

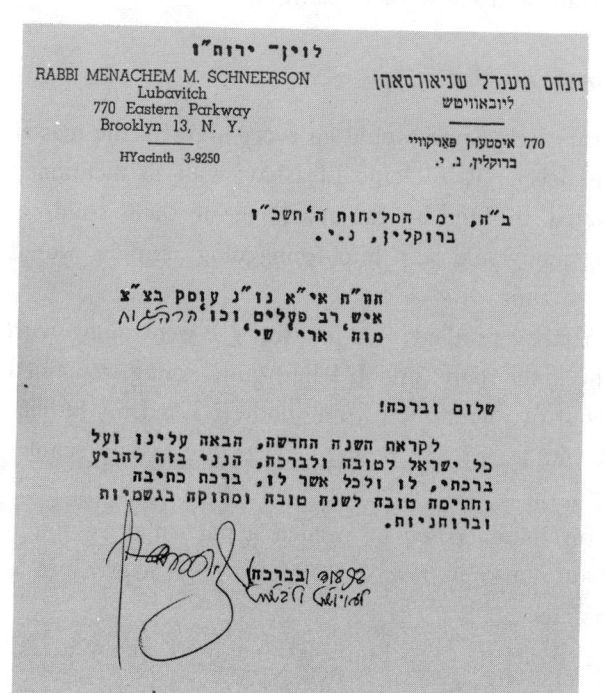

A letter of greeting for the Jewish new year, from the Rabbi of Lubavitch, addressed to Reb Aryeh as "the veteran ḥassid, the God-fearing, cherished, affectionate man occupied with the community's needs...."

This in essence was the reply of the Rabbi of Lubavitch: We read in *Pirkey Avoth* (iii 10), "Whoever finds the spirit of human beings pleased with him, the spirit of the omnipresent God is equally pleased with him." It does not say, "Whoever finds the spirit of the very righteous and pious people pleased with him," but simply the spirit of human beings—the ordinary man in the street. And few in Israel were as beloved as Reb Aryeh by the ordinary people who knew him.

on isolation

I met him once in the street, when he was returning from a visit to an extraordinarily learned scholar who lived in northern Jerusalem, isolated from others, devoted in solitude to piety and holiness. "Just think," said Reb Aryeh. "How admirable are the acts of that great scholar. Yet how are people to learn anything from his holy ways when he lives so utterly alone? A person is bound to say: That rabbi is a great man beyond any doubt; but how can I become like him when he is not like me? Does he walk through the streets of the city? Does he come in contact with human beings and deal with them, and know their pain?..."

in the service of a Torah scholar

For a period of three years Reb Aryeh would go every night to the master of *kabbalah* (Jewish mysticism) R. Sh'lomo Elyashav, who, as mentioned previously, became related to him by the marriage of their children. Neither cold, wind nor rain would stop him from going; and he would always stay for hours at a time.

His son R. Ḥayyim Yaakov recalled: "A few times I went along with him. They went into the inner room, and I, being quite young, remained in the anteroom, for about two hours. Returning home I asked my father: What did the two of you learn? He replied: That great holy scholar studied and delved into the sacred volumes, while I stood at his side holding the candle in my hand. When he needed a particular volume I handed it to him.... I do not know how I deserve so great a privilege as to serve this man of holiness...

"Well," said his son, "I never asked him anything more about it. His answer fitted in with his way of life—to reveal nothing of himself."

Rabbi Sh'lomo Elyashav

When Rabbi Elyashav died, however, Reb Aryeh wrote a short biography of the scholar of mysticism (privately published as a booklet; second edition, Jerusalem 1935); and in it he wrote:

> ... He finally permitted me to come night after night and read to him from his sacred volumes. Thus I would always spend several hours; and though I lack any human understanding of this wisdom of truth, nevertheless, as I sat in his presence I felt myself as if in an entirely different world, far from the matters that can drive a man out of this world. ...

Only after Reb Aryeh passed away did his oldest son learn, past all doubt, that the good rabbi had a great knowledge of *kabbalah* (Jewish mysticism). As he observed the seven days of mourning for his father, R. Shneor Kotler of Lakewood, New Jersey, a grandson of R. Isser Zalman Meltzer, visited him and told him so on the authority of R. Isser Zalman himself, Reb Aryeh's neighbor and former instructor.

the shoemaker and the Zohar

In a small corner, almost a hole in the wall, in the Maḥaneh Yehuda section of Jerusalem, an old Sephardic Jew used to sit through the day mending the worn-out shoes brought him for repair. Somehow the discerning eye of Reb Aryeh told him that the man hardly made enough to keep body and soul together; and every Friday, as he passed by, the rabbi made it a practice to drop off a sum of money and go his way. Had anyone stopped the good rabbi and asked him why he chose this particular shoemaker to support with a weekly stipend, he would have found it hard to give a rational answer. Some inner urge prompted him.

It was a custom that the good rabbi continued for years—until, one Friday, the Sephardic shoemaker called him back. "Rabbi," he said, "would you like to come to a *siyyum*?" (A *siyyum* is a small celebration to mark the end of the study of some major volume of Torah learning.) "I wish to invite you. Come next Thursday evening to my home"; and he gave Reb Aryeh his home address.

Always happy to attend religious celebrations, the good rabbi went there the following Thursday evening, and he found a *minyan* (quorum) of ten Sephardic Jews, including the shoemaker, gathered to complete their regular study of the *Zohar* (the Book of Splendor), the main text of Jewish mysticism. It was the shoemaker who served as the teacher, and now he taught the very last section of the book and went on to expound its meaning at length.

Reb Aryeh was taken by surprise. The entire group was obviously familiar with the abstruse and recondite principles of *kabbalah* (mysticism). He found himself caught up in an atmosphere of exalted spirit, raised to a sublime realm of thought far removed from the mundane world. A rare holiness, touched with ecstasy, filled the air....

The next day, Friday, he went as usual to the shoemaker's place of business, the hole in the wall—only to learn that the old Sephardic Jew had died in the night. Suddenly he thought of the section in the Zohar called *Idra Rabba*: the supreme lesson of mystic truth that Rabbi Shimon ben Yoḥai taught shortly before he died—in many ways the most profound and sublime part of the Zohar. And he knew that the old shoemaker had invited him to something slightly similar.

Now he knew, too, what had prompted him to support the man through the years, out of his charity funds....

Elijah's messenger?

It is possible, though, that the good rabbi often knew more than he revealed—through paranormal channels. Jacob David Abramsky, a son of the renowned Talmud scholar R. Yeḥezkel Abramsky, recalls a conversation of his with the famed author, winner of the Nobel prize, the late Samuel Joseph Agnon. Agnon told him that years earlier, Chief Rabbi Abraham Isaac Kook informed him, "You should know that Reb Aryeh has *giluy eliyahu* (the spirit of the prophet Elijah reveals himself to him)." Half in jest perhaps, Agnon asked, "Why does Elijah need Reb Aryeh?" Replied the chief rabbi, "There are many missions and errands of his for which Elijah needs him, so that things should appear natural and not miraculous."

his quality of devotion

About ten days before the end of his life, Reb Aryeh was visited by the head of the Yeshiva of Tchebin (in Jerusalem). When Reb Aryeh saw him he gathered his strength, and with an effort he rose from his sickbed and stood up. His visitor pleaded with him to remain seated; but Reb Aryeh would not yield. "In honor of a *rosh yeshiva* (head of a Torah academy)," he said, "one has to stand."

It is a commandment of the Torah, he insisted, to stand before a scholar. Not until the head of the Yeshiva of Tschebin left the room (which he did as soon as he understood the situation) would the good rabbi allow the man's brother (Dov Gneḥovsky), who was there too, to help him back into bed.

what he could not forgive

In his late seventies, when he needed a cane in walking, the good rabbi attended the funeral of Sh'muel Eden, director of the Diskin orphan home, with whom he had studied Torah for many years, for a set time each day, at the Etz Ḥayyim school. With him was Menaḥem Abramsky, the son of the famous Talmud scholar Rabbi Yeḥezkel Abramsky.

"Tell me," Reb Aryeh asked Menaḥem, "are you going out to the cemetery with the funeral procession?"

"No," said Menaḥem, "I have to go to a wedding soon." The bridegroom there was a grandson of R. Baruch Ber Lebowitz, the renowned head of the Yeshiva of Kamenitz, who had taught and studied with Reb Aryeh some sixty years earlier in the town of Halusk. This reminded the good rabbi that he too had to attend the wedding....

Suddenly he struck the ground with his cane, with great force. "I still cannot forgive him!" he exclaimed.

"Whom?" asked Menaḥem Abramsky. The good rabbi explained: R. Baruch Ber had lived in Halusk with his father-in-law, the rabbi of the town and a distinguished Talmud scholar. When it came time for Reb Aryeh to leave for the land of Israel, he went to bid farewell to R. Baruch Ber and his learned father-in-law. Said the father-in-law, "Don't go."

"Why not?" asked the young Aryeh, taken aback.

"You will not grow and flourish in your Torah learning there."

Sixty-odd years later, on a street in Jerusalem, Reb Aryeh explained to Menaḥem Abramsky that this was why he had never shone and excelled as a Talmudist in his adult years. He had an absolute faith (such was his ingrained belief in the Divine power of great Torah scholars) that it was the direct result of that noted rabbi's words—like a heavenly decree.

To the end of his days Reb Aryeh remained a bit envious of those who could create and publish original studies on the Talmud. In the Talmud, though, it is taught that a son brings his father merit (Sanhedrin 104a); indeed, a son is like a father's feet (see Eruvin 70b). If the good rabbi did not reach this "hall of distinction" himself, his eldest son took him there. Rabbi Ḥayyim Yaakov Levin, who served as a spiritual leader in America for some thirty years before returning to Israel, wrote two volumes of original studies on Rambam, the great code of law by Maimonides. One day it became Reb Aryeh's happy duty to go to Tel Aviv, to receive the Rabbi Kook prize for Torah literature on behalf of his son, who was then still in the United States.

the living memorial

Thus Reb Aryeh, soundly educated in the finest East European academies of Torah study, managed to live into his ninth decade without letting his range of Talmudic learning ever become widely known. As he moved through the streets of Jerusalem and traveled through the land of Israel on his innumerable errands of kindness for the prisoners under the British mandate, he used the time to review chapters of the Mishnah by heart. Yet that was no one's business but his own.

So well did he know the Mishnah that he made it a practice to review and learn through its entire six volumes once a month. Whether in silent study and meditation as he trudged through the streets on his humane errands, at his table at home, or in the *beth midrash* (house of study), he managed to review eighteen chapters of the Mishnah every day.

Every day of the week there was an hour that he devoted faithfully to teaching a small group of good Jews a daily lesson in the Talmud—a double-page, as it is studied regularly and concurrently by such groups the world over. The many volumes of the Talmud were familiar territory for him.

On the upper floor of his modest home, in his later years, he established a small yeshiva for older, advanced Talmud students—in addition to his regular employment at the Etz Ḥayyim elementary school. The financial burden of this yeshiva he bore entirely alone. It is easy to surmise that many were eager to proffer money in gratitude for the help and good

Every day he taught a group of neighbors, in the small local synagogue, the **daf yomi**, the daily lesson in Talmud studied by Jews the world over.

advice that he gave so freely, and finding that he would take absolutely nothing for himself, they gave their donations for his yeshiva. Yet he had an ironclad rule: Once he had enough for the month for his Torah school, he would take not a penny more till the following month. In this, it is said, he showed the lasting influence of his beloved wife (of blessed memory). It was she who imbued him with a sense of absolute trust in Divine providence, over and above all human relationships.

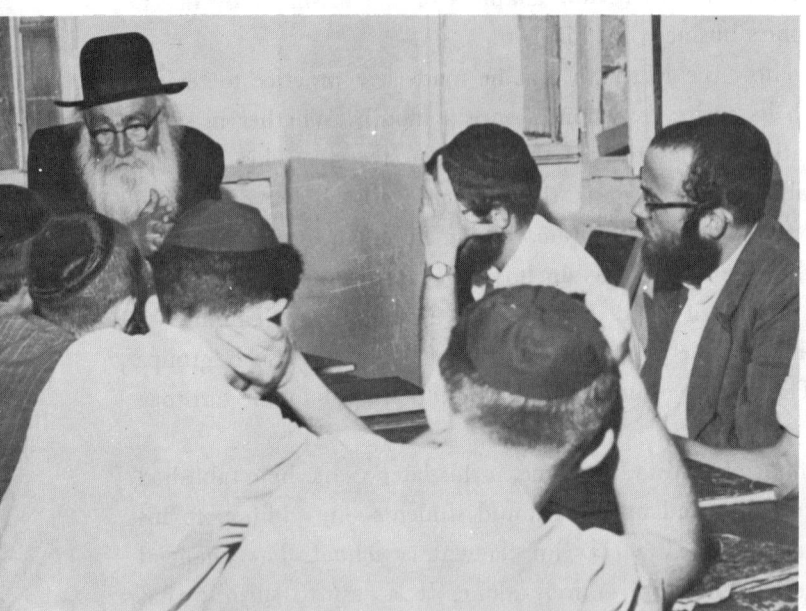

Teaching his beloved Torah at Beth Aryeh... and studying it in his old age

His devotion to Torah scholars and Torah study remained largely in the private, unpublicized and unknown side of his life. It is to this, however, that a living memorial stands and thrives today. On the upper floor of his lifelong home there is still the *kolel*, the small Torah academy for young married Talmud scholars, that he founded and ran in his lifetime. Called *Béth Aryeh*, it is headed now by his son R. Raphael Binyomin; and the physical setting and sweet sounds of sacred study are still as in his time.

In the beautiful, quiet region of M'vaseret Tziyyon, on the outskirts of Jerusalem, there is a modest yeshiva (*kolel*) named *Ne'oth Aryeh*, headed by his son R. Simḥa Sh'lomo; and many of the students are third and fourth generation members of the family. (Following in the good

IN THE WORLD OF TORAH

rabbi's footsteps, the yeshiva casts a benevolent educational influence, through lectures, classes and informal talks, on the youth and adults of M'vaseret Tziyyon, as well as the new immigrants in the well-known major absorption center.)

This is surely a most fitting memorial to his life, which made him a legend in Israel in his own time. For his incredible dedication to his people, his capacity to give of himself to help those who knew torment, misery and despair, came from the education he received in the sacred heritage of his people—the Torah.

His son R. Simḥa Sh'lomo heads **Ne'ot Aryeh,** a fine Torah academy in M'vaseret Tziyyon, for Reb Aryeh's descendants. The board of directors, under the presidency of R. Ḥayyim Yaakov Levin (Reb Aryeh's oldest son), includes the good rabbi's sons-in-law R. Yosef Shalom Elyashiv and R. Sh'muel Aaron Yudelevitch. In addition to intensive Talmud study, **Ne'ot Aryeh** brings the Torah's blessed influence into the lives of the local children and of immigrants at the nearby absorption center.

26

His sayings and maxims

truly good deeds

Truly good deeds, he used to insist, have to be done without any thought of receiving reward or payment. Once he explained this to me: At first thought we ought to go every morning to the policemen appointed to watch over us, in order to embrace them with the greatest affection and gratitude. For while we were sleeping they were at their posts protecting us. They do their work faithfully, even in the cold and the rain. Yet no one does anything of the kind—and the reason is only that the policeman receives a salary, even if but a small one, for his toil and trouble.... So we don't regard his activity as a good deed, warranting a show of gratitude.

At times he made the same point with a little story: A woman was once trudging along the street, wearily carrying some heavy bundles, when a man stepped up and offered to carry them for her. She accepted his offer gratefully, and with him now laden with the bundles they walked on to her home. All the way she thought of him as a blessing from heaven, a veritable angel if you will. When they reached her home and he set the bundles down, she said, "Here, let me give you something for your trouble"; and she held out, say, half a dollar. Somewhat to her surprise, he took it.

At that moment (said Reb Aryeh) the image of an angel started fading rapidly from her mind. She found herself thinking of him as a porter!

cleaning stains

For the Sabbath, Reb Aryeh would put on a long coat that was old and worn, but clean and stainless. His shirt too was far from new, but always freshly starched and ironed silken-smooth. Once he explained to his son Ḥayyim Ya'akov why he preferred these clothes: "You see, my son, when you put on a new garment, you have to be careful not to get it dirty. When you wear old clothing, however, you learn to clean stains."

Was it not symbolic? All his life he worked at cleaning stains, not only his own but others' as well. Gently, delicately he cleansed human spirits, never scrubbing or rubbing....

At a public gathering, with Abba Eban, Aryeh ben-Eliezer and former Chief Rabbi Unterman. He appeared many times with politicians and statesmen, but kept his political views to himself (see next page).

avoiding politics

In matters of politics he had his clear, firm views; but he was careful never to reveal them, so as to stir up no controversy against any members of Jewry, especially against a person whom it was granted to serve as a minister of the State of Israel.

Once Reb Aryeh dropped in for a visit at the home of Chief Rabbi, Isaac Herzog (of blessed memory); and as it happened, David Ben-Gurion, the prime minister, was there. The chief rabbi welcomed Reb Aryeh and asked him to give the prime minister a blessing. Unabashed, Reb Aryeh said, "I hereby bless you that you may soon vacate your position." At that Ben-Gurion gave him a puzzled glance, wondering if this smiling, undersized rabbi meant to arouse his ire. "Indeed?" he asked. "Yes," Reb Aryeh replied. "I pray that you may step down in favor of David, king of Israel, risen from the dead upon the advent of the Messiah!"

When he related this afterward, the good rabbi chuckled, "He could surely take no offense at that, could he?"

"good Jews at heart"

In his constant interaction with irreligious Jews he was occasionally asked, "Our Sages teach that 'the merciful God wants the heart.' The main thing is that we should be good Jews at heart. Then surely the *mitzvoth* (the things that the Torah commands us to do or forbids us to do) are only of minor importance?"

He would always answer with a true story: During the Six-Day War a woman in Jerusalem was notified that her son had been seriously wounded and was presently under medical treatment in the Tel Hashomer Hospital. Losing no time, she rushed off to see him.

As she entered the hospital, she met the head of the medical division in charge of her son's treatment. "How is my boy?" she asked him anxiously. "Thank God," the doctor replied, "there is no reason to worry." Somewhat heartened, she went on and found her son's bed. And then her world grew dark about her. The boy's foot had been amputated, his whole face was in bandages, and he had even lost an eye. Without a word she went out and found the head of the medical department again;

and she began wailing in anguish, "What in Heaven's name did you mean by telling me there was no reason to worry?"

In his most reassuring voice he replied, "The main thing is that the heart was not injured or affected in any way, and his life is out of danger."

"*Woe is me*," groaned the woman, "True, the heart is in order, but what about the limbs? *He is crippled!*"

It is true (Reb Aryeh would conclude) that "the merciful God wants the heart"; the main thing is to have a good heart. Yet of what value is the heart without whole and sound limbs? The 613 mitzvoth of the Torah correspond to the 248 limbs and parts, and the 365 sinews, in a human body. When a person treats a mitzvah injuriously (violating it) he injures a limb or part of his own spiritual self.

"I am rather short"

The former mayor of Rishon l'Tziyon once saw Reb Aryeh from afar, coming toward him. He wished there were some way he could avoid meeting the good rabbi, as he had no *kippah* (skull cap) on his head, and he felt uncomfortable at the embarrassment he faced. Still, there was the rabbi directly ahead, and there was no way out of it.

"Please forgive me, rabbi," he said as they met, "that I have no *kippah* on my head."

"Well," Reb Aryeh replied, "I am rather short, you know, and I generally cannot tell if a man is wearing a *kippah* or not. However, I see that your head is in the right place." And so with a pleasantry the embarrassment was removed.

the name of the Messiah

Speaking to his "children" in the Jerusalem prison (in the days of the British mandate) he once explained a Talmudic point:

The Talmud teaches that the name of the Messiah is among the things created even before the world came into existence. Why was that necessary? —because as you see, for our numerous sins we have to live without the Messiah; but how could we live for even one instant without the *name* of the Messiah? (The name is an endless source of comfort and hope, since it shows that he exists potentially, and is certain to appear one day.)

the sign of life

Once, shortly before the ninth of Av (the day of the year when the first and the second Temples in ancient Jerusalem were destroyed) he went to visit the grave of his departed wife, to pray there a bit. Turning in the direction of the Western Wall, he said to the members of the family with him: "How much does a man weep for a beloved person who has died: his wife, his mother or his son—his own flesh and blood, who was always near and dear to him? He sheds tears abundantly when the dear one passes away, and he continues to weep and mourn for him for some time afterward—and that is all. When a year or two have gone by, he has no more ability to weep. In the natural way of life, the fountain of tears dries up. The departed person has passed on to his world, and we turn back to our world; and as the Talmud teaches, it is a fate decreed upon the dead that he must be forgotten by the heart.

"Yet see how amazing this is: The holy Temple, a structure of stones, was destroyed so long ago. We never knew it in its period of glory. We never saw it close up, as a reality. Almost 2,000 years ago it was reduced to ruins. And over that Jews mourn and weep with flowing tears year after year, through the long centuries. For that, wherever they are, Jews find more tears and yet more tears.

"It is not really an amazing thing, but a manifest sign. It is to teach us that this is no dead entity that lies before us. The holy Temple did not succumb to the destruction of death. Over a dead person, even if he was ever so holy, distinguished and beloved, we weep once and perhaps another time—and no more. He is dead... and gone. The Almighty has taken him from us.

"Over this Sanctuary, though, if we still have the ability to weep, if we still have tears to shed, it is a sign that what we are mourning is alive and not dead.... It is a sign that there is hope!"

borrower and lender

In the *Shulḥan Aruch*, our code of religious law, there are laws which apply specifically to a man who borrows money: for example, that he should not be a "wicked borrower," who takes and does not pay back;

that he should repay his loan on time; that he should keep his word when he gives it.

On the other hand, there are laws set down specifically for one who lends money: for example, that he should not be unduly cruel in seeking payment; nor should he pass by the borrower's door continually when he knows the man is yet unable to repay the debt; and so on.

Said Reb Aryeh once: How good it is when a borrower learns the laws for him, and the lender learns the laws for him. If, however, the lender learns only the borrower's laws, and the borrower the lender's laws, human society will not benefit from that at all..."

the essential difference

In the Talmud we learn: Rabbi Akiva used to say, "Whatever the merciful God does, He does for good" [for a good purpose]. Nahum of Gamzu used to say [of whatever happened], "This too is for good." The difference between them (Reb Aryeh explained) is this: While Rabbi Akiva's approach is that whatever happens, some good will ultimately come out of it, Nahum of Gamzu's view is that whatever happens is goodness itself right now [although we may not perceive it].

so lofty a concept

We read in the Talmud that a non-Jew once came to Hillel the Elder and asked, "Convert me to Judaism, on condition that you teach me the entire Torah in the time that I can stand on one foot." Hillel accepted him and taught him, "You shall love your neighbor as yourself (Leviticus 19:18)—what is hateful to you, do not do to your neighbor."

Yet we find in the Talmud a more concise dictum by Rabbi Akiva: "You shall love your neighbor as yourself—this is the entire Torah." Why did Hillel not teach this to the would-be convert?—because so exalted a concept a non-Jew was not yet ready to understand.

you raise the other person with you

Our Sages speak of a person who is condoning and tolerant in regard to his esteem, and they speak of a person who judges his fellow-man favorably. Now, which of the two types is greater? At first sight we would say it is the one who is tolerant and forgiving in regard to his esteem, since he must swallow his pride and restrain himself when he is slighted or insulted. Actually it is not so. When a person overlooks an injury to his pride, he has done a fine thing, forgiving the one who treated him ill. The one who maltreated him, however, remains a miscreant. In contrast, when you judge another person favorably (giving him the benefit of the doubt), not only do you rise in spiritual status, but you also raise the other person with you to a higher spiritual level.

between loving truth and hating falsehood

Some people love truth, while others hate falsehood. Which of the two types is better?—the first kind. For in every person there are qualities of both truth and falsehood. If you are endowed with a nature that loves truth, you will see only the positive (good) elements in your fellow-man, and you will be happy. On the other hand, if you detest falsehood, you will perceive only the false, deceiving aspect in another human being; and as a result you will never find your place in the world, since you will see only the negative side in others, and thus you will live in a darkened world.

please to sit

At times a person imagines that happiness and wealth lie hidden somewhere else, to be sought and discovered; and he goes off in hot pursuit of them. He should bear well in mind, however, the Talmudic dictum, "To sit and not act is better"—which is to be understood so: Please to sit and stay in your own place, and do not act on the theory that it is better—elsewhere.

how to prepare for the Afterlife

When his oldest grandson was grown to manhood, he once told him: If you go to bed feeling as if you are going to lie in your grave, you will lie in the grave as if in your bed.

on unjust persecution

Quite often a person finds himself persecuted unjustly, only because he insisted on acting generously, beyond the letter of the law. Applying to this there is the verse in Scripture, *Only goodness and mercy shall pursue me all the days of my life* (Psalms 23:6), denoting that "I will be pursued and persecuted all my life for the good and the kindness that I did for people."

on saying No

If someone cannot say *No* to another person when it is necessary, neither will he be able to deny his evil impulse.

the important difference

When a person turns thirteen, we call him *bar mitzvah*; on the other hand, when a man becomes guilty of a sinful deed (or deeds) the standard term for him in rabbinic literature is *baal avéra*. Why do we use *bar* for the first and *baal* for the second?

The word *bar* means a son in Aramaic. When a boy becomes thirteen, he becomes obligated to keep the mitzvoth, the commandments of the Torah. So we call him literally a son of mitzvah—because a son can never end or cut off his relationship with his parents. Once born to them, he remains their son. Thus the link of the thirteen-year-old Jew with mitzvoth must remain equally lasting.

On the other hand, *baal* means an owner or master; but it is also the word for husband. The relationship of husband to wife is not permanent and indissoluble. Divorce is always possible. So we call a sinful man *baal avéra*, an owner or master of a bad deed—implying that he can always go and divorce himself from his sins.

on keeping a secret

Do not reveal your secret to another, because your friend will be no more careful than you to keep your secret.

on true reverence toward God

A person who is truly reverent in his fear of Heaven is one who lies awake at night worrying, "What have I done today to relieve the suffering of a Jew made wretched by his troubles?"

on true love of a Jew

To have affection for a fellow-Jew is a great fundamental principle of the Torah. However, we cannot fulfill our duty by thought alone, but by an inner feeling that touches our heart and moves us physically to act. Nor are we to look out in hope for any reward or recompense whatever. The Divine Master of compensation can be trusted to repay you your just reward.

on the expression of thoughts

Keep this rule in mind: If someone truly has something to say, he will strive to say it. As the Talmud puts it, "More than the calf wishes to suckle, the cow wishes to provide."

If a person phrases his thoughts in an inscrutable form, that is an indication that he really has nothing to say; and he therefore chooses an obscure way of expression, so as to try and capture an audience with his turns of phrase.

27
From his letters

on love of Jewry

What is love for Jewry? It is the great boundless love of the Holy Blessed One for His people, which was expressed in His selection of Jewry as the Chosen People.

Complete and perfect love of Jewry, without any flaws, can be ascribed only and solely to the Almighty. (He alone is capable of it.) We can only try to emulate His actions, so that we can take pride in having reached some modest level of love for Jews.

About affection for Jewry we can learn from Scripture's words, *you shall love your neighbor as yourself* (Leviticus 19:18). The truth, evidently, is that by his nature a man cannot love his neighbor in the full sense of the word. Hillel understood this when he paraphrased it as "What is hateful to you, do not do to your fellow-man." He meant: If it is hard for you to love a Jew, at least do not hate him.

It is clear that in love for fellow-Jews there are various and different levels. As great as a man is in Torah learning and good deeds, so great will be his love for the members of his people.

Come and see: It is a very noble level of behavior to fulfill the teaching, "Let the honor of your fellow-man be as dear to you as your own." Yet can anyone really be as happy over the honor that his neighbor receives as he would be over his own? Every person would admit that it is a difficult matter. Yet it is told in the Talmud that Hillel the Elder once ran for a distance of three parasangs before a poor man of a good (distinguished) family [as the man rode his horse, to give him prestige by acting as his servant]. The reason was that he sensed how much that poor man was missing honor and prestige, and he did all that he could to provide the man the honor for which he longed. This compassionate feeling, that Hillel acquired out of humility, patience and understanding, but mainly out of a proper love for fellow-Jews—this is the very highest level of love for Jewry.

* * * * * * * * *

Reproof is one of the qualities with which love of fellow-Jews has been graced. *You shall surely reprove your neighbor* (Leviticus 19:17)—this is the source of the command to give reproof and rebuke. A person who studies the Torah will note that before this verse we read, *You shall not hate your brother in your heart* (*ibid.*); after it we find, *you shall love your neighbor as yourself* (*ibid.* 18). In this order of the verses an important point about rebuke lies concealed: Which is the right kind of reproof, of which the Torah approves?—patently the kind that stems not from hatred but from love....

Reproof should be given when a person commits a sin, but then we should act with compassion.

It is told of a well-known rabbi that when he saw a Jew committing a sin, he would become altogether shaken and would burst into tears, out of his great compassion for the soul of the sinner (that was now doomed to punishment, unless the man repented); and he would try to bring the man back to the path of virtue. For you see, when a person notices someone fall and injure himself, it is human nature for him to rush to the other's aid; and if he does not do so, he has no pity in his heart for the other person. In the same way, if one sees another committing a sin, by which he injures his spiritual self, and he does not try to help the other person, he has no pity in his heart for the other person. And pity and compassion are among the outstanding characteristics of love for fellow-Jews.

The letter of R. Moses b. Naḥman (Ramban, Naḥmanides) to his son contains several pieces of good advice in connection with love for Jewry.

Ramban solemnly advises his son to "regard every single person as greater than he is"; that he should speak to everyone respectfully; and (Heaven forbid) he should stir up no accusation or controversy against anyone.

But more: The desired goal is not merely an attitude or relationship of respect, sympathy and brotherly affection. There should also be deeds and acts to show the love of fellow-Jews and give it tangible expression. We should help and assist our fellow-Jews.

* * * * * * * * *

Love for fellow-Jews derives from compassion, and compassion derives from love for fellow-Jews. The two are linked and interdependent.

Love for fellow-Jews means encouraging them—encouraging every single individual among them, even those who stray from the path of honesty and decency—for in truth they are spiritually sick.

I have had vast experience in encouraging and cheering up prisoners who were convicted of criminal activities. And I know how greatly the encouragement helped bring them back to the good, straight path and to return them to the Jewish community. They are not sundered and separate from the community. They are a limb of the body of Jewry, even if a slightly injured limb. And it is therefore our task to heal it, for the sake of the whole body.

* * * * * * * * *

Among the Jewish people, even the least one is a spark of Abraham, Isaac and Jacob. Even if he has sinned, he will return in penitence; and he will love his fellow-Jews in some measure or other....

Love for fellow-Jews needs to be inculcated and trained. One has to be educated not to hate another person, but only to speak favorably of him and never disparage him.

Love of fellow-Jews is the great source of light that has upheld the Jewish people through all the generations. It is that which carried our people safely through all the crises of our history. And it is that which has upheld every individual in Jewry in his time of trouble.

believing with perfect faith

Can there be a Jew who does not believe? Even if he says morning, noon and night, "I do not believe," can he then be believed? I for one do not believe him. Let him be a great philosopher; if he is a Jew, he believes. Take Rambam (R. Moses b. Maimon, Maimonides). Is there any doubt that he was a great philosopher? Yet what has remained of him for the generations of posterity?—his philosophical works, which few people read, or his thirteen principles of our faith, which every Jew says in the morning prayers, each of the thirteen beginning with the words, "I believe"?

A Jew cannot stop being a Jew, even if he has converted out of his faith. The distinctive characteristic of every Jew is that he is born with faith, having within him a spark of our father Abraham, the first of all believers. Only, with the passage of time, so much dust has gathered over that spark until it has completely covered up that faith. When troubles befall the Jews, though, they clean away the dust, and then the pure gold beneath is revealed.

Among others, all is gilt above, but within there is only dust, the dust of faith. When tribulations come, the gold on the surface—the golden veneer of civilization—is rubbed away, and what there is underneath is revealed. When some trouble comes upon a Jew, behold, he returns in repentance. As Scripture says, *In your distress, when all these things come upon you ... you will return to the Lord your God* (Deuteronomy 30:4). ... For a Jew, every Jew, there are always paths of repentance by which to return; and he has what to return to. He can revert to his own true self, to the essential spark of Abraham our father that burns within him. ...

To believe means more than to recognize. Our Sages teach that when he was but three years old, our father Abraham already recognized his Creator. Recognition, however, was not enough. Faith was necessary—as Scripture attests about Abraham much later, *And he believed in the Lord, and He reckoned it for him as righteousness* (Genesis 15:6).

The prophet Ḥabakkuk reduced all the principles (of our religion) to one principle: *the tzaddik lives by his faith* (Ḥabakkuk 2:4). My wife (may she rest in peace) used to derive this meaning from the prophet's words: Just as there can be no interruption of life, so there can be no interruption of faith. If someone does interrupt his faith and makes it cease, he interrupts his life and makes it (in essence) stop; whereas the believer lives till the day of his death.

The ways of the Lord are hidden, and human intelligence cannot grasp them. Do we then understand the regulation of the world? And yet how can we not understand and nevertheless go on living? Necessarily the answer is: by the strength of our faith. Long ago Moses asked the Almighty, *I pray Thee, show me Thy glory* (Exodus 33:18)—meaning, "Teach me, I pray Thee, the mystery of the regulation of the world." Yet even one so great as Moses found it impossible to know beforehand, in advance, the way of the Lord. This is what He meant by telling him, *but My face shall not be seen* (*ibid.* 23). Ahead of time we cannot possibly comprehend the ways of the regulation of the world. Only afterwards can we understand them; as He said, *and you shall see My back* (*ibid.*). Being believers, it is granted us to understand a little, at least after the events, looking back. If we have no faith, it will be impossible to comprehend anything at all of the world, neither before events happen nor afterward.

For those who have no belief, not only will it be difficult to understand the world, but it also becomes easy for them to sin. When he came to Abimelech, our father Abraham concealed the fact that Sarah was his wife and presented her as his sister (Genesis 20:2). Afterward, almost having come to grief as a result, Abimelech asked him, "Why did you see fit to deal so with me (*ibid.* 9), just as you acted in Egypt? There, before Pharaoh, your approach was well taken, since the Egyptians are steeped in immorality. We Philistines, however, are a civilized people. What anxiety did you have about us?"

To this Abraham replied, *It was because I thought: There is no fear of God at all in this place, and they will kill me on account of my wife* (Genesis 20:11). In a location where there is no fear of God, let civilization dwell there in all its glory, let its inhabitants be professors, intellectuals and philosophers—there is a need to be apprehensive of wrongdoing. Not all the civilizations in the world are proof against human craving. Only faith stands firm against craving and desire.

* * * * * * * * *

Faith brings us to prayer. When a man believes in his Father in heaven, how shall he not turn to Him? If you have a wonderful father on whom your whole life depends—a livelihood, health—and you never go to him, is that good? Is it possible to live like that?

I know people who ask, "Why do we need to pray with a congregation (formally), when everyone can pray alone, privately, in his own heart, in his own way?" Yet do those who say that ever really pray alone, in their heart? I have heard the well-known story of the innocent, unknowing Jew who gave a loud whistle on Yom Kippur, as his way of joining in the worship, because he did not know how to express his prayer in any other way. Yet if anyone whistled today, would he be praying at all?

There is a place and a need for individual, private prayer; but worship with a congregation is on a higher level than that, where the entire Jewish people is regarded in heaven as one individual. True, God hears the plea of every mouth, the groan of every heart; but prayer with a congregation is for our sake, not His. For since the Jewish people are mutual guarantors, mutually responsible for one another, if there is one sinner in the congregation, the merit of a tzaddik in the congregation will stand by him. Is that not a higher level of spirituality, when a man stands in entreaty not for himself alone but for the whole group with him? when an entire people stands in prayer not for itself alone but for every human created in the Divine image, indeed for the entire world?

True, our prayers are written out (in a set form and ritual). Yet who wrote them? It was the Men of the Great Assembly (in ancient times). By the holy spirit that rested on them, they composed prayers that speak from the hearts of all generations. Then why make changes? It is true that prayer rises and bursts from the depths of the heart. Yet its multitudinous thoughts that stream in profusion have to be channelled and focused; and this channelling requires holiness and concentration.

To give an analogy, if a man is given an appointment to see the king, would he not go to great pains to prepare himself physically and spiritually, in his appearance and dress, in good time, so that he be properly fit for this royal audience? Then if I have the opportunity, three times a day, for an audience with the supreme King of all kings, the Holy Blessed One—should I not hallow myself and attune my heart in good time beforehand, so that I will be prepared and fit to stand in His presence?

on the loss of a chief rabbi

[*written on the third of Elul 1936, at the first anniversary of the death of R. Abraham Isaac Kook, the first chief rabbi of the holy land*]

At the time that our great, holy, learned rabbi, Abraham Isaac Kook (of blessed memory) departed this life, I spoke the words that King David said (long ago) about Abner: "*Do you not know that a prince and a great man has fallen this day in Israel?* (II Samuel 3:38). You shall yet know and feel what you do not feel today." And true enough, in the course of a year we have felt the great misfortune that befell us. Our rabbi of blessed memory went to his eternal rest, and us he left bereft.

Our Sages recounted: When Rabbi Akiva fell ill, his disciples came to see him. "You are better," they said to him, "than the orb of the sun. For the orb of the sun is only in this world; but you are our rabbi [our instructor of Torah] both in this world and in the world-to-come." So was he to us, yet he left us to our woes, at the time we groan over the tribulations of Jewry in the holy land and the Diaspora—(in the words of the poet of lament:) "For foes have pillaged us, felling victims in our midst, the precious children of Zion. We thought to live in his shadow, and here came calamity upon calamity."

Our Sages taught: "Three days [after a death] are for weeping, and seven for mourning and lament. Thereafter the Holy Blessed One says: Do not be more pitying over him than I am" (Talmud, Moéd Katan 27b). Yet there are different grades of lament and mourning, and different grades of weeping. When they said, "Three days are for weeping," they meant in order to calm and assuage a person's mind over his dead—as we find about the death of Aaron's sons, that *Aaron grew still* (Leviticus 10:3); and he received Heaven's reward for his silence, as we read in the holy Zohar: Said the Holy Blessed One to the Israelites: You are certainly in the relationship of children [to Me] and it is not the way of a father to do his child harm. I take you up to precious, wondrous worlds; therefore do not be distressed at losing the world of vanity.

Yet in truth there is another kind of weeping, when we shed tears over the death of a tzaddik; and this is part of suffering over the distress of the *shechina* (the Divine Presence). For as it were, the removal of a tzaddik from the world is harder for the Holy Blessed One to bear than the destruction of the holy Temple was. About tears such as those, the Sages said that "the Holy Blessed One counts them and stores them away in His hidden archives." And regarding the death of men of virtue we find about Moses and Aaron that *the children of Israel wept thirty days* (Numbers 20:29, Deuteronomy 34:8).

On the other hand, the matter of eulogy in praise and lament is for the benefit of the deceased person. As we read in the holy Zohar, as a result of raising one's voice in eulogy, the spirit of the departed one becomes attached to the resonance of the voice and ascends upward to its place of abiding rest. Moreover, the purpose of the eulogy of lament is to relate the praises of the departed one, so as to arouse the people to cling to his good deeds. Through that he finds satisfaction of spirit in the world above.

The duty of giving a eulogy for the dead lies only on a person who knows how to give it, who is able to appreciate the worth of the lamented man. This is not the case, however, with weeping. That is a duty which lies on all Jews; as Scripture says, *let your brethren, the whole house of Israel, lament the burning which the Lord has kindled* (Leviticus 10:6). For this reason, about Samuel the prophet it is written that all the Israelites lamented him (I Samuel 25:1); but the verb for "lamented" is *safad,* denoting a eulogy or funeral oration; and so the Sages interpret: This is to teach you that everyone in Israel held a eulogy of lament for him in his own home and his own town, just as he was eulogized in Ramah. For all the Israelites recognized his great worth, each according to his perception, since Samuel would always make the rounds through all the towns of Israel and serve as their judge at the city gates.

I have no wish at all to tell here at length of the praises of our great rabbi, to describe his towering genius and piety. A full ark of the Lord was taken from us. The Babylonian and Jerusalem Talmud, the full range of Midrash, the holy Zohar, the works of *kabbalah* (mysticism) and research by our holy sages—no secret of theirs escaped him. We could apply to him the words of the Talmud, "Once Rabbi Akiva died, the glory of the Torah was no more" (Sotah 49b).... For a Torah of truth was on his lips, to arrive at clear religious law; and no wrong or unjust word ever escaped his mouth.

Our Sages recount that once R. Yoḥanan b. Zakkai died, the luster of wisdom was no more—because he would interpret the verses of Scripture like jewels (Talmud, Bava Bathra 115, Menaḥoth 65). For the sectarian heretics tried to find defects and shortcomings in our holy tradition, and R. Yoḥanan b. Zakkai strove to show the luminous radiance of the Torah to those who could not distinguish between light and dark.

Of our dear rabbi it could be said that he drew the luster of the Torah out of its container, both by his eloquent spoken word and by his fluent sparkling pen. Under his influence such people too began to see the luminosity in it.

Our Sages relate further that once Ben Azzai died, the diligent heedful students of Torah were no more. This too may be said of our rabbi of blessed memory. His diligent, heedful Torah study was extraordinary. Its words never left his mouth. He never walked four cubits without Torah. All his knowledge of it he acquired through the 48 ways by which Torah is gained (Avoth vi). His hallowed thoughts poured forth without limit, as from a boundless ever-flowing wellspring.

Yet his tremendous assiduous Torah study never prevented him from sharing, all his life, in the suffering of the Jewish people. He devoted himself to them, being literally ready to sacrifice himself for them. Like a faithful shepherd, he was ready to give his life for each and every member of Jewry.

I remember with a holy trembling those terrible, frightful moments, that remain etched on my heart, when I accompanied our dear rabbi (may his merit shield us) to the Hadassah Hospital in 1929, to find out by telephone about the welfare of our brethren in Hebron [at the time of the bloody riots]. When he learned of the murder of those holy martyrs, those most noble men of kindly piety, *he fell backwards to the ground and fainted.* When he returned to his senses, he wept bitterly and tore his clothing in grief, as we do over a Torah scroll that was burned, or over "the house of Israel and the people of the Lord that fell by the sword." He wallowed in the dust and exclaimed, "Blessed be the true judge."

From that moment old age overtook him, and he began sensing severe pains. Here was the cause of his mortal illness, from which he never recovered.

In the very midst of our rabbi's greatness, there you would find his humility. He was extremely modest, one of those who bore much insult and truly forgave even those who brought sorrow to his pure spirit. Many times I heard from his own lips that he used to pray for them every day, that they should not be punished (Heaven forbid) on his account. With all his power he would strive to do them good when it was necessary, as my own eyes saw.

His love for each and every member of Jewry was a mighty affection, and for students of the Torah his love was boundless. On his shoulders he bore the burden of his people, in its past and in its present. He grieved over its exile and prayed for its redemption.

Our rabbi never engaged in idle talk in all his life. His ordinary conversations would repay great study. In his words we find treasures of reverent fear of Heaven, love of the omnipresent God, love of human beings, and good qualities of behavior—for which he was ready to sacrifice himself.

Woe for what has been lost and cannot be forgotten. ... O man of kindly piety, O man of humility!

no compensation, no replacement

[*written for the fast day of the 10th of Teveth—the date chosen to observe the* yortzeit, *anniversary of death, of Nazi victims whose time of demise is unknown—1952*]

By the misfortune of the daughter of my people was I broken and blackened; desolation has possessed me.

There is no balm in Gilead, and no physician there to bandage and heal the calamity of our people, the destruction of six million martyrs bound on the altar, holy men of supreme virtue and piety. *Would that my head were water, and my eyes a fountain of tears, that I might weep day and night for the slain of the daughter of my people* (Jeremiah 8:23) —not alone for the victims of the sword, or even the victims of hunger, but for those felled by all kinds of strange deaths, and for those buried alive by that oppressive arch-tyrant Hitler, may his memory be blotted out and nevermore brought to mind.

The Lord told Cain, *the voice of your brother's blood cries out to Me from the ground* (Genesis 4:10)—because he had buried him in the ground.

Our Sages added a benediction in the Grace after meals, to thank the Lord "who is good and does good," on account of those killed at Betar, because they were granted proper burial. To those holy martyrs not even proper burial was given. Like waste matter on the face of the earth they remained, to make roads and soap out of them. Remember those martyrs. Remember those altars on which they were sacrificed.

In our prayers we seek to evoke the compassion of the Holy Blessed One, entreating Him to look down and see the ash of the ram that was offered up as a sacrifice in place of Isaac. We beseech Him to remember for us the binding of Isaac, his readiness to offer himself as a sacrifice, so that He may grant mercy to the descendants of Isaac. And there lies the hallowed ash of millions of Isaacs bound on the altar....

O God, put on garments of vengeance. Pour out Thy wrath on behalf of this abased people. Wilt Thou then take no revenge on Thy foes? Wilt Thou bear Thy enemies no hatred? *Sing, O nations, of His people; for He avenges the blood of His servants, and takes vengeance of His adversaries* (Deuteronomy 32:43). *Happy shall be the One who repays you as you have served us!* (Psalms 137:8).

to one who escaped

[*written to Dr Abba Aḥimeyer, a well-known Israeli journalist who was based in Poland till the outbreak of the Second World War. In those times of catastrophe, after many tribulations, he succeeded in returning to Israel. A few days afterward, he wrote Reb Aryeh of his safe arrival following his escape from the Holocaust. In response he received this letter:*]

With the Lord's help / 8 Tishri 1940 / Jerusalem, the holy city

My wishes for a verdict of a good year for [you] my brother and his precious family, brands plucked from the fire. God be thanked that He rescued you from there and brought you safely to the land of your forefathers. May the Lord keep you safe from all harm, and may He guard your lives from now forever.

An hour ago I returned home broken-hearted and melancholy from a visit to console mourners for victims of a terrible road accident, in which they were burned to death (may Heaven spare us). While I was yet in the doorway, my daughter came to greet me with the good news that a letter had arrived; and the handwriting on the envelope was that of my dear friend of Tel Aviv. I remained dumbfounded. Could it be?

I entered the home and took up the letter with my heart trembling. The handwriting was indeed my true friend's. I could not find the courage to tear open the envelope. Yet finally I did open it, and removed the envelope; and here is the writing before my eyes.

I began reading it word by word. I read it through once, again, and yet again—as uncontrollable tears from my eyes moistened the sheet.... *Would that my head were water and my eyes a fountain of tears, that I might weep day and night for the slain of the daughter of my people* (Jeremiah 8:23). *More fortunate were the victims of the sword than the victims of hunger* (Lamentations 4:10). O, what our enemies have done with our brethren... Woe, O woe, what has happened to them! May the mercies of the blessed Lord envelop the remnant of His people. With His mighty compassion, may He remember the kindly, pious, honest, innocent holy martyrs who were killed for the sanctification of God's name. And may He avenge the blood of His servants and pious ones that was shed.

I would embrace you, my brother—you brand plucked from the fire. I would weep with you for those precious holy souls. Remember these sacrifices bound on the altar, O God our lion; do not forget! And may I be the atonement for the daughter of my people, I who dwell in the east with my heart in the west!

There is no word on my tongue to say, there is no balm for my anguish, until the Lord shall look down from the heights of heaven and see the affliction of His people. Yet in truth, *the Rock, His work is perfect, for all His ways are justice... just and right is He* (Deuteronomy 32:4), *and by Him actions are weighed* (I Samuel 2:3). *As a man chastises his son, the Lord your God chastises you* (Deuteronomy 8:5). Out of this great misfortune may He bring them ransom and true relief; and may He grant us a verdict for a year of good life.

Forgive me for writing so, as my words are constrained. *May He, being merciful, pardon iniquity and not destroy.*

Your brother who prays to the blessed Lord with redoubled tears,

Aryeh

on dilemmas of a Jewish spirit

[*On the 26th of Nissan, Dr Abba Aḥimeyer wrote to Reb Aryeh, in part:*]
Dear Rabbi,

I was not educated in childhood in the performance of the mitzvoth [what the Torah commands us to do], and I am not able now, toward the evening of my life, to enter upon their practice. Yet I reverently fear the God of Israel, and in my spirit there is a profound sense that not with me was this world created and not with me will it end. I stand constantly before a great mystery that envelops me, which cannot be solved.

There is no possibility at all of living without recognizing the existence of a Creator of all and everything. Yet in these years a downgrade has been discernible; and even more important: prophecy has been bestowed on non-religious people, such as Theodor Herzl, Max Nordau, Vladimir Jabotinsky, and so many more. They were the "great rabbis" in the past two generations.

The situation is more serious than it appears to you, dear Rabbi, or to R. Tz'vi Judah Kook, *et al.* Our nation is undergoing a spiritual crisis, and there is no one to stem the tide. They become taken up with trivia, while the entire house is enveloped in flames. The problem is lengthy, and the hand quivers.... This is a fearful time, and we cannot acquit ourselves of the obligation of the hour by trivia. The problem is profound, and there is no one to stand in the breach. Nor is it enough to argue, "I have rescued my soul."

The God of Israel I do revere. There is no possibility at all to exist, in a meaningful sense, without a faith within the soul in the existence of a Father in heaven.

Writing in tears,
Abba Aḥimeyer

[*To this Reb Aryeh replied:*]
To my dear, noble and true friend—peace and blessing:

Your first letter as well as the second have reached me. Words written with tears are read with tears. My heart too is in tumult; my hand also quivers. Were I gifted with a writer's pen, I would answer you on every single point. My pen, however, is too deficient to express the thoughts of my heart. So my words will be brief.

You have exposed to me the hidden conviction of your heart, that you reverence God (I never thought otherwise of you) and you believe with perfect faith that no meaningful existence is possible without belief in God. You are "love-sick" with longing and yearning for the Creator of us all. Only, you have never become accustomed to the performance of the actual mitzvoth; and now you feel the lack of energy at the evening of life, at the approach of old age.

Not so, my brother. It is yet broad daylight for entering upon the way of religious observance. The blessed Lord will renew your youth with the vigor of an eagle. A righteous person lives by his faith. And through this you will find the solution to the great mystery that surrounds you; for solutions belong to God.

For who can penetrate the mystery and seek out the ways of supreme Providence? It is beyond us. Who can penetrate the mystery of the Lord, when His ways are sublime, and His thoughts are not ours? Yet a righteous person lives by his faith.

It is quite true that not with you was the world created, and not with you will it end. Yet the penultimate verse in the Book of Ecclesiastes closes with the words, *for this is the whole of man* (Ecclesiastes 12:13); and the Sages of blessed memory commented, "The world was created for nothing but the sake of this"—meaning that for the sake of every single person the world was created. And they taught further, "Man was created for no other purpose but to give this instruction" [as we read:] *in order that he may instruct his children ... to keep the way of the Lord* (Genesis 18:19).

An individual's prayer is very important. The tears of an individual are beyond value—now, when Heaven has called the world to account.

* * * * * * * *

You remark that prophecy has been bestowed on the non-religious Jews. Well, although we have no conception at present of the nature of prophecy, it is still known to all that true prophecy has its roots in the Torah, for the Torah is anterior and prerequisite to prophecy.

Let me respond now to your words in your first letter, the sharp critique which sprang from your pen against the great religious authorities of the previous generation; may the good Lord grant you forgiveness. As an example, my dear friend, you took one of the pillars of our world, on whom the whole house of Jewry relied—[R. Yitzḥak Elḥanan] the rabbi of Kovno, a man who, apart from his Talmudic genius, righteousness and piety, was devoted with all his heart and soul to a love of the Jewish people, collectively and singly. He was dedicated to the good of Jewry day and night; and his love for the land of Israel was known to all.

Of course, not all views are alike in all matters, in detail.

There are those whose consuming interest is the Torah, and the Jewish religion and faith is the purpose of their life, to build the edifice of the Jewish people on the foundations of the Written and the Oral Torah.

There are those who acknowledge Jewry's past and await its destined future. They are bound to the great community and strive to protect the Torah of Jewry, while they themselves do not observe it. They sing the praises of Jewry splendidly. It is called Jewish nationalism. Yet it is for them to know that just as a flame cannot possibly be separated from the wick, nor spirit from matter, so can our religion not possibly be separated from our nationhood. Without religion there is no nationhood.

Nevertheless, the Holy Blessed One deprives no one of his just reward who labors for Jewry's good. Each shall come and take his recompense—everyone who was stirred mightily by the spirit of God to assist in the construction of a permanent edifice for the house of Israel.

Then there are some for whom the "new ideals" are the main thing, and they want no part of the Torah of Israel. Any religious feeling is alien to them, while every nationalistic feeling is sacred to them. Their way is full of brambles and thorns. When the spirit of God left this people [in ancient times] it was condemned to exile. Over them we pray, *Let sins be abolished from the earth* (Psalms 104:35)—sins, not the sinners. Then *the earth shall be full of the knowledge of the Lord, as the waters cover the sea* (Isaiah 11:9).

Forgive me, dear friend, that I have written at such great length. I hope it will not be burdensome for you to read . . .

the power of self-sacrifice

We read in the Torah, *And you shall command the children of Israel that they bring you pure olive oil beaten for the light, to have a lamp burn continually* (Exodus 28:20). Elsewhere we read, *The Lord called your name a leafy olive tree, fair with goodly fruit* (Jeremiah 11:16). Consider: When the olives are yet on the tree, they are picked intermittently, taken off and pounded. Having been pounded, they are taken to an olive-press and put in a grinding-mill. Then they are ground up, whereupon [in the press] they are bound around with ropes and weighted down with stones; and after that they emit their oil.

So is it with the Jews: The heathen come and pound and pummel them about from one region to another. They imprison them and bind them with iron chains about the neck, and tie them about with ropes. Then they repent—and the Holy Blessed One answers them.... *In your distress, when all these things come upon you... you will return to the Lord your God* (Deuteronomy 4:30). [So we read in the Midrash—Exodus Rabbah 36, 1.]

For what great nation is there that has God so near to them? (*ibid.* 7). Of the heathen nations it is written, *and when they are hungry, they will be enraged and will curse their king and their god* (Isaiah 8:21). The Jewish people were differentiated from the heathen nations by virtue of our distinguished ancestry. As Rashi teaches, the Israelites were privileged to receive the Torah only on account of their distinguished ancestry (the three Patriarchs).

Our past is sacred and hallowed. *Look to the rock from which you were hewn... Look to Abraham your father, and to Sarah who bore you* (Isaiah 51:1-2). And that indicates our purpose and destiny in the future. *Remember the days of old... ask your father, and he will tell you* (Deuteronomy 32:7).

The faith and dedication of our father Abraham penetrated the very soul of Jewry and became absorbed by it, so that Jews could stroll even into the death chambers [of the Nazis] singing the praises of the Lord of the world with the chant of *ani ma'amin* ("I believe"), like fiery heavenly angels, until they gave up their spirits and their souls to the One who dwells in the highest heavens. This holy heritage of a capacity for self-sacrifice took root and burgeoned in our spirit from generation to generation—a readiness to give up our lives for the sake of the holiness of His name (blessed He be) and His Torah and mitzvoth; for the sake of our people, our holy land and the city of God—as we saw with our own eyes....

Writing this, I remember well my dear brothers and sisters, the precious children of Zion hidden away in the prisons and locked in the detention camps: those who have been exiled from home and family, and those sent off to another land. Who can evaluate the worth of the exiles sent to Kenya and the other detention camps?—scholars, poets and writers, skilled artisans in every craft. Such are the men banished to Latrun and Atlit, and the prisoners of Zion in Jerusalem—heroes of the spirit, courageous bearers of suffering and tribulation, precious sons and gentle daughters of Zion who ignore their travail and find comfort in sharing the troubles of their brethren, being filled with hopes of rescue and solace for our people and our holy land.

Who can describe the noble nature of the pure spirits of the gentle, delicate daughters of Jerusalem who guard their honor and chastity throughout, and our brethren of heroic spirit who have paved the way with body and soul, and with their chained hands wove and spun the flag of Israel....

the mitzvah is sufficient to provide protection

[*At some time in the midst of his activities on behalf of the political prisoners under the British mandate, Reb Aryeh received a letter from a spokesman of the prisoners, imploring him to stop the practice of carrying written messages, between the men and their families, hidden about his person, since he thus endangered his own liberty. On a Saturday night he took the time to reply:*]

For this I am most grateful, with abundant thanks from the depths of my heart to yourself and our circle of dear friends, since I clearly perceive from this how great is their devotion and affection for me.

However, my dear worthy friends, as much as possible I must minimize the value of my efforts. My devotion is absolutely nothing compared to the devotion of our brethren, who are ready to risk their lives on behalf of the blessed Lord, for our people in the holy land, and especially for the holy city. Lord, I pray Thee: Look down and see the righteousness of Thy servants, Thy devoted pious ones who have risked their lives.

As for me, by the grace of the blessed Lord, the guardian of Israel, I go into the prison by the officers' entrance. May the Almighty guard the goings and comings of all our brethren, myself included. With the Lord's help, no danger looms (Heaven forbid). How can it even be thought that in such times, when they are denied visits by their families and there is no link of communication between them and their parents and relatives, I should in addition sever this vital link of theirs? Never once did this come to my mind. And the mitzvah that I do is sufficient to protect me.

I remain in prayer to the Almighty that I may merit, with the whole Jewish community, to rejoice in the liberation of all our brethren, wherever they may be, and especially those hidden away in the prisons and cast away in the detention camps. Let the lame and the banished enter then from the ends of the earth, and may the children return within their borders. May we merit to see their happiness when the Lord returns the captives among His people, and those redeemed by the Lord will come back.

In hope of Heaven's mercy—O that the rescue of Israel be granted from Zion in the twinkling of an eye,

Aryeh Levin

28

Thoughts on prayer

envy

On a day before Yom Kippur (the Day of Atonement) Samuel Hugo Bergman, the late professor of philosophy at the Hebrew University, once came to visit him; and in the course of the conversation the man confessed that here, at nightfall, the most solemn day of the year would begin, and he still felt no spiritual awakening of a desire to pray. At that Reb Aryeh arose from his seat and took the professor's hand between his palms. "I envy you," said he with his unabashed sincerity. "You are a man of spiritual status: It distresses you that you are unable to pray; whereas I simply know I must go to the synagogue and pray as usual, like people with a lifetime habit."

just to stand on his feet again

Upon his entry into Hadassah Hospital, his friends and admirers wished him that for his merit he might yet be privileged to welcome the Messiah. "*Nu,*" he answered, "to welcome the Messiah there will be Jews more virtuous and worthy than I am. My prayer is that I may succeed in standing on my own two feet again, so that I will be able to go to the synagogue for the morning and evening prayers with a congregation."

the forgotten benediction

Once he took part in a festive meal marking some mitzvah, in the home of my grandmother. Having taken his leave of the family, and having already walked a good long stretch of the way home, he turned back and reentered that home. The guests were puzzled: Why had he returned? The good rabbi answered them simply, "I forgot to say the special blessing after cake; so I retraced my steps in order to say this final benediction at the place where the food was eaten."

the place in the heart

In the Talmud (B'rachoth 6b) it is taught: Whoever sets a fixed place for himself at prayer, the God of Abraham will come to his aid; and when he dies it will be said of him, "O man of humility, O man of kindly piety, of the disciples of our father Abraham!"

Now, why did the Sages of the Talmud attach so much importance to having a particular constant place for one's prayer, to the extent that they said that the God of Abraham will then be of aid to him? What difference can it really make if a person prays in this corner or that in the synagogue?

Reb Aryeh used to explain: Let us take as an example a prisoner who wishes to send an appeal for a pardon to the authorities. It is self-understood that he will not write his plea on wrinkled paper with erasures. He will take particular care that the paper should be flat and clean, the writing clear and legible, and the wording the finest that he can find.

This is what the Sages meant when they spoke of setting a fixed place for one's prayer. They meant not merely a specific permanent seat in the synagogue, but also a set place in the heart: a way of concentrating mind and heart on the words of prayer that he says.

to know one's place

The first of a group of benedictions in the early, personal part of the morning prayers runs: "Blessed art Thou, Lord our God, who gives the rooster understanding to distinguish between day and night." Now, what sense are we to make of this benediction, that a man is obligated to say each morning, shortly after he has risen?

The meaning is this: If you were to take a rooster to a distant land, it would sound its call when dawn comes up in that land where it has but arrived. It will not respond with its call to the time of morning in the land from which it was taken. So does a man need to use his intelligence to know and recognize his place where he finds himself, so as to attune his words to make them understood at that place, in that time. It is for this that we pray every morning shortly after rising.

the real point

In the grace after meals we pray, "Lord our God, let us not come to be in need of either the gift of flesh-and-blood or their loan." We do not ask to never be reduced to needing the help of a person, but "of flesh-and-blood": for the true point in this plea is that a man should never be in need of the gifts or support of his sons—his own flesh-and-blood.

speedily, before they can regret it

Toward the end of each of the three daily prayer-services we have the prayer of *aleynu* ("It is for us to praise the Lord of all"). In its second paragraph we say, "...when Thou wilt turn to Thyself all the wicked of the earth. May all who dwell in the world perceive and know that to Thee every knee must bend... let them all accept the yoke of Thy kingship, and do Thou reign over them speedily, and for ever and ever."

When all—the wicked of the earth and all the inhabitants of the world—will accept the yoke of Thy kingship, then Thou wilt reign over them (become their sovereign) speedily, before they can be sorry...since it is likely that their acceptance of the yoke of Thy kingship will be only superficial, in lip-service, and will not well up from within.

not merely covert

In the prayers of the Days of Awe (the high holy days) we beseech, "As a father has compassion on children, so have Thou compassion on us." Yet does the Almighty need to imitate a father in order to be compassionate? It rather means that just as a father's pity for his children is natural, and thus obvious and understandable to everyone, so, we plead, let the loving-kindness of the Almighty be toward us: not merely covert but evident, palpable for all to perceive.

no competition in the Garden of Eden

At a wedding ceremony, seven benedictions of *érusin* (betrothal) are recited. The sixth one runs, "O grant redoubled joy to the beloved companions, even as Thou didst gladden Thy human creations of old in the Garden of Eden."

Now, why was this included among the seven benedictions, which are not only recited under the wedding canopy but repeated at the end of meals during the seven days of celebration that follow?

At times, even after many years of married life, one of the two mates may muse secretly, "If only I had married so-and-so ... Ah, if only ..." Therefore, at the wedding and during the subsequent seven days of celebration, we pray that the spiritual force of this blessing may stand by the couple and protect the two all their lives. For you see, when Adam, the first man, rejoiced with Eve, the first woman, in the Garden, neither had any competition. Neither of the two could cast an eye on a possible alternative choice. ...

29
Thoughts on the Torah

the importance of self-sacrifice

Our Sages teach that "whoever sustains one human life in Jewry, it is as though he sustained the entire world" (Talmud, Sanhedrin 37). In that case, apparently Noaḥ should have been considered thoroughly righteous and good, since he saved an entire world, the totality of all kinds of living creatures, from total destruction—animals, birds, every species that the Lord created. He toiled over them day and night in the ark, to give them their food. Yet the upshot of it all is that we find the Sages of the Talmud divided in their views. Scripture states, *Noaḥ was a righteous man ...in his generations* (Genesis 6:9); and some interpret it to his credit, while others, to his discredit. Some say that if he could be righteous in *his* times, had he lived in a generation of piety he would have been far more righteous. Others, though, interpret it unfavorably: Relative only to his generation was he righteous. Had he lived, for example, in Abraham's time, he would have been insignificant (Talmud, Sanhedrin 109a).

Well, Reb Aryeh explained, it was because Noaḥ did not act properly. When the Almighty told him in advance about the flood, he did not pray for his contemporaries, but was satisfied to save himself and his family by taking them all into the ark.

Come and see: When it was decreed that Sodom and Gomorrah were to be turned into a pile of rubble, Abraham stood and pleaded with the Almighty: *And he said, "O let not the Lord be angry, and I will speak yet this once. Perhaps ten shall be found there"* (Genesis 18:32). He bargained with the Almighty until He promised that if there were even ten good and righteous persons in Sodom and Gomorrah, the cities would be spared. In a later time Moses our master arose with a readiness to sacrifice his own life to save the Israelites, unconditionally, even if there was not one good and righteous man among them. For he said to the Almighty, *if Thou wilt but forgive their sin—and if not, blot me, I pray Thee, out of Thy book* (Exodus 32:32).

On the other hand, when Noaḥ was already told by the Almighty to take his family and go into the ark, he offered no plea for anyone else. It is this that those Sages who view him unfavorably found particularly objectionable.

So we learn how important is dedication for the welfare of others—that it must include even a readiness for sacrificing oneself.

the same Sarah as before

In Genesis 16 we read how Sarah (still called Sarai then), having failed to bear Abraham (then called Abram) any children, had him take her bondservant Hagar for an added wife (verse 3). *And when she* [Hagar] *saw that she had conceived, her mistress became despised in her sight.... And Sarai dealt harshly with her, and she fled from her presence* (verses 4, 6). She fled into the wilderness, only to be told by an angel, *Return to your mistress and submit yourself under her hands* (verse 9).

At first sight this is very difficult. Sarah has always been known in our sacred tradition as the epitome of all good virtues. How could she turn cruel against her bondservant, because that woman grew overbearing upon becoming pregnant after Sarah herself had made her Abraham's added wife? And then, why should the angel tell Hagar to return to Sarah's domination if it was now harsh and cruel?

To this Reb Aryeh had his own answer: When a great ḥassidic rabbi tells a devoted disciple to do something for him or run an errand on his behalf, the disciple feels honored at having been chosen for the task. Nothing is too hard for him to do—because it is for his revered rabbi.

Suppose, however, that an ordinary person were to ask him to do that very task. Then he would take offense and bristle: "What? Am I your servant?" And if he is forced to perform the deed for the plain man— the same thing that he would do for the ḥassidic rabbi with zest—it will seem utter drudgery to him.

This, said Reb Aryeh, explains the words of Scripture. All along, Hagar regarded Sarah as a great woman of noble virtue. Our Sages teach that Hagar was a daughter of a Pharaoh, an Egyptian princess; and yet she willingly became Sarah's servant because Sarah was so highly esteemed. So until then she served her mistress willingly and easily. Once she conceived, however, as Abraham's added wife, her attitude changed. She no longer regarded Sarah as a great person but as an ordinary human being. Then automatically, when Sarah continued treating her as always, Hagar felt it as cruel, harsh treatment—because she saw and felt about Sarah differently. Gone was the eager wish to serve her. It was only drudgery now. And hence she fled into the wilderness, unable to bear it— although Sarah had changed not a bit toward her.

Well, the angel therefore gave her a simple answer: "Return to your mistress." No matter what has happened, you must see her as your mistress; she is the same noble, exalted Matriarch as before. Return and serve her as before.

why Jacob imperilled his life

And Jacob was left alone (Genesis 32:25). Our Sages teach that having taken his family and belongings across the stream of the Yabbok, Jacob returned alone. Why did he retrace his steps and go back to a place of danger? Rabbi Elazar answers in the Talmud: Because he had forgotten some small jars, and he went back for them. From this we learn that the possessions of righteous men of piety are more precious to them than their own persons. Why this extreme attitude of theirs?—because they never set their hand to rob or steal (Talmud, Ḥullin 91a).

True enough, we learn from this that the righteous would sorely miss any lost property of theirs. Yet why did Jacob put *himself* in danger to retrieve his possessions that would otherwise be lost? He could surely have sent one of his bondservants for the same purpose?

However, Reb Aryeh explained, had our father Jacob sent one of his bond-servants, we could not have learned from this that the property of righteous men of piety is more precious to them than their own persons. On the contrary: we might have concluded that (Heaven forbid) human life is expendable—for here Jacob thought nothing of putting someone else's life into mortal peril, even if it was his bond-servant, sending him into that dangerous place merely to bring him back some trivial things that he had forgotten.

Therefore our father Jacob, in all his eminence, took the trouble to go himself—in order to teach us the regard that a man who never sets his hand to robbery or theft should have for the possessions that he has acquired by honest labor.

to see only the good

And Israel stretched out his right hand and put it on the head of Ephraim, who was the younger, and his left hand on the head of Manasseh, crossing his hands sagaciously, for Manasseh was the firstborn (Genesis 48:14).

When one person faces another, his right hand is directly opposite the other's left, while his left is opposite the other's right hand. In our rabbinic and mystic tradition, the right side denotes the good, and the left side, the "not good"; hence this denotes (symbolically) that one person sees another's shortcomings quite well, with a clear eye, whereas the other's virtues he perceives only with a dimmed and faulty vision.

Here our father Jacob came to teach us that it has to be the reverse: our right hand directly opposite the other's right, and our left facing his left—meaning that we should see another person's virtues clearly and sharply, but his negative aspects only in a blurred vision.

(At another time Reb Aryeh made the point a bit differently: When one person faces another, his right hand is directly opposite the other's left. He generally sees what he does as "right" and good; and what the other person does, as "not good." When the other does something "right" and good, he sees it with his "left side": critically and negatively. When we look in a mirror, whatever we do with our right, we see the same thing in the mirror. Whatever we do that we believe to be "right," we see it that way.... We must rather learn to see others as we see ourselves.)

imaginary pursuit

When the Torah foretells the dire punishments that will come for the disobedience of the Almighty's commandments, it states, *and you shall flee when none pursues you* (Leviticus 26:17). Evidently, though, if we apply logic, it would seem to be a worse fate for a man to flee from his hostile enemy who *is* there, pursuing him to do him serious harm. Then why the threatening prediction, "when none pursues you"?

However, we read elsewhere that *God seeks out the one who is pursued* (Ecclesiastes 3:15). Thus it is far worse a punishment when a man flees in desperation and no one is pursuing him: for then not even the Almighty will come to his aid, since He gives aid only to those who are really pursued.

yours, not His

Scripture states, *If you will follow My statutes and will keep My commandments and do them, then I shall give you your rains in their season* (Leviticus 26:3-4). Note that the term is "your rains": The Almighty will send not His rains but your own, that belong to you. We find the same thing in the Book of Deuteronomy (7:13): *and He will love you and bless you and multiply you; He will also bless the fruit of your womb and the fruit of your land, your grain and your wine and your oil*—not His, but all yours. When will it be so?—"If you will follow His statutes," etc.

on choosing life

I call heaven and earth to witness against you this day, that I have set before you life and death, the blessing and the curse, therefore choose life (Deuteronomy 30:19). It is difficult to understand the need for this charge. Who would not prefer life to death? Moreover, the Hebrew means literally, not "therefore choose life," but "therefore choose *in* life." What does *that* mean?

In truth, though, this concerns man's free will. We are commanded to choose the good over the bad, the fine over the shoddy. For indeed, there is life, and there is life. There are many things which a man believes derive from the good inclination, though in truth they come from the evil impulse (Heaven spare us). Hence the Torah warns us, "therefore choose *in* life"— among its forms and varieties.

the hope of our mother Rachel

Thus says the Lord: Restrain your voice from weeping, and your eyes from tears; for your work shall be rewarded, says the Lord, and they shall come back from the land of the enemy. There is hope for your future, says the Lord, and the children shall return to their own country (Jeremiah 31:15-16).

In these words of reassurance and hope by the Almighty to Rachel, we find "says the Lord" repeated, apparently needlessly. Yet there is a reason for the repetition. For there are two stages to the redemption: the first, when they will return from the enemy land; and as it were, Rachel will look well at those returning, and she will find no consolation. "Are these *my* children?" she will ask. "Was it for them I longed so desperately?" and she will raise her voice in weeping once more.

Hence "says the Lord" is repeated, and she is reassured that "there is hope for your future ... and the children shall return to their country." This time they will look like her children. They will yet return to their roots and sources—their spiritual heritage of the Jewish faith.

For such is the process of the ultimate redemption: first, the emergence or exodus from the land of the enemy, a physical rescue which is not, as yet, linked with any spiritual renewal. Here the emphasis in the Scriptural text is not on the destination but on the point of origin: "the land of the enemy." When they will return "within their borders," however, to the Rock from which they were hewed, to their spiritual origins and sources, then they will be called her children. And that is the hope and solace of our weeping mother Rachel.

as long as there is hope

This is something the good rabbi once told in the name of his beloved wife (of blessed memory): There is the well-known account in the Bible of the child born miraculously to the woman of Shunem in her older years, by the great spiritual influence of Elisha the prophet (II Kings 4).

When the little boy died, she set out to fetch the prophet swiftly, and he revived the child. Before she left, however, her husband asked her, "Why are you going to him [Elisha] today? It is neither new-moon-day nor Sabbath"; and she said, "Shalom" (II Kings 4:23), meaning "It is all right."

Why wouldn't she tell her husband the truth, that the child had died? The answer is that had she said this, the prophet would never have been able to revive the child afterward. Once she said it in words, she would have acknowledged the death as an irrevocable fact, and despair would have possessed her. As long as there is hope, one must not yield to despair.

His evaluation of a good deed

And to Thee, O Lord, belongs loving-kindness. For Thou dost recompense a man according to his work (Psalms 62:13). Yet what loving-kindness does the Almighty show when He rewards a man according to his work? Surely he deserves his recompense, in simple justice, for what he has done?

Reb Aryeh explained: Let us take as an example a shopkeeper who finds it difficult to tear himself away from his place of business in order to go to the synagogue and say the afternoon prayers with a congregation. Perhaps, in the time he is away, customers will come to his store and not find him in; so he will lose money. Yet with an effort, he picks himself up and goes, locking the door behind him.

Now, how much merchandise might he have sold in the time he is away? Let us say, thirty dollars' worth. How much of that would have been profit?—perhaps ten dollars. Suppose that after the prayer-service you went over to this storekeeper and said, "Dear friend, sell me the merit of the mitzvoth you performed by locking your store and going to the synagogue—the merit of the benedictions you said; the *kedusha* you recited; the amens you said in response. Here is twenty dollars." Do you think the storekeeper would ever agree to sell that? Definitely not.

This is the meaning of the verse in Scripture: "To Thee, O Lord, belongs loving-kindness because Thou dost recompense every man according to his deed"—a really good reward according to his deed after he has performed it, when he is unwilling to sell its merit for any price.

the repudiated angry oath

For forty years I was wearied with that generation, and said: They are a people who err at heart, and have not known My ways (Psalms 95:10). These forty years, when the Israelites who were liberated from slavery in Egypt wandered through the wilderness, were indeed a long and striking period. In that time those Israelites saw signs and mighty wonders of the Lord which no other generation was privileged to see. Yet that generation turned out to be a trial to the Lord, failing in their faith and trust in Him.

The education of our people today has remained, similarly, sadly incomplete. Part of the flock of Jewry wanders and strays today too, not knowing the ways of the Lord. They grope their way in the spiritual dark, straying in error.

Now, Scripture continues, *Therefore I swore in My anger* (ibid. 11). Said R. Joshua "I swore, but I retracted" (Talmud, Ḥagiga 10a). The oath taken in anger was annulled. Chanting this psalm in the prayer-service of Friday evening, we therefore end it always particularly with a joyful melody, since there is consolation in that. The verse ends, literally, *if they should ever enter My rest* (*ibid.*): If the erring people will ever arrive, it will be, so to speak, in "My rest," and not in their own. For *I am with him in tribulation* (Psalms 91:15), says the Lord. The Almighty too, if we might so speak, did not achieve His purpose with the generation of the wilderness, just as they did not manage to attain their destination.

quality and quantity

Regarding the wisdom of the Torah, Scripture says, *Gold and glass cannot equal it, nor can its barter be vessels of fine gold* (Job 28:17). In the Book of Proverbs (3:15) we read, *It is more precious than jewels, and all you can desire cannot compare with it.* This is the meaning:

Fine gold has a fixed, specific value; its worth is measured quantitatively (so much money for a unit of weight); therefore, the greater the weight of the gold, the greater its value. On the other hand, when a jewel is slightly larger, its value is considerably greater. In other words, if one gem is twice the size of another, its value is not merely twice the worth of the other, but far more than that. Here quality is the significant factor, and thus its worth is measured not by its weight but by its size.

In the study and knowledge of Torah, both criteria of value apply: both quantity and quality. One scholar may be greater than another in Torah learning because his fluent familiarity with the contents of several Talmud tractates is greater than the other's familiarity, and the routes through the sea of the Talmud are clear to him. On the other hand, there is a Torah scholar who probes more deeply in his Talmudic study, plumbing the depths of religious law, so that his understanding is broader. Then of course his knowledge of Torah becomes wider and more encompassing than that of the scholar who excels in his expert familiarity with the texts.

For this reason it is said of the Torah that its worth is greater not only than gold but also than jewels. And it thus follows that it is quite difficult to appraise the level of a Torah scholar. We lack the criteria or yardsticks by which we could measure and say who surpasses whom in greatness of learning.

finding once or finding always

On the one hand we read, *He who has found a wife has found a good thing* (Proverbs 18:22); whereas in Ecclesiastes (7:26) we have, *and I find more bitter than death the woman.* In something of a light vein, the contradiction can be explained so: If a man finds his true partner for life, once and for all, it is well—he has found "a good thing." If, however, (Heaven forbid) it is not so, but he is the kind who *continually* "finds"—a new woman every day, supposedly better than the wife he has, so that she is the one who ought to be married to him, then it is "more bitter than death."

At one of the innumerable gatherings he attended with distinguished Torah scholars. To the left of him is R. Yeḥiel Mordecai Gordon, late head of the Yeshiva of Lomza.

a time to harden the heart

In the State of Israel, Baruch Duvdevani became a leading member of the National Religious Party; but in 1935 he was a young sheltered yeshiva student, unaccustomed to the harsh aspects of life, when suddenly he found himself imprisoned by the British, because his passionate convictions and beliefs had led him to aid the underground fighters. When Reb Aryeh first saw him on a Saturday morning visit to Jerusalem's central prison, the good rabbi was surprised to see an innocent, unscarred yeshiva student there. Before the prayer-service he said not a word to him; but afterward he took the young man's hand between his palms. There were sorrow and pain in his eyes, and the suggestion of a tear, as after a few moments of silence he told him, "Baruch, remember this verse: *Fortunate is the man who fears always; but he who hardens his heart shall fall into evil trouble* (Proverbs 28:14). A man should always be fearful and cautious; he should take care. But if he falls into evil trouble, then particularly it is for him to 'harden his heart' and be resolute to accept his afflictions with love, strength and courage."

the metaphor of a dove

Behold, you are beautiful, my love; behold you are beautiful, your eyes are doves (Song of Songs 1:15).

On Friday afternoons Reb Aryeh would always go early to the synagogue and chant the Song of Songs in great gladness. Once his tutor of Torah, the illustrious scholar R. Ḥayyim Berlin (of blessed memory), the rabbi of Jerusalem, was sitting next to him, chanting the Song of Songs with him. When they came to the verse cited above, the eyes of his master instructor began shedding tears.

"Why are you weeping?" Reb Aryeh asked him. "These verses are such a moving description of the abiding affection between the Almighty and the community of Jewry."

Rabbi Ḥayyim Berlin answered with a story:

When I served as a rabbi in Moscow (he said), a distinguished man approached me and asked to speak with me in private. Then the man told me, "I have become the father of a son, and I should like you, dear rabbi, to perform the circumcision."

"Why, of course," I replied. "That will be fine. But why the need for secrecy about this?"

"I am a man of considerable means, dealing in crosses to the Christian market. No one in my neighborhood knows that I am Jewish. I therefore wish to have the circumcision take place in secrecy; and I have come to ask your advice how it may be kept hidden from my neighbors."

Well, I advised him to let the Christian servant-girls in his home have the day off; and he did so. This man held the child on his knees, and I performed the circumcision, all in secrecy, without a minimum congregation of ten Jews present. When it was over I asked the infant's father to let me know three days later how the child was faring.

Three days later, he came to see me, and he put down a sum of money on the table, for my trouble. "I do not take money for that mitzvah," I told him. With his commercially trained mind, he thought I meant that the amount was too small to satisfy me, and he put down the same amount again, and yet again; but of course I remained firm in my refusal. Finally I asked him, "Tell me something: I was in your home, and I found there not a trace of our Jewish heritage. In addition, you yourself make every effort to hide your Jewish identity. You want no one to suspect that you are a Jew. Whatever then made you want to have your son circumcised? What made you go to all that trouble, with such sacrifice, just for this mitzvah?"

"Rabbi," he replied, "I know how completely estranged I am from Judaism. Frankly, I doubt if I will ever be able to undo everything and return to my people's faith. As for this child of mine that was now born to me, it is well-nigh certain that he will never even know what Judaism is. I at least grew up among Jews.... Nevertheless, should the boy find out when he grows up that he is Jewish, and should he wish to be a complete Jew, I want that nothing should stand in his way..."

You see (R. Ḥayyim Berlin concluded), whenever I read this verse—*Behold, you are beautiful, my love; behold, you are beautiful, your eyes are doves*—I am reminded of that incident. Through that I understand why Scripture repeats the phrase, "behold, you are beautiful." You know how the Sages interpret it, about the Jewish people: "Behold, you are beautiful" before sinning; "behold, you are beautiful" even after sinning. Why are the Jewish people "beautiful" (still held in the Almighty's affection) even after sinning?—because "your eyes are doves": As the Talmud (Bava Bathra 23a) indicates, even when a dove flies off from the dovecote, it tries to go not too far away, and remains within the range where its eyes can keep the dovecote in view.

It is, then, as we said: The community of Jewry is "beautiful" before sinning, and "beautiful" as well afterward....

overtly and covertly

Behold, He stands behind our wall, He looks in through the windows, He peers through the lattice (Song of Songs 2:9).

"He looks in through the windows": When a man stands at a window and looks out, he sees the people walking in the street, and they can see him too. "He peers through the lattice": When a man does that (or similarly looks through blinds) he sees the people in the street, but they cannot see him.

Divine providence functions in the same way. The Almighty watches over His Jewish people constantly, sometimes openly and sometimes in a concealed, unperceived way; and not always can we recognize or sense it. Then it is as if "He peers through the lattice."

without imagined superiority

"Love labor and hate lordship" (Avoth i 6). The Hebrew for "lordship" generally means the rabbinate (the position of a rabbi). Could this then mean that it is better for a man to be a bricklayer, as long as he avoids serving as a rabbi? That would be amazing indeed.

We must rather understand that to every public task or duty there are two aspects: the side of lordship and authority, and the element of labor, the practical task to be done. This dictum means to teach you to "love the labor" in the rabbinate: spreading a knowledge of the Torah, making peace among human beings, and so forth; but "hate the lordship," the imperial aspect, of the rabbinate. Do not exalt yourself, imagining that you are of the élite, above the people, being superior to them in knowledge of the Torah, and that therefore everyone owes you honor.

the main ingredient

"These are the things whose fruits a man enjoys in this world, while the principal remains for him for the world-to-come: ... but the study of Torah is the equal of them all together" (Mishnah, Pé'ah i 1). What exactly does this mean to teach us?

Reb Aryeh explained: When we bake a cake, we put in a few eggs, baking powder, sugar, oil, etc. All well and good—yet without flour it is impossible to bake the cake, in spite of all the fine ingredients. Well, it is the same thing here: The Mishnah lists first doing acts of kindness, visiting the sick, helping a couple to marry, accompanying the dead in the funeral procession, and making peace between a man and his neighbor. These are all fine ways of behavior; yet "the study of Torah is the equal of them all": it is in the nature of the flour.

the innate cleansing power

"Afflictions cleanse away the misdeeds of a man" (Talmud, B'rachoth 5a). The power of suffering to cleanse away sinful deeds operates even for a person who does not sense that it is the hand of God which has thus stricken him. For we find this teaching of R. Shim'on b. Lakish in the Talmud (*ibid.*): The Hebrew term for "covenant" occurs in Scripture both about salt (Leviticus 2:13) and about afflictions (Deuteronomy 28:69). Just as salt cures meat, so do afflictions purify.

Now, it clearly makes no difference if the meat belongs to the owner of the salt or not. It is simply the nature of salt to cure (preserve) meat. It is similarly the innate nature of distressing conditions that of themselves they cleanse away a man's misdeeds, even if he is not aware that they have befallen him to atone for his wrongdoing.

the conflict between the inclinations

'A man should always incite his good inclination against the evil impulse" Talmud, B'rachoth 5a).

There were two shopkeepers who sold the same merchandise. Yet as luck would have it, one grew rich while the other did poorly. The first was busy with customers the entire day, but hardly a soul ever came to the other's store, and he merely stood there idle.

One evening, as they were about to close up, a customer suddenly appeared at the door of the second one's store. From across the street the first storekeeper called out, "Sir, come over to me. I have a fine selection of wares. You are sure to find anything you want."

This quite enraged the poor second storekeeper. "Look," he called out. "The entire day, so many people come to you, and no one ever steps into my shop. Still, I make no complaint. I accept it as my fate. Now, in the evening, one solitary customer comes to me—and you cannot bear it but must go pulling him to you?"

What is the moral of this parable?

All day long, a man is burdened and busy earning a living for his family, and the affairs of the marketplace give him no chance to think of his duties to his Creator. Finally, toward evening, he goes to the synagogue for the afternoon prayers. Then, waiting for the evening prayer-service, he listens to a lesson in the daily double-page of the Talmud, or looks into a holy volume of Torah study. Then lo and behold, his evil impulse comes and distracts him with all kinds of other thoughts.... At that the good inclination must become incensed and protest, "All day long, this customer is with you. You get his business. Now that he finally comes to do a mitzvah, a religious good deed, you refuse to let him?"

the value of suffering

"The Holy Blessed One gave three good gifts to the Jewish people, and He gave them all only through suffering. These are: the Torah, the land of Israel, and the world-to-come" (Talmud, B'rachoth 5a).

In the Midrash we learn: R. Pinḥas... said: In time to come all the other animal sacrifices will be abolished, but the *toda,* the thank-offering will never be abolished. All other acknowledgments of gratitude will become null and void, but the acknowledgment of the thank-offering will never be voided. Hence it is written [that in the ultimate future there will be] *the voice of those who say: Give thanks to the Lord of hosts, for the Lord is good* (Jeremiah 33:11), meaning acknowledgments of gratitude.... And thus David said, *Thy vows are upon me, O God; I will render thank-offerings to Thee* (Psalms 56:13) ... meaning both acknowledgment of gratitude and the thank-offering (Va-yikra Rabba 27, 12).

At first sight it is puzzling: What good news for rejoicing is this? A *toda*, a thank-offering, would be brought to the Sanctuary when a person was saved from some mortal trouble or danger. Surely a man does not wish to rejoice over the promise of continued dire troubles and perils, even if he is certain that he will be rescued from them?

In truth, however, the Almighty declared through his prophet, *My thoughts are not your thoughts* (Isaiah 55:8). Moses asked the Lord, "Why hast Thou done harm to this people? Why didst Thou thus send me?" (Exodus 5:22). And the Almighty answered him that now he would see how out of the midst of every tribulation He would provide rescue and relief; how after all the afflictions and vicissitudes that this Israelite-Jewish people have suffered and are suffering, the complete redemption will come, in all its glory and splendor.

For you see, without the troubles we do not arrive at rejoicing. Every happiness that we attain comes to us only on account of the previous miseries that we have suffered. On the verse, *that I may be hallowed in the midst of the children of Israel* (Leviticus 22:32) Rashi comments: Sacrifice yourself and sanctify His name, that we may be embraced and bound by our Father in heaven.

The Midrash relates that before the slavery in Egypt began, the Israelites there wanted to become assimilated. When Joseph died, they abolished the covenant of circumcision, saying, "Let us be like the Egyptians." At that, the Almighty turned the heart of the Egyptians to hate them and enact evil decrees against them. The suffering and oppression that they underwent bound and united them, so that they became one distinct body, brothers in trouble. If not for the slavery, they would have become (Heaven forbid) assimilated.

The gift of the land of Israel has been granted us through suffering—the suffering of oppression and bondage. Do not imagine that these "vicissitudes of Egypt" were meant to do us harm. Not at all. *You should know in your heart that as a man chastens his son, the Lord your God chastens you* (Deuteronomy 8:5). The afflictions are for your good, *for the Lord your God is bringing you into a good land* (*ibid.* 7). If not for the bondage we suffered, we would not have come into a good land.

ample room or crowded conditions

"It was taught: That day, the guard at the door was removed, and the students were given permission to enter. For R. Gamliel used to proclaim and say, 'Any student who is not the same internally as externally, is not to enter the house of study.' That day, many seats were added. Said R. Yoḥanan: Abba Yosef b. Dostai and the Sages differed. One view was that 400 seats were added, and the other view, 700 seats" (Talmud, B'rachoth 28a).

Now, why did the students need so very many seats? Could they not have squeezed in a bit on the benches to sit and study? And how did such a wide difference arise in the estimate of the number of seats?

Well, a blessing was bestowed on Jerusalem that in it people should be able to "stand packed close together, and bow down with comfort and ease"; and "never did anyone tell his fellow man: There is insufficient place for me to spend the night in Jerusalem" (Avoth v 5). What was the reason?—because Jerusalem was graced with the blessing of peace. As the Sages said: *as a city that is bound together* (Psalms 122:3)—it unites the Jewish people into a bond with one another (Jerusalem Talmud, Ḥagiga iii 6). For that reason there was always a readiness in everyone to use less space and make room for others. Even if they were pressed in, they did not notice it, on account of the great friendliness—just as a mother who invites her grown children to visit her never feels how crowded the house is.

However, on that day of which the Talmud tells, R. Eliezer b. Azarya ruled that even students who were not the same internally as externally were to be admitted into the house of study—students who only gave the appearance of piety and good qualities. Every one of them needed a very spacious seat, since each was sure to complain and grumble that the one near him was pressing him in, and he would push the other off, so as to sit comfortably, apart from the others.

in honor of the Sabbath

For expenses for the Sabbath, it is taught, the Almighty tells his people, "Borrow on My account and observe the holiness of the day; and trust in

Me that I will pay it back" (Talmud, Bétza 15b). Yet elsewhere in the Talmud (Shabbath 118a) it is taught: Treat your Sabbath as a weekday [as regards expenses for it] and do not be in need of people's help!

There is, however, no contradiction between the two passages. If you wish to spend money to honor the Divine Sovereign of the world, then "borrow on My account... and I will pay it back." But if you want to spend money for your own pleasure, then "treat your Sabbath as a weekday."

the main virtue in a wife

The School of Shammai says: A man should not divorce his wife unless he has found something very blameworthy about her. The School of Hillel says: He may do so even if she overcooked his food. R. Akiva says: Even if he found someone more beautiful (Talmud, Gittin 90a).

In his commentary on the Mishnah, Rambam (Maimonides) considers R. Akiva's view difficult: If a man finds a woman more beautiful than his wife, why would R. Akiva permit him to divorce his wife so freely? In R. Akiva's time it was permissible to take more than one wife. Then why should he not merely marry the prettier woman in addition to his wife?

Well, in the Talmud tractate Shabbath (25b) we find that R. Akiva taught: Who is wealthy?—whoever has a wife beautiful in her deeds. And Maharsha explains: It means a woman who makes do with little.

Now all can be understood. R. Akiva himself was blessed with a wife—Rachel the daughter of Kalba Savua—whose way it was to make do with little. She lived happily with him during their first years, in poverty. Then he realized that if a man has a wife who is not "beautiful"—in her deeds, meaning (as Maharsha explained) that she does not make do with little, he would want to marry "another woman, more beautiful than she": He would want a wife who *can* make do with little. After marrying the second woman, with this good quality, he will no longer be able to accept the presence of the first one, since the virtues of his second wife will make the shortcomings of the first wife only too blatant.

And that answers the difficulty of Rambam.

the reward for personal devoted service

The elders in that generation [their contemporaries] said, "The countenance of Moses was like the face of the sun; the countenance of Joshua was like the face of the moon. Woe for that disgrace, woe for that shame!" (Talmud, Bava Bathra 75a).

On the surface it would seem that those elders were being offensive to Joshua, since they pointed to the "generation gap" between him and Moses. Then too, why did Joshua the son of Nun, of the tribe of Ephraim, merit the privilege of this elevation, to become Moses' successor? There were people greater than he in that generation: for example, Othniel the son of Kenaz, of the tribe of Judah—the brother of Caleb the son of Yephuneh—of whom the Talmud (T'mura 16a) tells: 1700 definitive laws on both minor and serious matters, laws derived from the identity of terms in Scriptural verse, and the inferences of scholars, were forgotten in the days of mourning over Moses' death—and Othniel the son of Kenaz restored them out of his sharp deductive reasoning.

Well, this great privilege was granted Joshua only because he was the personal attendant and assistant of Moses. In the words of the Midrash: Said the Holy Blessed One to Moses, "Joshua has attended upon you and accorded you great respect. Late and early he was there in your meeting room. He would arrange the seats and spread the mats on the floor. Since he has served you with all his strength, he is worthy to serve the Israelites, so that he will not lose his just reward" (Ba-midbar Rabba 21, 14).

This evidently means that Joshua was not ashamed to attend to all those tasks that are entailed in running errands and giving service. Later the elders took to murmuring among themselves, "What made Joshua privileged to become Moses' successor?—the fact that he was not ashamed of his work, to fetch and carry. He was ready to be a servitor in matters of holiness. Had we been similarly unashamed, who knows if we too might not have been similarly elevated and promoted. Woe for that disgrace, woe for that shame—that because of this we lost our golden chances and did not attain any grandeur."

to give insight into personal tragedy

"Said R. Yoḥanan: When any man loses his first wife, it is as though the Sanctuary had been destroyed in his lifetime. Said R. Alexandri: When any man's wife dies in his lifetime, his world grows dark for him. R. Yosé b. R. Ḥanina said: His footsteps become shortened" (Talmud, Sanhedrin 22a).

Now, why do the Talmudic Sages paint such a bleak, melancholy picture? Furthermore, when a man loses his wife, he realizes only too well the tragedy that has befallen him. Then he surely has no need at all of this mournful description?

In truth, though, this sad delineation is not intended for the grieving husband at all, but for his neighbor. Sometimes a man asks his friend, "Has so-and-so recovered from that tragedy which he suffered?" And the friend answers, "Oh yes, he has adjusted to it; he is coming back to his old spirits again . . ." Therefore the Sages come to teach you that in such a case it is not so: You should know that if such a tragedy has struck your friend, it is as though the Sanctuary had been destroyed in his days; his world has grown dark around him; and his footsteps have become shortened.

the measure of a man's stature

"Whoever wants to know what the height of a palm tree is, let him measure its shadow and the shadow of its height, and thus he can know the palm tree's height" (Talmud, Eruvin 43b).

Actually, it is difficult to measure the height of a palm tree. Even the shadow that it casts about it can be deceptive at times, since it depends on the angle at which the shadow is cast. When can we really measure a palm tree's height?—when it has been cut down and it lies on the ground.

It is the same with a man. As long as he is alive, there are times when he is praised in order to flatter him, or because a favor is needed of him. When can we know if he is really a fine or great man?—when he departs this life. Then, when his body lies prone and still, "cut down" and awaiting only burial, if behind his coffin people speak his praises, you can be sure he deserves them.

from despondency to encouragement

In the description of the Festival of Water-drawing at the Sanctuary on the second night of Sukkoth, the Mishnah relates: "They came to the gate that led out to the east; they then turned their faces westward and said: Our forefathers [idol-worshippers] who were on this site used to have their backs toward [the site of] the Temple of the Lord and their faces toward the east, and they would bow down in prostration to the sun; but as for us, our eyes are turned toward God" (Mishnah, Sukkah v 4).

This is rather strange. In that holy festive setting, what point was there for them to mention the sins of their forefathers? Surely it would have been enough to note their own praiseworthy behavior: "As for us, our eyes are turned toward God"?

However, as a spur to self-improvement, a touch of despair should first be planted in the heart: "The earlier generations were better than the later ones. Each generation grows worse and worse..." Then the people of the current generation have the task of giving themselves encouragement: "On the contrary: quite likely, we are better. Our ancestors were sun-worshippers, whereas our eyes are lifted up in hope to Heaven."

the two approaches to a mitzvah

"In time to come the Almighty will bring the evil inclination and slaughter it in the presence of both the righteous men of piety and the wicked people. To the righteous ones it will appear like a mountain; to the wicked it will seem like a single hair" (Talmud, Sukkah 52a).

Now, how could one thing have two such extremely divergent appearances?

The answer is that to every mitzvah (religious good deed) there are two possible approaches: It can be done merely to fulfill the obligation, or to enhance and beautify it, so that it is done to perfection. Take t'fillin (phylacteries): One man may buy a pair for a relatively small price, with which he acquits himself of his obligation. Another may take the trouble to seek out a pair of t'fillin made out of one piece of leather, from the skin of cattle, for which the portions of Scripture within the boxes were written by a scribe of great piety who took care over each grace-line of a letter—and it may cost quite a sum. A person who buys such t'fillin is trying for perfection and spiritual splendor in observing a mitzvah.

In the ultimate future everyone will make an account of his life on earth: what were the tests and trials that he had to withstand, what battles he had to wage against the evil inclination, and so forth. The tzaddik will look behind him and say, "How did I ever succeed in overcoming my evil impulse? How was I ever able to keep those mitzvoth, which cost me so much hard effort—like a mountain?" On the other hand, a wicked person will reflect and say, "I could have acquitted myself of my obligation so easily, without any undue effort. There was just a hairsbreadth between fulfilling a mitzvah and violating it..."

(This is what Reb Aryeh taught Abraham Axelrod, who wished to return to authentic religious observance, but did not know how to go about it, and feared that it might be too much for him. By this teaching Reb Aryeh drove home the point that contrary to the popular Yiddish saying, "It is hard to be a Jew," a mitzvah *can* be observed simply and easily. Thus Axelrod, who served as a deputy mayor of Jerusalem, returned to the orthodox faith.)

finite versus infinite charity

"Every single day a heavenly voice sounds and proclaims: The entire world is sustained for the sake of My son Ḥanina, yet for Ḥanina a measure of carob fruit is enough from one Friday to the next" (Talmud, Ta'anith 24b).

The Talmud relates further: His wife [finally] asked Ḥanina, "How long shall we go on suffering like this?"

"Then what shall we do?" he asked in turn.

"Beseech Heaven's mercy to be given something of the good reward stored away for the tzaddikim in the ultimate future."

He prayed, and something like the palm of a hand emerged and gave him one leg of a golden table. Then he saw in his dream that all the tzaddikim were eating each at a table with three legs, but they [his wife and he] at a table with two legs. He asked her, "Is it agreeable to you that every tzaddik there will be eating at a table with three legs, and we at a table with one of its legs missing?"

"Then what shall we do?" she replied. "You had better pray that this be taken from you." He prayed, and it was taken back.

Now, we have a tradition from our great rabbis that the three table-legs are Torah, Divine worship, and acts of loving-kindness—on which the world stands. And the leg that Ḥanina b. Dosa found himself missing was that of acts of kindness.

Then this begs a question: Suppose Ḥanina had kept the table-leg, and it made him rich. What would he have done with his money? He would surely have given generously to charity, bestowed gifts on the poor. Then how could his heavenly account became defective in the area of acts of kindness? And more: In the life he lived, even if he wanted to distribute money to charity, he absolutely could not, since he was so desperately poor. Then why was he to be reckoned as defective in the quality of loving-kindness if he retained the golden table-leg?

Consider, though: Even if Ḥanina b. Dosa became very wealthy, how much charity and kindness could he do with the money made available to him by means of the table-leg? He would have enough to sustain perhaps a hundred families. Whatever he did, it would be a limited number of people whom he could benefit. It would be far beyond him, though, to sustain the whole world. In other words, his ability in this direction would be limited and finite.

This—when he held the table-leg in his hand—an object of gold, whose worth could be appraised and ascertained. When he was impoverished, however, the effects of the loving-kindness bestowed on the world through his great virtue was boundless.

This is why the Sages stated specifically, "The *entire* world is sustained for the sake of My son Ḥanina": All find their sustenance by his merit, since he finds a measure of carob enough for him; and they do not obtain their sustenance from his personal wealth. Once he became potentially rich, however, he was no longer the same Ḥanina b. Dosa. He was now simply a wealthy man. True, he could now own a great amount of money. True, he would busy himself with giving huge amounts to charity—nevertheless, to some limited extent, since he had only a finite amount of money. The *entire* world would no longer be sustained by his prodigious virtue.

Therefore he prayed for Heaven to take back the golden table-leg.

the lot of the Almighty

"The Holy, Blessed One is happy with His lot" (Tanna d'vey Eliyahu). Yet why should the Almighty not be happy with His lot? *The earth is the Lord's, and the fullness of it* (Psalms 24:1). *Mine is the silver, and mine the gold, says the Lord* (Haggai 2:8).

In truth, though, what is the Almighty's lot or portion? Scripture tells us: *the portion of the Lord is His people, Jacob the lot of His inheritance* (Deuteronomy 32:9). Well, all the Jews are not Godfearing and wholehearted in their faith—and nevertheless, the Almighty is happy with them.

A human being must learn from this to be similarly happy with his lot, even if he finds it not altogether splendid.

out of innate love

"R. Abba used to kiss the stones of Acco. R. Ḥanina used to fix its broken places that could cause accidents. R. Ḥiyya b. Gamda used to roll in its dust; for it is stated, *Thy servants hold her stones dear, and cherish her dust* (Psalms 102:15)" (Talmud, K'thuboth 110a).

In his commentary on the Talmud, Rashi cites this without the term "for it is stated." The reason is that R. Ḥiyya b. Gamda used to wallow in the dust of the land of Israel not because "it is stated," not because of words in Scripture, but out of an inner, innate emotion, a strong yearning of love that possessed him, once he realized that he was treading on the soil of the holy land...

groundless love or groundless hate

It happened once that a heathen came to Shammai. Said he, "Convert me to Judaism on condition that you teach me the entire Torah in the time that I can stand on one foot." Shammai drove him off with the builder's measure that he held in his hand. The man then came to Hillel, and he converted him. Later, the Talmud continues, the convert came to Hillel and said, "May blessings abide about your head, that you drew me close under the wings of the *shechina* (the Divine Presence)" (Talmud, Shabbath 31a).

A difficult question has remained: Whose approach should be followed—Hillel's or Shammai's? If we say Hillel's, to draw such a would-be convert close under the wings of the *shechina,* are we then to disapprove of Shammai for thrusting him away from the *shechina*? Yet to this day we do not know which of the two was greater, Hillel or Shammai.

The truth is that the intentions of both Hillel and Shammai were for the sake of Heaven. They differed, however, in their religious outlook and approach. What Shammai achieved for the sake of Heaven by rejection, out of anxiety that the generation might become unrestrained, Hillel achieved by friendship and affection.

From this we can learn and teach ourselves a valuable lesson: It is better to make a serious error in religious law and practice by drawing people near than to do so by rejection and withdrawal. This is exactly what the chief rabbi of the holy land, R. Abraham Isaac Kook, was wont to say: "It were better that I err seriously through unjustified love than through unjustified hate."

Our Sages taught: Be among the disciples of Aaron, loving peace and pursuing peace (Avoth i 12). Aaron and Moses were brothers; and of the two, the Sages teach us to choose Aaron's way and not that of Moses, although we never had anyone greater than Moses, with whom the Lord spoke face to face. Yet the reason for this is quite similar: If it is a question of ways of behavior, it is better to take Aaron's ways. Then if a man will thus err seriously in a matter involving law, it will be on account of groundless love.

30
From his last will

nothing new

...I have determined in my heart to fulfill the mitzvah, *that he may command his children...to keep the way of the Lord* (Genesis 18:19); but in this I have nothing new to write you. For the way of the Lord is paved and set in the *shulḥan aruch* (the code of religious law), everything for its time and place. For everything there is time (time being a Divine matter)...and I have nothing to add for you.

prayer with a group

It would be worthwhile, however, to convey to you certain good ways of behavior that I inherited from my rabbis (instructors of Torah), the great scholars and luminaries of the world (may their merit protect us) whom I was privileged by the blessed Lord to serve in some small way: I was careful to attend prayer-services with a group (congregation) at the proper times, as much as possible—occasionally with tears. As one wise scholar said: When is prayer heard?—when the eye sets a tear to flow, and the spirit in reverence bows low. From the time I began, I have never stopped this practice. It has stood by me, and the merit will never abandon me.

trust and faith

It was always my purpose to implant in my heart a strong faith in Heaven's providential, watchful care of the individual... I strove to implant in my heart the quality of trust, according to my poor intelligence. For whoever has the quality of trust certainly has the quality of faith—since a man trusts only one in whom he believes.... I never was greatly distressed over any loss. *Praise the Lord, that He is good* (Psalms 118:1)—for He collects His debt in His own good way.

between man and man

I paid attention as much as possible, in my own small way, to the mitzvoth (sacred duties) between a man and his fellow-man. As Scripture says, *and what does the Lord require of you, but to act justly and to love kindness, and to walk humbly* (Micah 6:8).

second nature

I was very careful to receive everyone cheerfully, until this became second nature for me. I was careful, too, to take the initiative in greeting everyone.

gratitude

I was most careful not to be ungrateful (Heaven forbid) to anyone who had done me a favor. As the Sages said: Whoever does not acknowledge the favor of another person, it is as though he refused to acknowledge the favor of the Almighty (Jerusalem Talmud, B'rachoth ix). And it was taught in the Midrash Rabba: If someone opens a passageway for another, the other has a duty to be ready to give his life for him.

This has always stood by me. I learned a great deal about the quality of gratitude from my dear brethren, the former prisoners of Zion [under the British mandate] may they live and be well.

to accept and not retaliate

I always made a strong effort to be among those who accept insult and do not give insult, listen to their disgrace and make no answer; and I would immediately pray that no man might be punished by Heaven on my account.

love for human beings

I have tried with all my power to implant in the hearts of the members of my family a love of human beings. Instead of sowing a dislike for the irreligious, I have striven to implant love, respect and esteem for the devout.

no political party

I was careful not to be allied with any political party or group, in keeping with the teaching I received from my tutors, the great and holy Torah scholars: *And truth was* ne'edereth, *lacking* (Isaiah 59:15)—because they became *adarim*, separate little herds, in which a person would strive only for the good of the members of his group and vote only for a candidate from his group, even if that person was unfit for the position under consideration, rejecting a fit and qualified candidate. Moreover, this brings misfortune for generations; and it is in contradiction to our principles of faith and trust in Divine providence: For a man acts in this way in order that they—his group—should work for his benefit, at a time of his need. To this the verse of Scripture applies, *Cursed is the man that trusts in man ... Blessed is the man that trusts in the Lord* (Jeremiah 17:5,7).

not to press

I have seen and realized that it is not worth striving, in order to attain a position, to force matters importunately. You will be called by your name, and will be seated in your place; you will be given your due.

for the prisoners

As it is well known, I held firmly to the mitzvah of visiting our unfortunate brethren in Jerusalem's central prison and in the *kishle* [the British reception-center for prisoners, near the Jaffa Gate] since the year 1927, every Sabbath and festival day. Not once was I restrained by rain or snow, cold or heat. It was literally with self-sacrifice. Even at the times of the "incidents" [disturbances, when there was physical danger] I went.

God be praised that through me several significant things, of the highest importance, were achieved:

(1) At my request to the prison director, Warsley, the Jews and the Arabs were divided into separate cells.

(2) A special [kosher] kitchen was built for our Jewish brethren.

(3) It is clearly known to the Holy Blessed One that in every instance where someone sentenced to death here in the holy city was saved by Heaven's mercy, I had a share.

(4) In those instances also where a prisoner was sentenced for life and in the course of time, by Heaven's grace, he was set free, it was through my intervention, with the Lord's help, for which I received no recompense whatever from anyone.

(5) There were a good number of prisoners whom I worked to release by giving surety for them.

Now you, my dear cherished son ... since you have also taken to observing this mitzvah to some extent, do not abandon it. It will cause you no interruption of your Torah studies, since it involves only the Sabbath and festival days. Even if you do it for compensation, I would not mind; for it is a great mitzvah, with which many mitzvoth are involved. "Captivity is the hardest fate of all" (Talmud, Bava Bathra 8b).

to speak or keep silent

It is easier to learn several languages and become accustomed to speaking them, than to refrain from saying unnecessary things.

FROM HIS LAST WILL

no domineering position

It is better even to work at cleaning sewage than to try to become an official. Would that we can acquit ourselves of our obligations. This especially applies to the acceptance of responsibility to serve as a public steward or administrator. We have seen with our own eyes how people take the reins by force and act in holy matters as their heart desires, even contrary to the principles of the Torah. Let not their lot be yours. May the Lord guard you from all evil.

no controversy

Do not become involved (Heaven forbid) in any controversy in the world. Maintain no quarrel or contention, even for the sake of Heaven.

no printed announcements

I earnestly request that no institution or society print any notice of my departure from life, even the holy institution [the Etz Ḥayyim school] where I have been employed for decades. Only my family is to do so, in the name of the family, with this wording: "Aryeh Levin, of the Etz Ḥayyim elementary school, who shared in the suffering of the prisoners of Zion ... The funeral procession will commence from his home in the courtyard of Zalman Sendler in the neighborhood of Mishk'noth, at the hour of ..."

no eulogy

I implore with every kind of appeal not to eulogize me with any funeral oration whatsoever ... nor after the seven days of mourning, nor after thirty days have passed—and especially not the holy Yeshiva Etz Ḥayyim, so as not to cause any loss of time for Torah study—particularly since greater and better people than myself, worthy teachers for decades, were not eulogized there.

Woe, woe for the disgrace and the shame when one is praised for things that are not so, and especially myself: I have no knowledge of Torah,

467

being properly fluent in not even one chapter of the Mishnah. Even of Scripture I have no sound knowledge, never having studied it through with a teacher.

the inscription

I strongly insist that no more than one row of simple, undressed stones be placed over the grave; the tombstone should be of modest size, and the inscription should not vary in the least from what I have written herewith: "Here lies Aryeh Leyb the son of Binyomin Beynish of blessed memory, known as Rabbi Aryeh Levin..." I insist that not even one word of praise is to be added. For I possess no Torah learning, being fluent in not even one chapter; nor have I a proper reverent fear of Heaven, or good deeds to my credit. If I did something of worth, I have been accorded honor for it seven times over; and perhaps I have thus (Heaven forfend) already received my reward for it?

let all affirm their faith

After the grave has been sealed shut, let all those assembled say aloud: "I believe with perfect faith that there will be a resurrection of the dead at a time when it will please the Creator, blessed be His name and exalted His fame for ever, through all eternity."

I shall not forget

All those with whom I formed a bond in my lifetime, especially those who were close to me in a Divine intimate bond wherein I felt their pain and suffering—I shall not forget them, if I have any merit after twelve months to implore mercy before the Divine throne of glory....

addendum

This anecdote came to my attention after the book had gone to press, and there was no way of inserting it in proper place. I have nevertheless determined, at the risk of anti-climax, to add it here, because it reveals so much of the man.

It was related by Sh'néor Meisels, who in his childhood had been a pupil at the Etz Ḥayyim school, in the periodical Gur Aryeh, no. 8 — Netanya, Nissan 1976. (c.w.)

Whenever a boy at the Etz Ḥayyim school reached his thirteenth birthday, it was an old established custom for his classmates to give him a *séfer,* some holy book of Torah learning, as a gift in honor of his bar mitzvah. Every pupil gave his share of the cost; and when the séfer was bought, it was never given the bar mitzvah boy before Reb Aryeh wrote on the flyleaf a few words of dedication and good wishes in the name of the class. Without those few lines, in his unique crystal-clear hand, we all felt the gift would be like a lifeless thing, hollow and empty.

Well, one boy came from a desperately poor home. His parents' financial situation was such that there was just no way for him to give his share for any of the bar mitzvah presents that the class bought.

In time, however, *his* thirteenth birthday approached; and because young boys cannot temper the cruelty of justice with the mercy of understanding, the members of the class refused to buy him a séfer. Unable to think further, they decided he should get as good as he gave; and that was that.

Two days before the boy was to observe his bar mitzvah, Reb Aryeh happened to meet me in the school courtyard. "Tell me," he asked: "why hasn't anyone brought me the séfer for So-and-so, so that I can write the dedication in it? In two days he will be bar mitzvah!" Of course, I told him the truth: because this youngster never gave anything for others' presents, the boys would not buy anything for him.

"Go to my home," said Reb Aryeh, "and tell my wife to give you the *ḥumashim* [Pentateuch, the Five Books of Moses] on the top shelf of the bookcase; and bring them to me." I went and did so; but when I brought the five volumes to him, he gave a small groan: *"Ai vey,* I did not mean these. Go back and tell my wife (she should live and be well) that on the very top shelf there is a brand-new set of *ḥumashim* which were given to Ḥayyim Yaakov [my oldest son] as a bar mitzvah present. Those are brand-new: my son never used them; and now that he is grown-up and gone, he will never really need them. These, however, are worn with use. It won't do at all to give these as a bar mitzvah present. Just be a good lad and take them back."

Soon enough he had the set of *ḥumashim* he wanted; and as I watched, he wrote in the dedication. "Who knows," he mused as his pen formed the gemlike Hebrew letters, "who knows how much anguish this boy would have suffered if he saw his classmates coming empty-handed to his bar mitzvah celebration? It would have been murder! Was it his fault that he could not share in buying presents for others? Of course not. So if there is a way to save a poor boy from distress, we have to do everything we can — to gain such a great mitzvah as that!" And he finished the dedication, in the name of all the boys in the class.